A PHOTO-LOCATION AND VISI

# PHOTOGRAPHING
# LONDON

## GEORGE JOHNSON

**VOLUME 1**
**CENTRAL LONDON**

*fotoVUE*

# PHOTOGRAPHING **LONDON**
## VOLUME ONE – CENTRAL LONDON
### BY GEORGE JOHNSON

First published in the United Kingdom in 2019 by fotoVUE.
**www.fotovue.com**

Edited by Mick Ryan and Susie Ryder.
Design and layout by Ryder Design – *www.ryderdesign.studio*
Book project managed by Mick Ryan.
Author management by Lisa Johnson.

All maps within this publication were produced by Don Williams of Bute Cartographics.
Map location overlay and graphics by Mick Ryan. Maps contain Ordnance Survey data
© Crown copyright and database right 2016.

A CIP catalogue record for this book is available from the British Library.

ISBN 978-1-9160145-1-0
10 9 8 7 6 5 4 3 2 1

**Front cover**: *Big Ben by Westminster Bridge through the eastern arch (page 248). Sony NEX-C3, 18–55mm, ISO 200, 18mm, f4.5, 1200s. Jan.*

**Rear cover left**: *Queen Elizabeth II and the Duke of Edinburgh passing during Trooping the Colour (page 312). Canon 5D II, 70–200mm at 200mm, ISO 400, 1/180s at f/6.7. June.*

**Rear cover right**: *Artillery Passage in the rain, Spitalfields (page 52). Canon 5D IV, 24–70mm at 24mm, ISO 5000, 1/30s at f/4. Sept.*

**Opposite**: *Below Big Ben (page 248). Sony A6000, 16–50mm at 16mm, ISO 100, 1/400s at f/5. Nov.*

Printed and bound in Europe by Latitude Press Ltd.

*The streets of London have their map; but our passions are uncharted.*
*What are you going to meet if you turn this corner?*

**Virginia Woolf,** *Jacob's Room***, 1922**

# CONTENTS

## THE CITY

## BOROUGH

# CONTENTS

## BARBICAN, TEMPLE & ST PAUL'S CATHEDRAL

### FEATURE PAGES

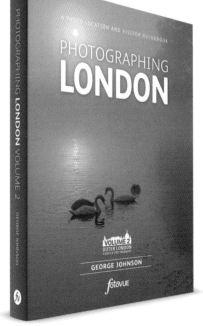

PHOTOGRAPHING **LONDON**
VOLUME 2 – OUTER LONDON & SECRETS
OF STREET PHOTOGRAPHY
See page 588 for details

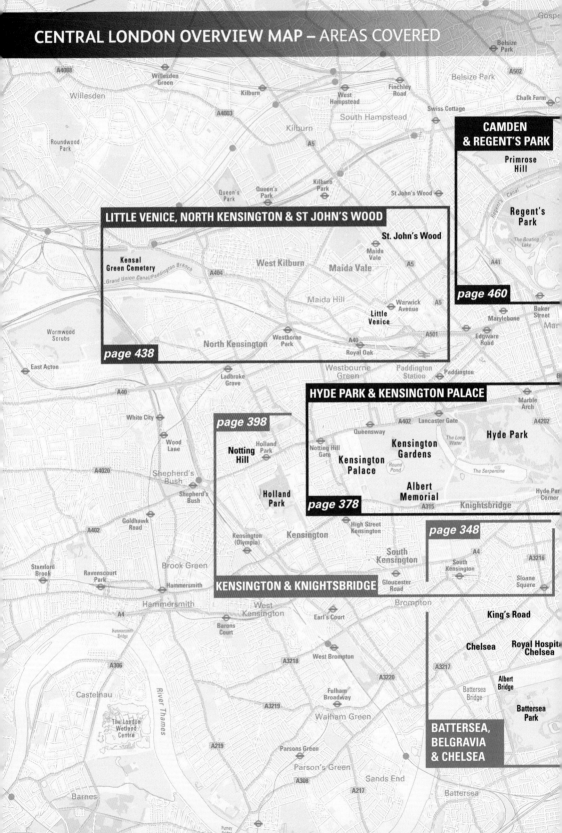

**CAMDEN & REGENT'S PARK**

page 460

**LITTLE VENICE, NORTH KENSINGTON & ST JOHN'S WOOD**

page 438

**HYDE PARK & KENSINGTON PALACE**

page 398

page 378

page 348

**KENSINGTON & KNIGHTSBRIDGE**

**BATTERSEA, BELGRAVIA & CHELSEA**

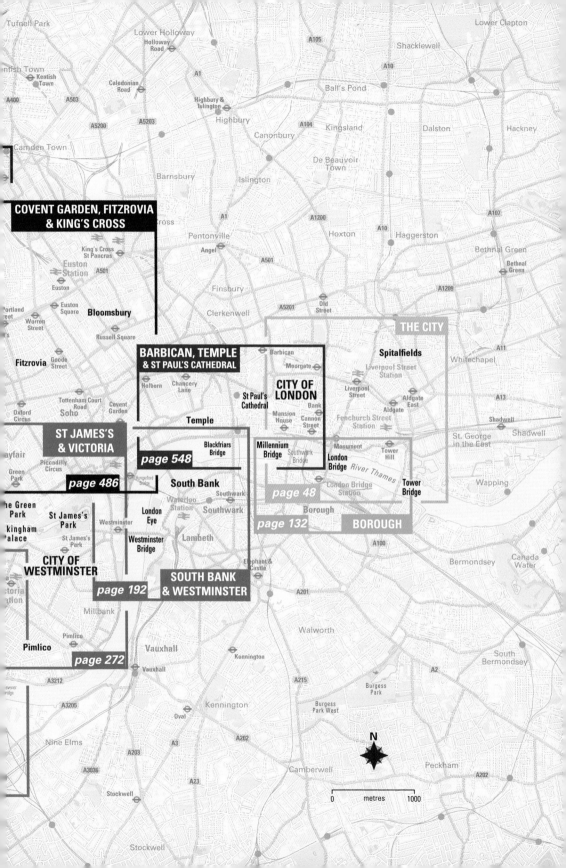

**COVENT GARDEN, FITZROVIA & KING'S CROSS**

**BARBICAN, TEMPLE & ST PAUL'S CATHEDRAL**

**THE CITY**

**CITY OF LONDON**

**ST JAMES'S & VICTORIA**

page 548

page 486

page 48

page 132

**BOROUGH**

**CITY OF WESTMINSTER**

page 192

**SOUTH BANK & WESTMINSTER**

page 272

N

0    metres    1000

# ACKNOWLEDGEMENTS

**Huge projects are never just one person's work; there's always a dedicated team of people behind the name on the cover and this book is no exception.**

Mick Ryan approached me with an idea to write a book about photographing London and I agreed as I thought it might be fun. I'd take some snaps and write about them – just a couple of months later we'd be done … Here we are, seven years, 100,000 images and five cameras later!

It's been a major part of my life – juggling a full time IT career and making time to photograph the city has been a huge challenge. I've faltered far too many times; felt nothing was good enough to the point I wanted to quit photography. I put immense pressure on myself to get the very best pictures I was capable of. During that time two people have shown the most incredible patience with me and without them you wouldn't be reading this now.

The first of course is Mick Ryan. He has far too much energy for just one man – it's frightening! He's pushed, badgered, annoyed, poked and prodded me, but all with my very best interests at heart. He is now a colleague and, of course, a wonderful friend.

The second is my wife, Lisa. She bore the brunt of my moaning, whinging and self-criticism, every time I came home empty handed, fed up and (often) soaking wet. She told me exactly what I needed to hear to get the pictures I eventually got. She's worked tirelessly behind the scenes to keep me on track, organising tickets, trips, maps and images to allow me to get on with the jobs of shooting and writing. This book would never have happened without her pushing me.

To all the people who wouldn't stop bugging me with "You finished that book yet?" Yep – Volume One is finally done! I started off my photographic life as a pure landscape shooter and many of my online acquaintances are landscape photographers who wouldn't set foot in a city, yet they've been the most vocal with support for me in getting this done. To all my online friends, my work colleagues and family, a *huge* thank you for the support.

A huge thank you also to Nathan Ryder and Susie Ryder for doing a superb job with design, layout and editing, and for turning my crude offerings into a real book. And of course, not forgetting Don 'the Map' Williams and his wonderful maps – we really made him work for his supper on this book.

Finally, I want to dedicate this book to three people: Winnie, Anne and Bill. I can never thank you for all you did for me. You showed me the beauty in this world and handed me a camera to capture it with. Although, sadly, two of you are no longer with us, I know you'd be proud of me Nan and Mum.

Thank you.
**George Johnson**
September, 2019.

*London skyline at dawn on Primrose Hill (page 470). Canon 5D IV, 70–200mm at 200mm, ISO 1600, 1/60s at f/4. Oct.*

***Overleaf**: Queen Elizabeth II and the Duke of Edinburgh passing during Trooping the Colour. Canon 5D II, 70–200mm at 200mm, ISO 400, 1/180s at f/6.7. June.*

## Foreword by Lee Frost

**London is one of the world's most iconic cities, and for photographers one of the most inspiring. From classic views along the Thames and magnificent historic architecture, to candid characters and quirky details hidden down little-known backstreets, there's something for everyone and, day or night, rain or shine, it's difficult not to come away with at least one or two great images.**

I started making frequent trips to the Big Smoke soon after I became interested in photography in my teens, and almost 40 years later, I still get a buzz when I'm there with my camera. London is exciting, intoxicating, fast-moving and ever-changing. No matter how many times you visit, there's always something new to discover and photograph and it's the perfect place to hone both your technical skills and creative vision.

The biggest hurdle photographers have to overcome when they visit a city like London, especially for the first time, is knowing where to be and when to be there. Being in the right place at the right time is far more important than owning the latest fancy camera, or a truck-load of lenses, and when you miss a great shot because you're not where you needed to be, the frustration is immense. I know that feeling!

Now, thanks to George Johnson's superb guide, the chance of this happening is dramatically reduced. You no longer need to waste hours or days wandering around aimlessly; everything you need to know about photographing the city of London is right here in these pages. There's information and instruction to guide you and hundreds of fantastic images to inspire. What more could any photographer wish for?

I've been an admirer of George's photography for several years now and I'm envious of that fact that he gets to see and photograph London on a daily basis. If anything special is happening, whether natural or manmade, he's usually there with his camera to capture it, and the fruits of his labour are now here for all to enjoy. I'm so pleased he has decided to share his immense knowledge and experience by writing this book. In my opinion it's by far the best photographer's guide to London ever published, and no photographer should head there without a copy tucked away in their backpack.

**Lee Frost**
September, 2019.

*Lee Frost picked up a camera for the first time aged 15 and has been obsessed with photography pretty much ever since. For the last two decades he has been regarded as one of the UK's best-known landscape and travel photographers. He spends several months each year exploring the globe with his camera, and his images are sold and published worldwide.*

*Lee is also a prolific author, with over a thousand articles and more than twenty books on the art and craft of photography to his name. He has organised and led more than two hundred photographic workshops and tours around the world.*

*www.leefrost.co.uk*

*Night in Parliament Square (page 248). Canon 5D II, 17–40mm at 24mm, ISO 100, 30s at f/20, tripod, LEE ND 0.9 grad. May.*

# INTRODUCTION

**The perception**: a crowded, noisy, dirty, concrete jungle. **The reality**: the crown-jewel of England. A diverse metropolis abuzz with people of all races, creeds and cultures, rich with breathtaking architecture and over two-thousand years of history. Vibrant, non-stop … in short: one of the most exciting places in the world.

This book is my personal take on London. It's where I was born and where I work. The city has so much more to offer than half a dozen famous sights; it has hundreds, if not thousands, of fascinating places to explore.

My desire was to write a book that anyone keen on photography could use – irrespective of ability or experience. Whether you have a mobile phone or are lucky enough to own the latest medium format Hasselblad camera, you'll be able to capture something special from a visit to this great city. I'm an IT technician by trade, not an artist, so if I can create interesting images, then anyone can.

A huge number of images in this book were taken with a pocket camera (and a dose of good luck, of course). There are snapshots taken on my daily commute alongside other images that took time and patience as I waited for the right conditions. And one thing I learned was this: no matter what mood you're in, no matter what the weather, there is *always* something interesting happening on the streets of London.

This first volume covers Central London – home to world-famous landmarks and sights, but to so much more. I hope you visit London, enjoy it, take photographs and go home with your own unique images of this glorious city.

**George Johnson**
September, 2019.

*Opposite*: St Paul's Cathedral puddle reflection, Festival Gardens (page 556). Sony A6000. 16–50mm at 16mm, ISO 100, 1/640s at f/5. Apr.

*Next spread*: Perfect dawn slacktide reflection by Tower Bridge. (page 112) Canon 5D IV, 24–70mm at 24mm, ISO 200, 1/125s at f/11. Apr.

# GETTING TO AND AROUND LONDON

London is the most connected city in the UK; it's well served by road, rail and air. When in the city, a combination of public transport and walking is the best way to get around.

## GETTING TO LONDON
### Car
All roads lead to London; its outer orbital road, the M25, links to the north via the M11 and the M1; to the west by the M40, M4 and the M3, and the M20 connects it to the south east.

### Driving distances to London
| | | |
|---|---|---|
| Edinburgh/Glasgow to London | 403 miles | 7hrs 30mins |
| Newcastle to London | 289 miles | 5hrs 11mins |
| Manchester to London | 200 miles | 4hrs 25mins |
| Birmingham to London | 127 miles | 2hrs 35mins |
| Swansea to London | 187 miles | 4hrs 10mins |
| Bristol to London | 118 miles | 2hrs 43mins |

### Rail
The main central London railway stations are **Waterloo, Paddington, King's Cross, St Pancras, Euston, Charing Cross, Victoria** and **London Bridge**.

Tickets are cheaper if you book in advance and are usually released 12 weeks before the date of travel. Try individual rail companies (there are several) or an online ticket agency such as *thetrainline.com* or *thetrainpal.co.uk*

### Bus
Travelling to London by bus can be very cheap. The two main nationwide operators are National Express (*nationalexpress.com*) and Megabus (*uk.megabus.com*)

### Airports
The main airports serving London are **London Heathrow** – the main gateway into the UK for visitors from outside Europe – **Gatwick, Stansted** and **Luton**. There is also **City Airport**, based in London's Docklands, which serves mainly business passengers. All the airports have train and bus links to central London.

## GETTING AROUND LONDON
London has some of the worst traffic congestion, parking is expensive and, of course, for those visiting from overseas, we drive on the 'wrong' side of the road – the left. So when it comes to getting around London, opt to use a combination of public transport and walking; how far you walk depends on you – an underground station or bus stop, a black cab or an Uber ride is never far away. All locations in this book are well served by public transport and you never have to walk too far. Take advantage of London's extensive public transport system: with a little familiarisation, it's faster, cheaper and more environmentally friendly than driving a car.

For more information visit *tfl.gov.uk* and *visitlondon.com*

**Each of our location chapters has directions, co-ordinates (postcode and lat-long) and public transport information. (See example below)**

### How to get here
Take the Circle line to Tower Hill station, exit the station and follow the steps down under Tower Hill (the road). You will come out on the path that leads west around the Tower of London to its entrance. An alternative is to find your way to the river then simply head towards Tower Bridge, which is situated right next to the Tower of London.

*Type the lat-long or postcode into a map service such as Google maps or Bing maps to find the location:*

**Location Lat/Long:** 51.50814, -0.07610
**Location Postcode:** EC3N 4AB

*There is also information about public transport links, the nearest cycle hire and car parks:*

**Underground & Lines:** Tower Hill: *Circle & District*
*(the nearest underground stations and lines)*

**Main Station:** Fenchurch Street, London Bridge
*(nearest overground mainline railway stations)*

**DLR:** Tower Gateway
*(nearest Docklands Light Railway station)*

**Riverboat:** Tower Pier
*(nearest Riverboat pier)*

**Bus:** 15, 42, 78, 100, RV1
*(buses that stop at a location)*

**Cycle Hire:** Tower Gardens, Tower
*(nearest cycle-hire stations)*

**Car Park:** Tower Hill Car Park, EC3R 6DT
*(nearest car park)*

*The London Underground or the Tube is the best way to get around London, just beware rush hour.*
*Canon 5D IV, 24–70mm at 30mm, ISO 800, 1/6s at f/8. Apr.*

## Plan your journey at the Transport for London (TfL) website – *tfl.gov.uk*

For detailed travel information on which stations to use and suggestions for the best route to reach your destination, visit *tfl.gov.uk* and enter your current location and where you want to go. You can also download transport maps and get updates on any delays.

## Payment for travel

Pre-paid **Oyster** cards, contactless payments using your debit/credit card, a Travelcard or Apple and Android Pay are the most cost-effective ways to pay for public transport in London.

An Oyster card is a smart card that you add money to, so you can pay as you go. It gives you access to all London Transport Networks:

• London Underground (Tube)
• Buses
• Docklands Light Railway
• Overground Trains

Children under 11 years of age can travel for free on London Transport if accompanied by an adult holding a valid Oyster card. Children between 11 and 15 with a 1, 2, 3 and 6-day London Pass + Travel package will receive a paper Travelcard, not an Oyster card.

## Save money

Oyster cards are available from railway stations and airports. As of 2019, an adult cash fare on the London metro for a single journey in zone 1 is £4.90. The same journey with a Visitor Oyster card, an Oyster card or a contactless-payment card is £2.40.

An alternative is a pre-paid Travelcard, which gives unlimited travel on all public transport for a day or 12 months. These are available at most stations. >>

## London Underground – the Tube

Make sure you grab a London Underground map at: *tfl.gov.uk/maps* to plan your visit to your chosen location and landmark. The Underground is divided into nine zones: central London is covered by zone 1, which includes the loop of the Circle line, whose stations are close to many of the locations in this book. There are eleven Tube lines and the fare depends on how far you travel, the time of day and how you pay. Tube services usually run from 5am until midnight, with night services on some lines on Friday and Saturday evenings. Fares can be paid by Oyster card, Travelcard or by contactless payment.

## London Overground Rail

London Overground is a suburban rail network serving London and its environs. Established in 2007 to take over Silverlink Metro routes, it now serves a large part of the city, as well as the home county of Hertfordshire, with 112 stations on nine different routes. It is complementary to the London Underground and fares can be paid by Oyster card, Travelcard or contactless.

## London buses

London's iconic double-decker buses are a cheap and convenient way to travel around the city. Buses are cashless though, so you will need to use an Oyster card, Travelcard or contactless payment. A bus fare is £1.50 and a day of bus-only travel will cost a maximum of £4.50. You can hop on unlimited buses or trams for free within one hour of touching in for your first journey. Night buses run all night between the close of the Tube and the start of daytime bus services.

## Docklands Light Railway

The Docklands Light Railway (**DLR**) is an automated metro system that serves the Docklands of East London, which lie to the east of Tower Bridge. Use an Oyster card, Travelcard or contactless payment to pay your fare.

## Riverboat

London River Services Limited is a division of Transport for London. It does not own or operate any boats but licenses the services of operators – Thames Clipper being one of the most visible. These operators provide commuter, ferry and leisure services along the River Thames. The boats pick up and drop off passengers at twenty-one piers along the Thames and connect with the land-based public transport. Buy tickets at the piers – there's sometimes a discount for Oyster card-holders.

## Cycle hire

**Cycling in London is not for the faint hearted and we only recommend travelling by bike if you are an experienced and confident cyclist.** Santander Cycles (formerly called Boris bikes) is the most popular cycle-hire scheme in London – there are over 13,600 bikes with 839 docking stations across the capital. You pay for your bike at a docking station; it costs £2 to hire a bike and £2 for every additional 30 minutes. There are several other cycle hire schemes, Mobike Lite being the most popular.

## The London black cab and the Knowledge

You must take a ride at least once in a London black cab. Fares range between £6–£9.40 for a journey of a single mile. Black cabs, unlike other cab services, can be hailed by customers and it's worth getting one just to chat to a cab driver, who has taken three years to master the Knowledge. There are thousands of streets and landmarks within a six-mile radius of Charing Cross – anyone who wants to drive an iconic London cab must memorise them all. This is known as the *Knowledge of London*.

Unbooked minicabs are illegal. You may be approached by minicab drivers – avoid using them as they may be unsafe, unlicensed and uninsured.

*Opposite*: *Gants Hill Underground Station. Sony A6000, Fisheye 8mm at 8mm, ISO 250, 1/25s at f/8. June.*

This is a quick guide to accommodation and eating in London. Whilst we can't provide a comprehensive list of accommodation and eating choices, we can point you in the right direction.

## Accommodation

Whilst there are numerous accommodation resources and booking websites, our purpose here is to give you a general guide to your options. For more detailed accommodation information go to: *visitlondon.com*

### Which part of London should I stay in?

You can pay a premium for the convenience of staying in central London next to all the attractions and sights, but everything will be on your doorstep. It's cheaper (and some may say more authentic) to stay in neighbourhoods just beyond the outskirts of central London and either walk in or catch public transport.

- In North London look at Hampstead, Camden Town and Fitzrovia
- In South London look at Southwark, Vauxhall and Greenwich
- In East London look at Shoreditch, Whitechapel and Hoxton
- In West London look at Earl's Court, Bayswater and Kensington

London has accommodation of all types and for all budgets.

### Hotels and Bed & Breakfasts

The main hotel chains are all represented in London and rates can be very competitive even in high season (largely because of the success of Airbnb) with prices starting at £50 a night. Similarly, smaller bed and breakfasts can offer great value. If you're flexible about where you want to stay, sites like *lastminute.com* offer mystery deals (a 4 or 5 star hotel room at half price for 2 nights). You pay up then they tell you where it is.

There are many historic luxury hotels in London including The Savoy, The Dorchester, Claridge's and The Ritz, all starting at around £500 a night. Visit: *luxuryhotelsguides.com* You can also rent luxury serviced-apartments in some prestigious areas.

### Airbnb – airbnb.co.uk

There are over 80,000 Airbnb listings in London, with single rooms for two adults in a shared house starting around £50 a night but these go fast. The average price is over £100 per night, but for that you can get a studio apartment all to yourself. It's wise to restrict yourself to looking for Airbnbs in central London and adjoining neighbourhoods.

### Halls of Residence

Several London universities offer their student rooms for visitors outside term time in the summer, over the Christmas period and at Easter. The London School of Economics (LSE) has rooms starting at £49 per night (breakfast and Wi-Fi included), and offer a choice of different locations. See what LSE has to offer at: *lsevacations.co.uk* or for more choice go to: *universityrooms.com*

### Hostels

There are several traveller or backpacker hostels in London that offer bunk beds in shared rooms (£20 per night) twin rooms (£50 per night)) and dormitory rooms for six people (£99 per night). Many are self-catering but some have their own restaurants. Options include private or shared bathrooms and most offer free Wi-Fi. The Youth Hostel Association (YHA) has six centrally located hostels. Visit: *yha.org.uk/places-to-stay/london*

### Others

**Generator Hostel London** – 37 Tavistock Place, Saint Pancras, London WC1H 9SE ......... *staygenerator.com*

**The Dictionary Hostel** – 10–20 Kingsland Road, Shoreditch, London E2 8DA ........... *thedictionaryhostel.com*

**Rest Up** – Driscoll House, 172 New Kent Road, London SE1 4YT ................................. *restup.co.uk*

**Wombat's City Hostel London** – 7 Dock Street, Whitechapel, London E1 8LL .............. *wombats-hostels.com*

**St Christopher's Village** – 165 Borough High Street, London SE1 1HR ........................ *st-christophers.co.uk*

*A Chinese buffet in China Town. Canon 5D IV, 24–70mm at 24mm, ISO 1250, 1/45s at f/6.7. Dec.*

## Caravan and camping

There are over forty campsites and caravan parks within 40 miles of London. Prices start from £12 a night for a single tent. Go to: *pitchup.com* for a full listing of places to stay.

# Eating 🍴

To say that you are spoilt for choice when it comes to eating in London is an understatement – every taste is catered for – therefore all we can provide is some general guidance.

## On the go

Need a snack whilst you are out and about? You're never far from cafes and coffee shops, fast food takeaways and delis, street food and pubs to suit all budgets, but it's more expensive in central London especially close to the sights. A budget option is to visit one of the many mini-supermarkets that offer meal deals: a sandwich or wrap, a drink and some fruit or crisps, usually for under £5.

## Afternoon Tea

Afternoon Tea is a 19th-century English tradition consisting of sandwiches, scones with clotted cream and jam, cakes or pastries and, of course, a pot of tea. It was originally a social event for high society ladies before the main evening meal, which was served at 8pm and it is most definitely part of the London experience.

Recommended but expensive (over £50) is afternoon tea at The Ritz, Fortnum and Mason or the Mad Hatter's Afternoon Tea at the Sanderson Hotel. For these and other options visit: *afternoontea.co.uk*

## Restaurants

For restaurants the choice is vast and the best policy is to study the listings online at Time Out, Visit London and Design My Night: *timeout.com*, *visitlondon.com* and *designmynight.com/london*

## Street Food and Market Food

Camden Market offers really good food and is great value but again, you're spoilt for choice in London. Such is the popularity of street and market food that new places are opening all the time.

### Here's my top five.

**1  Borough Market**

*8 Southwark Street  SE1 1TL*

As well as being one of the locations in this book, Borough Market is highly recommended for street food. Food stalls sell everything from French confit duck sandwiches to aromatic Ethiopian stews, Spanish chorizo sarnies, Tuscan porchetta-inspired spit roast and even gussied-up Scotch eggs.

**2  Berwick Street Market**

*Berwick Street, Soho, London  W1F 0PH*

With over twenty street food vendors including Afghan Delights, Greek2Go, Paella Fellas, Savage Salads and The Jerk Drum, this is a great market to wander round, though there's no seating.

**3  Boxpark, Shoreditch**

*2–10 Bethnal Green Road, Hackney  E1 6GY*

A shipping container, pop-up mall for independent and global fashion and lifestyle stores. The cafes include Eat Chay (Vietnamese/Korean vegan), Voodoo Ray's (monster pizzas), Snog (frozen yoghurt), Rudie's Jerk Shack (Jamaican) and more.

**4  The Kitchens in Spitalfields**

*16 Commercial Street, Spitalfields  E1 6EW*

Included are Flank, Rök, Yum Bun, Sood Family, Bar Barbarian, Thousand Knives and Dumpling Shack, Berber & Q and Breddos Tacos with more to come.

**5  Southbank Centre Food Market**

*Southbank Centre, Belvedere Road, Lambeth  SE1 8XX*

Beside the Royal Festival Hall on the Southbank. Try Street Pig BBQ or Spit & Roast (buttermilk fried chicken baps). Others fill up at the Curry Shack, Crêpes à la Carte, Crust Bros (pizzas) or Korrito (Korean barbecue in burritos, rice, bowls and salad boxes).

*Rear of the Globe Pub. NEX-C3, E 18–55mm at 18mm, ISO 1600, 1/60s at f/3.5. Jan.*

## Something different for the evening

Recommended in the evening is **Brixton Village and Market Row** (SW9 8PS), a shopping arcade with global food kitchens and local independent traders, dating back to the 1960s. Here you'll find European, Indian, Asian, African, South American and Caribbean cuisine and a lovely atmosphere. Head over to the large selection of Indian restaurants on **Brick Lane in Spitalfields** (E1 6PU).

## Pubs 🍺

The great British pub is a British institution, and London is packed with them, some of them dating back to the 1500s. Many pubs in the UK have really upped their game in the last ten years, especially since the indoor smoking ban. Most serve decent food and have a welcoming atmosphere.

On the maps at the beginning of each section we've marked some recommended traditional pubs with the pub icon 🍺 and its name.

*Cafes by Southwark Cathedral. Canon 5D IV, 24–70mm at 24mm, ISO 200, 1/10s at f/11. June*

## Here is a selection of the oldest pubs in London:

**The Grapes** – established 1583
*76 Narrow Street, Limehouse, London  E14 8BP*

**The Prospect of Whitby** – established 1520
*57 Wapping Wall, Wapping, London  E1W 3SH*

**Angel** – established 1850
*101 Bermondsey Wall East, Rotherhithe, London  SE16 4NB*

**The George Inn** – established 1677
*75–77 Borough High Street, Southwark,*
*Greater London  SE1 1NH*

**The Mayflower** – established 1550
*117 Rotherhithe Street, Rotherhithe, London  SE16 4NF*

**Spaniards Inn** – established 1585
*Spaniards Road, Hampstead, London,*
*Greater London  NW3 7JJ*

**Ye Olde Cheshire Cheese** – established 1667
*145 Fleet Street, London  EC4A 2BU,*

**Lamb & Flag** – established 1772
*33 Rose Street, Covent Garden, London  WC2E 9EB*

**Old Bell Tavern** – established 1670
*95 Fleet St., London  EC4Y 1DH*

**Ye Olde Mitre** – established 1546
*1 Ely Court, Ely Place, London  EC1N 6SJ*

And of course, there are always the pub chains:
Taylor-Walker and Wetherspoons have around one
hundred pubs in London. You can get a burger & chips
and a pint for about £15.

If you're not a city dweller and feel a little apprehensive about your visit, there's no need to be; London is a warm, inviting and friendly place and the natives only bite when provoked. Like any city, it can be a bit overwhelming on that first visit but never fear – this handy cut-out-and-keep guide will ensure you survive the 'Big Smoke', leave happy with your sanity intact and, most importantly, make you want to return.

## SO WHAT SHOULD YOU EXPECT?

### It's Expensive

London is probably one of the most expensive cities in Europe, especially if you're a tourist. Pay attention and keep a sharp eye out to ensure you don't get fleeced. Everything in the city costs more than elsewhere, however, there are things you can do to save the pennies.

### It's Busy

True. It *is* very busy. Some parts of the city simply never stop – they're on the go 24 hours a day, 7 days a week. In fact some shops and cafes even open on Christmas Day! This can be a plus: you're rarely alone and you can always find what you need. If you want to avoid crowds however, much of London is very quiet in the early hours, especially at weekends.

### It's Dirty

That's unfair, though with so many people and so much traffic the air can get very dirty and if you suffer from any respiratory conditions such as asthma (as I do) ensure you have your reliever medications with you. Sometimes in the heat of summer when the humidity soars, the air can get thick, making breathing difficult. At times like that you may find it helpful to seek refuge in one of the air-conditioned museums and galleries to get some relief. One unpleasant side effect from a visit to London is that after a day in the city, the inside of your nostrils will often be black from grime. It's something you have to tolerate, so have a pack of tissues handy. Being in close contact with so many people means germs can spread quickly; you'll be touching handles and handrails on Tubes, stairs, doors, etc. so it's a good idea to carry one of those small bottles of antibacterial hand-gels in your pocket – especially if you have children. Before you eat, give your hands a quick once over with cleaning gel.

## Tube Travel Etiquette

Here are a few DOs and DON'Ts about travelling on the Underground network. They aren't hard and fast rules but more of a guide to help make your stay that bit easier.

**Stand on the right on the escalators** – On escalators at rush hour (or indeed anytime) people keep moving on the left. If you don't wish to walk up the escalators, stand stationary on the right hand side – the conventions on the Underground escalators are different to those in shopping centres. Generally, if you are moving, stay on the left. If you stand still on the left, you may be asked to move and not always politely!

**Don't stop moving** – When you reach the top of an escalator, travelator or a building entrance, don't stop to look at your map or phone as you may be shoved aside. People won't necessarily ask politely and will rarely apologise as standing in the way is considered a sign of rudeness. If you need to stop, simply move out of the flow of people, check where you're heading and rejoin the flow.

**Let passengers off the train before getting on** – Stand to one side and let passengers off before getting on. If the train is full, it's better to wait for the next one, which is usually only a few minutes later.

**Don't carry big bags on your back on the underground** – When using public transport, avoid carrying a bulky bag on your back. Take it off and place it by your side or between your legs so it can be moved more easily to make room for others. During rush hour, public transport will be extremely busy with thousands of people trying to get home. Don't make it harder for them! Besides, carrying a bag on your back makes you the perfect target for pickpockets, who will happily unzip pockets and take whatever they find. You won't know about it until later, when there's nothing you can do. Be safe, sensible and considerate.

**Don't give pickpockets a chance** – Don't put your wallet, phone, tablet or anything valuable in an unzipped pocket. Pickpockets operate on public transport – it's their main 'place of work'. With everyone jammed in they can take things without you even noticing. If you're carrying a handbag, ensure it has a zip or snap-shut clasp so you can close it securely. Handbags make an even better target as stealing from them is less risky than pilfering from pockets. Thieves on the Underground are very skilled at what they do so don't give them the opportunity.

**Move along to the end of the platform** – At busy times always head to the end of the platform, where it will be less busy. The station guards will encourage you to do this and as a veteran commuter I can promise you a better ride – perhaps even a seat – if you move to the platform's far end to board a train. Standing by the platform entrances when it's crowded means there's a danger of getting pushed on to the tracks. Platform entrances are almost always in the middle of platforms, so by moving to the end you'll stand more chance of getting on during busy periods.

## AVOID THE RUSH HOURS

### Travel

There are nine million people living in London with around four million coming into the city every day to work. If you want to experience the heady excitement of rush hour, the busiest times are always Monday to Friday and at three key times: 8am to 9.30am – the morning rush; 11.30am to 1.30pm – the lunchtime rush and 4.30pm to 7pm – the evening rush. If you don't like crowds, avoid public transport during the rush hours or, at least, avoid long journeys. Some Tube and bus lines will be so busy you won't be able to get on and may have to wait 15 minutes or longer for one with enough room.

### Lunch

Lunch is best bought in advance at 11am. You'll find it incredibly busy in shops and cafes during the lunchtime rush hour, when office workers go out for supplies.

### Pushchairs

If you have a pushchair, I strongly advise you avoid travelling during rush hours. Most commuters will accommodate children who are walking or being carried but they generally won't have much patience for large pushchairs being wheeled on to packed trains and buses. If you have to use one, fold it up and carry the child on board.

**Keep young children close** – Don't let children anywhere near the edge of the Underground platform under any circumstances. Stay close to the wall, hold their hands then go to board once the train has arrived. Underground rail lines are live and carry 400 volts so please take special care when walking along station platforms.

### Eating

Don't buy food from stalls near well-known landmarks – they are overpriced. To save money, head away from the main centres of interest and down some of the side streets, where you'll find independent cafes that will charge a sensible amount for tea, coffee and snacks. For example, if you find yourself on Regent Street, make your way to Soho, where you'll find lots of little, inexpensive cafes tucked away. When eating during the day, fast food may be the way to save time and money. Another option is to use supermarkets. The main ones have stores all over the city and offer meal deals: a sandwich, drink and snack for under a fiver.

If dining out, you'll have your pick of places to eat at a price range to suit you. I would advise saving your money during the day and enjoying a good meal in the evening. Pub chains such as Taylor-Walker offer good, honest, traditional pub grub all day long at fair prices. They can be considerably cheaper than some of the restaurants. Another option to save cash is to take advantage of London's diverse culture. Brick Lane, for example, has food from India and Bangladesh at very reasonable prices. And for beer lovers: at the time of writing the average cost of a pint of beer is just over £5 in most inner city pubs.

Spring Daffodils in St James's Park. Sony A6000, 16–50mm at 26mm, ISO 100, 1/320s at f/5.0. Mar.

Summer Days in Battersea Park. Canon 5D IV, 24–70mm at 27mm, ISO 200, 1/180s at f/8.0. June.

Photography in London, as in any city, is not quite so affected by the seasons as it is in the countryside. And with so much happening there's no reason not to shoot images all year round. However, London's extensive parks – both large and small – with their trees, grass and tended flowerbeds are at their peak at certain times of year. Summer can be very humid as heat gets trapped between buildings but for the most part the seasons don't generally affect activity in the built-up parts of the capital.

## When is the best time to visit London

### SPRING – March, April, May

Flowerbeds in the parks start showing colour in late February/early March with huge explosions of yellow daffodils heralding the spring. These early flowers make exciting foregrounds as the trees are still bare and buildings are visible through the branches. St James's Park and Green Park are great places to capture daffodils in front of Buckingham Palace. Around the city, the weather becomes much less dreary with more hours of sunshine and longer days. As the daffodils begin to fade, buds and leaves start to appear on the trees and greenery sprouts around the city in nooks and crannies. March and April are often wet months and this means the chance to shoot wet streets

and people with umbrellas. When it rains, the streets clear as people seek shelter but these are the times to head out. Nothing beats the mood and atmosphere of an image of a single person with a brolly on a wet street – just remember to bring your own!

### SUMMER – June, July, August

Summer in the city can sometimes be tough, especially for those with respiratory issues. Hotter, drier weather increases the dirt and dust in the air, which can make it harder to breathe. On hot days the city traps the heat and it tends not to dissipate until late into the evening. In June, the longest day of the year arrives and with longer days more sunshine reaches the darker parts of the city much earlier in the day. Shooting during the day in July and August can be hard work if the sky is clear of clouds. Light is reflected from every surface, especially glass and white stone, which means you have to compensate exposures down to stop blown highlights. Seek refuge in parks; you'll find fountains and cool shade under trees now heavy with foliage. The longer days mean dawn arrives around 4am and early morning offers much longer stretches of time in which to shoot the city with fewer people around, especially at key landmarks along the river, though you'll need to walk or take night buses to visit locations at sunrise. Longer, hotter days also mean more people will sit outside cafes and bars and this offers

*View of Wellington Arch, Hyde Park Corner. Canon 5D IV, 24–70mm at 34mm, ISO 400, 1/180s at f/8.0. Nov.*

*Frosty Fountains, Trafalgar Square. Canon 5D IV, 24–70mm at 70mm, ISO 1600, 1/125s at f/8.0. Mar.*

opportunities to photograph people at many more places around the city. The parks are by now a riot of colour with flowerbeds in full bloom and the warm weather brings out street performers and city characters.

## AUTUMN – September, October, November

Temperatures start to cool by mid-September, the days take longer to heat up and it can be quite chilly by the Thames at sunrise, which is now around 6am. By late October, the sight of almost every tree ablaze with colour is not to be missed. Autumn is my favourite season in London, with vibrant hues lighting up every park, children kicking up leaves and people enjoying the last bright sunny days they'll see for a while. There's plenty to photograph. During autumn, especially from late October to mid-November, stay close to the parks at the western end of central London, where on calm days you'll see reflections in the ponds and lakes, leaf-covered paths and people wrapped up against the cold. All this makes for atmospheric shots. While visitors come to the city all year round, with school holidays now long over and summer gone, the number of visitors in the city drops dramatically and the streets and public transport are not so crowded. Be aware that the parks departments often do two or three sweeps to gather up fallen leaves, so be sure to take those autumn shots when you have the chance – the next day the leaves that lay on the ground could all be gone.

## WINTER – December, January, February

Around the beginning of December with the leaves almost all gone, the city has lost a lot of its colour. There will be few flowers and no green or brown leaves to add subtle shades to your shots. The only bright colours left are those on the buildings themselves. I tend to shoot more long-exposure night shots during the winter months; shorter days means the evenings are far longer, so you can take your time getting to more locations for light trails from the traffic, whilst still catching the last Tube or train home. Sunrise is later – around 8am – but over more quickly so be mindful of this when shooting along the river at dawn. A walk through a city park in winter makes it apparent just how much of the cityscape is blocked by foliage during the rest of the year. The city noise reaches deeper into the parks and shooting from within these spaces requires a little more care as the taller buildings are now visible at the edges of every frame. In winter, among the buildings there is often very little difference from summer, other than perhaps duller light and the sight of people wrapped up against the elements. Shooting along the Thames or outside the central areas of the city you'll find temperatures more akin to those outside London, so wrap up warm if you head out to open spaces like Hyde Park or along the river.

*Dog-walking in the rain, Victoria Embankment. Sony A6000, 16–50mm at 21mm, ISO 200, 1/160s at f/4. Sept.*

**Despite the preponderance of umbrella photographs in this book, it doesn't always rain in London. In fact, London is far from the wettest place in the UK – you'd need to visit the mountains of Snowdonia, the Lake District or the Highlands of Scotland for that, where 200 inches (5000mm) a year is not unheard of, to experience that. London, in contrast, gets a mere 20 inches/ 500mm of rain a year – less than New York city or Washington DC. It rains approximately 100 days of the year with the wettest months being October through to January.**

It is however often overcast, although the sun does shine a lot in spring and summer, averaging 7 hours a day with temperatures that average 20°C or 70°F.

London has mild winters, though snow does cover the pavements every now and then, with frosty mornings occurring most often in January and February, around six or seven days a month.

The best description of London's weather is mixed: winters are generally mild, and summers temperate, with the occasional mini heatwave.

Whilst you'll rarely need a down jacket, they're useful for cold dawn shoots in autumn and winter, and a good rain jacket and umbrella are handy all year round.

Misty mornings – especially if close to bodies of water and in depressions – are most common from September through to spring. Clear cool nights, particularly after a warm or wet day, means a high chance of fog and mist.

*Dawn in Victoria Park Gardens in Westminster. Canon 5D IV, 24–70mm at 24mm, ISO 200, 1/45s at f/19. May.*

## Met office weather station averages

Greenwich Park, London

**Location**: 51.477, 0.004        **Altitude**: 47m above mean sea level

**Hottest month**: July (19 °C avg)        **Coldest month**: January (6 °C avg)
**Wettest month**: November (72.0mm avg)        **Windiest Month**: January (10mph avg)
**Annual rainfall**: 596.5mm (per year)

☀ **SUN** / Average hours of sunshine per month

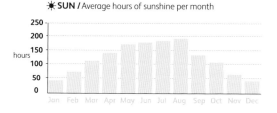

🌡 **TEMPERATURE** / Average min/max per month C/F

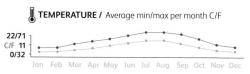

🌧 **RAIN** / Average days rain/month and precipitation in mm

❄ **FROST** / Average days of frost per month

# USING THIS GUIDEBOOK TO GET THE BEST IMAGES

Great photographs can require being in the right place at the right time, regardless of whether you use a digital, film or mobile phone camera. This is what fotoVUE photo-location guidebooks are about – giving you the information and the inspiration to get to great locations in the best photographic conditions.

## In the right place

Each location chapter in this guidebook describes a place or an area where you can take superb photographs in London. We provide comprehensive directions to each location, including postcodes and lat-long co-ordinates that you can type into your smartphone, along with all public transport options.

Before you set off, it's a good idea study a map so you know where you're going and allow yourself plenty of time to get there. Whilst there are detailed maps in this guidebook, which along with the directions will get you to a location and its viewpoints, for finer navigation we recommend popping a printed map in your rucksack or camera bag. The Collins Pocket Maps of London is a good one or the A–Z Handy Map – Central London. There are also various apps available, including Visit London and Transport for London Tube Map.

### Our map symbols

Our maps are detailed but with few symbols. The important symbols are as follows:

### A location chapter

A location chapter is marked by a numbered circle or pin and its name.

### A viewpoint

A viewpoint – a specific place to take a photograph – is marked by a small circle and sometimes accompanied by the name of the viewpoint. Not all locations have specific viewpoints; in some location chapters you'll be directed to an area that has photographic potential and interesting subjects, but they are yours to discover.

## Pub symbols

The best pubs are marked with a pint symbol and the pub name. These are included as they make useful way markers, provide much-needed refreshment (before or between photographic excursions) and often make good photographic subjects in their own right.

## At the right time

Great photographs depend on good light, texture and colour. In each location chapter you'll find notes on the best time of year and day to visit and capture the best results. Good light can occur at any time however and often the best time to visit a location is when conditions are rapidly changing, like after a storm.

The topography, sun position and weather determine how light falls on the land. Use the sun position compass on the front flap of this guidebook for sunrise and sunset times, to find out where the sun rises and sets on the compass (it changes throughout the year) and for sun elevation (how high the sun rises in the sky).

Useful websites include *suncalc.org* and the Photographer's Ephemeris: *www.photoephemeris.com*. A new 3D version renders the landscape in three dimensions, painting the light on the artificial landscape as it would appear on a clear day at any given time. Photopills – another app – lacks the 3D feature of TPE but has the advantage of many other photography tools, including depth of field and exposure calculators: *www.photopills.com*

## Weather forecast

Check the weather forecast in the days leading up to your photography outing. It's best to have several weather apps on your phone or to check on a website. We recommend the following:

- Yr is a weather app from the Norwegian Meteorological Institute and NRK, the Norwegian public broadcasting company. Many photographers swear by its reliability: *www.yr.no*
- Met Office Weather app: *www.metoffice.gov.uk*

## Exploration

The photographic interpretation of viewpoints is entirely down to prevailing conditions as well as your own personal style and skill as a photographer.

This guidebook will help you get to some of the best photographic locations and subjects in London but the list is by no means exhaustive; use it as a springboard to discover your own photo locations. There are countless other fascinating places in the city – both known or waiting to be discovered and photographed. Study a map to search for possible locations or just follow your nose and discover your own.

*Infrared image of the Peace Pagoda in Battersea Park, Canon 5D II, 17–40mm at 17mm, ISO 100, 1/45s at f/11. June.*

*Top: Looking across the Tower of London moat towards Tower Bridge. Canon 5D II, 24–70mm at 59mm, ISO 100, 30s at f/13, tripod. Dec.*

*Middle: Close up of the Underground roundel in front of Anteros in Piccadilly Circus. Canon 5D IV, 70–200mm at 127mm, ISO 1250, 1/90s at f/8. Dec.*

# CAMERA, LENSES AND CAPTIONS

This project took close to a decade to complete and during that time I've used many cameras. I started with a Canon 350D, then various DSLRs, right up to the full-frame Canon 5D MkIV I use today. I use both the full-frame DSLR and a small Sony A6000 camera to shoot city images, occasionally using a full-frame camera converted for infrared photography.

I use few lenses, having owned the same ones for seven years – I find too much kit weighs you down while in the city. I stick with a 17–40mm wide-angle, 24–70mm and 70–200mm zoom with stabilisation. With my Sony A6000 I just use a Sony 16–55mm kit lens and a Samyang 8mm fisheye for extreme wide angle. Some people sneer at kit lenses but my Sony kit lens has netted me several award-winning images.

I will only use a tripod in the city before dawn and after dusk, other times I shoot handheld. When shooting on a tripod I use a LEE ND filtration as there is no colour cast and reliable contrast control. Most of the images in this book were shot handheld, as lugging a tripod around on a 6–7 hour walking trip is just not feasible during the day when the city is busy. A tripod can become a crutch for many but in the city you quickly learn whether you truly need one or not.

"Failure to plan is planning to fail" as they say. And so I'll pick three to five key locations and use the Photographer's Ephemeris, Google Maps and MetOffice desktop websites before going out and the corresponding mobile apps during the day. Picking and sticking to locations forces you to focus on the images you want; when you arrive you're ready to take the shots you imagined. If it doesn't work, change your perspective by a few yards. Some of my best shots have come from changing perspective rather than giving up on a location.

I rarely use HDR, bracketing or stacking methods. I prefer to capture the shot in a single frame, which is perfectly doable with today's modern cameras. I use Lightroom to prep the RAW image, selective edits in Photoshop and then save back to Lightroom to make final tweaks to contrast, warmth and saturation.

## Equipment list

### Camera bodies
- Canon 5D MkIV
- Canon 5D MkII (converted for infrared)
- Sony A6000

### Lenses
- Canon 17–40mm f/4L
- Canon 24–70mm f/2.8L
- Canon 70–200mm f/4L
- Sony 16–55mm f/5.6
- Samyang 8mm fisheye

### Filters
- LEE Filters combinations of soft and hard ND graduated.

### Tripods
- Manfrotto C55 legs with 420 RC2 head
- K travel tripod

### Software
- Adobe Photographer's CC package: Adobe Lightroom & Photoshop
- Photographer's Ephemeris
- Google Maps
- MetOffice

*George's kit.*

*George at work in King's Meads Nature Reserve, Hertford, Hertfordshire.*

## Photo captions

The photo captions in fotoVUE guidebooks are in two parts:

### 1 Descriptive caption

First is a descriptive caption that describes where the photograph was taken, mentioning any references to viewpoints (e.g. VP1) in the accompanying text and any other useful information.

### 2 Photographic information

The second part of the caption lists the camera, lens, exposure, filter used (if any) and the month the photograph was taken. This information is from the Exchangeable Image File Format (Exif data) that is recorded on each image file when you take a photograph.

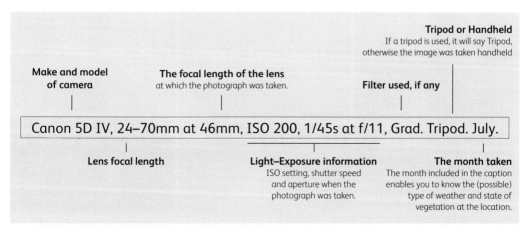

**Tripod or Handheld**
If a tripod is used, it will say Tripod, otherwise the image was taken handheld

**Make and model of camera**

**The focal length of the lens**
at which the photograph was taken.

**Filter used, if any**

Canon 5D IV, 24–70mm at 46mm, ISO 200, 1/45s at f/11, Grad. Tripod. July.

**Lens focal length**

**Light–Exposure information**
ISO setting, shutter speed and aperture when the photograph was taken.

**The month taken**
The month included in the caption enables you to know the (possible) type of weather and state of vegetation at the location.

If you want to visit the main London sights in one day, we've devised a walking tour of just under six miles that takes in the top 25 landmarks. As well as being great fun, this tour will orientate you and make you more familiar with central London. Although it's possible to do this walk in half a day, it's best enjoyed at a more leisurely pace, with a few stops for refreshments. Alternatively, break it down into sections and do it over several days.

In these directions, each location has a page number so you can read more about the landmark, as well as discovering the best viewpoints for photography.

## THE ROUTE

We start at **1** **Trafalgar Square** (p536) and the National Gallery then south of the square, cross the Strand to **2** **The Mall** (p316), passing Admiralty Arch and heading along The Mall to **3** **Buckingham Palace** (p320). From the Palace, double back and walk through **4** **St James's Park** (p306) with an optional trip to the Blue Bridge in the park itself. Head south to **5** **Birdcage Walk** (p311) and take a left turn all the way to Westminster, visiting **6** **Westminster Abbey** (p254), **7** **Houses of Parliament** (p248) and **8** **Big Ben** (p260).

*1  Trafalgar Square*

*2  The Mall*

*3  Buckingham Palace*

*4  St James's Park*

*5  Birdcage Walk*

*6  Westminster Abbey*

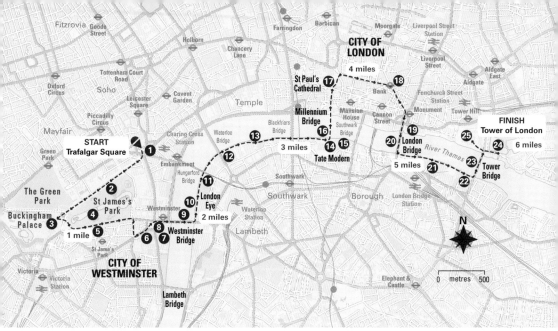

*7 Houses of Parliament*

*8 Big Ben*

*9 Westminster Bridge*

*10 London Eye*

Cross **9** **Westminster Bridge** (p260) then head north towards **10** **London Eye** (p242) along the Queen's Walk, which follows the Thames. You may wish to take a break in **11** **Jubilee Gardens** (p239). Continue along the Thames Path to Waterloo Bridge (see the book sellers under the arches) and **12** **National Theatre** (p220), before enjoying the wonderful views from **13** **Gabriel's Wharf** (p216) and **OXO Tower** (p212). Continue past Blackfriars Bridge to **14** **Tate Modern** (p178) and **15** **Shakespeare's Globe** (p176) then cross **16** **Millennium Bridge** (p552). »

*11* Jubilee Gardens

*12* National Theatre

*13* Gabriel's Wharf and OXO Tower

*14* Tate Modern

*15* Shakespeare's Globe

*16* Millennium Bridge

*17* St Paul's Cathedral

*18* Bank of England/Royal Exchange

*19* The Monument

*20* London Bridge

*21* HMS Belfast and Hay's Galleria

*22* City Hall

After crossing the bridge, head straight on to **17 St Paul's Cathedral** (p556) After a look around, walk down Cheapside to Bank underground station and **18 Bank of England/Royal Exchange** (p90). From here, walk down King William Street to **19 The Monument** (p78). Cross **20 London Bridge** (p106) with its superb views and go back to the South Bank. Head west to **21 HMS Belfast** and **Hay's Galleria** (p140) and catch great views of

Tower Bridge from **22 City Hall** (p136). Cross **23 Tower Bridge** (p112) to **24** Tower of London (p60). Finish at **25 St Katharine Docks** (p124), where you can enjoy food and drinks at the **The Dickens Inn**.

*23* Tower Bridge

*24* Tower of London

*25* St Katharine Docks

# GEORGE'S TOP 10 LOCATIONS

If you want to visit and photograph London's most
beautiful and classic photography locations, here,
in no particular order, is my top ten.

1 WESTMINSTER — P.248

2 PRIMROSE HILL — P.470

3 LEADENHALL MARKET — P.80

4 THE CHURCHILL ARMS — P.404

## 5 BUTLER'S WHARF                  P.120

## 6 BATTERSEA POWER STATION         P.352

## 7 MILLENNIUM BRIDGE               P.552

## 8 HYDE PARK                       P.384

## 9 LONDON EYE                      P.242

## 10 SMITHFIELD                     P.566

Please note that none of the information given here can be construed as legal advice. The information is presented in good faith and collected from various resources and guidelines from both the Home Office and the Metropolitan Police Federation.

## Private and Public Property

There is a lot of private property in London, with land values being some of the most expensive in the world. Generally speaking, the streets around London are owned and maintained by the local councils and you are free to shoot on these and photograph any of the buildings. Private land around buildings is often easy to spot: look for rows of steel, nickel or brass studs in the pavements around buildings – these denote private-public boundaries. You can shoot from the public side with no issues but if you shoot from the private side, the building owners can ask you to move.

The general guidelines for photography apply in the city as they do in the countryside however, in the city, some building owners' understanding of public rights is limited. If you're on public land, only the police can request you cease or move on. When on private land – for example taking photos on a public right-of-way through a privately owned piece of land – then you may be asked to cease taking photographs by the building security. You should abide by this – simply being on a public right-of-way does not mean you have explicit permission to take photos. Private security cannot detain you, request you delete any images or seize your equipment however. The police can only seize equipment or detain you if they feel you are committing a criminal act and you are being formally charged with an offence. Nor can the police delete any images as this can be regarded as destruction of potential evidence that may be required later.

If you visit quieter locations where there are buildings – the London Docklands for example – there's a good chance you'll be questioned by private security personnel. Don't be aggressive or abusive, this will only inflame the situation and you'll lose the opportunity to continue shooting. Instead, be polite, offer to show the security guard some of your images and tell them why you find the sight so interesting. They simply want to make sure you're not collecting information for any subsequent illegal activity and they often need to log this in their records. Set their mind at rest and they will often provide you with a quick guide to the best places to go for better shots. Engage in a friendly manner and you will often benefit. If they are insistent that you cease immediately, politely ask the reason, inquire where the public can take pictures and then leave if they request you do so.

## Tripod Use

Generally speaking, you can use tripods almost anywhere in London. The days of the 'tripod police' arresting people were over a decade ago now. The only objection to tripod use is usually for health and safety reasons; if a member of the public were to trip over one, the landowner is liable and as they have no control over you or your tripod, it's easier and safer for them to ban tripod use outright. Public streets, parks and council-owned land rarely have an issue with tripod use. Unless you're causing an obstruction to the public on a pavement or the traffic on a road, then you're free to use a tripod. However, you're advised to show due diligence, care and attention and bear in mind that you as an individual are responsible for the safety of those around you. If you cause an accident you could well face a private prosecution, so be careful where you set up. When I use my tripod in crowded public places like bridges and along the river, I check it's safe to do so. I also keep an eye on people around me and discourage them from getting too close to the tripod feet for their own safety (without hindering them). When on private land, you need to be more careful. Check location websites beforehand. I have endeavoured to state tripod usage for all locations but rules change so if you have any doubts, always check in advance.

## Street Photography

Many labour under the misapprehension that they can't be photographed in public. I'm afraid that's simply not true in the UK. Despite this incorrect assumption being touted in the media, there are also no laws forbidding anyone from taking pictures of children in public places. There is no law stating you cannot be photographed in public; the general guideline is there is 'no expectation to privacy in a public place.' The issues begin when photography causes distress or obstruction to others and there are laws and conventions covering these. You must not impede someone's progress by your acts or cause unnecessary distress. Street photography, both candid and formal, is about telling a story and everyone you photograph deserves dignity and respect. The skill of the good street photographer is capturing the story in a single frame, adding something to the subject being photographed, rather than taking anything away.

## Commercial Use of Pictures

You may take pictures of people and places for personal use and many places will have a sign offering their social media IDs and hashtags so you can share your images. You may take images for artistic use – source material for painting for example – and even print your own images. You may even sell your images through stock agencies such as Getty Images for use as editorial or educational images. You cannot however sell images for commercial use without permission. This is especially true when it comes to well-known landmarks and people. If pictures are to be used to promote products or services in such a way as to endorse a product, then you will need to obtain property releases from the landowner. For people, you'll require model releases if you wish to use their face in promotional materials or product advertising. If you have any doubts as to whether your images can be used commercially, seek legal advice before selling them. I sell images through Getty Images and they have a very comprehensive screening process that checks if a model or property release is required. They won't accept an image for commercial use without the correct paperwork.

## Being a respectful photographer

The key to making the best impression is by showing respect to others. Every time you visit somewhere, remember you are a guest. This is doubly important if you plan to use your camera in public places.

- **Do not** erect a tripod in the middle of a crowded place. It's rude, dangerous and you could end up with a hefty legal bill if someone trips.
- Show consideration and respect when photographing strangers on the streets.
- Cities are crowded places and shots can be tricky to get sometimes. Make sure you're not blocking someone else's shot when you shoot. I always allow others to complete their shot first.

## Limited mobility and wheelchair users &#9855;

If you have limited mobility, use a wheelchair, crutches or a walking stick and need to know whether a location is suitable for you, each location chapter has a brief access notes section, describing the terrain and distance from the road to a viewpoint. This is a city so you're never very far from each location, and many places and attractions now have full accessibility. If a location or viewpoint has the wheelchair symbol, part or all of it will be accessible by wheelchair. Bear in mind though that access for wheelchair users may not be exactly as described in the text; use your own judgement at any given location.

## Step Free

Buses are almost all wheelchair accessible with ramps available on request from the driver as you board. The Underground is over 150 years old and so not all the central London stations are fully accessible. Transport for London (TfL) is making huge strides to improve older stations and installing accessibility features as each station is built or revamped. Currently, 78 Tube stations, 58 Overground stations and nine TfL Rail stations have step-free access. All DLR stations are step-free.

For more details and maps:
*tfl.gov.uk/transport-accessibility*

THE CITY

# THE CITY – INTRODUCTION

## Welcome to the City of London.

We begin our exploration with a tale of two cities. When the Romans arrived in 43AD they settled Londinium and built a fortified wall around the fledgling town. The boundary known as London Wall still encompasses the City of London today. When the Normans invaded in 1066, one of William the Conquerer's first duties was to make his mark by building the much feared and loathed Tower of London, a frightening fortress that stated in no uncertain terms exactly who was in charge. Over the centuries London began to grow through worldwide trade and commerce and it subsumed the surrounding towns such as Shoreditch, Greenwich and City of Westminster. They in turn became the twenty-eight boroughs within Greater London that encircle the original City boundary.

This first section covers the City of London – a town founded by the Romans over 2000 years ago. London is steeped in history with the aforementioned Tower of London (incidentally, the last prisoners to be held there were the Kray twins in 1952), London Bridge, which inspired the children's nursery rhyme and Monument, the location close to where the Great Fire of London began in 1666. Fans of Harry Potter will appreciate a visit to Leadenhall Market, used as a location for the Leaky Cauldron and Diagon Alley. We'll also visit some lesser-known places you may not have heard of but may recognise, including Shad Thames and St Katharine Docks. Of course, the City itself is the financial powerhouse that drives the UK's economy and the Square Mile is home to incredible concrete, glass and steel skyscrapers.

There's a lot of ancient and modern ground to cover, so let's get cracking.

*Previous spread*: Looking south from London Bridge to Tower Bridge. Canon 5D IV, 24–70mm at 70mm, ISO 200, 1/500s at f/11. Apr.

*Next spread*: Spitalfields printers. Canon 5D II, 17–40mm at 39mm, ISO 200, 1/180s at f/8. Aug.

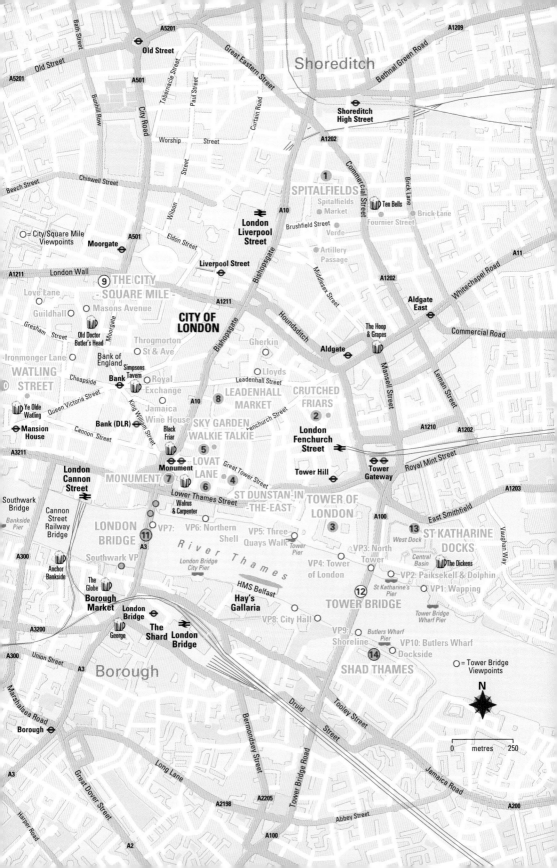

46 DONO

The noted hou

FLORISTS'
PACKING
TISSUE,

GREASEPROOFS
&
COLOURED PAPERS.

TRONG CAR

AN BROS 46
for PAPER BAGS

PRICE
TICKETS
of every description

PRINTED BAGS
&
CARRIE
TO ORD

ER BAGS

Spitalfields is located on the boundary of the classic East End of London and the City of London. The area has been known as Spitalfields since 1197 when the land belonged to the St Mary Spital Priory and Hospital. In the 17th century the Huguenot silk weavers arrived with nothing but their skills and it was through the efforts to alleviate their poverty in the area that Spitalfields was expanded to encompass Bethnal Green, Shoreditch and Whitechapel.

This area, like so much of the East End, deteriorated during the Victorian era, many of the houses degenerated into slums and the area became notorious as a bolthole for London's worst criminals. In the latter half of the 20th century there was a huge influx of Bangladeshi immigrants, who came to work in the local textile industry, and the area's fortunes changed dramatically. They brought with them their customs and, of course, their cuisine and with the help of their community, were able to set up their own businesses including the many restaurants that line Brick Lane. It is now one of the best places to enjoy fine Asian cuisine in London. But be warned: on an evening visit to Brick Lane you will find the restaurant owners offering deals in person at the door of their premises to every passer-by and they are very persistent.

## What to shoot and viewpoints

### Spitalfields ♿

The centre of Spitalfields is primarily all about the market. It was established during the reign of Charles I in 1638 and today, housed in its modern building, the market is still very popular. Wander around taking shots of the stalls, being mindful of those who don't wish to have their stall photographed. Seek to capture some of the ambience of the busy market, especially if you visit on a weekend, then head to the streets directly surrounding the market building; here you will find intriguing buildings and art: the Verde restaurant across the road with its classic French decoration, the printers around the corner and the various novel pieces of art. Keep an eye out for interesting characters to isolate from the crowds and so create an interesting street image.

*Opposite top: Street art in Spitalfields. Sony A6000, 16–50mm at 16mm, ISO 250, 1/160s at f/4. May.*

*Opposite bottom: Brick Lane Sunday market. Canon 5D II, 17–40mm at 29mm, ISO 200, 1/125s at f/8. Aug.*

## How to get here

### Spitalfields

Start from Liverpool Street Station, having arrived by Tube or bus. Proceed to the A10 Bishopsgate, then head north until you find Brushfield Street (to the right.) Spitalfields Market is on the left-hand side of Brushfield Street.

| | |
|---|---|
| **Location Lat/Long**: | 51.51946, -0.07445 |
| **Location Postcode**: | E1 6LY |
| **Underground & Lines**: | Liverpool Street: *Central, Circle* |
| **Main station**: | Liverpool Street |
| **DLR**: | Tower Gateway |
| **Bus**: | 8, 26, 35, 48, 78 |

*Old houses on Fournier Street, Spitalfields. Canon 5D II, 70–200mm at 116mm, ISO 200, 1/45s at f/8. Aug.*

## Brick Lane ♿

There are two good reasons to visit Brick Lane: excellent food and superb street art. You will find a multitude of restaurants here, usually packed to the rafters during the evenings. As you enter the gaudily lit street full of noise and activity, taking photos can seem a tad overwhelming with so much going on. The trick is to isolate something interesting – a person, a shop front, a sign. Don't rush things. Take your time and see what catches your eye, then take a few seconds to plan the shot. If it's at night, a high ISO is the order of the day. No one will stop you setting up a tripod but you'll probably find yourself in the way. What's more the restaurant 'gatherers' will spy you and see you as a potential customer if you're not on the move, so expect to be asked many times if you want to come in for food! Brick Lane has some of the best street art London has to offer, so visit during the day and take your time. Explore the side streets off it too; there are hundreds of artworks, large and small. Dull overcast days work best for shooting street art because bright, sunny days tend to bleach the colours. The paints used are often reflective, so a polariser can be useful to reduce glare.

## Fournier Street ♿

As you emerge from Spitalfields Market on the east entrance, you will come out on to Commercial Road. Walk south until you see the large white church – the road that lies to the north is Fournier Street and, with its connected streets Wilkes and Princelet, it's like stepping back in time to the 1800s. The houses have old ornate entrances and wooden window frames; almost every house is unique in design and decoration. Try using a zoom lens and shooting along the street from the western end; you'll get a very tightly compressed and intriguing shot of the doorways. Look out for Number 11 and its neighbour, 'Number 11 and a Half'. To bring a bit of life to your images, wait for someone to pass by and capture them as they move along this fascinating part of the city.

*Opposite top left*: Brick Lane street signs. Sony A6000, 16–50mm at 50mm, ISO 100, 1/200s at f/5.6. May. **Right**: Largescale street art, Spitalfields. Sony A6000, 16–50mm at 16mm, ISO 100, 1/100s at f/4.5. July.

## How to get here

### Brick Lane
At the far eastern end of Brushfield Street, cross over Leman Street and take Fournier Street, which runs along the northern side of Christ Church (which you can see at the end of Brushfield Street.) Brick Lane is situated at the end of Fournier Street.

| | |
|---|---|
| **Location Lat/Long**: | 51.51915, -0.07173 |
| **Location Postcode**: | E1 6RE |

### Fournier Street
From Liverpool Street Station, take the A10 Bishopsgate. Take a right along Brushfield Street, cross over Leman Street, and Fournier Street is located on the northern side of Christ Church. If you're on Brick Lane, head south. The Brick Lane Mosque marks the corner of Brick Lane and Fournier Street.

| | |
|---|---|
| **Location Lat/Long**: | 51.51927, -0.07371 |
| **Location Postcode**: | E1 6LY |

*Mobile coffee shop in Brick Lane market. Sony A6000, 16–50mm at 16mm, ISO 100, 1/250s at f/4.5. May.*

*Opposite left*: Doors in Spitalfields. Sony A6000, 16–50mm at 21mm, ISO 1000, 1/160s at f/4. Oct.

*Above*: Brick Lane curry restaurant signs. Canon 5D IV, 24–70mm at 70mm, ISO 640, 1/60s at f/2.8. Sept.

*Below*: Wilkes Street in Spitalfields. Canon 5D II, 17–40mm at 26mm, ISO 640, 1/80s at f/4. Oct.

## Verde and Company ♿

Located on the western side of Spitalfields Market, situated on Brushfield Street is Verde and Company coffee shop. It's a super location, quaint and incredibly photogenic. During the summer, this small coffee shop has a very continental feel to it. With wicker baskets hanging under the canopy, and people sitting outside on the pavement, it just begs to be photographed. From here, walk east to the corner of Crispin Street, turn to your right and capture the faded paint of the front of Number 46, Donovan Brothers paper bag makers – another special image for your collection.

## Artillery Passage ♿

Leaving Liverpool Street Station and heading down Artillery Lane you will find much of interest to photograph. The narrow streets around Artillery Passage and Gun Lane have a lively, bohemian feel and this is the place to get personal with the city. Using the widest lens you have, look for solid compositions that incorporate the long length of Artillery Passage while also capturing the shops and buildings that close over it. Anything under 40mm focal length will work here. This is another place that works well when it rains; lights come on in the evening and the location takes on an ominous feeling as darkness battles meagre streetlights in the pouring rain.

*Opposite*: Artillery Passage in the rain, Spitalfields. Canon 5D IV, 24–70mm at 24mm, ISO 5000, 1/30s at f/4. Sept.

*Verde and Co, Spitalfields. Canon 5D II, 70–200mm at 135mm, ISO 400, 1/30s at f/11. Aug.*

## How to get here

### Verde and Company

This coffee shop lies on Brushfield Street, opposite Spitalfields Market.

| | |
|---|---|
| **Location Lat/Long**: | 51.51900, -0.07699 |
| **Location Postcode**: | E1 6AG |

### Artillery Passage

From Liverpool Street Station, head east to the A10 Bishopsgate, cross over and turn right by Dirty Dicks pub along Middlesex Street. Cross the road and take the left side of the fork that heads down Widegate Street. Where Widegate Street crosses Sandy's Row (you should see the Kings Stores pub on the corner) you will find Artillery Passage, it's a very narrow pedestrian-only passageway.

| | |
|---|---|
| **Location Lat/Long**: | 51.51814, -0.07742 |
| **Location Postcode**: | E1 6AG |

### Accessibility ♿

This is an ordinary city street, which should present no accessibility issues.

### Best time of year/day

This location can be shot all year round. The quietest time to shoot the street art is in the morning an hour or so after sunrise when there's plenty of light. At weekends you will find more markets and shops open. For Verde and Company, during summer days, the outside is more likely to be decorated, providing more interest to your shots.

**Walk from the Tower of London north through Aldgate heading back into the City and make time to take this interesting little diversion.**

As you pass Trinity House, head along Coopers Row then turn right along Crutched Friars. When you reach the corner of Crutched Friars and Rangoon Street, you'll find two stone figures tucked out of the way at the rear of the distinctive brown Friary Court building. The statue recognises one of the four orders of the *Fratres Cruciferi* (the cross-bearing brethren) – the Crutched Friars who settled in London in 1249 close to Tower Hill.

This is one of my favourite statues, partly because it's so hard to find and quite different from the usual white marble statues set high on plinths. But there's another reason it's special to me: when I was taking pictures of it, a local man approached me and we began talking about London and photography. As we parted company, he whispered that it's considered good luck to rub the foot of each statue and say "Thank you Father" to each figure. Whether you're superstitious or not, this is just one example of the special experiences you can have while walking and taking photos around London if you're open to them. I always advise people to walk the streets of the city, only using the Tube and bus when really necessary so you can experience London face-to-face. So make time to see these statues as you pass from location to location, take some pictures and gather your own little piece of London's good fortune.

*The Crutched Friars near Tower of London. Canon 5D II, 17–40mm at 17mm, ISO 200, 1/60s at f/11. July.*

*Opposite: The Crutched Friars near Tower of London. Canon 5D II, 70–200mm at 70mm, ISO 200, 1/60s at f/8. July.*

## How to get here

Start from Tower Hill Tube station and head north to Trinity Square, which leads directly on to Coopers Row. Keep heading north until you meet the crossroads with Crosswall. Cross over and this will lead you on to Crutched Friars Road which veers north-easterly. Head past Northumberland Alley, where you will see a pink stone building. Keep walking until you see the statue.

| | |
|---|---|
| **Location Lat/Long**: | 51.51211, -0.07687 |
| **Location Postcode**: | EC3N 2HT |
| **Underground & Lines**: | Tower Hill: *Circle & District* |
| **Main Station**: | Fenchurch Street |
| **Bus**: | 15, 42, 78, 100 |
| **Cycle Hire**: | Crosswall, Tower |

## Accessibility ♿

This is an ordinary city street, which should present no accessibility issues.

## Best time of year/day

This location can be shot all year round.

There has been a castle or fort here since just after 1066 when the Normans, led by William the Conqueror, seized control of Britain. The Normans built the central White Tower that housed the king and the famous landmark is now the most complete 11th-century palace in Europe. Her Majesty's Royal Palace and Fortress of the Tower of London has had many uses over its thousand-year history; as a palace, prison, armoury, treasury and royal mint. The Crown Jewels are still displayed here and, for a while, it housed a menagerie of exotic wild animals.

Many famous historical figures were sent to the Tower when they fell from favour and were brutally dealt with by the monarch they had displeased. The warders and Beefeaters who guard the Tower and give tours will tell you of ghosts – in particular Anne Boleyn, who in 1536 was beheaded at the Tower for treason. She allegedly roams the White Tower carrying her head under her arm. So while you're taking pictures don't be surprised if you get more in your photographs than you bargained for! Lions, leopards, hyenas and even a polar bear – gifts to the reigning monarch of the time – were once kept at the Tower and in the 18th century the menagerie was open to the public for an admission of three pence. You could even gain free entry, if you supplied a cat or dog to feed to the lions housed there! The animals were eventually relocated to London and Regent's Park zoos and today, only the ravens remain. Six ravens, under the care of the Ravenmaster, are kept at the Tower at all times or, legend has it, the kingdom will fall.

*Above*: *Tower of London with display of ceramic. Canon 5D II, 17–40mm at 17mm, ISO 200, 1/5s at f/6.3, tripod. Sept.*

*Opposite*: *Beefeaters in the Tower of London. Canon 5D II, 17–40mm at 40mm, ISO 200, 1/125s at f/8. July.*

## What to shoot and viewpoints

### Outside in the grounds ♿

The Tower of London is a superb place to photograph. Although the entrance fee is quite expensive, with so many areas within the Tower now open to the public it is good value for money. Allow at least half a day to enjoy all the Tower has to offer. Head here on a bright day if you can and benefit from good light, in which to secure excellent images of the exterior of the various buildings.

There are many walkways and paths that provide great lead lines to the different sections of the Tower complex. The old cottages that face directly towards the White Tower in the centre of the complex are themselves wonderful buildings to shoot; you can't get too close but by using a 50mm lens, you can get some great shots. Use the walkways by the cottages and you may be lucky enough to catch a Beefeater on the way to his post. If you're quick off the mark, you'll get them in front of the White Tower. The cottage walkway by the Beauchamp Tower offers a high enough platform to allow you to incorporate Tower Bridge as background interest in your images. »

## How to get here

Take the Circle Line to Tower Hill station, then exit the station and follow the steps down under Tower Hill (the road). You will come out to the path that leads west around the Tower of London to the entrance. An alternative is to find your way to the river then simply head towards Tower Bridge, which is situated right next to the Tower of London.

| | |
|---|---|
| **Location Lat/Long**: | 51.50814, -0.07610 |
| **Location Postcode**: | EC3N 4AB |
| **Underground & Lines**: | Tower Hill: *Circle & District* |
| **Main Station**: | Fenchurch Street, London Bridge |
| **DLR**: | Tower Gateway |
| **Riverboat**: | Tower Pier |
| **Bus**: | 15, 42, 78, 100, RV1 |
| **Cycle Hire**: | Tower Gardens, Tower |
| **Car Park**: | Tower Hill Car Park, EC3R 6DT |

## Accessibility &#9855;

Most areas within the Tower are fully accessible including the Jewel House, though some areas like the White Tower and battlements are not. There are several cobbled areas and some steps, so if you're concerned, it's best to head to the Royal Palaces and check their statement on accessibility within the Tower complex.

## Best time of year/day

The Tower of London can be shot all year round but summer is best when the grass, foliage and flowerbeds are lush and look great set against the buildings' stonework.

*Flower boxes in Tower of London. Canon 5D II, 17–40mm at 27mm, ISO 200, 1/250s at f/8. July.*

*Tower of London gateway. Canon 5D II, 24–70mm at 24mm, ISO 200, 1/30s at f/13. Apr.*

The entire site is quite small and contains various styles of buildings that have been added over the centuries. From the central White Tower to the houses and cottages at the outer edges for employees and Beefeaters, this eclectic mix of architectural styles offers yet more picture opportunities. Keep an eye out for unique compositions, in which you can juxtapose different styles of building. Another interesting possibility is to use arches as frames for photographs. If you make your way to the southern most area (by the gift shop), there is one arch that allows you to frame the White Tower, and this works really well on a sunny day. Alternatively, on colder, cloudy days, try heading up to the southern battlements for a more sombre, moody image of this place of murder, mystery and intrigue.

## Inside &

Shooting inside the buildings will require high ISO abilities and fast lenses, and tripods are not allowed anywhere in the main site. Some areas within the site do not allow photography at all – the Jewel House being one of them, for security reasons.

*Opposite top: Beefeater heading towards the White Tower. Canon 5D II, 17–40mm at 17mm, ISO 200 1/500s at f/8. July.*

*Famous Tower of London raven. Canon 5D II, 70–200mm at 200mm, ISO 400, 1/90s at f/5.6. Apr.*

*Gardens at the Tower of London. Canon 5D II, 24–70mm at 24mm, ISO 200, 1/500s at f/8. July.*

*Tower Bridge from Tower of London. Canon 5D II, 24–70mm at 24mm, ISO 100, 1/15s at f/8, tripod, LEE ND 0.6 hard grad. Sept.*

### From the Thames Path ♿

You can use tripods along the walkway by the Thames, which is especially good when the riverside is clear early in the mornings. The Tower is generally open from 7am to 7pm. During the winter months it's worth getting there when the gates open, as you'll be able to catch some superb shots of the buildings and Tower Bridge from a unique angle during blue hour. The Beefeaters sometimes take breaks away from the main building by the Thames riverside, offering unusual photo opportunities. See page 112 Tower Bridge.

### Events

Events are held at the Tower during the summer months, particularly during school holidays, and these are the best times to visit. Not only will you get to shoot pictures of the Tower buildings but also be able to capture images of people in period costume performing various tasks such as metal working, jewellery making, creating weapons and armour, even performing plays involving the visitors and combat recreations. While shooting these events, try to compose and frame the subjects without any modern trappings – try to isolate faces and hands. If you set your camera to sport/action mode, you'll be able to fire off many shots in quick succession and capture some interesting expressions in the actors' faces and gestures.

*Next spread: The White Tower, Tower of London. Canon 5D II, 17–40mm at 20mm, ISO 200, 1/750s at f/8. July.*

*Opposite top left: Medieval recreationist, Tower of London re-enactment day. Canon 5D II, 70–200mm at 70mm, ISO 400, 1/250s at f/9.5. Apr. Top right: Tower of London re-enactment day. Canon 5D II, 70–200mm at 200mm, ISO 200, 1/125s at f/8. Apr.*

*Opposite bottom left: Tower of London re-enactment day. Canon 5D II, 70–200mm at 200mm, ISO 200, 1/1500s at f/4. Apr. Bottom right: Tower of London re-enactment day. Canon 5D II, 70–200mm at 135mm, ISO 200, 1/125s at f/11. Apr.*

**A church ruin situated right in the heart of London's financial district is certainly a unique location to take photos. Originally built in 1100, St Dunstan-in-the-East was almost destroyed by the Great Fire of 1666. Its rather sad history continued with the church being repaired many times and parts of the building removed in case of possible structural collapse.**

It was repaired during the 19th century only to be completely gutted during the Blitz in World War II, when only the steeple and tower survived. The decision not to rebuild was made in 1967 and instead it was turned into a public garden. As you pass through the City, most probably on your way from the Tower of London, it's well worth stopping off for ten minutes to enjoy this peaceful spot.

## What to shoot and viewpoints

If ever the phrase 'oasis in the city' was fitting, it certainly applies to St Dunstan-in-the-East. The strong walls and large open window frames, having had all the stained glass removed or destroyed during the Blitz, make it a wonderful place to take photos. The many arches of the old church can be used for framing your shots, giving you the opportunity to experiment with depth and focus. If you have a friend or family member with you, the benches and arches make the perfect place to shoot portraits. Harsh light on sunny days creates strong bold shapes which complement the array of grass areas and flowerbeds, as the open nature of the broken architecture allows the light to cast interesting shadow

*Opposite left*: St Dunstan-in-the-East Gardens. Canon 5D II, 17–40mm at 29mm, ISO 200, 1/45s at f/8. July.

*Opposite right*: Magpie at St Dunstan-in-the-East churchyard. Canon 5D II, 70–200mm at 183mm, ISO 200, 1/60s at f/4.5. Apr.

patterns. The north garden, with its winding pathway that leads to the east end of the church, is a must-see. Empty window frames are covered by ivy and moss that form wonderful, natural patterns ornamenting the lime-washed walls of what's left of the church. The location is often used as a venue to host photo shoots and weddings due to its open areas, which trap the bright sunlight so well.

*Opposite left*: St Dunstan-in-the-East gardens. Canon 5D II, 17–40mm at 17mm, ISO 200, 1/90s at f/8. July.
*Top right*: St Dunstan-in-the-East gardens. Canon 5D II, 17–40mm at 17mm, ISO 200, 1/500s at f/8. July.
*Middle right*: St Dunstan-in-the-East gardens. Canon 5D II, 24–70mm at 38mm, ISO 200, 1/45s at f/8. July.

## How to get here

If coming from Monument Station (Circle line), exit the station and head east along Eastcheap. Keep walking for about five minutes, until you find St Dunstan's Hill to your right. Head south and you'll find the church garden on your right. If coming from Tower Hill, head west along Great Tower Street passing the Hung Drawn and Quartered pub to your left. Head east until you find St Dunstan's Hill to your left, then head south until you find the church garden on your right. You can also walk east along Lower Thames Street from the Tower of London; from here, turn right up St Dunstan's Hill – a pedestrian-only entrance – and you will see the church garden directly in front of you.

**Location Lat/Long**: 51.50969, -0.08259
**Location Postcode**: EC3R 5DD
**Underground & Lines**: Monument: *Circle & District*
**Main Station**: Fenchurch Street, Cannon Street
**Riverboat**: Tower Pier
**Bus**: 15

### Accessibility

The church garden itself is flat with just one of two small steps. However, there are about half-a-dozen steps leading up to the entrance, so it's not easily accessible to wheelchairs.

### Best time of year/day

The best time of year to visit is summer or autumn. The flowers are all in bloom in summer, which really gives an oasis feeling to this location, and the backdrop of steel and concrete buildings works well with lush, green summer foliage. In autumn, these leaves turn a rich browns and oranges and the ivy on the old stonework looks good any time of year. The main consideration though is to aim to shoot at midday, when the light gets right into this tucked-away spot.

The Sky Garden is a large 360° viewing area located at the top of 20 Fenchurch Street – a 160m skyscraper close to the Tower of London. The striking building is more fondly known as the Walkie Talkie due its concave shape, which, several years ago, acted as a mirror, reflecting and focussing sunlight on to the streets below. The heat generated – over 100°C – melted the bodywork of cars parked in the street directly below the building and a news reporter was able to fry an egg in a pan set on the ground! This issue has since been resolved; in 2014 the building was fitted with a 'sunshade' – a *brise soleil* – to reduce solar glare.

The primary reason for visiting the Sky Garden is, of course, the incredible view looking south over the whole of London. The front-facing gallery allows a full 180° view that encompasses Tower Bridge to the east and Westminster to the west. It is one of the best views of London and is free to visit. However, in order to visit the Sky Garden you must first register for tickets on the Sky Garden website (skygarden.london). The waiting list for tickets is usually about three to four weeks, so ensure you book early to avoid missing out. Tickets are not available from the building itself; the website is the only place to obtain tickets for entry.

Photography is actively encouraged at the Sky Garden and, within reason, you are welcome to use any camera you wish, though monopods, tripods or selfie-sticks are not permitted and any attempt to use these items will result in a swift rebuke from one of the many security guards. This is a private location, so commercial photography requires prior agreement. The main viewing balcony has a two-metre-high glass partition that is open at the top, so security are acutely aware people may attempt to raise cameras and phones above the glass partition, potentially dropping them several hundred feet to the street below. You are free to walk around the entire Sky Garden area and take as many pictures as you wish. In my experience, staff are very helpful and friendly towards photographers.

## What to shoot and viewpoints

The best time to visit is shortly before dusk in order to catch the sunset. The main viewing balcony has a very thick glass partition with a slight green hue to it, so be prepared to remove that during the editing process. Shooting long exposures as the light starts to fade is tricky as you can't use any form of tripod – not even a small one.

### Use a sweater or jacket as a camera rest
The trick is to place a sweater on the balcony handrail, then place the camera on top, pulling a sleeve over the lens to ensure no reflected light bounces between the lens and the main glass partition. This does pique the interest of staff but they're usually just curious about the novel ways people find to get pictures of the view. Using this technique I was able to secure several images of about 20–30 seconds of traffic crossing London Bridge and the soft glow of the city lights around the Shard as blue hour arrived. Be aware: once dusk hits, the interior of the Sky Garden becomes brighter than the area outside, causing reflections in the glass that will inevitably be on your images. In addition to this, the Sky Garden staff begin to place purple and pink lanterns around the bar area, so aim to capture all your evening shots before the lanterns appear.

The Sky Garden viewing area is not the only thing to see at 20 Fenchurch Street; if you visit on a bright sunny day, arrive early and take a good walk right around the building itself, always looking up. A blue sky with white wispy cloud makes a perfect background to the steel and glass architecture of the Walkie Talkie. You can construct some intriguing abstract images, using the steel lines of the building against the sky.

*Opposite top*: View looking east from the top of the Walkie-Talkie building. Canon 5D II, 24–70mm at 57mm, ISO 400, 1/60s at f/8. Oct. **Middle left**: Abstract lines of the building. Canon 5D II, 70–200mm at 127mm, ISO 200, 1/250s at f/8. Oct. **Middle right**: Restaurant and bar area. Canon 5D II, 24–70mm at 24mm, ISO 1600, 1/8s at f/2.8. Oct.

*Next spread*: Looking south from top of the building. Canon 5D II, 24–70mm at 24mm, ISO 200, 6s at f/8. Oct.

## How to get here

From Monument Station (Circle line ) exit the station and head
east along Eastcheap. Keep walking for about five minutes until
you find Philpot Lane to your left. Head north up this lane until
you find yourself at the foot of the building.

| | |
|---|---|
| **Location Lat/Long**: | 51.51114, -0.08384 |
| **Location Postcode**: | EC3M 8AF |
| **Underground & Lines**: | Monument: *Circle & District* |
| **Main Station**: | Fenchurch Street, Cannon Street |
| **Riverboat**: | Tower Pier |
| **Bus**: | 15, 48 |

## Accessibility ♿

This location is fully accessible with excellent service for
wheelchair users and those with limited mobility.

## Best time of year/day

Any time of year is good for a visit but the best time of day is
at dusk, when you can catch the city as it heads from day
into early evening.

*The bar, Walkie-Talkie building. Canon 5D II, 24–70mm
at 43mm, ISO 400, 1/20s at f/8. Oct.*

Like most cities, London has undergone much construction and demolition over hundreds of years and this has led to a very eclectic mix of new and old. Lovat Lane falls into the latter camp; it's a steep, cobbled pedestrian lane leading from Eastcheap to Lower Thames Street. Previously called Love Lane, this narrow city path feels very closed in as you walk past St Mary-at-Hill Church at the top, down the S-shaped curve of the lane towards the Thames.

## What to shoot and viewpoints

The secret to this location lies as you emerge from the s-shape to behold a perfect view of the Shard framed by other buildings. The foreground buildings are constructed from modern concrete but as you approach the bottom of the lane you'll find a traditional old London pub, decked out in black and gold decoration: the unusually named The Walrus and The Carpenter pub (a nod to the poem by Lewis Carroll). »

## How to get here

From Monument Station (Circle line) exit the station and head east along Eastcheap. Walk for five minutes until you find Lovat Lane to your right. Turn on to it and head south. It's an S-shaped, pedestrian-only lane that leads all the way down to Lower Thames Street.

| | |
|---|---|
| **Location Lat/Long**: | 51.50999, -0.08409 |
| **Location Postcode**: | EC3R 8EE |
| **Underground & Lines**: | Monument: *Circle & District* |
| **Main Station**: | Fenchurch Street, Cannon Street |
| **Riverboat**: | Tower Pier |
| **Bus**: | 15, 48 |

## Accessibility

This is a relatively steep cobbled lane. If you have mobility problems, you may be OK to proceed but ensure you have sensible footwear and some assistance in case you find yourself in trouble. You may find it easier to approach the lane from the southern end, entering from Lower Thames Street. There you won't have to descend the steep lane, but only partially ascend it to get a photograph. The street is cobbled and therefore not easily accessible for wheelchair users, though with assistance you may be able to head up enough of the lower part of the lane to capture the pub in a foreground photo.

## Best time of year/day

This spot can be shot all year round. The best time to visit is late evening or early morning before sunrise.

*Top*: Early morning on Lovat Lane by Monument. Canon 5D II, 17–40mm at 17mm, ISO 200, 1s at f/8, tripod. Mar. ***Above***: Artwork on Philpot Lane by Tower of London. Canon 5D II, 70–200mm at 200mm, ISO 200, 1/250s at f/4.5. May.

*Left*: Rainy day. Canon 5D II, 17–40mm at 21mm, ISO 100, 0s at f/8. Mar.

*Opposite*: Early morning on Lovat Lane. Canon 5D II, 17–40mm at 19mm, ISO 100, 1s at f/8, tripod. Mar.

*Keeping dry. Sony A6000, 16–50mm at 17mm, ISO 1250, 1/160s at f/4. Mar.*

*Wet cobbles. Canon 5D II, 17–40mm at 21mm, ISO 100, 1s at f/8, tripod. Mar.*

This location is not done giving up its secrets just yet … for the ultimate photograph, visit on a dark wet evening, when the cobbles glisten in the rain, the lights from the pub glow and, in the distance, the summit of the Shard glows eerily in the sodden London sky. All of this, combined with the atmosphere of the closed-in lane makes it one of the must-shoot spots in London and without a doubt, it's one of my favourites.

If you do decide to visit Lovat Lane, take a small five-minute detour to see what's considered to be London's smallest sculpture, the Philpot Mice. Walk north up Lovat Lane back on to Eastcheap, take a left and then the

first right into Philpot Lane. On the side of the very first building (on the corner of Philpot Lane and Eastcheap), about 2m above the ground, you'll find a tiny sculpture of two purple mice nibbling at a piece of cheese. Whilst you might not make a special journey to see it, this sculpture makes an interesting diversion and many people simply pass by without even realising it's there.

*Opposite: Looking towards the Shard. Canon 5D IV, 24–70mm at 27mm, ISO 6400, 1/30s at f/2.8, tripod. Sept.*

The Great Fire of London occurred in 1666, starting off in Pudding Lane, from where it swept ferociously through east London before it was finally stopped near Smithfield. In the end 13,000 buildings were destroyed and 430 acres of London devastated. The 202-ft-tall Monument is a Doric column of Portland stone situated on Pudding Lane, where the first church to be razed to the ground was located. It's not the site where the fire actually started, as many believe. Designed by Robert Hooke and Christopher Wren, the Monument was completed in 1677 and it is the tallest free-standing column of its kind in the world.

## What to shoot and viewpoints

Many images can be taken of the Monument from the roads leading to it, including some interesting juxtapositions with the surrounding architecture. The view from the top is worthwhile despite the punishing 311 steps but is somewhat marred by a very fine wire mesh cage. It is possible however to focus past the cage and obtain some spectacular views of London. One of the most interesting parts of the structure in photographic terms is the staircase that leads up the inside. Shooting inside the monument is quite tricky as it's very dark – you'll need fast lenses and a camera with good low-light capabilities. I found that an f/2.8 to f/4 lens worked fine and shooting at ISO800 or greater was required along with a steady hand. The busiest times are always in the middle of the day, and the narrow steps are easily congested, so I would advise visiting around dusk. At this time, you can catch the city lights as they begin to glow against a deep blue sky. The best time of year would be October/November, when you can time your visit to coincide with dusk leading into night before the Monument closes. No tripods are allowed so a small, flexible mini-tripod is ideal. The cage does have a small ledge for you to place your camera on and if you have a smaller aperture lens, this can be pushed up against one of the gaps in the cage to obtain a clear view of the city below.

The company that operates the Monument also operates Tower Bridge so you can buy a combined ticket for both attractions from their website. This will save you money as, being just a short walk apart, both attractions can be visited in the same day.

*Opposite top: The Monument's spiral stairs. Canon 5D II, 17–40mm at 17mm, ISO 800, 0s at f/4. July.*

*Opposite bottom left: Monument at dawn. Sony A6000, 16–50mm at 45mm, ISO 100, 1/80s at f/5.6. Apr.*
*Right: Shard and Monument. Sony A6000, 16–50mm at 50mm, ISO 100, 1/400s at f/5.6. May.*

## How to get here

The Monument is located right next door to Monument Station; simply follow the signs from within the station. If you're coming from along the River Thames, keep walking towards London Bridge, climb the stairs and walk north towards the Monument Station entrance. The Monument is located at the junction of Monument Street and Fish Street Hill.

| | |
|---|---|
| Location Lat/Long: | 51.51014, -0.08593 |
| Location Postcode: | EC3R 8AH |
| Underground & Lines: | Monument: *Circle & District* |
| Main Station: | Fenchurch Street, Cannon Street |
| Riverboat: | Tower Pier |
| Bus: | 15, 17, 35, 43 |

## Accessibility &#x267F;

Exterior shots should present no problems as the streets around the Monument are flat and level. However the steps within the Monument itself are very narrow and with over 300 of them, you need to be mobile *and* fairly fit to climb to the top.

## Best time of year/day

This location can be shot all year round but the view from the top is only accessible during opening hours.

## Opening hours

| | |
|---|---|
| Summer hours: | Apr–Sep 9.30am–6pm daily (last admission 5.30pm) |
| Winter hours: | Oct–Mar 9.30am–5.30pm daily (last admission 5pm) |

The Monument is closed from 24th–26th Dec.

## Admission prices (2019)

Please note that payment is by cash only.

| | |
|---|---|
| **Adults:** | **£4.50** |
| **Children** (aged 5–15): | **£2.30** |
| **Students** (with ID): | **£3.00** |
| **Seniors** (aged 60+): | **£3.00** |

Leadenhall Market sits in the centre of the main financial district of London, just a stone's throw from the Bank of England. Originally a poultry market, it stands on what is believed to be the centre of Roman London, and the current covered marketplace structure was designed by Sir Horace Jones in 1881. However, the second most people see it they remember one thing: Diagon Alley!

The marketplace was used for exterior scenes in the film adaptations of JK Rowling's beloved Harry Potter books. The market has in fact been used for exterior shoots in many films and music videos. No longer an open-air marketplace, it now serves as a shopping arcade and covered space, where restaurants and bars offer al fresco refreshment all year round.

## What to shoot and viewpoints

During the evenings the market place can be very busy, especially on a Friday night in summer when City workers like to let their hair down after a busy week. At weekends, the marketplace (like much of the financial district) is practically a ghost town. For busy shots of city folk, arrive around 4pm and stay for an hour or so. >>

## How to get here

Coming from Bank Station (Central line) proceed east along Cornhill
and turn right at Gracechurch Street. Keep an eye to the left, until you
spot the entrance to Leadenhall Market. Coming from Monument
Station, head north along Gracechurch Street for about 5 minutes
until you spot the entrance to Leadenhall Market to your right.

**Location Lat/Long**:   51.5128, -0.08348
**Location Postcode**:   EC3V 1LT
**Underground & Lines**:   Bank: *Circle*
**Main Station**:   Liverpool Street
**Bus**:   35, 48

## Accessibility ♿

The main paths that lead through the market are cobbled, which
may make it tricky for wheelchair users. However, there are flat
paths to the side of the cobbled sections in most places, which will
allow you access to the market. If you do have limited mobility,
I would advise you visit during quieter times such as the weekend,
as the lanes within the market are often full of visitors, chairs
and tables, which inevitably impede movement.

## Best time of year/day

The market can be shot all year round, although weekends
are quieter. Late evenings offer a rich, warm light within
the interior.

*Above: Leadenhall Market at Christmastime. Canon 5D II,
17–40mm at 19mm, ISO 100, 6s at f/11, tripod. Jan.*

*Opposite: Ultra-wide-angle image of Leadenhall Market.
Canon 5D II, 17–40mm at 17mm, ISO 400,
1/45s at f/8. July.*

*Leadenhall Market at Christmas. Canon 5D II, 17–40mm at 17mm, ISO 100, 1s at f/11, tripod. Nov.*

To capture the marketplace completely empty, visit on a Saturday or Sunday morning before 9am and you'll have the place to yourself. The same can be said for late evening shoots at the weekend; visit after 9pm on a Saturday and you're likely to be the only one there. It's private land but I've never had any issues shooting with a tripod, however I would advise only shooting handheld in busy evening periods, otherwise you'll quickly find yourself in the way.

Visiting during the day is a treat as it allows you to shoot the interior details, such as the large number of dragons in their 'roosts' atop various pillars and the decorated ceiling in the central crossroads section – deep blue with painted stars. You'll need something around 100mm to capture a lot of the smaller details but even a 70mm lens should be adequate for capturing the stunning paintwork. If you have a very wide-angle or fish-eye lens, a classic shot is to stand in the centre and shoot two of the arched areas leading off in different directions.

During the evenings, when the lights come on inside the market, a soft amber colour creates a cosy feeling within the large open halls; this is the time to shoot. The rich, red ironwork with gold detail (signs and other fixtures) makes for a very rich image indeed. There's no special equipment required; a tripod and camera is all you need. Aim for a deep depth-of-field with a large f-stop and shoot away.

*Opposite top: Leadenhall Market ceiling. Sony A6000, Fisheye 8mm at 8mm, ISO 640, 1/320s at f/8. May.*

*Opposite left: Dining and drinks on St George's Day. Sony A6000, 16–50mm at 16mm, ISO 1000, 1/160s at f/4. Apr.*
*Right: Dragons, Leadenhall Market. Canon 5D II, 70–200mm at 200mm, ISO 800, 1/30s at f/5.6. July.*

Situated at the heart of London, the City of London – the Square Mile (as opposed to the city of London) – is a county in its own right that lies amidst the other 33 London boroughs. Its purpose? Business – specifically, the business of making money. The financial industry dominates here; from Monday to Friday more than 300,000 people commute to the City to work, although only 9,000 reside here. Amongst the mix of skyscrapers and old buildings, the wheels of business, finance, insurance, law and commerce are turned; 500 banks have their offices here, as well as the London Stock Exchange, Lloyd's of London and the Bank of England. It is this mix of old and new, along with the volume of people in such a compact area that makes the City so interesting for photography.

The area has been a centre of commerce since the Romans established a settlement here in 43AD, when it was known as Londinium. To the western side of the City is the Temple, with the Royal Courts of Justice and many firms of solicitors and barristers. The City has some unique attributes, including its own Mayor – the Lord Mayor of the City of London – a completely separate office from the Mayor of London and the one referred to in the story of Dick Whittington.

*30 St Mary Axe during Winter. Canon 5D II, 24–70mm at 52mm, ISO 400, 1/80s at f/16. Jan.*

## What to shoot and viewpoints

Old and new architecture rubs shoulders here; for every huge monolithic glass temple there are dozens of smaller buildings nestled in the backstreets of the City. The area around Cornhill, where the Royal Exchange is located, has many alleys and passages to explore.

### Viewpoint 1 – 30 St Mary Axe (The Gherkin) &

Designed by world-famous architect Norman Foster and built in 2003, the Gherkin is easily one of London's most recognisable contemporary buildings. Its distinctive shape is a wonderful counterbalance to the rest of the regimented square buildings in the City of London, making it interesting for placing in compositions. One of the best places to get photos of it is from Leadenhall Street, on the corner where the Lloyd's building stands. From this spot you'll get a very clear view of the building. Additionally you can compose images using St Andrew Undershaft church in the foreground. For something slightly more unusual, zoom in on the Gherkin on a very bright day, especially if a sunrise or sunset is in progress and you'll be treated to a snakeskin effect as its diamond-shaped panes of glass appear to twist, each piece catching the light at different angles and reflecting it with varied intensity.

*Opposite: The Gherkin from Leadenhall Street. Canon 5D II, 17–40mm at 17mm, ISO 200, 1/45s at f/16. July.*

The Gherkin behind buildings on St Helen's Place. Canon 5D II, 70–200mm at 70mm, ISO 200, 1/125s at f/8. July.

## Viewpoint 2 – The Lloyd's Building &

Designed by Richard Rogers architects and opened in 1986, it is a classic example of Bowellism architecture, in which the functional infrastructure of the building is visible on the outside. The Lloyds building makes for interesting images with its duct work and other functional fittings creating incredible textures. I recommend a walk along Lime Street, where it is located, and shooting directly up to the sky. If you have a very wide-angle lens or even a fisheye, this is a superb place to capture an unusual view of the City architecture. Extreme fisheye lenses of 8mm will be able to capture the Gherkin on the edge of the frame, and on sunny days the light bouncing between the glass and steel is a sight to behold.

*Opposite top left: Lloyd's building at sunset. Sony A6000, Fisheye 8mm at 8mm, ISO 400, 1/160s at f/8. June. **Right**: Lloyd's at dusk. Canon 5D II, 17–40mm at 17mm, ISO 1600, 1/40s at f/4.5. Oct.*

*Opposite bottom left: Lloyd's, City of London. Sony A6000, 16–50mm at 50mm, ISO 200, 1/80s at f/5.6. Apr. **Right**: Lloyd's, City of London. Canon 5D II, 24–70mm at 50mm, ISO 200, 1/180s at f/11. July.*

*Next spread: City of London financial district. Sony A6000, Fisheye 8mm at 8mm, ISO 125, 1/160s at f/8. June.*

## How to get here

### The Square Mile

The nearest station from which to start exploration of the Square Mile is Bank Station, where you'll find yourself outside Cornhill Royal Exchange.

**Underground & Lines:** Bank, Monument, Aldgate, Liverpool Street: *Central, Circle*
**Main Station:** Liverpool Street

### Accessibility &

Most areas within the Square Mile are standard streets; some are cobbled streets but most are flat with no steps and, where required, ramps are in place to ensure full accessibility for wheelchairs.

### Best time of year/day

Can be shot all year round.

### VP 1 – 30 St Mary Axe (The Gherkin)

From the Bank of England outside Bank Station, head east along Cornhill, cross over Gracechurch Street and head east along Leadenhall Street. You'll find St Mary Axe that leads to the Gherkin building around 500m on the left.

**Location Lat/Long:** 51.51459, -0.08051
**Location Postcode:** EC3A 8EP
**Underground & Lines:** Aldgate: *Circle*
**Main Station:** Fenchurch Street
**Bus:** 25

### VP 2 – The Lloyd's Building

The Lloyd's building can be found at the junction of St Mary Axe and Leadenhall Street. Follow the directions to 30 St Mary Axe and you will pass the Lloyd's building.

**Location Lat/Long:** 51.51323, -0.0823
**Location Postcode:** EC3A 4AX
**Underground & Lines:** Aldgate: *Circle*
**Main Station:** Fenchurch Street
**Bus:** 25, 40

*Backstreets of Cornhill, the City. Canon 5D II, 17–40mm at 19mm, ISO 100, 8s at f/8, tripod. Jan.*

### Viewpoint 3 – The Jamaica Winehouse ♿

This small establishment located in St Michael's Alley is now a pub and restaurant but was originally London's first coffee house, opened in 1652 and often frequented by the famous diarist Samuel Pepys. It's a superb building to photograph with its bright red facade and huge coffee pot sign. Even in the confines of the tight alleyway, a standard mid-range lens of 24–70mm will allow you to get a good picture of this interesting little venue. Rain or shine, this location makes for a great image, particularly if you incorporate the large signage.

### Viewpoint 4 – The Royal Exchange ♿

Located next door to the Bank of England on Threadneedle Street is the Royal Exchange. Once a centre for banking and commerce, it now houses high-end shops

#### VP 3 – The Jamaica Winehouse

This can be a little tricky to find: leave Bank Station and head east along Cornhill. Keep an eye out for a small, narrow church tucked away to your right; running alongside the church is St Michael's Alley. Keep heading south until you see the huge coffee pot sign hanging outside the Jamaica Winehouse.

| | |
|---|---|
| **Location Lat/Long**: | 51.51293, -0.08571 |
| **Location Postcode**: | EC3V 9DS |
| **Underground & Lines**: | Bank: *Central* |
| **Main Station**: | Fenchurch Street, Liverpool Street |
| **Bus**: | 25 |

#### VP 4 – Royal Exchange

Alight at Bank Station. The Royal Exchange is right next to the station and the Bank of England.

| | |
|---|---|
| **Location Lat/Long**: | 51.51359, -0.08743 |
| **Location Postcode**: | EC3V 3BT |
| **Underground & Lines**: | Bank: *Central* |
| **Main Station**: | Liverpool Street |
| **Bus**: | 8, 25 |

*Jamaica Winehouse, Cornhill, City of London. Canon 5D II, 17–40mm at 17mm, ISO 100, 30s at f/8, tripod. Jan.*

*Threadneedle Street. Canon 5D II, 24–70mm at 58mm, ISO 100, 6s at f/11, tripod, LEE ND 0.6 grad. Oct.*

and restaurants. Within the building, a courtyard is home to exclusive shops such as Louis Vuitton, situated in just the right spot to entice rich city bankers looking for presents. It's also a great place to find interesting street photography opportunities as people rush through on their way to places of business. Walk south, turn on to Cornhill and head west to the front of the Exchange. Here you'll find another open space in view of the Lord Mayor's office and the Bank of England. There are some interesting compositions to be had here, especially if you use the ornate streetlights. If you have a telephoto or zoom lens, use it to isolate details among the clutter; the dragons (the symbol of the City) can be found atop streetlights and when juxtaposed with the old stone buildings, form classic images you'll have seen on the cover of countless London guidebooks.

*Lamppost and statue of James Henry Greathead on Cornhill, City of London. Canon 5D II, 70–200mm at 192mm, ISO 200, 1/250s at f/8. Apr.*

*Top*: Buses by the Bank of England, Threadneedle Street. Canon 5D II, 17–40mm at 17mm, ISO 200, 1/350s at f/8. July.

*Above*: Threadneedle Street, Royal Exchange. Canon 5D II, 70–200mm at 121mm, ISO 200, 1/350s at f/8. Apr.

*Above*: Royal Exchange building at night. Canon 5D II, 17–40mm at 20mm, ISO 100, 1s at f/8, tripod. Jan.

**Top**: *Royal Exchange, Cornhill, City of London. Canon 5D II, 17–40mm at 17mm, ISO 200, 1/180s at f/11. July.*

**Above**: *Bus light trails along Threadneedle Street. Canon 5D II, 24–70mm at 24mm, ISO 100, 3s at f/4.5, tripod. Oct.*

**Above right**: *Cornhill clock in the morning sun, Royal Exchange. Canon 5D II, 70–200mm at 200mm, ISO 200, 1/500s at f/8. Apr.*

*Looking up Throgmorton Avenue at dawn. Canon 5D IV, 24–70mm at 70mm, ISO 400, 1/30s at f/11. Apr.*

*Throgmorton Avenue. Canon 5D II, 70–200mm at 70mm, ISO 250, 1/25s at f/7.1. May.*

### Viewpoint 5 – Throgmorton Street and Avenue ♿

Throgmorton Street was named after Nicholas Throckmorton, Queen Elizabeth I's chief banker. This is another great example of the eclectic nature of the City architecture that makes for fascinating images: lining the street are a number of small shops with quaint signs over the doors, whilst all around loom the giant steel and glass buildings of various corporations. The road is curved so by standing at one end you'll be treated to the sight of Tower 42 appearing to fill the gap between the buildings at the far end. Many people use the street to reach the rear of the Bank of England and it's another superb place to get some lively street photography images of busy city workers. In the evening as the City goes quiet,

darkness descends and the lights come on; it's a good place to capture a more sombre image with one or two people passing by on their way home. Along this street you'll find the Drapers' Hall. It's easy to spot as the entrance has wrought-iron gates flanked by two enormous stone statues. Leading directly off Throgmorton Street is Throgmorton Avenue, a private cut-through only open from 7am–7pm each day. One end is owned by Drapers' livery company and the other owned by the Carpenters' livery company and both operate their own sets of gates at either end – an example of some of the unusual arrangements that have come into existence in the City.

*Opposite left: Entrance to the Drapers' Hall. Canon 5D II, 17–40mm at 17mm, ISO 200, 1/45s at f/8. July.*

*Mary Poppins spotted in Ironmonger Lane. Sony A6000, 16–50mm at 16mm, ISO 1600, 1/160s at f/4. Mar.*

## VP 5 – Throgmorton Street and Avenue

Leave Bank Station and take Threadneedle Street northeast. Take a left along Bartholomew Lane next to the Bank of England. The lane will split in two: to the left is Lothbury that continues along the outside of the Bank of England; to the right is Throgmorton Street. Head east until you see the blue railings that mark the entrance to Throgmorton Avenue.

**Location Lat/Long**: 51.51488, -0.08634
**Location Postcode**: EC2N 2DQ
**Underground & Lines**: Bank: *Central*
**Main Station**: Liverpool Street
**Bus**: 8, 11, 133

### Best time of year/day

The streets can be shot all year round, although Throgmorton Avenue is only open Monday to Friday from 7am–7pm.

## VP 6 – Ironmonger Lane

Head west from Bank Station and take the street named Poultry, (not Queen Victoria Street). Keep walking for about five minutes until you see a very narrow paved lane to your right – this is Ironmonger Lane.

**Location Lat/Long**: 51.51424, -0.09191
**Location Postcode**: EC2V 8AU
**Underground & Lines**: Bank: *Central*
**Main Station**: Fenchurch Street, Liverpool Street
**Bus**: 8, 25

## Viewpoint 6 – Ironmonger Lane ♿

This one-way lane located just off Cheapside has been known as Ironmonger Lane since the 12th century and it is believed Thomas Becket (murdered in Canterbury by followers of Henry II) was born in this particular street. At first glance it looks rather bland but the regimented architecture of the buildings and the cobbles in the lane offer a superb backdrop to capture street photography images. Using a wide-angle lens increases the perception of space; as people approach from the northern end of the lane, capture them in the frame and they will seem to dominate the scene. My favourite time to visit is when it's raining; I like to wait for that evocative shot of a single person walking over the glistening cobbles perfectly framed between the buildings.

*Early morning, Masons Avenue. Canon 5D II, 24–70mm at 24mm, ISO 100, 20s at f/7.1, tripod. Mar.*

### Viewpoint 7 – Mason's Avenue &

North of the Bank of England lie Mason's Avenue and Whalebone Court – two quaint backstreets next to the Guildhall. The streets are part of the Bassishaw ward. Mason's Avenue is the location of the pub, The Old Doctor Butler's Head. Butler was the chief physician at the court of James I. Whalebone Court is so named because whalebone was boiled here before being used to make corsets.

Not many people tend to come down these streets and therefore this particular location is one of the best to capture that classic intimate city feeling, especially after hours, when City workers relax in the various bars and pubs. Here are two ways to approach shooting these particular scenes: visit during the evening when the Dr Butler's Head is open, shoot handheld, high ISO and aim to capture a sense of workers taking a breather after a busy day.

Alternatively, visit early in the morning after overnight rain. The pavement will glisten, reflecting the meagre light of the avenue floor, and the rich artwork of signage contrasts wonderfully with the cold, harsh tones of the stonework, creating an intimate feeling.

### Viewpoint 8 – Guildhall &

Located just off Gresham Street – a road that runs parallel to Cheapside – Guildhall (never called 'the' Guildhall) is the ceremonial and administrative office of the City of London Corporation. It consists of a U-shaped set of buildings surrounding a large open courtyard. The primary focus of your visit should be the facade of the old building that houses the Great Hall. There's no need for any special equipment; it's an easy location to shoot due to the large open space. After dark the outside of the Great Hall is lit up, usually with purple lights, making a beautiful image.

*Guildhall at night. Canon 5D II, 17–40mm at 32mm, ISO 100, 4s at f/11, tripod, LEE ND 0.9 grad. Sept.*

Note that tripods are not allowed on the main concourse. Security here is very strict and you'll be asked to put it away. My advice is to stand in Guildhall Yard or further back in Gresham Street and simply zoom in to shoot images of the building at night. The Great Hall is open from May to September, from 10am–4pm. It's free to visit and, if you have time, it's well worth checking out the stunning interior.

## VP 7 – Mason's Avenue

Head north from Bank Station hugging the western side of the Bank of England along Princes Street, then take a left at the crossroads into Lothbury. Head west until you spot Coleman Street to your right then head north. Keep an eye out to your left for the pedestrian entrance to Mason's Avenue; you should see the pub about 20m inside the avenue.

| | |
|---|---|
| **Location Lat/Long**: | 51.51554, -0.09089 |
| **Location Postcode**: | EC2V 5BQ |
| **Underground & Lines**: | Bank: *Central* |
| **Main Station**: | Moorgate, Liverpool Street, Fenchurch Street |
| **Bus**: | 8, 25 |

## VP 8 – Guildhall

Head north from Bank Station hugging the western side of the Bank of England along Princes Street, then take a left at the crossroads into Lothbury, heading west. Continue as Lothbury becomes Gresham Street and keep an eye out to your right for a small lane called Guildhall Yard. Beyond it you should see Guildhall.

| | |
|---|---|
| **Location Lat/Long**: | 51.5158, -0.09196 |
| **Location Postcode**: | EC2V 7HH |
| **Underground & Lines**: | Bank: *Central* |
| **Main Station**: | Moorgate, Liverpool Street, Fenchurch Street |
| **Bus**: | 8, 25 |

*Guildhall charity event. Canon 5D II, 70–200mm at 106mm, ISO 200, 1/250s at f/8. Sept.*

*Guildhall charity event. Canon 5D II, 70–200mm at 200mm, ISO 200, 1/60s at f/8. Sept.*

## Viewpoint 9 – Love Lane ♿

Love Lane is very short road located about two minutes from the major highway of London Wall. Tucked out of sight, it links the St Alban Tower to the City of London Corporation office. St Mary Aldermanbury Garden is another of the little green havens that dot the City. Located in the centre of this oasis is a bust of William Shakespeare, dedicated to his fellow actors, Condell and Hemmings, who assisted the playwright in getting his first folio of works into print. Whilst you won't need to spend long here, it does offer some interesting picture opportunities, specifically the bust of Shakespeare positioned among the foliage that turns green in summer and golden brown in autumn. Another great little shot is found from the back of the park; from there you can capture the street's name carved into the building facade and with careful composition you can capture the words 'Love London' behind an old lamppost. It might not win any photography awards but it's a great little souvenir shot and may even gain you a few more followers on social media!

*Top left: Re-enactment actors, Guildhall. Canon 5D II at 155mm, ISO 200, 1/125s at f/6.7. Sept.*

*Opposite top left: Shakespeare bust, Love Lane. Canon 5D II, 70–200mm at 89mm, ISO 200, 1/60s at f/5.6. July.*
*Top right: Church Tower, Love Lane. Sony A6000, 16–50mm at 18mm, ISO 100, 1/320s at f/4.5. May.*

## VP 9 – Love Lane

Head north from Bank Station hugging the western side of the Bank of England along Princes Street, then take a left at the crossroads into Lothbury, heading west. Continue as Lothbury becomes Gresham Street and keep walking for five to ten minutes until you find the street Aldermanbury to your right. Head north along Aldermanbury until you reach the very small park at the far end – Love Lane is to the left.

| | |
|---|---|
| **Location Lat/Long**: | 51.51643, -0.09374 |
| **Location Postcode**: | EC2V 7AF |
| **Underground & Lines**: | Bank: *Central* |
| **Main Station**: | Moorgate, Liverpool Street, Fenchurch Street |
| **Bus**: | 100, 388 |

### Best time of year/day

The small park can be shot all year round. Summer is best for foliage and flowers.

*One Love Lane London. Canon 5D II, 70–200mm at 127mm, ISO 400, 1/45s at f/11. July.*

# [10] WATLING STREET

Watling Street is the name for an ancient trackway used by the pre-Roman Britons. The track led from near Shrewsbury on the Welsh border through England, past St Albans, through what is now London and all the way down to Dover on the Kent coast. When the Romans arrived they paved the track and turned it into a road.

You will find many Watling Streets through the towns of England marking the existence of this ancient road. Here in London there is only a small section left around the St Paul's area, no more than 100m long. It's exciting to think that this small back lane in London was once part of a tremendous track that stretched hundreds of miles from Dover almost to North Wales.

## What to shoot and viewpoints

The little back alleys around Watling Street are a wonderful example of the 'rat's nest' of streets that old cities like London are well known for. It can be quite busy during the week with the City crowd making use of the shops and bars. At weekends like most of the City, it is very quiet. There are some great photo opportunities here, shooting down the maze of pedestrian alleys, capturing busy city folk as they rush by. It will be busy during the week from dawn and well into the evening – a perfect time to capture both hectic city life images as well as the city slowing down for the evening. Visit early morning just after dawn during the summer, walk in from Cheapside and if you're lucky you may find a slight mist at the far end of Watling Street, a not-to-be-missed photo opportunity. At weekends, when it's quiet, very few of the shops and bars will be open, so this the time to be shooting those intriguing empty city images. Shoot before dawn or after dusk at weekends and there will be more atmosphere, the soft light from the lamps casting shadows over the street. At Christmastime the street is festooned with strings of lamps and these can make for perfect lead lines along the street to give your images a dynamic but cosy feeling.

*Watling Street pub. Canon 5D II, 17–40mm at 20mm, ISO 100, 4s at f/8, tripod. Jan.*

*Previous spread: City workers during rush hour. NEX-C3, E 18–55mm at 18mm, ISO 1600, 1/40s at f/3.5. Jan.*

*Opposite: Late night workers on Watling Street. Canon 5D II, 24–70mm at 24mm, ISO 100, 4s at f/8, tripod, LEE ND 0.9 grad. Apr.*

## How to get here

Coming from Bank Station, take Poultry (not Queen Victoria Street) and keep walking for about 5–10 minutes, you will eventually reach the famous St Mary-le-Bow Church (the one that defines Cockneys) and follow Bow Lane (which is just before the church) to Watling Street.

**Location Lat/Long**: 51.51274, -0.09371
**Location Postcode**: EC2V 6AU (St Mary-le-Bow Church)
**Underground & Lines**: Mansion House: *Circle & District*
**Bus**: 8, 25, 11

## Accessibility

The lane is cobbled in places and can be busy midday on weekdays. Visit during quieter times in the late evenings and weekends to ensure you won't be jostled by crowds.

## Best time of year/day

Can be shot all year round. It's quieter at weekends and at sunrise is the time to catch the best light.

*Top left: Late night on Bow Lane. Canon 5D II, 17–40mm at 17mm, ISO 100, 15s at f/11, tripod. Sept. **Right**: Reflections of St Paul's in One New Change. Sony A6000, 16–50mm at 16mm, ISO 100, 1/100s at f/4.5. Apr.*

*Above left: Bow Lane. Canon 5D II, 70–200mm at 173mm, ISO 200, 1/250s at f/8. Sept. **Right**: Along Watling Street towards St Paul's. Sony A6000, 16–50mm at 20mm, ISO 3200, 1/50s at f/4. Oct.*

*Opposite: Heading towards St Paul's along Watling Street. Sony A6000, 16–50mm at 17mm, ISO 1600, 1/160s at f/3.5. Mar.*

Often confused with Tower Bridge, London Bridge is the plain cousin of the famous Gothic construction and famed for being the subject of the nursery rhyme, *London Bridge is Falling Down*. The current bridge's predecessor (built from granite in 1831) was sold to American businessman Robert McCulloch in 1968 and is now sited at Lake Havasu in the Arizona desert. The original London Bridge (and the first to cross the Thames) was built by the Romans. Thereafter, a series of wooden and stone bridges replaced each other. In the Tudor period, there were 200 buildings on the bridge and its narrow arches slowed the ebb and flow of the tide so that during some winters, during the Little Ice Age (in the 1600s) the river would freeze and frost fairs would be held on its surface.

Construction on the current bridge was completed in 1972 and it crosses the river just thirty metres along from the original medieval bridge. Tragedy struck on June 3rd 2017 when terrorists drove a van over the bridge and into a crowd. Eight people died in the attack. All London's bridges are now fitted with barriers between the road and the pavement to prevent anyone causing such carnage again.

## What to shoot and viewpoints

### North Side &

London Bridge is one of the few bridges to have retained its red illumination, which was fitted in 2004 to mark Remembrance Day. At night the spectacle of the red glow under the bridge against the blue of the evening sky, dark water and light from the buildings marks it as one of the London's finer bridges. Position yourself to the northeast side of the bridge (north of the river) for a wonderful lead line that stretches to the collection of buildings at the foot of the Shard. Shoot at night or before dawn to capture that perfect combination of blue and orange. »

*Looking south to the Shard and London Bridge. Canon 5D II, 17–40mm at 17mm, ISO 100, 10s at f/8, tripod, LEE ND 0.9 hard grad. Jan.*

*Looking south over London Bridge to the Shard. Canon 5D II, 17–40mm at 17mm, ISO 100, 30s at f/16, tripod, LEE ND 0.9 grad. Oct.*

## How to get here

Head to London Bridge Station, exit and walk north towards the river. If you're coming from Monument station, exit the station and head south to the river. London Bridge is the next crossing west along the river from Tower Bridge so you can also walk along the river path from there.

| | |
|---|---|
| **Location Lat/Long**: | 51.50787, -0.08767 |
| **Location Postcode**: | SE1 9RA |
| **Underground & Lines**: | Monument, London Bridge: |
| | *Circle & District, Northern* |
| **Main Station**: | London Bridge |
| **Riverboat**: | London Bridge City Pier |
| **Bus**: | 17, 40, 47, 521 |

## Accessibility

This is an ordinary city street that should present no accessibility issues.

## Best time of year/day

Can be shot all year round and at any time of day, though dawn and dusk are rewarding times for a visit.

*A carpeted London Bridge. Sony A6000, 16–50mm at 16mm, ISO 100, 1/320s at f/5. June.*

*London Bridge and the Shard. Canon 5D II, 17–40mm at 40mm, ISO 200, 1/250s at f/11. July.*

As you head back towards the bridge be sure to ascend the 'wireframe' staircase on the northeast side; there are some wonderful views and a superb diamond-shaped framed composition to be had at the foot the stairs. Note that tripods are not allowed here for safety reasons so you'll need high ISO for handheld shots. You can use your tripod at the top of the stairs but make sure you're standing on the bridge pavement. Use the metallic frame of the staircase as a lead line to the Shard.

## On the bridge ♿

Crossing the bridge night or day offers a stunning view of Tower Bridge and HMS Belfast in the foreground. Tripods are permitted on the bridge and you'll often find photographers taking photos, videos and time-lapses of the Pool of London (the stretch of the Thames from London Bridge to below Limehouse). One of the best

times to visit is just before sunrise on a clear day. When the sun rises it casts an incredible orange glow over the whole scene, and if you're lucky enough to have a windless morning and a slack tide, the scene is probably one of the finest views of the Thames from anywhere.

As you cross over to the south side, stop off at No 1 London Bridge – an impressive construction built as office space. Walk down the steps and look up; reflective surfaces and stark brown stone make an interesting view. Try using different lenses to capture something abstract.

*Opposite: East to Tower Bridge from Northern Shell. Canon 5D II, 17–40mm at 22mm, ISO 200, 1/8s at f/18, tripod, LEE ND 0.9 hard grad. Jan.*

*The Preacher, London Bridge. Sony A6000, 16–50mm at 39mm, ISO 100, 1/200s at f/5.6. May.*

*Evening looking north over London Bridge towards the City. Canon 5D IV, 24–70mm at 28mm, ISO 100, 30s at f/11, tripod, LEE ND 0.9 grad. June.*

*Opposite: Dawn over London Bridge and the Shard. Canon 5D II, 17–40mm at 17mm, ISO 400, 1/8s at f/11, tripod, LEE ND 09 grad. Jan.*

## South side – Southwark viewpoint ♿

Once on the south side of the bridge, cross over the road towards London Grind located at N°. 2 London Bridge. A set of steps leads down to Montague Close, which runs underneath London Bridge Road. Walk about 100m west along Montague Close until you see an open area to your right – this is Southwark Viewpoint. This location offers a perfectly clear view of London Bridge as it leads to the tall buildings of the City of London. Shoot from this quiet spot at dawn or dusk and use a long exposure to blur the water of the Thames. Shooting during darker hours ensures the bridge's streetlights are switched on. Use a tight aperture of f/16 or above to 'star effect' the lights of the city and those on the bridge.

There can be no more iconic structure in London than Tower Bridge. The bridge was designed by Sir Horace Jones and Sir John Wolfe Barry, completed in 1894 and opened by the Prince of Wales. With over 70,000 tons of concrete in the two bases and over 11,000 tons of steel, the structure is clad in Cornish granite and Portland stone.

The bridge carries over 40,000 people every day and raises its bascules over a thousand times a year to let ships pass. Interesting fact: the bridge usually only raises enough to allow the vessel to pass under, except if the reigning monarch is aboard, in which case the bridge bascules raise fully, no matter the size of the vessel.

## What to shoot and viewpoints

Tower Bridge is an easy subject to shoot both night and day, and can be easily reached by bus and underground. There are some considerations to be aware of before planning your shoot: all the land surrounding the bridge is private property so there are restrictions. You can shoot from anywhere along the south bank of the Thames both night and day and use a tripod. To the north, you may only shoot from the walkway in front of the Tower of London during daylight hours as the walkway is locked at night. To the northeast are St Katharine Docks and private property owned by the Guoman Hotel. There is 24-hour access to walk through to St Katharine Docks, however if you attempt to take any pictures of the bridge from here using a tripod, hotel security may ask you stop immediately. Handheld shots of the fountain with bridge behind are usually acceptable but tripods will certainly draw their attention.

### Viewpoint 1 – View from Wapping ♿

This spot is a five-to-ten minute walk and is only open between 8am and 11pm, however it's one of the least-known spots from which to obtain images of Tower Bridge. Proceed through St Katharine Docks to St Katharine's Way and keep an eye out to your right for the signpost to the Thames Path. Walk down the

*VP1. The Shard and Tower Bridge from Wapping. Canon 5D IV, 24–70mm at 46mm, ISO 100, 106s at f/11, tripod, LEE ND 0.9 grad. Jan.*

## How to get here

### Tower Bridge

The easiest way to get Tower Bridge is to exit Tower Hill station and walk around the Tower of London until you see the bridge; it should be visible above the Tower of London.

| | |
|---|---|
| **Location Lat/Long:** | 51.50543, -0.07536 |
| **Location Postcode:** | SE1 2UP |
| **Underground & Lines:** | Tower Hill, London Bridge: |
| | *Circle & District, Northern* |
| **Main Station:** | London Bridge, Fenchurch Street |
| **DLR:** | Towergateway |
| **Riverboat:** | St Katharine's Pier, Tower Pier |
| **Bus:** | 42, 78, RV1 |
| **Cycle Hire:** | St Katharine's Way, Tooley Street, |
| | One Tower Bridge |
| **Car Park:** | Tower Hill Car Park EC3R 6DT |

### Accessibility &

On the bridge itself, if approaching by road, there are no accessibility issues. There is a lift at the southeast corner of the bridge to allow anyone with limited mobility to descend from the bridge deck to Shad Thames and City Hall area.

### Best time of year/day

Can be shot all year round.

### VP 1 – View from Wapping

Starting from the riverside in front of the Tower of London, head under the A100 to the east of the Tower of London, then follow the Thames Path in front of the hotel towards St Katharine Docks. You will pass the Girl with a Dolphin Fountain and the Paiksekell sundial. Cross the small wooden bridge into St Katharine Docks then continue around 100m until you reach a main road – this is St Katharine's Way. Follow it to the junction of Mews Street then take a right. Continue along St Katharine's Way for five to ten minutes until you come to another junction with Thomas More Street. Just before this junction and to the right is a small alley with blue gates, where Thames Path signs direct you towards the river; follow these. You will enter an open platform in front of an apartment block.

| | |
|---|---|
| **Location Lat/Long:** | 51.50478, -0.06902 |
| **Location Postcode:** | E1W 1DD |

### Accessibility &

This is an ordinary city street that should present no accessibility issues. Ramps are in place on the path, allowing access to the barrier of the viewing area.

### Best time of year/day

Can be shot all year round and at any time of day, though note that this spot is only open from 8am to 11pm each day.

*VP1. The Shard from Wapping. Canon 5D IV, 70–200mm at 85mm, ISO 100, 15s at f/19, tripod, LEE ND 0.9 grad. Jan.*

path towards the river and it will bring to a large riverside area with a few benches. Set up your tripod in the corner to get the clearest view of the bridge. If you arrive in the early evening, you can catch the golden hour, as you'll be looking west. The sky shifts from golden sunset through the blue hour and into night, and all the time more city lights will illuminate as you take your pictures.

## Viewpoint 2 – The Girl with a Dolphin Fountain (Paiksekell) ♿

This is by far the most popular location from which to shoot the bridge. The Girl with a Dolphin Fountain makes for perfect foreground interest when set against the huge bridge behind. The area is technically private property but the landowners are tolerant of personal photography with tripods if you get your shots quickly and move on.

## Viewpoint 3 – View of the North Tower ♿

This spot has a great view of the northern tower inside the arch of the southern tower. Use a relatively wide-angle lens (24mm or less) to capture the sign on the tower. If you line up your shot carefully, you should be able to place the Shard between the supports of the bridge. If you're shooting at night, use a long exposure to capture those classic traffic streaks. The traffic is limited to 20mph so it all moves at a steady and predictable pace making the shot a must if you have a tripod with you.

### VP 2 – The Girl with a Dolphin Fountain
Starting from the riverside in front of the Tower of London, head under the A100 to the east of the Tower of London, then follow the Thames Path in front of the hotel towards St Katharine Docks. You will pass the Girl with a Dolphin Fountain and the Paiksekell sundial.

**Location Lat/Long**:  51.50621, -0.07303
**Location Postcode**:  E1W 1DD

#### Accessibility ♿
Ordinary city street – should present no accessibility issues.

#### Best time of year/day
Can be shot all year round.

### VP 3 – View through North Tower
Simply cross the bridge from north or south and align yourself (either side of the road) until you can capture most of the arch at the opposite side within the arch nearest to you. If you need to cross over, you'll have to walk to the nearest end of the bridge and walk back up.

**Location Lat/Long**:  51.50711, -0.07432
**Location Postcode**:  E1W 1LE

#### Accessibility ♿
This is an ordinary city street that should present no accessibility issues.

#### Best time of year/day
Can be shot all year round at any time.

*VP2. Dolphin fountain and Tower Bridge. Canon 5D II, 17–40mm at 17mm, ISO 100, 51s at f/14, tripod, LEE ND 0.6 grad. Oct.*

*Opposite left: VP2. Fountain in front of Tower Bridge. Canon 5D IV, 17–40mm at 17mm, ISO 200, 1/90s at f/8. Mar.*

*Opposite right: VP3. Tower Bridge light trails through the northern arch. Canon 5D II, 17–40mm at 19mm, ISO 100, 15s at f/11, tripod. Oct.*

### Viewpoint 4 – Tower of London

Between dusk and dawn the walkway directly between the Tower of London and the Thames is open to the public. This affords a superb (if nowadays a little clichéd) view of the bridge. It is private land and you should ask before using a tripod, though just after the dawn opening in summer there are very few people there so using a tripod for a few shots is rarely a problem. Simply shoot the bridge over the railing or, for something a little more special, shoot the bridge with one of the lamps in the foreground – especially worthwhile when the lamp is lit. Lots of people visit this spot so it's an interesting place to shoot street images of people enjoying the view.

### Viewpoint 5 – Three Quays Walk ♿

Just before the Tower of London a small walkway leads to the edge of the river. Proceed east along Lower Thames Street; as it turns abruptly left into Petty Wales, head right and follow your nose to the edge of the river. This is the classic pods shot, where you'll find glassed domed pods outside the Coppa bar and restaurant. Try shooting from the wall to get a shot of the bridge in the distance with the riverboat dock in front of you – it works really well at night. Another option is to shoot using the glass pods as foreground interest – a shot that works well at dusk during the magic moment when the light begins to balance between the sky and the lights in buildings and streets.

## VP 4 – Tower of London

Make your way to the Tower of London, then proceed towards the river. Directly in front of the Tower of London is a cobbled walkway.

**Location Lat/Long:**     51.50715, -0.07656
**Location Postcode:**     E1W 1DD

### Accessibility

This section is cobbled and while there are some smooth paths, it may be tricky to navigate in a wheelchair, particularly as the area is very busy during the afternoon.

### Best time of year/day

Can be shot all year round.

*Opposite: VP4. Tower Bridge at dawn on a slack tide. Canon 5D IV, 24–70mm at 24mm, ISO 200, 1/60s at f/11. Apr.*

## VP 5 – Three Quays Walk

Starting from the western side of the Tower of London, proceed north around the Tower of London shop and head west to the corner of Lower Thames Street and Petty Wales. Heading directly south towards the river is a pedestrian walkway known as Three Quays Walk.

**Location Lat/Long:**     51.50779, -0.07947
**Location Postcode:**     EC3R 6AG

### Accessibility ♿

This is an ordinary city street that should present no accessibility issues.

### Best time of year/day

Can be shot all year round.

*Above: VP5. Tower Bridge from Tower Dock. Canon 5D II, 24–70mm at 42mm, ISO 100, 10s at f/8, tripod. Nov.*

## Viewpoint 6 – Northern Shell

Located along Lower Thames Street is a rather striking blue glass building. Make your way between the buildings to the riverside and you'll find not one, but two superb viewpoints. Walk west around 100m along the river path and keep an eye out to your right: you'll see an odd triangular donut sculpture, which sits in the stairwell to a public viewing terrace. The terrace is open 24 hours a day and offers yet another of those little known but special views of London – this time 50m above the river and with a clear view of the southern Thames bank from London Bridge to Tower Bridge. It's the perfect spot to create a multi-shot panoramic image. For the second viewpoint, head back down the stairs then head east to the far corner just outside the old customs house. This shot can often seem a little busy with boats moored just in front of you, but in the right morning sunrise, with a red or orange sky, it's a composition that's busy without being cluttered.

## Viewpoint 7 – London Bridge

Probably the second most popular spot to take pictures of Tower Bridge is London Bridge. Walk across the bridge until you find a suitable spot somewhere in the middle, then simply shoot towards Tower Bridge. On bright sunny mornings you won't be alone here; it's very popular at dawn and dusk with photographers so arrive early to get the best spot. The perfect time to shoot is dawn when the sun casts orange light over the bridge, HMS Belfast and the surrounding buildings, and if you're especially lucky a slack tide reflects the bridge and the old Navy warship. At night, when the bridge and surrounding buildings are lit, the darkness will create naturally long exposures if you have your ISO kept low. When the Thames is flowing fast, it creates dynamic lines that lead and converge at Tower Bridge.

*Above*: VP6. Dawn breaking over Tower Bridge. Canon 5D II, 17–40mm at 33mm, ISO 100, 0s at f/8, tripod. LEE ND 0.9 hard grad Jan.

*Opposite top*: VP6. East to Tower Bridge from Northern Shell. Canon 5D II, 17–40mm at 22mm, ISO 400, 1/40s at f/11, tripod, LEE ND 0.9 hard grad. Jan. *Bottom*: VP7. Evening looking east past HMS Belfast towards Tower Bridge from London Bridge. Canon 5D IV, 70–200mm at 93mm, ISO 800, 1/20s at f/4. Feb.

### VP 6 – Northern Shell

Follow directions to Three Quays Walk (dockside viewpoint) and head west hugging the Thames Path until you pass a blue glass building to the left of the old custom house. Proceed for another 100m along the path until you see a triangular sculpture set into concrete steps. Ascend the steps to the public viewing gallery at the top.

**Location Lat/Long:** 51.50847, -0.08428
**Location Postcode:** EC3R 6DX

#### Accessibility

This area requires climbing several flights of steps and there is no lift, so may be inaccessible to anyone with limited mobility.

#### Best time of year/day

Can be shot all year round.

### VP 7 – London Bridge

Proceed to London Bridge along the river then cross the bridge on the eastern side and you'll see Tower Bridge in the distance.

**Location Lat/Long:** 51.5083, -0.08748
**Location Postcode:** SE1 2PF

#### Accessibility &

Ordinary city street – should present no accessibility issues.

#### Best time of year/day

Can be shot all year round.

## Viewpoint 8 – City Hall ♿

If you love lead lines, then the area directly in front of City Hall is where you need to be. The Scoop is a performance area used to stage plays and other performances, and the curved rows of 'seats' make the perfect lead lines towards both the bridge and City Hall. The area directly in front of City Hall is covered with hundreds of narrow-cut pieces of stone, which offer hundreds of photogenic lead lines, all pointing towards the bridge. It's an added bonus when it rains here: the stone floor glistens and reflects City Hall and the bridge. During autumn the small number of trees in front of the buildings above The Scoop take on their end-of-summer colours and if you're lucky enough to be there before the leaves are cleared away, there's a rare chance to capture autumn leaves on lead lines in front of Tower Bridge. The area around City Hall is private but, having been in touch with the landowners myself, they assure me anyone is free to take pictures for non-commercial purposes, and you can use any reasonable equipment you wish, including a tripod.

## Viewpoint 9 – Shoreline of Butler's Wharf

The River Thames is tidal and as the tide drops, beaches are revealed along the edge of the river. Just how much beach is determined by the tidal range that day. Head east under Tower Bridge for about 100m along Butler's Wharf. The first building has a very narrow walkway with steps down to the beach. At the bottom of the steps is a little-known spot for taking images of the bridge lowdown and at low tide. Due to the sticky estuary silt, Thames beaches can be very slippery so wear appropriate footwear and watch the tide as it moves very quickly. Study the tide timetables and aim to be there around an hour before low tide. A wide-angle lens is a must; you'll be very close to this vast structure and a midrange 24–70mm lens will only net you so much. Look for two spots: the first is the old dockside cobbled jetty that is revealed at low tide. Covered in dirty muddy water as the tide recedes, it glistens in the light from the bridge, forming a perfect lead line. The second spot lies about 10m east of the bridge. From here you can capture the tall buildings of the City underneath the road that leads on to the bridge. Shooting from these two spots at dawn or dusk will provide you with some enviable pictures for your collection.

*VP8. City Hall. Canon 5D IV, 24–70mm at 24mm, ISO 800, 1/20s at f/6.7. Sept.*

## VP 8 – City Hall

As you cross Tower Bridge you will see the dome-shaped building of City Hall to the southwest. Steps at the southern end of Tower Bridge lead down to the riverside; head down the steps and towards City Hall pedestrian area.

**Location Lat/Long:** 51.50502, -0.07827
**Location Postcode:** SE1 2AP

## Accessibility ♿

Some of the lower sections of The Scoop have a curved ramp that allows access to the floor of The Scoop. All other areas are flat and fully accessible to those with limited mobility.

## Best time of year/day

Can be shot all year round.

## VP 9 – Shoreline of Butler's Wharf

As you cross Tower Bridge, steps at the southern end of Tower Bridge lead down to the riverside. Head down here then proceed directly east – this leads you along Shad Thames. Look for the first, most westerly building as you head away from the bridge, and you'll find a set of steps leading down to the shoreline.

**Warning**: do not descend the steps unless you are wearing sturdy footwear; the shoreline is littered with broken stones, glass and other dangerous objects. Also, do not head to the shoreline if the tide is coming in. Please check tide times before coming here. The Thames tide rises very quickly indeed and it simply isn't worth risking life or limb for a photo.

**Location Lat/Long:** 51.5042, -0.07480
**Location Postcode:** SE1 2NJ

## Accessibility

This location is only accessible to those with full mobility.

## Best time of year/day

Can be shot all year round.

VP8. Tower Bridge at dawn from The Scoop. Canon 5D II, 24–70mm at 24mm, ISO 100, 0s at f/16, tripod, LEE ND 0.6 grad. May.

*VP9. Tower Bridge from the shoreline. Canon 5D II, 17–40mm at 17mm, ISO 100, 30s at f/11, tripod, LEE ND 0.9 grad Sept.*

*VP8. Autumn by City Hall and Tower Bridge. Canon 5D II, 24–70mm at 24mm, ISO 200, 0s at f/11, tripod, LEE ND 0.6 grad. Oct.*

### Viewpoint 10 – Butler's Wharf – Dockside ♿

I revisit this location time and time again to shoot at dawn and catch subtle colours in the sky behind the bridge and the City, and in the evenings when it's pouring with rain. Walk under Tower Bridge, head along Shad Thames and take a left to the dockside in front of the Mississippi Riverboat moored at the quayside. Arrive as dawn is about to break and you will often be the only person there. It's worth it: you'll be treated to the wonderful sight of the city waking up to the morning sun as it falls over the bridge and the buildings behind. The lamps that light the dockside have bulbs strung between them and these provide a great lead line that helps hold the composition in check. This is a cityscape so standard kit and a normal midrange 24–70mm lens will work just fine, plus there's no issue using a tripod here. Position yourself by the anchor or propeller on the dockside around 100m from the boats, or shoot handheld with a high ISO of around 400 or 800 for that perfect shot of a couple huddling under an umbrella. As they head towards the city, wet paving slabs not only reflect all you see, but bounce light back up into the scene. The key with this type of shot is to isolate the people from anything around them; ensure they're not in front of any street furniture like benches or lampposts. This allows them to 'breathe' within the composition – they become the focus, just as they should be.

## VP 10 – Butler's Wharf – Dockside

Using the directions to Butler's Wharf viewpoint, proceed along Shad Thames and keep an eye out to the left for the entrance to the dockside. If you miss it and end up at the end of Shad Thames, simply turn left on to the dockside and walk back east along the river; you'll see the bridge in the distance.

**Location Lat/Long**: 51.5038, -0.07362
**Location Postcode**: SE1 2NJ

### Accessibility ♿

This is and ordinary city street that should present no accessibility issues.

### Best time of year/day

Can be shot all year round

*Above*: *VP9. Shoreline view: Tower Bridge at dawn during slack tide. Canon 5D II, 17–40mm at 17mm, ISO 100, 8s at f/8, tripod, LEE ND 0.6 grad. Oct.*

*VP10. Brighter skies coming, Shad Thames. Canon 5D IV, 24–70mm at 30mm, ISO 400, 1/350s at f/4. Dec.*

St Katharine Docks is named after a hospital that once stood here amidst a 19th-century slum. An act of Parliament saw the entire area demolished with its redevelopment designed by Thomas Telford to increase the commercial opportunities for shipping. It was not a great success as large ships were unable to dock and unload.

The area was heavily bombed during World War II and underwent a huge commercial redevelopment during the 1980s and 1990s. It's now a mix of restaurants, offices and private dwellings with the dock home to an array of boats ranging from small dinghies to multi-million pound playthings of the rich and famous, and the Queen's barge.

## What to shoot and viewpoints

For the photographer the area holds much interest: to the southwest you'll find the famous Girl with a Dolphin Fountain and Sundial installation (see Tower Bridge chapter page 112) that make the perfect foreground complement to Tower Bridge. These can be shot any time, night or day, and rank as classics to shoot while in London. »

*Quiet dawn in Wapping. Sony A6000, 16–50mm at 16mm, ISO 100, 1/125s at f/4.5. Mar.*

*St Katharine Docks. Canon 5D IV, 70–200mm at 200mm, ISO 200, 1/30s at f/8. Mar.*

## How to get here

Starting from the northern side of Tower Bridge, either head down the steps next to the northern tower or (before the bridge) take the road that runs parallel to it. This drops away towards the riverside. Once in front of the hotel, head east until you pass the sundial. A small wooden bridge will lead you into St Katharine Docks.

| | |
|---|---|
| **Location Lat/Long**: | 51.50600, -0.07198 |
| **Location Postcode**: | E1W 1LA |
| **Underground & Lines**: | Tower Hill: *Circle & District* |
| **Main Station**: | London Bridge, Fenchurch Street |
| **DLR**: | Tower Gateway |
| **Riverboat**: | St Katharine's Pier, Tower Pier |
| **Bus**: | 15, 25, 42, 78, 100, N15, N551, RV1 |
| **Cycle Hire**: | St Katharine's Way |
| **Car Park**: | City Quay Car Park, E1W 1YW |

## Accessibility ♿

This is an ordinary city street that should present no accessibility issues.

## Best time of year/day

Can be shot all year round, but is especially good in autumn and early in the morning.

*St Katharine Docks. Canon 5D II, 17–40mm at 40mm, ISO 100, 1/125s at f/4. Oct.*

*Boats moored in the docks. Canon 5D IV, 70–200mm at 89mm, ISO 400, 1/750s at f/4. Mar.*

The dock itself has a lot of character with its cobbled quayside walkways and array of boats. With crafts moored in the dock and some of the older buildings such as the Dickens Inn on site, there's always something to shoot. Early on bright sunny mornings you'll find the sun makes its way into the dock, casting warm light over the boats and, being secluded, the water in the dock is often still offering some superb reflections. The Queen's Barge, with its ornate red and gold paintwork, is moored here and is usually easy to find.

A visit during autumn offers yet more interesting compositions, with leaves falling over the cobbles and the old red telephone box and postbox contributing to some exciting compositions. Visit in the early evening to shoot images of the Dickens Inn; you'll capture some wonderfully atmospheric images of a hidden London gem. With so many expensive boats moored in the dock, security is tight and patrols frequent. You won't be prevented from taking pictures but security will take an interest and won't allow the use of tripods.

*Opposite top: The Dickens Inn, St Katharine Docks. Canon 5D IV, 70–200mm at 138mm, ISO 400, 1/20s at f/9.5. Mar.*

*Opposite bottom left: St Katharine Docks signage. Canon 5D IV, 70–200mm at 121mm, ISO 400, 1/350s at f/4. Mar.*
*Right: Sunny morning in the docks. Canon 5D IV, 24–70mm at 24mm, ISO 400, 1/90s at f/11. Apr.*

To the southeast corner of Tower Bridge is an area known as Shad Thames with the partly cobbled Shad Thames Lane leading east away from the southern end of Tower Bridge. It runs parallel to the River Thames between tall warehouse buildings that used to house tea, coffee, spices, grain and other commodities. When the Port of London was at its height and ships were constantly coming and going, Shad Thames was the largest warehouse complex in London. The warehouses are now apartments, shops, restaurants and offices but many have retained their original names, such as X Wharf, Cardamom Building and Y Wharf.

## What to shoot and viewpoints

The main focus of interest here is Shad Thames Lane, a long, slightly curved street with very tall caramel-coloured buildings on either side. High above you, criss-crossing the lane are metal walkways that allowed the dockworkers to get from building to building quickly without having to run up and downstairs when carrying cargo. It is this mixture of tight-knit architecture and features such as the walkways that make this a great place to get photographs. Look to shoot along the lane from the western end, then walk along and shoot directly upwards. Finally, shoot back the way you came. Seek to use the walkways to frame the scene; this works especially well if you shoot in portrait orientation with a wide-angle lens. Obviously, this is a great place to capture street images especially during a rainstorm with people huddling under a brolly as they walk towards or away from you along the curved road.

*Opposite left*: Shad Thames in the morning. Canon 5D IV, 70–200mm at 176mm, ISO 400, 1/45s at f/8. Mar.

*Opposite right*: Impossible to get film for this camera, Shad Thames. Canon 5D II, 17–40mm at 29mm, ISO 400, 1/40s at f/8. Sept.

*Building signage, Shad Thames. Canon 5D IV, 70–200mm at 70mm, ISO 400, 1/60s at f/4. Mar.*

## How to get here

As you cross Tower Bridge, you'll find steps at its southern end that lead down to the riverside. Head down next to the river path and then proceed directly east, this leads you along Shad Thames Lane.

**Location Lat/Long**: 51.50357, -0.07392
**Location Postcode**: SE1 2YE
**Underground & Lines**: Tower Hill, London Bridge: *Circle & District, Northern*
**Main Station**: London Bridge
**Riverboat**: Butler's Wharf Pier
**Bus**: 42, 78, RV1

## Accessibility &#9855;

This should present no accessibility issues. Although the street is cobbled there are smooth paths at the side for wheelchairs.

## Best time of year/day

Can be shot all year round and at any time of day.

*Shad Thames. Canon 5D II, 17–40mm at 17mm, ISO 100, 8s at f/6.3, tripod. Sept.*

# BOROUGH

# BOROUGH – INTRODUCTION

**On the opposite riverbank to the City of London are Southwark and Borough, although the area of Borough is a small part of the London Borough of Southwark. The area known today as Southwark was one of the places the Romans first tried to establish a settlement – they later abandoned it in favour of the northern side of the river.**

The name Southwark comes from a fortified settlement established by King Alfred in the 9th century. In 1965, when Greater London was officially formed, many areas of London were amalgamated to form the twenty-eight key boroughs, making it easier to manage services and amenities. Southwark was formed from three existing boroughs and kept the original Saxon name.

I've chosen to use the name Borough for this section as it primarily concentrates on places along the side of the Thames – key locations as City Hall, the famous Shard skyscraper, Borough Market and Shakespeare's Globe. Sometimes regarded as a a poor cousin to the wealthy City of London, Borough boasts as much if not more history than the City as it grew at a slower pace. As the city expanded, areas such as Borough were in huge demand – the docks, wharfs and warehouses that dominate the southern side of the river begin in Borough and extend through the Pool of London by Tower Bridge and along the Thames towards the East End. Just by Borough Market stands Southwark Cathedral, which was founded on the site of a 7th-century convent. To the south of Borough lies Crossbones Garden, graveyard of the outcast dead and the final resting place of 15,000 paupers and prostitutes.

History and intrigue awaits as we cross to the other side of the Thames …

*Previous spread*: Southwark Bridge tunnel at sunrise, southside. Canon 5D IV, 24–70mm at 34mm, ISO 3200, 1/60s at f/6.7. Apr.

*Next spread*: Well-stocked stall, Borough Market. Sony A6000, 16–50mm at 16mm, ISO 500, 1/160s at f/4. July.

Barbican

A1

A1211

London Wall

Moorgate

A501

Wilson Street

Eldon Street

Bishopsgate

London Liverpool Street

Spitalfields

Brick Lane

A10

A1211

Moorgate

A1211

Houndsditch

Middlesex Street

A1202

Newgate Street

Gresham Street

Cheapside

Aldgate

A1210

Mansell Street

Aldgate East

St Paul's

Saint Paul's Cathedral

Bank

The City

Leadenhall Street

Queen Victoria Street

Bank (DLR)

Cannon Street

King William Street

Fenchurch Street

London Fenchurch Street

Royal Mint Street

Queen Victoria Street

Mansion House

The Blackfriar

Great Tower Street

Tower Hill

Tower Gateway

A3211

Monument

The Monument

Lower Thames Street

Tower of London

Blackfriars Pier

Millennium Bridge

Southwark Bridge

London Cannon Street

West Dock

Central Basin

SHAKESPEARE'S GLOBE THEATRE **9**

THE TATE MODERN **10**

Bankside Pier

Cannon Street Railway Bridge

Golden Hind

London Bridge

River Thames

Tower Millennium Pier

A100

St Katherine's Pier

Tower Bridge

**8** SOUTHWARK BRIDGE

**7** THE ANCHOR PUB

London Bridge City Pier

HMS Belfast

A3200

A300

**6** CLINK STREET

**4** SOUTHWARK CATHEDRAL

**2**

Butlers Wharf Pier

Southwark Tavem

**5** The Globe

London Bridge

HAY'S GALLERIA AND HMS BELFAST

Tower Bridge

A3200

BOROUGH MARKET

George

London Bridge

THE SHARD

**3**

The Shipwrights Arms

**1**

**11** CROSSBONES GARDEN

Union Street

Union Street

CITY HALL

RED CROSS GARDEN **12**

Southwark

Borough

Marshalsea Road

Borough

Druid Street

Tooley Street

A300

A3

Long Lane

Bermondsey Street

A300

Great Dover Street

A2198

A2205

Tower Bridge Road

Abbey Street

Elephant and Castle

Harper Road

A2

A100

A201

Elephant & Castle

A100

A2206

A302

N

New Kent Road

A201

Elephant & Castle

0 metres 250

A3

Heygate Street

Rodney Road

Old Kent Road

A2

B203

Dunton Road

Designed by the architect Norman Foster and built in 2002, this oddly shaped building next to Tower Bridge on the Thames' South Bank is the functional HQ of the Greater London Authority (GLA) and the Mayor of London. City Hall was built on a site previously occupied by wharves that once served ships docking at the Pool of London.

City Hall's shape and the reduced surface area it covers was designed with the intention of making it more energy efficient. The building is ten storeys high, with a helical walkway linking the lower floors, and is home to the mayoral offices and the staff of the GLA. The London Assembly meet on the ground floor and the public are welcome to visit the lower two floors of the building Monday to Friday. There is also free WiFi and a public cafe. During the open-house weekend the public are allowed to visit the ninth-floor viewing gallery (dates at *www.london.gov.uk*). Like so many uniquely shaped buildings in London, the structure has some colourful nicknames; former London Mayor Boris Johnson once described the building as 'The Glass Gonad'!

## What to shoot and viewpoints

City Hall is an interesting shape to work into photographic compositions, especially given its older and more distinguished neighbours, Tower Bridge and the Tower of London. There are several locations around the building that work well. The Scoop, an outdoor, terraced performance area next to the building, with its curved lines of seat terraces, works incredibly well as lead lines to draw the viewer's eye through the scene, past City Hall and on towards Tower Bridge. The modern design of City Hall at first appears at odds with the bridge but the more you begin to work the compositions, the more comfortable it feels. Move to the upper terraces of The Scoop and you'll find even more ways to utilise the lines of the terraces, especially the large tubular 'handrails'. The large open area between the river and The Scoop is often used for public events and its vast, open feeling provides the opportunity to capture the colours and textures of the sky and clouds in your shots.

*Opposite: Looking east past City Hall to Tower Bridge. Canon 5D II, 17–40mm at 17mm, ISO 200, 15s at f/8, tripod, LEE ND 0.9 grad. Oct.*

*Golden dawn light striking the City during slack tide. Canon 5D II, 17–40mm at 22mm, ISO 100, 1/30s at f/14, tripod, LEE ND 0.9 grad. Oct.*

*City Hall and The Scoop. Sony A6000, Fisheye 8mm at 8mm, ISO 200, 1/125s at f/8. May.*

## Inside City Hall ♿

You can visit the City Hall interior most days, unless there is a special event; the lower two floors are open to the public. Once through security, head up the helical walkway to take images of its unique curves. These become especially intriguing when using a wide-angle or fisheye lens to distort perception of the composition. Bright sunny days work best, creating lots of interesting patterns that give a much-needed sense of depth.

*Opposite top left: Lone reader, The Scoop. Canon 5D IV, 70–200mm at 70mm, ISO 800, 1/180s at f/4. Dec.*
*Right: City Hall interior, north-facing windows. Sony A6000, Fisheye 8mm at 8mm, ISO 125, 1/160s at f/8. Apr.*

## How to get here

Follow directions to Tower Bridge from Tower Hill station. Cross Tower Bridge and City Hall is located to the southwest side of the bridge.

| | |
|---|---|
| **Location Lat/Long:** | 51.50516, -0.07878 |
| **Location Postcode:** | SE1 2AA |
| **Underground & Lines:** | London Bridge, Tower Hill: |
| | Circle & District, Jubilee, Northern |
| **Main Station:** | London Bridge |
| **DLR:** | Tower Gateway |
| **Riverboat:** | London Bridge City Pier, |
| | St Katharine's Pier, Tower Pier |
| **Bus:** | 42, 47, 48, 78, 381, RV1 |
| **Cycle Hire:** | Potters Fields Park |

## Accessibility ♿

Ordinary city street – should present no accessibility issues.

## Best time of year/day

Can be shot all year round.

## Opening hours

Parts of City Hall are open to the public:
Mon to Thur: 8.30am–6pm
Fri: 8.30am–5.30pm

## Admission price (2019)

Free.

*Opposite: The spiral walkway. Sony A6000, Fisheye 8mm at 8mm, ISO 500, 1/60s at f/8. Apr.*

Launched in 1938, HMS Belfast saw extensive service in both World War II and the Korean conflict in the early 1950s. She remained in active service until 1967, when a joint initiative between the Ministry of Defence and the Imperial War Museum (IWM) set up the HMS Belfast Trust to preserve the ship as a museum piece. The ship is now wholly owned and run by the IWM. Moored in the Pool of London between London Bridge and Tower Bridge, it receives over a quarter of million visitors a year.

Next to HMS Belfast you will find the Hay's Galleria, named after Alexander Hay, who acquired the property in 1651 when it was a brewhouse. The Galleria was a wharf for several hundred years and nicknamed 'the Larder of London' such was the volume of tea and other dry goods that passed through it. Due to containerisation in the shipping industry, the wharf closed in 1970 and was eventually redeveloped in the 1980s as a location for shops and restaurants, making it one of the first visitor attractions on the newly developed South Bank. Make a note to shoot David Kemp's unusual sculpture, *The Navigators*.

## What to shoot and viewpoints

### Hay's Galleria ♿

Hay's Galleria is an intriguing structure to shoot, as its large vaulted roof lets in a huge amount of light in the morning. Aim to arrive during the golden hours (early morning or early evening) and use a wide angle lens to capture the breadth and height of the main hall. Face towards the Thames to capture the 'Walkie Talkie' skyscraper framed by the opening at the southern end of the building. Make time also to visit the northern end of the main hall, where the old narrow passages funnel the sunlight into complex patterns, offering a chance to experiment with light-based compositions and architecture. Note the Galleria is closed at night, so night shots need to be taken at dusk in the winter months.

*Top*: *Dawn over HMS Belfast by Hay's Galleria. Canon 5D II, 24–70mm at 34mm, ISO 200, 1/100s at f/8. Sept.*

*Looking east towards Tower Bridge from Hay's Galleria. Sony A6000, Fisheye 8mm at 8mm, ISO 400, 1/250s at f/8. May.*

*Looking north from Hay's Galleria. Sony A6000, 16–50mm at 19mm, ISO 100, 1/320s at f/5. Mar.*

*Riverside by Hay's Galleria. Canon 5D II, 17–40mm at 17mm, ISO 100, 13s at f/8, tripod. Oct.*

*Passing through Hay's Galleria in the morning. Sony A6000, 16–50mm at 16mm, ISO 100, 1/400s at f/4.5. Mar.*

## HMS Belfast ♿

HMS Belfast is an impressive ship to photograph as its close position to the shore (the South Bank) and its proximity to Tower Bridge provide ample opportunities to shoot compositions – in particular the ship juxtaposed with the London skyline. It makes a great foreground component in most Thames-based compositions and the hull (being slightly reflective) captures the morning colour from the east. Look to arrive on a clear, bright sunny morning to capture it from London Bridge (see page 106, London Bridge) with a medium zoom and place Tower Bridge behind. Alternatively, shoot from the South Bank to place Tower Bridge behind. Tripods are permitted on London Bridge but not in the area directly by HMS Belfast on the South Bank. Luckily, the railings make excellent resting places for cameras.

*Opposite top left: Quiet morning in Hay's Galleria. Sony A6000, 16–50mm at 18mm, ISO 1000, 1/160s at f/4. Mar.*
*Top right: The Navigator. Sony A6000, Fisheye 8mm at 8mm, ISO 400, 1/125s at f/8. May.*

### How to get here

Coming from Tower Bridge and City Hall, walk along the river path until you find yourself at the riverside end of the Hay's Galleria building. If approaching from London Bridge, take the steps down by N°. 1 London Bridge to the river path and follow it along to HMS Belfast moored outside Hay's Galleria. If you're unable to take the steps by London Bridge, head towards London Bridge station, take a left at Tooley Street and keep walking until you find the rear entrance to Hay's Galleria; this is much easier access for the less mobile.

| | |
|---|---|
| **Location Lat/Long**: | 51.50615, -0.08259 |
| **Location Postcode**: | SE1 2HD |
| **Underground & Lines**: | London Bridge, Tower Hill: Circle & District, Jubilee, Northern |
| **Main Station**: | London Bridge |
| **DLR**: | Tower Gateway |
| **Riverboat**: | London Bridge City Pier, St Katharine's Pier, Tower Pier |
| **Bus**: | 42, 47, 48, 78, 381, RV1 |
| **Cycle Hire**: | Potters Fields Park |

### Accessibility ♿

Ordinary city street – should present no accessibility issues.

### Best time of year/day

Can be shot all year round.

### Opening hours

| | |
|---|---|
| **Hay's Galleria** | Mon to Fri: 8am–11pm |
| | Sat: 9am–11pm |
| | Sun: 9am–10.30pm |
| **HMS Belfast** | Mon to Sun: 10am–6pm |
| | (last admission 5pm) |

HMS Belfast is closed from 24th–26th December.

### Admission prices (2019)

HMS Belfast

| | Online | On the day |
|---|---|---|
| **Adults**: | £16.20 | £18.00 |
| **Children** (aged 5–15): | £8.10 | £9.00 |
| **Concessions** (students, seniors, disabled): | £12.95 | £14.40 |
| **Family 1** (adult and up to 3 children): | £27.90 | £31.00 |
| **Family 2** (adult and up to 6 children): | £41.40 | £46.00 |
| **IWM Member** | Free | Free |

For more information visit: *www.iwm.org.uk*

*Opposite left: Hay's Galleria rear entrance. Sony A6000, Fisheye 8mm at 8mm, ISO 250, 1/160s at f/8. Apr. Right: Hay's Galleria rear entrance. Canon 5D IV, 24–70mm at 24mm, ISO 400, 1/30s at f/6.7. June*

*Tower Bridge from the Shard. Canon 5D II, 24–70mm at 40mm, ISO 200, 1/125s at f/9.5. May.*

**The views of London from the top of the Shard are spectacular and allow you to see for at least five miles in all directions – even further on clear days.**

Standing 310m tall, the Shard is one of the most recognisable buildings on the London skyline and the tallest building in the United Kingdom. Designed by architect Renzo Piano, who shunned what he saw as dull conventional building design, favouring instead something radical but practical. Work began in 2007 during a time of financial upheaval and there was a risk the project would be abandoned. However, investment to proceed was found in the Middle East and work was finally completed in 2012. Sixty-seven of the Shard's ninety-five floors are given over to office space, hotels and restaurants. Floors 68–72 house the public observation decks and floors 73–95 complete the spire.

The observation decks are open from 10am–10pm most days, except when private functions are being held. As a photographer you will wish to plan your visit carefully in order to maximise the potential –

I share my tips to do just that in this chapter. There are no restrictions on the amount of time you can spend at the top of the Shard once there so you're able to take full advantage of the ticket price.

On the subject of photographing the city, I have included a list of some of the best locations for exterior images at the end of this chapter.

## What to shoot and viewpoints

Shooting from top of the Shard has limitations but these can be overcome with a little bit of careful planning. Tripods and monopods are not allowed on the observation decks for safety reasons. You will be shooting through glass and when it rains the droplets cling to the glass, making clear shots tricky to obtain. The upper observation decks are open to the elements meaning you can get quite cold and wet while there.

***Opposite**: Looking west from the Shard. Canon 5D II, 24–70mm at 45mm, ISO 200, 1s at f/4. Feb.*

*Sunset view from the Shard. Canon 5D II, 24–70mm at 24mm, ISO 200, 1/30s at f/16. May.*

**Top**: *Looking east. Canon 5D II, 24–70mm at 24mm, ISO 200, 1s at f/4. Feb.*
**Above**: *Tower of London from the Shard. Canon 5D II, 70–200mm at 85mm, ISO 200, 1/15s at f/16. May.*

## How to get here

The Shard is one of the easiest landmarks to spot from almost anywhere in London and is located directly over London Bridge station. Take the Northern or Jubilee lines and exit London Bridge station. This will lead you to the entrance of the Shard. It is easily reached by taking the river paths and walking across London Bridge. Proceed towards the station then pass through towards the south side, following signs to the entrance of the Shard.

| | |
|---|---|
| **Location Lat/Long**: | 51.50455, -0.08649 |
| **Location Postcode**: | SE1 9SG |
| **Underground & Lines**: | London Bridge: *Jubilee, Northern* |
| **Main Station**: | London Bridge |
| **Riverboat**: | London Bridge City Pier |
| **Bus**: | 47, 133, 343, RV1 |
| **Cycle Hire**: | Snowfields, Southwark Street, Tooley Street |

## Accessibility

The viewing gallery is fully accessible, as are most viewpoints around the city for exterior shots.

### Best time of year/day

Views from the top of the building must be enjoyed during the Shard's opening hours, whilst the exterior can obviously be shot any time of year, day and night.

### Opening hours

Sun to Wed 10am–8pm
Thur to Sat 10am–10pm

Opening times may vary due to events taking place. Please check Opening Times before you visit. For more information visit: *www.the-shard.com*

## Admission prices (2019)

|  | Online | On the day |
|---|---|---|
| Standard ticket: | £24.00 | £32.00* |
| Premium ticket: | £31.00 | £42.00** |
| All inclusive ticket: | £39.00 | £52.00*** |
| Family ticket: | £65.00 | £80.00**** |

*Guaranteed entry only. **Guaranteed entry, weather guarantee, fast track, panoramic guide booklet. ***Guaranteed entry, weather guarantee, fast track, panoramic guide booklet, glass of Champagne or soft drink, souvenir digital photograph. ****Guaranteed entry (1 adult & 3 children or 2 adults & 2 children), weather guarantee, fast track, panoramic guide booklet, souvenir digital photograph.

*Above*: St Paul's Cathedral from the Shard. Canon 5D II, 70–200mm at 116mm, ISO 100, 0s at f/4. Feb.

## City Lights

Two of the main factors that will affect your ability to secure great images are the time of year and the notorious British weather. During the middle of summer it can be difficult to shoot dusk when the lights of the city below come on; sunset often begins after 9.30pm – very close to closing time. The best time of year to visit for night photography is between October and April, when dusk falls in the early evening allowing plenty of time to be in place and get the shots you want.

## Which deck?

There are two public observation decks: the lower, fully enclosed deck and the upper open deck. I would advise heading to the upper deck, as there are fewer people and slightly less obstructed views.

### Lenses

If possible, take a range of lenses from 24mm to 300mm. This range will provide the best opportunities to capture both the wider view and to zoom in to buildings, the river and other features.

### The Views

The wider views are best looking directly east and west.

### To the East

To the east, capture the view along the Thames to Canary Wharf. Be sure to capture Tower Bridge in the foreground and the river Thames winding around Rotherhithe leading to the Isle of Dogs; during sunset this changes from drab grey to soft yellow and orange.

### To the West

To the west, the Thames curves around Southwark as it heads past Westminster and off towards Richmond. You'll be able to capture a very wide view of most of London's attractions from this side.

### To the North

To the north, and if you are using a telephoto lens, you'll be able to capture the detail of St Paul's as dusk arrives; the tall buildings around Fenchurch Street, such as the 'Walkie Talkie', and details of the Tower of London and Tower Bridge. Once again these come into their own as dusk descends and evening approaches.

### The small room

While here, try to find time to visit the toilets at the top of the Shard; they make a very interesting experience to say the least … There's nothing quite as novel as sitting by a 7ft x 3ft window that's open to the whole of London while you 'take the throne'!

*Top*: *Throne with a view. Canon 5D II, 17–40mm at 17mm, ISO 100, 1/30s at f/14. May.*

*Above*: *Tower Bridge with raised bascules. Canon 5D II, 70–200mm at 135mm, ISO 200, 1/60s at f/8. May.*

*Opposite*: *Looking west over London. Canon 5D II, 24–70mm at 43mm, ISO 800, 1/10s at f/4.5. May.*

*The Shard from Tower Bridge. Canon 5D IV, 70–200mm at 127mm, ISO 200, 1/500s at f/8. Mar.*

Here are my top tips for shooting from the Shard's observation decks:

- During sunset lots of people will camp out on the floor of the west side and will not move; if you want a sunset, you'll have to lean over them or get there early enough to camp in the spot you want.
- There are limitations on the size of the bag you can to take up to the viewing decks, so use a small camera bag but one that's able to stand on its own. This can then be used as a makeshift platform for resting your camera.
- Ensure you take at least one thick jumper, preferably two, or take a small beanbag. These can be placed on your camera bag to create an adaptable platform, on which to put the camera. This will become increasingly important as the light fades and exposures easily increase to thirty seconds or more.
- Ensure you have lens hoods, as you will be shooting through thick glass that easily catches reflections. I always carry a cloth hat with me, which I use as a flexible lens hood to stop glass flare and reflections getting into shot. You could also use a bellows, placing this against the glass too.
- At night, lights are switched on just underneath the viewing decks and they cast a white glow into the lower area of the frame. To counteract this you can rest your camera bag on the railing, using the jumper/beanbag trick to overcome the worst of the light glow.

## External locations from which to shoot the Shard

The Shard, like any modern building, is designed to be functional but has an incredible aesthetic that just begs to be shot. The building itself has over 11,000 panes of glass covering its exterior and with such a huge surface area it can't help but catch myriad facets of the light that hits it. Combine the reflective glass with atmospheric weather; overcast days with shafts of light piercing the clouds are a favourite and you can take some terrific images.

Here are some of the best places you can really appreciate this superb building, either in the context of its surroundings or by isolating smaller sections of the Shard.

*Looking east along the Thames at dawn. Sony A6000, 16–50mm at 22mm, ISO 100, 1/160s at f/4. Dec.*

## One New Change ♿
### 1 New Change, London  EC4M 9A
Located next to St Paul's (page 556) and designed to be a viewing platform primarily to observe St Paul's Cathedral, it also offers a unique high vantage point from which to shoot photos of the Shard, which can clearly be seen over the tops of the buildings. From here, the Shard is quite a long way away, so a 100mm or greater telephoto lens is needed to really isolate it from the buildings below it.

## Tate Modern Viewing Gallery ♿
### Bankside, London  SE1 9TG
Take the lift to the tenth floor of the Tate Modern gallery's 360° viewing platform (page 182) and you'll be rewarded with a view of London like no other. Included in that view, of course, is the Shard. This is one of the best places to get an unobstructed view and, on cloudy days, strong light breaking through cloud casts strong tones and textures over the Shard's surface. Again, the building is some distance away but, by using a lens of about 100mm, it's easy to isolate the Shard either in portrait to centre it or in landscape, where you can create a sense of negative space by framing it in sky and cloud.

*Looking south across the river towards the Shard at dawn. Canon 5D IV, 17–40mm at 20mm, ISO 200, 1/90s at f/11. Apr.*

*View south from Lovat Lane. Canon 5D II, 17–40mm at 21mm, ISO 100, 15s at f/8, tripod, LEE ND 0.9 grad. Oct.*

## North side of London Bridge &

### Adelaide House, London Bridge, London EC4R 9HA

London Bridge (page 106) offers a great selection of viewpoints from which to shoot the Shard. You can simply shoot from either path and use the bridge itself as a lead line towards the tower. Stand at the top of the steel stairwell located to the northeast side of the bridge and use the stairwell as a foreground point of interest. Continue down the stairs to the bottom and on to the Thames Path, then turn and position yourself so the Shard's pointed shape fits neatly into the diamond-shaped frame formed by the steel stairwell and the bridge's stonework. Shot after dark, this makes an incredible night image.

## Lovat Lane &

### Monument Street, London EC3R 8BU

See the location chapter on Lovat Lane (page 74). From this location the Shard itself becomes part of a new-with-old juxtaposition: the cobbles of this pedestrian street combine with the old pub on Lower Thames Street, whilst the huge gleaming tower fills the only area of sky between the buildings. The result is a very interesting composition.

*Opposite: View from under London Bridge (north side) towards the Shard. Canon 5D II, 17–40mm at 17mm, ISO 100, 15s at f/11, tripod. Oct.*

*Shard reflected in Northern Shell building. Canon 5D II, 24–70mm at 24mm, ISO 100, 1/60s at f/6.3. May.*

*The Shard from One New Change. Canon 5D II, 70–200mm at 78mm, ISO 100, 1/180s at f/8. July.*

## The Daily Express Building ♿
### 10 Lower Thames Street, London  EC3R 6EN
Located alongside the Old Billingsgate building on the northern side of the Thames opposite the HMS Belfast is a blue glass-covered building resembling something from the Minecraft video game. On bright days, when the sky is blue and sunlight illuminates the buildings on the south side of the Thames, shoot reflections of the Shard captured in the blue glass. You'll have a low viewpoint but the unusual blue tones and the reflection make for an interesting image.

## Corner of Bermondsey Street and Tooley Street ♿
### 88 Tooley St, London  SE1 2TF
In London there are countless opportunities to find new-with-old compositions and this location is one such place. Where Bermondsey Street meets Tooley Street, just outside London Bridge station, you will find the Shipwrights

Arms pub. Position yourself across the road, where you can place the old buildings directly below the Shard. This shot works well as a monochrome image, especially when paired with a cloudy sky.

## Wapping and Tower Bridge ♿
### St Katharine's & Wapping, London  E1W 1UJ
See page 112 and the Wapping viewpoint for Tower Bridge. From this location you can obtain a wonderful composition of the Shard from top to bottom, slightly set aside from the south tower of Tower Bridge. This works well in the evening, when dusk falls, with a long exposure to smooth the water and the whole composition shot in portrait. Move back along the Wapping viewpoint platform and you can shoot a wider, longer image that incorporates the boats in the foreground and the whole of Tower Bridge. The Shard's sheer scale dominates the scene, so be careful to balance your composition carefully.

*Monochrome of the Shard from the rear of Hay's Galleria. Sony A6000, 16–50mm at 17mm, ISO 100, 1/250s at f/5. Mar.*

One legendary tale about the cathedral's beginnings has it that during the 10th century, a ferry owned by John Overs operated between the north and south banks of the Thames. Overs – a known miser – tried to fool his workers into thinking he was dead so they would mourn him and stop eating his food. Unfortunately, his employees were so overjoyed at the news of his death they stopped work and began to feast! Enraged by this, Overs leapt from his coffin, prompting the shocked workers (believing the 'corpse' possessed) to beat him to death. The ferry owner's grieving daughter, Mary, sent for her lover, intending to claim the inheritance but when he arrived, he fell from his horse and died. Mary was so grief stricken she used her inheritance to found the convent of St Mary Overie (over-the-river) and devoted her life to helping the poor.

Sadly, this is all just legend, albeit a wonderful one. The truth is less whimsical: it is believed there has been a convent on the site since the 7th century. The Bishop of Winchester converted the convent into a college for priests in the 9th century. Re-founded as a church in 1109 by two Norman knights, it has passed through the hands of various owners. It was renamed St Saviour's Church during the Reformation and finally renamed Southwark Cathedral in 1905. Famous patrons include William Shakespeare and Charles Dickens.

*Opposite top: Southwark Cathedral ceiling. Sony A6000, Fisheye 8mm at 8mm, ISO 800, 1/20s at f/8. Apr.*

*Opposite bottom left: Southwark Cathedral by Borough Market. Sony A6000, 16–50mm at 16mm, ISO 100, 1/250s at f/5. June. Right: Cathedral interior. Canon 5D IV, 17–40mm at 17mm, ISO 800, 1/15s at f/4. Apr.*

## What to shoot and viewpoints

### Outside the cathedral ♿

The cathedral is tightly packed into the surrounding area so it's quite tricky to shoot the exterior. Try positioning yourself on the steps that lead from London Bridge down into Borough Market; there is an entrance directly level with the bridge road. This is a great spot for taking evening shots, when the cathedral is lit.

Proceed through Borough Market and north along Cathedral Street to the western side of the churchyard. From here you can obtain some interesting shots of the main building, often with flowers in the foreground offering summer-in-the-city images.

### Inside the cathedral ♿

Enter the cathedral for some fantastic images of the interior, including the incredible vaulted ceiling. Use a zoom lens to locate and isolate interesting pieces of architecture. The best time to do this is on bright sunny days at any time of year, as the light pours in through upper windows to flood the interior. Make time to photograph delights such as the reclining statue of Shakespeare and the wonderfully ornate final resting place of the poet John Gower, who was in residence in the 14th century when the cathedral was still a convent.

### Permit for a £1

Please note the following with regards to interior photography: a personal photography permit should be purchased before taking any photos. At present this is just £1 – superb value for money – and any one of the curators or gift shop staff can help with this.

Most importantly, note that this is an active place of worship and people often attend the short services given throughout the day. You are requested to be mindful and show respect for others during these times. There is no time limit on your stay so if you wish to obtain a particular image, please wait while people complete their prayers before taking photos.

*Top*: *Memorial to Shakespeare. Canon 5D IV, 24–70mm at 30mm, ISO 1600, 1/10s at f/4. Apr.* ***Above***: *Cathedral interior. Canon 5D IV, 17–40mm at 21mm, ISO 800, 1/8s at f/5.6. Apr.*

*Top*: *Cathedral interior. Sony A6000, Fisheye 8mm at 8mm, ISO 400, 1/20s at f/8. Apr.* ***Above***: *Decoration inside cathedral. Canon 5D IV, 17–40mm at 22mm, ISO 1600, 1/15s at f/8. Apr.*

## How to get here

Exit London Bridge Station on to Tooley Street, walk west towards, the Barrowboy and Banker pub, and you'll see the cathedral located behind the pub. Take the steps to the left that lead into Borough Market and walk around the cathedral until you find the small entrance on the western side, located on Montague Close.

| | |
|---|---|
| **Location Lat/Long**: | 51.50617, -0.08959 |
| **Location Postcode**: | SE1 9DA |
| **Underground & Lines**: | London Bridge: *Jubilee, Northern* |
| **Main Station**: | London Bridge |
| **Riverboat**: | London Bridge City Pier |
| **Bus**: | 47,133, 343, RV1 |
| **Cycle Hire**: | Southwark Street, Tooley Street |

## Accessibility &#9855;

The main entrance has wheelchair access and a lift; the southern entrance, when open, leads directly on a level footing into the nave.

## Best time of year/day

Sunny days are best at any time of year.

## Opening hours

Visit during the following times as access to parts of the cathedral are restricted during services. Photography is not permitted during any of the services or events.

Sun 12.30pm–3pm & 4pm–6pm
Mon to Fri 9am–5pm
Sat 9.30am–3.45pm & 5pm–6:00pm

## Admission price (2019)

It's free to enter the cathedral but a personal photography permit, currently priced at £1, is required to take photos.

*Cathedral interior. Sony A6000, Fisheye 8mm at 8mm, ISO 640, 1/20s at f/8. Apr.*

Located to the south of Southwark Cathedral and London Bridge is Borough Market. There has been a market on or around this site for over a thousand years, and today the market is arguably the most famous food market in the UK. It sells a wide variety of fresh produce from the sea and the field, prepared food (and drink) and street food – both homegrown and international. It is a riot of colour, aromas and humanity, and a joy to wander around with a camera and catch a bite to eat.

The public food market is open on most days between 10am and 5pm and the wholesale food market is open between 2am and 8am on weekdays. It's another superb place to buy good quality, low-cost food to go, when you're on the move through the city and, on Saturday lunchtimes, the place is absolutely throbbing with visitors buying their lunch.

*Above*: Western entrance to Borough Market. Canon 5D II, 24–70mm at 24mm, ISO 200, 1/180s at f/8. July.

## What to shoot and viewpoints

### The market ♿

The market can be considered bisected by Bedale Street with the street food market to the east and the permanent stalls to the west. With so much activity and history it's a wonderful place to people-watch, and that means street photography in abundance. Using any camera with a typical mid-range focal length of 24–70mm you can work your way through the crowds, shooting images of the throng, the food, the stalls and – where they agree to it – the stall holders. Obviously they are working, so be mindful not to be a nuisance and please respect any signs that request no photography.

Alternatively, if you're not a street photographer or simply find crowds too much, then visit Borough Market before it opens early in the morning, when the place is completely deserted. This will allow you to wander around freely and obtain images of the architecture unhindered. The vaulted roof of the western market site is superb, catching light and pulling it into the lanes between the stalls. Obviously, outside working hours the market lacks life but a visit at both times will allow you to appreciate the contrast.

**Above**: Inside Borough Market. Canon 5D II, 24–70mm at 24mm, ISO 400, 1/250s at f/5.6. July.

**Above**: Stall holder at Borough Market. Sony A6000, 16–50mm at 28mm, ISO 2000, 1/160s at f/4.5. May.

**Above**: Fruiterer in Borough Market. Canon 5D II, 24–70mm at 50mm, ISO 800, 1/30s at f/9. Jan.

**Left**: Bread stall. Sony A6000, 16–50mm at 16mm, ISO 1250, 1/160s at f/4. May.

**Opposite**: Umbrella sculpture, Vinopolis, Borough Market. Sony A6000, 16–50mm at 16mm, ISO 100, 1/320s at f/4.5. Apr.

*Quiet morning in Borough Market. Sony A6000, 16–50mm at 16mm, ISO 3200, 1/160s at f/3.5. Feb.*

## The Globe Tavern and *Lock, Stock and Two Smoking Barrels* ♿

While taking photos around the market, make sure you visit some of the interesting sights to be found here. The Globe pub at the centre of the markets underwent a full overhaul during 2016. Some of the grubby punters may have moved on during its refurbishment but it's still a superb sight to shoot. If you're a fan of Guy Ritchie movies, then you mustn't miss a walk to the bend at the end of Park Street to the west of the market; this was where most of the exterior shots in the film *Lock, Stock and Two Smoking Barrels* were taken.

Located on the wall under the railway bridge on Storey Street is a mural consisting of eight pink hearts, dedicated

*Park Street buildings from Lock, Stock and Two Smoking Barrels. Canon 5D II, 24–70mm at 24mm, ISO 200, 1/180s at f/8. July.*

to those who lost their lives in the terrorist attacks of 3rd June 2017. The attackers crashed their van on London Bridge and ran into the market, randomly attacking innocent people. Each time I pass this way I spare a thought for those to whom this important piece is dedicated.

## How to get here

Coming from London Bridge, head into Borough Market by way of either Bedale Street (directly off Borough High Street) or head down the steps by Southwark Cathedral.

| | |
|---|---|
| **Location Lat/Long**: | 51.50560, -0.09067 |
| **Location Postcode**: | SE1 1TL |
| **Underground & Lines**: | London Bridge: *Jubilee, Northern* |
| **Main Station**: | London Bridge |
| **Bus**: | 43, 141, 149, 521 |
| **Cycle Hire**: | Park Street, Southwark Street |

## Accessibility ♿

The market itself is completely flat and level, however during busy periods (Saturday lunchtime for instance) the market is packed with hundreds of people buying from the stalls. If your mobility is limited, try to visit before or after the busy times (generally lunchtime), when it's easier to move around and through the market.

## Best time of year/day

It can be shot all year round but note the opening times if you want to get shots of the people and stalls.

## Opening hours

| | |
|---|---|
| **Full Market**: | Wed & Thur 10am–5pm |
| | Fri 10am–6pm |
| | Sat 8am–5pm |
| **Limited Market**: | Mon & Tue 10am–5pm |
| | Closed Sun. |

There is a fascinating history of the market at: *www.boroughmarket.org.uk*

*Above*: Borough Market memorial to the London Bridge attack victims. Sony A6000, 16–50mm at 21mm, ISO 250, 1/160s at f/4. June

*Below*: Cafes by Southwark Cathedral. Canon 5D IV, 24–70mm at 24mm, ISO 200, 1/10s at f/11. June

Clink Street is located close to the Thames, just west of Borough Market, and today it forms part of the southern Thames Path. The street is named after the infamous prison that once stood here. The Clink was originally a debtors prison owned by the Bishop of Winchester but as religious intolerance grew during the 17th century it housed mostly heretics.

The prison was rebuilt after the Peasants Revolt in 1382 and again in 1450 – the latter resulting in a two-storey men's prison. The slang word 'clink' is still used as a generic term for prison, as in 'he's going to the clink' and thought to have come from the sound of the rusty chains prisoners wore. The site now houses the Clink Prison Museum, identifiable by a skeleton housed in a cage that hangs outside this visitor attraction.

## What to shoot and viewpoints

The street itself is tiny – no more than 200m long in total – but it is a very important thoroughfare that links the Golden Hind exhibit to the east with the Thames Path, which leads past the Anchor Pub and on to Millennium Bridge. The street is always busy and it's another one of those great little 'crossroads' to shoot street photography. So many people pass through here as they move along the Thames Path and towards the river. The key to this location is the huge contrast in lighting between the sections under the railway bridge, the Clink Prison Museum, the open area that meets Storey Street (leading up to Borough Market) and the closed-in section leading east to the Golden Hind (the first UK ship to circumnavigate the globe, famously captained by Sir Francis Drake). >>

*Opposite top left: Coffee in Clink Street, Sony A6000, 16–50mm at 34mm, ISO 250, 1/160s at f/5. June **Right**: Cafe table in Clink Street. NEX-C3, E 18–55mm at 18mm, ISO 1600, 1/250s at f/4. Jan.*

*Opposite bottom left: Illuminated tunnel in Clink Street. Sony A6000, 16–50mm at 16mm, ISO 3200, 1/30s at f/3.5. Feb. **Right**: Painter at work. Canon 5D II, 24–70mm at 50mm, ISO 400, 1/350s at f/6.7. Sept.*

*Lone bicycle on Clink Street. NEX-C3, E 18–55mm at 19mm, ISO 1600, 1/50s at f/3.5. Jan.*

*Early morning in Clink Street NEX-C3, E 18–55mm at 26mm, ISO 1600, 1/30s at f/4. Feb.*

## How to get here

Coming in from London Bridge, head into Borough Market by way of either Bedale Street, directly off Borough High Street, or head down the steps by Southwark Cathedral. Pass through Borough Market until you reach the other side and emerge on to Stoney Street. Proceed north towards the river and at the end of Stoney Street you'll be on Clink Street. Turn left for the museum and river walk, or turn right for The Golden Hind.

| | |
|---|---|
| **Location Lat/Long**: | 51.50694,-0.09092 |
| **Location Postcode**: | SE1 9DG |
| **Underground & Lines**: | London Bridge: *Jubilee, Northern* |
| **Main Station**: | London Bridge |
| **Riverboat**: | Bankside Pier |
| **Bus**: | 43, 141, 149, 344, 521 |
| **Cycle Hire**: | Duke Street Hill |

## Accessibility &

This is an ordinary city street and should present no accessibility issues, though the Clink Prison Museum is not wheelchair accessible.

## Best time of year/day

All year round.

## Opening hours

The Clink Prison Museum is open seven days a week (closed on Christmas Day).

| | |
|---|---|
| **Summer hours**: | **July–Sept** 10am–9pm daily (last admission 8.30pm) |
| **Winter hours**: | **Oct–June** Mon to Fri 10am–6pm (last admission 5.30pm) Sat to Sun 10am–7.30pm (last admission 7pm) |

## Admission prices (2019)

### The Clink Prison Museum

| | |
|---|---|
| **Adults**: | **£7.50** |
| **Children** (under 16) | **£5.50** |
| **Students** (with ID): | **£5.50** |
| **Seniors** (aged 60+): | **£5.50** |
| **Family** (2 adults & 2 children under 16): | **£18.00** |

For more information visit: *www.clink.co.uk*

It's these stark differences in light through the street's various short sections that offer the best photographic opportunities. On bright sunny days you can catch people moving through the shadowy areas, capturing how their shapes play with the light. Early in the morning, and under the right conditions, (when there's moisture in the air) a thin veil of mist shrouds the edge of the shadowed areas; with fewer people around early in the morning, you should be able to isolate them and utilise their shapes most effectively. Obviously, when rain falls, the hard paved street glistens and throws light back up like a reflector. It's a perfect place to shoot individuals with umbrellas. Streetlights add yet another layer of interplay between light and shadow.

*Opposite top: Hiding in the shadows, Clink Street. Canon 5D II, 24–70mm at 42mm, ISO 400, 1/125s at f/6.7. Sept.*

*Opposite left: Early morning in Borough Market. NEX-C3, E 18–55mm at 20mm, ISO 1600, 1/160s at f/4. Feb.*
*Right: The Gherkin from Clink Street. Canon 5D IV, 24–70mm at 70mm, ISO 800, 1/1000s at f/4. Apr.*

The Anchor Bankside pub (or just Anchor Bankside or The Anchor) is located along the Thames Path between London Bridge and Southwark Bridge, which it's closer to. Originally built in 1616 as a brewery tap room – the brewery was at the rear of the building – it has been rebuilt several times over the last 400 years.

When the pub was first built, the area formed London's theatreland district, and its many inns were frequented by actors, playwrights and writers, including William Shakespeare and Dr Samuel Johnson. It is also reputed to be the place where diarist Samuel Pepys first observed the Great Fire of London in 1666. Rebuilt after another fire in the 1770s, it became a tavern frequented by lowlifes and pirates, who came up the Thames with stolen and contraband goods; it was even a brothel for a while. In 2008 it underwent one of the most costly pub refurbishments in history at £2.8m.

## What to shoot and viewpoints

There are many, many pubs in London all with their own charm but there's something truly special about the Anchor Bankside, especially at dusk. The old brickwork exterior of the building has several lamps attached to it and the wooden fixtures are painted red. These details combine to create a building that is beautiful to shoot at dusk, as the golden hour gives way to the blue hour. The pub is very popular, especially its terrace, which sits opposite. This area is dark and you'll need a tripod to really capture this gem of a location, which can be shot from either side – both angles work perfectly well. However, shooting from the western side looking east might offer more opportunity to capture the crowds, the people hurrying past and the towering presence of the Shard. The Anchor Bankside is a magical picture opportunity.

Apart from using a tripod, you won't need any special equipment but please be careful where you place your tripod, as you'll be working around people who may not see you in the dark.

*Opposite left: The Anchor Bankside Pub, Southwark. Sony A6000, 16–50mm at 16mm, ISO 100, 1/500s at f/4.5. May.*

*Opposite right: Pub patrons. Sony A6000, 16–50mm at 50mm, ISO 400, 1/160s at f/5.6. May.*

### How to get here
Following the directions to the Globe Theatre, continue along the river path that leads through the tunnel under Southwark Bridge. Keep walking along the river path and, as you spot the Shard in the distance, you'll come across the Anchor Bankside. If coming from Borough Market, head along Clink Street, past the Clink Prison Museum and under the railway bridge. Turn right towards the river and the Anchor Bankside is to your left.

| | |
|---|---|
| **Location Lat/Long**: | 51.50727, -0.09287 |
| **Location Postcode**: | SE1 9EF |
| **Underground & Lines**: | London Bridge: *Jubilee, Northern* |
| **Main Station**: | London Bridge |
| **Riverboat**: | Bankside Pier |
| **Bus**: | 43, 141, 149, 344, 521 |

### Accessibility ♿
This is an ordinary city street and should present no accessibility issues.

### Best time of year/day
Can be shot all year round. Late evening's best for capturing the warmth of the crowds.

### Opening hours
Mon to Wed 11am–11pm (food served 11.30am–10pm)
Thur to Sat 11am–11.30pm (food served 11.30am–10pm)
Sun 12pm–10.30pm (food served 12–9.30pm)

*Opposite: The Anchor early hours. Canon 5D II, 24–70mm at 24mm, ISO 100, 3s at f/8, tripod. Nov.*

There have been two bridges at the current site of Southwark Bridge; the original bridge, designed by John Rennie and opened in 1819, was toll only – a penny to cross. The owners of the toll bridge went bankrupt and it was acquired by the Bridge House Estates company in 1864, which immediately made it toll-free. The current structure was opened in 1921 by King George V.

The bridge has appeared in several films including *Harry Potter and the Order of the Phoenix* and *Mary Poppins*. It's also mentioned in Charles Dickens' novel *Little Dorrit*. The Thames Path foot tunnel passes under the southern end of the bridge. As you walk through it, take time to observe the Thames' Freeze Frost Fairs Frieze (a tongue-twister!) depicting the fairs that were set up between the 17th and 19th centuries, when the Thames would freeze during harsh winters.

## What to shoot and viewpoints

While the bridge itself is quite picturesque, to my mind, of most interest to the photographer is the Thames Path foot tunnel, which passes under the southern end of the bridge. The tunnel itself has several facets that make for some very interesting pictures throughout the day: at dawn, the sun rises and casts its light directly into the eastern end of the tunnel, causing a bright orange eclipse over the brickwork. As you proceed along the path, take time to observe the patterns that have appeared

where rainwater has leaked through the ceiling and run down the brickwork. These make effective backdrops for pictures of passers-by.

As you emerge at the western end of the tunnel, you will notice a drainage trough in the floor, which creates a perfect lead-in line in either direction. Shooting to the west, you will catch the dome of St Paul's Cathedral and the cityscape can be framed in the arch of the tunnel. Walk a little further, then turn to look behind you; once again – using the drainage trough as a lead-in line – capture passers-by on foot and bikes as the head through the tunnel. This composition works very well in the evening as the light fades and the lights from the tunnel dominate. On wet days, people often keep their umbrellas up as they pass through; use the natural framing of the arched entrance to the tunnel to secure a composition.

*Opposite: Southwark Bridge tunnel at sunrise, southside. Canon 5D IV, 24–70mm at 34mm, ISO 3200, 1/60s at f/6.7. Apr.*

## How to get here

Proceed from the Anchor Bankside pub, walk west along the Thames Path until you reach the green-arched Southwark Bridge. The tunnel lies directly to the left of the steps that lead up to Southwark Bridge Road. If approaching from the Tate Modern, walk east along the Thames Path until you reach Southwark Bridge.

| | |
|---|---|
| **Location Lat/Long**: | 51.50802, -0.09457 |
| **Location Postcode**: | SE1 9HA |
| **Underground & Lines**: | London Bridge: *Jubilee, Northern* |
| **Main Station**: | London Bridge |
| **Riverboat**: | Bankside Pier |
| **Bus**: | 43, 141, 149, 344, 521 |
| **Cycle Hire**: | Hop Exchange, Borough, Borough High Street |

## Accessibility ♿

Ordinary city street that should present no accessibility issues.

### Best time of year/day

Can be shot all year round. Late evening is a good time to capture passers-by.

*Above: Passing under Southwark bridge towards St Paul's. Sony A6000, 16–50mm at 20mm, ISO 100, 1/160s at f/4.5. June.*

*Opposite left: Looking east towards Southwark Bridge from the Globe Theatre. Canon 5D IV, 24–70mm at 46mm, ISO 200, 1/90s at f/11. Apr. Right: Late night under Southwark Bridge. Sony A6000, 16–50mm at 23mm, ISO 3200, 1/60s at f/4. Mar.*

The original Globe theatre was built in 1599 by the Lord Chamberlain's Men – the name given to a company of actors that included Shakespeare. The playhouse burned down in 1613, caused by a theatrical cannon set off during a performance of *Henry VIII*, and was rebuilt in 1614. It was open until 1642 when an act of Parliament closed all theatres; the Puritan view was that plays represented 'lascivious Mirth and Levity'.

The modern Globe Theatre, located roughly 250m from the site of the original 17th-century playhouse was built in 1997. It was the actor Sam Wanamaker who organised the construction and funding for the modern playhouse we see today and it is considered a very accurate replica of the original, the only major difference being the size of the audience: modern safety regulations only allow half of the 3,000 people who would have been admitted to the original theatre.

## What to shoot and viewpoints

The main reason for visiting the Globe is to see a play and with only so much of the building visible from the Thames Path, it's not a location you would go out of your way to see, just to photograph. However, it does have historical appeal, it's a unique structure and is accessible for photos night and day (from the riverside path). The best time to get good photos of this unusual building is late evening, as the blue hour commences and the building is illuminated. Even when the gates are closed, the theatre remains illuminated. When shot from the Millennium Bridge looking towards the Shard, it makes an attractive

### How to get here

As you cross south over the Millennium Bridge, you'll see the Globe to your left on the southern bank. Simply exit the bridge and head east along the river path towards your destination.

| | |
|---|---|
| **Location Lat/Long**: | 51.50815, -0.09727 |
| **Location Postcode**: | SE1 9DT |
| **Underground & Lines**: | Blackfriars, Southwark, St Paul's: *Central, Circle & District, Jubilee* |
| **Main Station**: | Blackfriars, London Bridge |
| **Riverboat**: | Millbank Pier, Bankside Pier |
| **Bus**: | 45, 63, 100, 344, RV1 |
| **Cycle Hire**: | New Globe Walk, Southwark Street |

### Accessibility &#9855;

The theatre has separate entrances that offer easy passage for the less mobile. The river path is completely accessible to anyone with mobility problems.

### Best time of year/day

Can be shot all year round.

### Opening hours

Theatre Tours 9.30am–5pm. Performance times vary so please check the website for details.

### Admission prices (2019)

**Globe theatre guided tour (40 minutes)**

| | |
|---|---|
| **Adults**: | £17.00 |
| **Children** | £10.00 |
| **Students** (16+, with ID): | £13.50 |
| **Seniors** (aged 60+): | £3.00 |

**Performance ticket prices**

| | |
|---|---|
| **Yard** (standing): | £5.00 |
| **Gallery** (seated) from: | £23.00 |

**Under 18s** – £3 off all seats

*The Globe Theatre, South Bank. Canon 5D II, 17–40mm at 19mm, ISO 100, 15s at f/19, tripod 0.6 grad. Oct.*

subject to incorporate into compositions of the South Bank. The classic juxtaposition of old and new within the frame makes for an interesting take on the London skyline.

When shooting up close from the river path, you'll need a wide-angle lens – probably something 17mm or lower – as the building is quite tall. Shooting from a distance, isolation is key, and to capture the old and new composition, shoot with a 100mm+ lens from the bridge. From the Millennium Bridge, using a tripod is tricky at busy times due to the vibrations from passers-by; you may find handheld is more effective if your camera or lens has built-in stabilisation.

Claims that the original Globe theatre was located in Hoxton on New Inn Street are unfounded. That was in fact another theatre that performed Shakespeare's plays. But if you visit Brick Lane, be sure to head to New Inn Street, where you'll find a huge mural depicting Shakespeare's Romeo and Juliet (next to a sign that incorrectly claims the original Globe theatre was situated here). If you want to visit the actual site of the original playhouse, proceed eastwards from the current theatre along New Globe Walk, then turn right on to Park Street. Proceed for about 100m until you see a large plaque on the south side of the road (about N°. 40) – this marks the spot of the original 17th-century theatre.

Britain's national gallery of international modern art, the Tate Modern, is housed inside the old Bankside Power Station, located directly south over the Thames from St Paul's Cathedral. Crossing the Millennium Bridge will lead you right to the building's entrance. The building was due for demolition after the power station was shut down in 1981 but many campaigned to keep the building and obtain listed status.

The Tate Group stepped in and, after six years of work, the Tate Modern was completed, opening its doors in January 2000. Admission is free and the building is comprised of three main sections: the main Turbine Hall in the centre, the Boiler House to the north and the ten-storey Blavatnik Building (or Switch House) in the south, which has 360° views of the London skyline from its viewing terrace.

*Tate Modern cafe overlooking the Thames. Canon 5D II, 70–200mm at 70mm, ISO 200, 1/250s at f/8. July.*

*Panoramic view from the 10th floor of the Tate Modern. Canon 5D II, 24–70mm at 24mm, ISO 200, 1/180s at f/13. July.*

As well as offering some of the best views of the city, intriguing artworks and exhibitions, the vast concrete interior of the Tate Modern is a goldmine of photographic opportunities. Unlike many galleries in London, photography is permitted inside the Tate, although commercial photography requires prior agreement.

## What to shoot and viewpoints

### The Turbine Hall ♿

The vast Turbine Hall is a cathedral of light – a wonderful place to shoot images using light as the main medium for the composition. The best time to shoot is on a bright sunny day, late in the afternoon, as the sun moves around to the west side of the building, where it will cast light through five narrow windows. As the sun moves, the lines of light become longer and brighter until they reach peak point, lying directly down the main hall. I would advise timing your arrival as the light enters the windows, then situate yourself on the gallery just one floor above the main hall. From this elevated viewpoint you can shoot

*The Turbine Hall, Tate Modern. Canon 5D IV, 70–200mm at 121mm, ISO 400, 1/2000s at f/16. June*

the lines of light and capture people as they pass through the long shadows, making excellent compositions. As the light moves around, follow it and shoot either from the first floor walkway, looking towards the light, or head down to the main hall. When processing, consider monochromatic and harsh contrast to emphasise the bold lines of light and subjects caught within them.

*Tate Modern tower on a summer morning. Sony A6000, 16–50mm at 16mm, ISO 100, 1/250s at f/4.5. May.*

*Late afternoon sun in the Turbine Hall. Canon 5D IV, 17–40mm at 17mm, ISO 400, 1/60s at f/16. June*

*Tate Modern. Canon 5D II, 70–200mm at 200mm, ISO 400, 1/350s at f/5.6. July.*

*View from Tate Modern viewing gallery. Canon 5D II, 17–40mm at 17mm, ISO 100, 1/60s at f/8. July.*

## The Blavatnik Building and the 360˚ Viewing Terrace ♿

At the top of the Blavatnik Building sits the 10th-floor viewing terrace – another of those wonderful hidden–but-getting-increasingly-popular gems that London has to offer. Head through the gift shop to the lifts and they will take you to the main viewing gallery. The 360˚ view encompasses the Shard and beyond, views north over the river to St Paul's and the city, and west up river towards Temple. Use a mid-range lens to capture a broad vista or a zoom lens to isolate details in the city skyline. A word of caution: the residents of the buildings behind the Tate have requested that visitors don't take photographs of their apartments. While it's not illegal, my advice would be to respect their wishes and concentrate on shooting from the north side of the building, especially in the evening. While on the balcony of the viewing area, consider taking street-style images of people enjoying the view. These offer not only a sense of scale but imbue the cityscape with a human touch.

## How to get here

Starting from the south entrance at St Paul's Cathedral, cross over to Peter's Hill, through Carter Lane Gardens. Go past the National Firefighters Memorial and head south towards the river. Cross over the Millennium Bridge and the Tate Modern is directly in front of you.

| | |
|---|---|
| **Location Lat/Long**: | 51.50759, -0.09935 |
| **Location Postcode**: | SE1 9TG |
| **Underground & Lines**: | Blackfriars, Southwark, St Paul's: *Central, Circle & District, Jubilee* |
| **Main Station**: | Blackfriars, London Bridge |
| **Riverboat**: | Bankside Pier, Millbank Pier |
| **Bus**: | 45, 63, 100, 344, RV1 |
| **Cycle Hire**: | New Glove Street, Southwark Street |
| **Tate to Tate Tours**: | The Tate Boat runs every 40 minutes during gallery opening times between Tate Britain and Tate Modern. The Tate Boat is operated by MBNA Thames Clippers. |

## Accessibility &#9855;

Most areas within the Tate are fully accessible to those with limited mobility.

## Best time of year/day

The exterior of Tate Modern can be shot all year round. It's open 10am–8pm most days. Afternoons in summer are best for Turbine Hall shots.

## Opening hours

Sun to Thurs 10am–6pm
Fri to Sat 10am–10pm

## Admission price (2019)

**Free** (some special exhibitions may incur a charge).

*Above*: *View from Tate Modern viewing gallery. Canon 5D II, 17–40mm at 17mm, ISO 100, 1/90s at f/8. July.*

*Interior of Tate Modern. Canon 5D II, 17–40mm at 17mm, ISO 800, 1/15s at f/8. July.*

## Spiral Staircase

If you're able, I would advise taking the stairs back down. There are some interesting architectural features in the harsh concrete interior of the building that offer unusual compositions, especially on bright days when the light is filtered into the building. Keep an eye out for the spiral staircase, which a wide-angle lens will best capture.

## Cafe with a View ♿

Once back on the ground floor, cross back through the gift shop and take the lift up to the restaurant and cafe on the north side of the complex. From here you will have an uninterrupted view looking directly over the Thames to St Paul's. Make use of the silhouettes of people in the foreground, in front of the windows, to create a composition with a unique perspective of the London skyline.

## The Exhibits and a Donation

Please do make time to enjoy the galleries and leave a small donation or purchase something from the gift shop. The Tate is free to everyone to enjoy, it's funded without

needing to charge entrance fees and it's up to visitors to keep such a wonderful place open. Viewing the abstract art that the Tate houses is a great way to detach from photographic subjects and I find it helps me think more carefully about the compositions I create and the way light interacts with objects.

*Dividing glass partition in the Turbine Hall. Canon 5D II, 70–200mm at 70mm, ISO 800, 1/60s at f/4. July.*

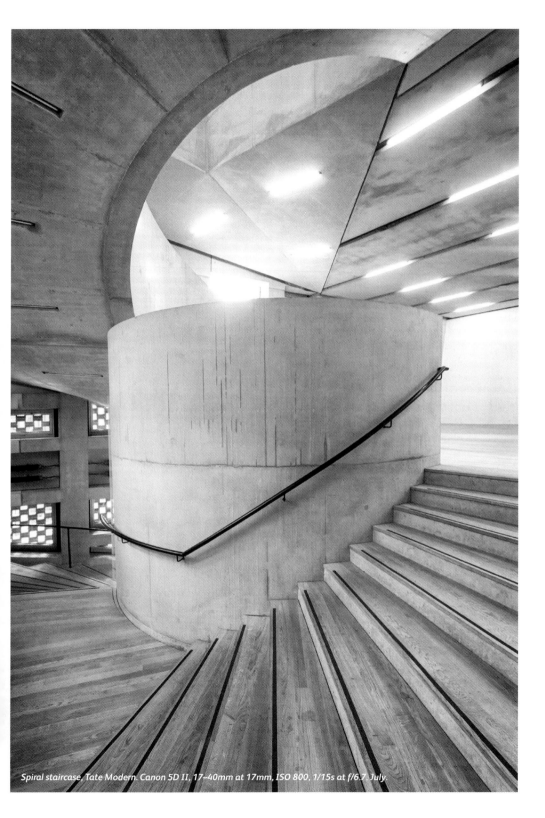

*Spiral staircase, Tate Modern. Canon 5D II, 17–40mm at 17mm, ISO 800, 1/15s at f/6.7. July.*

**R.I.P. The Outcast Dead. Crossbones Garden was a paupers burial ground dating back to medieval times. It's thought that over 15,000 paupers from the surrounding slums have been buried here, including 'single women' – a euphemism for prostitutes who, due to their 'sinful' lives were denied the right to a standard Christian burial. And yet, many brothels or 'stews' that used to be situated in Southwark were in fact licensed by the Bishop of Winchester and consequently, these working women were known as 'Winchester Geese'. When it was time to lay them to rest however, they were denied the dignity of a proper burial. Instead, the Crossbones, the outcasts' graveyard, became their final resting place, in unhallowed and unconsecrated ground.**

By the 19th century there were so many bodies buried at Crossbones that it was declared a severe health risk and it closed in 1853. When Transport for London was in the process of building the Jubilee extension at the end of the 20th century, 150 skeletons were removed from the site.

Since 1996, the writer and playwright John Constable along with Katy Nicholls, the friends of Crossbones and Bankside Open Spaces Trust have transformed the graveyard into a beautiful place, *'a garden of remembrance, a sacred place and sanctuary in the heart of the city, dedicated to the outcast dead and to living sex workers, outcasts and outsiders.'*

## What to shoot and viewpoints

If you're in the Southwark area I recommend you visit this natural and bohemian place. It's a small area and amongst the shrubs, flowers and trees are statues of the Madonna, skulls, small shrines, displays of artistic artifacts, snatches of poetry and quotes from John Constable. All this makes for a contemplative environment in which to take photos. There are two distinct ways to approach taking photos: close ups of the variety of interesting objects or shooting wider to give a sense of the location.

Towering over the garden is the Shard, which helps to offer not only a sense of location but also a sense of scale. Wildflowers in spring and summer add colour and vibrancy to this otherwise rather melancholy place.

The derogatory name of 'Winchester Geese' is a prominent theme throughout the garden, illustrated both in writing and objects and thanks to the tireless work of the volunteers, who tend the garden and make time to keep it open for visitors a few hours a week, this poignant piece of London's history is remembered.

*Opposite left: The Crossbones Garden, Southwark. Canon 5D IV, 24–70mm at 24mm, ISO 200, 1/180s at f/8. Apr. **Right**: Crossbones memorials, Southwark. Canon 5D IV, 24–70mm at 46mm, ISO 200, 1/90s at f/5.6. Apr. **Middle**: Statues in the garden, Southwark. Canon 5D IV, 24–70mm at 28mm, ISO 200, 1/500s at f/8. Apr.*

## How to get here

Leaving London Bridge station, walk west on Tooley Street for about 250m. Take a left under the railway bridge and head south along the A3. Pass Borough Market to your right and, as you pass London Bridge underground station, take the fork in the road on to Southwark Street. Keep walking west for about 250m and you will see Redcross Way to your left. Walk south until you see the railings of the garden festooned with ribbons.

| | |
|---|---|
| **Location Lat/Long**: | 51.50391, -0.09342 |
| **Location Postcode**: | SE1 1SD |
| **Underground & Lines**: | Borough, London Bridge: *Jubilee, Northern* |
| **Main Station**: | London Bridge |
| **Riverboat**: | London Bridge City Pier |
| **Bus**: | 133, 344, 381, RV1 |
| **Cycle Hire**: | Hop Exchange, Borough, Borough High Street |

### Accessibility ♿
The garden is very flat and has wide paths that lead around it. It should present no accessibility issues.

### Best time of year/day
Crossbones Garden can be photographed any time of the year but has very restricted opening hours so check opening times before your visit. For more information visit: *www.crossbones.org.uk* and *www.bost.org.uk*

### Opening hours
Wed to Sun 12pm– 2pm.

### Admission price (2019)
Free.

*Beehive, Crossbones Garden, Southwark. Canon 5D IV, 24–70mm at 32mm, ISO 200, 1/90s at f/8. Apr.*

*Ornaments, Crossbones Garden, Southwark. Canon 5D IV, 24–70mm at 70mm, ISO 200, 1/250s at f/8. Apr.*

This little park and its cottages were designed and established in 1887 by renowned social reformer Octavia Hill. Hill believed that working families should have access to good quality housing and public spaces for their wellbeing. She also played an important part in the founding of the National Trust in 1894. The garden had fallen into decay and it is through the efforts of the volunteers from the Bankside Open Spaces Trust that the garden was restored to its former glory for all to enjoy and photograph.

## What to shoot and viewpoints

Much like Crossbones just along the road, this is a small but delightful space in which to take photos. In spring and summer the flowerbeds are alive with blooms, while trees create shady canopies over the benches, making for superb urban-park scenes – a must to shoot. The park's winding paths offer wonderful lead-in lines to the cottages and provide direction and flow within the images you'll make. The contrast of soft natural colours in the trees, shrubs and flowers set against the harsh urban setting that surrounds the park offers yet more opportunities to make stunning images. The centrepiece pond and its fountain add a sense of life-in-motion to shots.

*The Red Cross Garden, Southwark. Sony A6000, Fisheye 8mm at 8mm, ISO 100, 1/160s at f/8. Apr.*

## How to get here

Follow the same directions as for Crossbones Garden but keep heading south on Redcross Way until you find Red Cross Garden to your right. It lies just opposite the Cathedral School of St Saviour & St Mary Overy.

| | |
|---|---|
| **Location Lat/Long**: | 51.50316, -0.09459 |
| **Location Postcode**: | SE1 1HA |
| **Underground & Lines**: | Borough, London Bridge: *Jubilee, Northern* |
| **Main Station**: | London Bridge |
| **Riverboat**: | London Bridge City Pier |
| **Bus**: | 133, 344, 381, RV1 |
| **Cycle Hire**: | Hop Exchange, Borough, Borough High Street |

## Accessibility ♿

The garden is very flat with wide paths that lead around it and should present no accessibility issues.

## Best time of year/day

Red Cross Garden can be photographed any time of the year, though spring to autumn is best. For more information visit: *www.bost.org.uk/red-cross-garden*

## Opening hours

Mon to Sun 8am–8pm.

## Admission price (2019)

Free.

*Opposite left: The Red Cross Garden. Canon 5D IV, 24–70mm at 30mm, ISO 200, 1/125s at f/8. Apr. **Middle**: Traffic light, Southwark. Canon 5D IV, 24–70mm at 70mm, ISO 200, 1/350s at f/5.6. Apr. **Right**: The Red Cross Garden, Southwark. Sony A6000, Fisheye 8mm at 8mm, ISO 125, 1/160s at f/8. Apr.*

# THE SOUTH BANK
# & WESTMINSTER

After the Square Mile, the South Bank is probably the most dynamic and constantly changing area of London. The western side of Southwark and Lambeth contains many places that have only been established in the last 100 years, including the OXO Tower, Waterloo Bridge, the National Theatre and, most recently, the world-famous London Eye. Concluding this section is Westminster, the United Kingdom's seat of political power.

Lambeth first appears on record in 1062 and its name, meaning *landing of lambs*, marked it as a riverside dock where sheep were traded. It remained distinctly rural, predominantly marshland in fact up until the 18th century, when it was drained. Several street names reflect this hidden past, including Lower Marsh Street. Lambeth was badly bombed during World War II, resulting in the loss of thirty-seven lives and a huge amount of devastation. The area was rejuvenated during the late 20th century and now hosts many shops, restaurants and galleries.

To the western edge of this area, lies Westminster. The Palace of Westminster is on record as having been the residence of one of the last kings of England, prior to the Norman invasion – King Canute lived here from 1016–1035. The first meeting of parliamentarians took place when rebel Simon de Montfort and others assembled here in 1265. The palace ceased to be a royal residence in the 15th century and has since become the primary meeting place for the government.

There is a vast range of eclectic locations to discover in this section – the street art and graffiti of the Leake Street tunnel, the architecture of the London Eye (as well as the stunning views a trip on it offers) and the ancient history of Westminster.

*Previous spread*: Looking east along the Thames from Waterloo Bridge. Canon 5D IV, 24–70mm at 70mm, ISO 100, 20.0s at f/11, tripod, ND 0.6 grad. May.

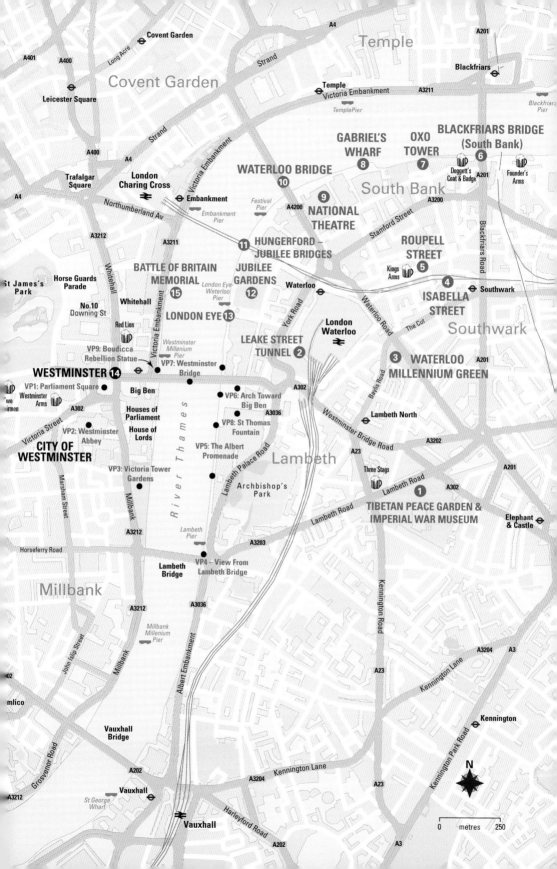

**The Tibetan Peace Garden is located in the grounds of the Imperial War Museum (IWM) and was consecrated in 1999 by the Dalai Lama. The garden is a gift to the people of Britain to help us understand the need for compassion and peace in our troubled world.**

The central Kalachakra mandala – cast from bronze – confers peace upon the garden and those who visit. Around the garden are sculptures that represent the four elements: earth, air, fire and water, with eight seats, each representing the tenets of the Tibetan religion. The garden is also a monument to the ongoing courage of the Tibetan people's commitment to non-violence and desire to find peace. In contrast, and somewhat ironically, photographing the Peace Garden also gives you an opportunity to photograph the 15-inch guns from *HMS Ramillies* and *HMS Resolution*, which take pride of place outside the Imperial War Museum.

## What to shoot and viewpoints

### The Tibetan Peace Garden ♿

Although just a tiny part of the Imperial War Museum grounds, the Peace Garden is a beautiful place to visit in summer when the flowers and shrubs are in full bloom amongst the stone memorials. The white stone reflects light into the central area, offering some compelling photographic compositions. If you're lucky, you may see one or two monks visiting the garden.

### Imperial War Museum ♿

You will find monuments to warfare and peace around the grounds of the IWM, and most notable are the huge guns situated at the entrance to the main museum. When shot on a bright day with a wide-angle lens, they offer a superb image of the power of mankind's engineering prowess but also a sobering reminder of our ability to make weapons of destruction.

I've visited the museum many times on my own and with my family, most recently to see the Holocaust exhibition – a reminder that we must never forget one of the most horrendous periods of human history. I would strongly encourage you visit the museum; there are some amazing exhibits and admission is free. The IWM is financed by donations and grants so leave a donation or buy something from the gift shop if you do visit.

## How to get here

If using the Underground, take the Bakerloo Line to get to Lambeth North station. Turn left on leaving the station and proceed southeast along the A302 for about ten minutes until you reach the junction of the A3203 and Lambeth Road, where you'll see the Imperial War Museum ahead to your right. You can access the Peace Garden through the main IWM entrance or continue for another 200m along the A302 and take one of the entrances to the park situated to the east of the main building. There are three bus stops at the museum's entrance and the number 12 bus from Elephant and Castle Underground station will drop you off outside the Peace Garden. The alternative is the number 344 from Liverpool Street station, which goes direct to the IWM bus stop on Lambeth Road.

| | |
|---|---|
| **Location Lat/Long**: | 51.49689, -0.10784 |
| **Location Postcode**: | SE1 6HZ |
| **Underground & Lines**: | Elephant & Castle, Lambeth North: *Bakerloo, Northern* |
| **Main Station**: | Waterloo |
| **Bus**: | 12, 53, 148, 344, 453, C10 |

## Accessibility ♿

The museum is fully accessible with excellent service for wheelchair users and visitors with limited mobility.

## Best time of year/day

During spring and summer the flowers around the gardens are in full bloom. The best time to visit is during the day when the most light is available. There are no exterior lights overnight.

## Opening hours

**Imperial War Museum**
10am–6pm daily
The Imperial War Museum is closed 24th–26th Dec.

## Admission price (2019)

Free.

*Opposite top: Tibetan Peace Garden, Lambeth. Canon 5D IV, 24–70mm at 28mm, ISO 200, 1/125s at f/8. July.*

*Opposite left: Tibetan Peace Garden, Lambeth. Canon 5D IV, 24–70mm at 24mm, ISO 200, 1/350s at f/8. July. Right: Imperial War Museum gardens, Lambeth. Sony A6000, Fisheye 8mm at 8mm, ISO 100, 1/160s at f/8. July.*

The Leake Street tunnel is located under the tracks that enter Waterloo Station. The tunnel became a temporary graffiti area in 2008 during a street art festival organised by the renowned street artist Banksy, but is now a permanently designated graffiti and street art space. This is a great place to shoot urban art and the adjacent bars and restaurants are also worth a visit.

## What to shoot and viewpoints

At 300m long and with only basic street lighting, the tunnel can seem quite intimidating on first glance but, much like Brick Lane in the East End, it is a rich source of street art concentrated in one compact area. The art here is regularly replaced and if you visit during the middle of the day – and if you're lucky – you may witness an artist adding a new piece of work. The tunnel also contains art-space-come-gallery, The Vaults, which is open when work is being exhibited.

Shooting in the tunnel can be tricky due to the very low light; you'll need a camera with good performance at high ISO, a flash and/or a tripod. A medium range lens (24–70mm) is useful to capture small samples of work on the walls, or use a wide-angle lens to capture a sense of the vast array of work on display. The best time to visit is early morning during the week when the tunnel is used by commuters heading from and to Waterloo Station. That way, you won't find yourself alone. The lighting is subdued and CCTV is only installed at either end of the tunnel, so avoid visiting alone in the evening or late at night. Another word of caution: wear stout footwear and watch your step as broken glass, paint cans and other rubbish tends to litter the floor.

*Top*: Leake Street tunnel ceiling decoration. Canon 5D II, 17–40mm at 17mm, ISO 100, 10s at f/11. June.

*Bottom*: Art in the Leake Street tunnel. Canon 5D II, 17–40mm at 17mm, ISO 100, 20s at f/11. June.

*Opposite left*: Leake Street tunnel. Canon 5D IV, 24–70mm at 32mm, ISO 3200, 1/45s at f/4. July. **Right**: The Vaults, Leake Street tunnel. Canon 5D IV, 24–70mm at 34mm, ISO 1600, 1/30s at f/4.5. Apr.

## How to get here

The tunnel runs directly under Waterloo Station. To get here take the Underground Bakerloo, Northern or Jubilee line to Waterloo Station. Exit the main station entrance on to Cab Road, then take a left and continue until you reach the junction with the A3200 (about 50m from the station entrance.) Take another left and continue west for about 500m – you will see Leake Street to your left. The north tunnel entrance is about 50m from the A3200 that you've just walked along. An alternative route is to come from Waterloo Millennium Green. Cross the road to the north of the park and enter Lower Marsh Street. Continue for about 500m and you will see the entrance to Leake Street on the right-hand side located between two buildings, one of which has about twenty identical bird houses on the wall. Finally, if you arrive from Westminster, cross the bridge heading east and keep walking until you see Belvedere Road to your left. Proceed along this road until you find Forum Magnum Square, a huge open piazza, to your right,. Cross the square towards the A3200, take a left and you will find Leake Street on your right.

| | |
|---|---|
| **Location Lat/Long**: | 51.50138, -0.11475 |
| **Location Postcode**: | SE1 7NN |
| **Underground & Lines**: | Lambeth North, Waterloo: *Bakerloo, Jubilee, Northern, Waterloo & City* |
| **Main Station**: | Waterloo |
| **Riverboat**: | Waterloo Pier |
| **Bus**: | 12, 53, 148, 453, C10, RV1 |
| **Cycle Hire**: | Lower Marsh, Southwark Station |

## Accessibility

The tunnel is fully accessible with excellent access for wheelchairs and those with mobility problems. Please be aware that there can be broken glass in the tunnel; wear sturdy footwear and supervise children carefully.

## Best time of year/day

This location can be visited all year round as it never closes. The best time of day to visit is between 10am and 6pm as the tunnel is quite dark even on bright days. The area is quite safe during the day when there are lots of people passing through but I would advise that late in the evening, you only visit as part of a group or guided tour just to be on the safe side.

*Top*: Birdhouses by Leake Street tunnel, Southwark. Canon 5D IV, 24–70mm at 70mm, ISO 200, 1/90s at f/8. Apr.

*Above*: Leake Street tunnel. Canon 5D IV, 24–70mm at 25mm, ISO 3200, 1/60s at f/4. July.

*Opposite Top*: Looking south along the Leake Street tunnel. Canon 5D II, 17–40mm at 17mm, ISO 100, 10s at f/11. June.

*Opposite*: Bar in the Leake Street tunnel, Southwark. Canon 5D IV, 24–70mm at 25mm, ISO 1600, 1/10s at f/4.5. Apr.

**Middle**: *Leake Street tunnel. Canon 5D IV, 24–70mm at 24mm, ISO 3200, 1/90s at f/4. July.*

**Above**: *Leake Street tunnel. Canon 5D IV, 24–70mm at 24mm, ISO 800, 1/10s at f/4. May.*

Waterloo Millennium Green, located south of its namesake station, is one of the Bankside Open Spaces Trust (B.O.S.T) projects. Created by the local community but managed by B.O.S.T. it is great place to escape from the city bustle.

The small water garden, the wildflower beds, the winding path and the wonderful array of trees make the green a must-stop place to photograph if you're in the area. Though the Bankside Trust makes design decisions, the garden is staffed and maintained by local volunteers – a perfect example of what can be achieved when local communities have the drive, a goal and come together to improve their own areas.

## What to shoot and viewpoints

The best time to visit is in spring and summer when the garden is awash with greenery. In springtime you'll find the wildflowers a riot of colour and the trees in full blossom, which helps mask the buildings and noise of the roads that run on three sides of the park. The most prominent feature to be seen from this small park is the London Eye, just behind Waterloo Station, and it makes a great backdrop for shots taken through the trees and flowerbeds on the south side of the garden. The real trick to shooting this sort of

location is to make your compositions mostly greenery, whilst trying to incorporate one third or less of the surrounding urban structures or other clues as to the garden's location. This will help to highlight the location as a 'city oasis'.

The small natural water garden with its bridges and seating areas adds motion and life to the park environment and there's a good number of shots to be had mixing grass, flowers and trees with the bridges and rockeries. Look to position yourself among the trees and wild areas to the northeast side of the garden, where the contrast of light and shade on sunny days combined with the winding paths is hard to resist.

*Top*: *Millennium Green. Canon 5D IV, 24–70mm at 24mm, ISO 200, 1/500s at f/8. Apr.* ***Above***:*Millennium Green. Canon 5D IV, 24–70mm at 24mm, ISO 200, 1/180s at f/8. Apr.*

*Opposite top*: *Millennium Green. Canon 5D IV, 24–70mm at 28mm, ISO 200, 1/350s at f/8. Apr.*

*Opposite*: *Millennium Green, Waterloo. Canon 5D IV, 24–70mm at 24mm, ISO 200, 1/250s at f/8. Apr.*

## How to get here

If arriving from Waterloo Station's main entrance, walk north about 50m and turn right on to Mepham Street. Keep walking east until you reach the junction with A301 Waterloo Road, then continue southeast along Waterloo Road for about 200m. You will find the park to your right on the corner of Waterloo Road and Baylis Road. The Old Vic theatre is located across the road from the park and there are many bus stops located straight opposite the park. Bus stop Q is next to the park and is serviced by the 176 bus from Trafalgar Square.

| | |
|---|---|
| **Location Lat/Long:** | 51.50153, -0.10981 |
| **Location Postcode:** | SE1 7AA |
| **Underground & Lines:** | Waterloo: *Bakerloo, Jubilee, Northern, Waterloo & City* |
| **Main Station:** | Waterloo |
| **Riverboat:** | Waterloo Pier |
| **Bus:** | 1, 68, 168, 171, 172, 176, 188 |
| **Cycle Hire:** | Baylis Road |

## Accessibility

The park is fully accessible with excellent service for wheelchair users and those with limited mobility.

## Best time of year/day

Any time between March and October is a rewarding time for a visit. In spring and early summer the flowers around the gardens are in full bloom, and in autumn warm colours set the park aglow. The best time to visit is during the day when the most light is available. There are no exterior lights overnight. For more information visit: *www.bost.org.uk*

Located just behind Southwark Underground station is the little-known Isabella Street. It's another of those tucked-away places you suddenly come across when wandering the city streets looking for photos. At about 200m long it's essentially a series of local restaurants – and a great place to go out for a meal – located under the arches of the railway line that runs into London Bridge. This location's magic is that the restaurant owners have given the street a stunning makeover using nothing more than vast numbers of pot plants, from huge yucca plants to small rose bushes. The result is it feels like you're walking through a botanical garden.

## What to shoot and viewpoints

The scope of compositions you can shoot within this confined space is quite limited, so look to shoot long shots offering hints at the urban expanse lying just beyond the greenery. Starting at the western end of the street there are good compositions straight down the avenue of greenery; use a telephoto lens for detail or a wide-angle lens to make the scene appear deeper than it actually is. From the far western end of the street, you can shoot straight down the main line of the greenery or move to your right, where you'll find a smaller, more dense set of plants surrounding trees. There will be ample opportunity to position the Shard in the distance among the foliage.

Move back to the main walkway and proceed east, aiming to capture the blooms as foreground interest along with the Shard and railway viaduct as lead lines in the upper portion of your compositions. As you approach the eastern end of the street, the foliage will thin out and the balance of plants-to-buildings will shift towards harsh architecture. Right at the eastern end of Isabella Street you will find a strange half-moon structure; its rich blue tiles act as a useful counterpoint to the greenery of the main walkway.

## How to get here

Follow the directions to Southwark Station then exit the station before walking east for around 50m along The Cut (B300). Take a right along Joan Street and you should see Isabella Street's greenery to your left.

**Location Lat/Long**: 51.50415, -0.10652
**Location Postcode**: SE1 8DD
**Underground & Lines**: Southwark: *Jubilee*
**Main Station**: Waterloo East
**Bus**: 4, 63, 388, N63, N89
**Cycle Hire**: Southwark Station

## Accessibility &#9855;

This is a fully accessible street with standard street-level access for wheelchair users and those with restricted mobility.

## Best time of year/day

It's best to visit in spring and summer, when the flowers are in bloom and the trees and shrubs are in full leaf. Consider a visit during the evening and shoot handheld to capture some interesting shots of the nightlife. The street is open 24 hours a day and it can get busy in the evenings when the restaurants are open. If you want fewer people in your photos, visit during the middle of the day.

*Above: Isabella Street, Southwark. Canon 5D IV, 24–70mm at 24mm, ISO 200, 1/60s at f/11. Apr.*

*Opposite left: Tree-lined walkway of Isabella Street. Canon 5D IV, 24–70mm at 27mm, ISO 200, 1/90s at f/11. Apr. **Middle**: Flowers in Isabella Street. Canon 5D IV, 24–70mm at 70mm, ISO 200, 1/750s at f/4.5. Apr. **Right**: Isabella Street. Canon 5D IV, 24–70mm at 70mm, ISO 200, 1/45s at f/11. Apr.*

Located just a stone's throw from Waterloo Station is Roupell Street, an area of perfectly preserved two-storey Georgian houses. Were it not for the cars parked on the street, you could almost believe you'd stepped through a portal into the late Georgian or Victorian era. With the King's Arms pub at its heart and old-fashioned corner shops at the far end, a stroll down this street is like stepping back in time.

John Roupell, a successful metal refiner, began building dwellings in the early 1820s on Lambeth Marsh, south of the River Thames. They were home to artisans and skilled workers – joiners, metal workers, stonemasons and blacksmiths. Roupell named all the local streets after his family: John Street, Catherine Street and Richard Street. However, this caused confusion for the Royal Mail, as there were other similarly named streets in the area, and so the streets were rechristened with unique names such as Theed Street and Whittlesey Street.

Fortunately, this 19th-century time capsule survived the Blitz and the development consortiums that have erected so many modern buildings around the Waterloo area.

## What to shoot and viewpoints

Head to the King's Arms pub, which stands at the junction of Windmill Walk and Roupell Street, where you can capture the corner of the houses on Windmill Walk and the narrow pedestrian alley. A wide-angle lens will help exaggerate the buildings and size of the alley but a standard mid-range 24–70mm lens will do just as well. Head north up Windmill Walk, then turn around and shoot back along the alley, aiming to include the lamps and the pub at the far end. Head south along Windmill Walk, past the pub and consider a composition that includes the pub to your left and the crossroads. »

*Houses on Roupell Street. Canon 5D II, 24–70mm at 24mm, ISO 200, 1/125s at f/8. July.*

***Opposite left**: Roupell Street. Canon 5D II, 24–70mm at 28mm, ISO 200, 1/125s at f/8. July. **Right**: Roupell Street. Canon 5D II, 24–70mm at 24mm, ISO 200, 1/45s at f/11. July.*

Next, proceed east along Roupell Street to the junction with Theed Street, where there is a wonderful curved composition to be shot in either direction. Theed Street is a 'double yellow' area so there will be no parked vehicles to blight your photographs. Being able to shoot this street from both directions means that on bright sunny days you'll still be able to take photos from the southern end, shooting north if the light is too bright to the south.

The key to getting the best shots from this area is to exclude the cars. It's not easy to do at weekends – when the residents are home – so the best time to visit is during the week when there are likely to be fewer vehicles.

*Roupell Street. Canon 5D II, 24–70mm at 43mm, ISO 200, 1/60s at f/8. July.*

*Opposite top: Roupell Street. Canon 5D IV, 24–70mm at 35mm, ISO 200, 1/125s at f/8. May. Bottom left: Monochrome view of Roupell Street. Canon 5D II, 17–40mm at 22mm, ISO 100, 1/15s at f/13. June. Right: The pub on Roupell Street. Canon 5D II, 17–40mm at 17mm, ISO 100, 1/10s at f/13. June.*

*Below: Roupell Street. Sony A6000, 16–50mm at 16mm, ISO 125, 1/160s at f/4. May.*

## How to get here

Follow the Southwark Station location information. Exit Southwark Station and turn right on to the road called The Cut heading west. Look for the road called simply Hatfields that lies along The Cut, about 150m west from Southwark Station. Follow Hatfield in an S-shaped curve for about 250m until you find Roupell Street to your left.

| | |
|---|---|
| **Location Lat/Long**: | 51.50473, -0.10806 |
| **Location Postcode**: | SE1 8SU |
| **Underground & Lines**: | Southwark, Waterloo: *Bakerloo, Jubilee, Northern, Waterloo & City* |
| **Main Station**: | Waterloo East |
| **Bus**: | 4, 63, 388, N63, N89 |
| **Cycle Hire**: | Southwark Station |

## Accessibility

This is a fully accessible street with standard street-level access for wheelchairs.

## Best time of year/day

This location is great to visit at any time of year, although summer means some of the buildings will be decked in flowers. Note this is a residential street so please show courtesy and respect for those who live there. Make your visit during the day, when the most light is available and you can take advantage of the strong contrast on the buildings. During midweek, there will be fewer cars parked on the street allowing wider-angle shots. The area has street lighting and it's safe to visit in the evening and at night.

Blackfriars is more of a district than a single place and is located just to the southwest of the City of London. The area was established in the 14th century when Dominican friars, known for their distinctive black robes, moved their priory from Holborn to the area just south of Ludgate Hill. This chapter will focus solely on locations to the south of Blackfriars Bridge. For the north side of Blackfriars Bridge, see page 572.

## What to shoot and viewpoints

To the south side, take stock of the huge, painted wrought-iron panel of the London Chatham and Dover Railway that adorns the old railway bridge (which closed in 1885.) Here you will also find one of the smaller City Boundary Dragons.

Make your way under the south side of Blackfriars Bridge by taking the steps by Doggett's Coat and Badge pub, and here you will find another of London's hidden viewpoints: using the old railway bridge as a frame, you can capture a wonderful vista of the distant City of London and its skyscrapers. This particular view works well first thing in the morning when the sun comes up and over the buildings. Using a very tight aperture and 'squeezing' the sun among the many edges you'll find you can force a sunburst that will splay beams through the image and make for a very unusual take on a London vista.

*City skyline from under Blackfriars Rail Bridge. Canon 5D IV,*
*17–40mm at 17mm, ISO 100, 30s at f/11, tripod. May.*

## How to get here

To get to Blackfriars (South Bank) take the Underground Circle Line to Blackfriars Station, exit the station and cross the bridge to its south side. Both the 45 and 63 buses leave King's Cross Station and stop at Blackfriars – stop L on the north side of the bridge and stop D on the south side.

**Location Lat/Long**: 51.50854, -0.10392
**Location Postcode**: SE1 9UD
**Underground & Lines**: Blackfriars: *Circle & District*
**Main Station**: Blackfriars
**Riverboat**: Blackfriars Pier
**Bus**: 45, 63, 388, 388, N63, N89
**Cycle Hire**: Milroy Walk, Poured Lines

## Accessibility ♿

This is a fully accessible street with standard street-level access for wheelchair users. Note some parts, such as the steps from the bridge to the Thames Path, may not be directly accessible and you may have to make a small round-trip at street level via Upper Ground and Marigold Alley to get to the Thames Path.

## Best time of year/day

Blackfriars can be visited at any time of year and any time of day. As advised in this chapter, there are various times of night and day when some shots will work better than others.

# [7] OXO TOWER

Built at the end of the 19th century the OXO Tower was originally a power station that supplied electricity to the Royal Mail. In the 1920s it was purchased by the Liebig Extract of Meat company – owners of the OXO brand – to be used as a cold store. The firm gutted the building and had the exterior redesigned in the Art Deco style. Liebig had been refused its request to advertise the OXO product on the exterior of the building, as there was a ban on skyline advertising at the time. However, when the building was rebuilt, the main tower had gained new windows that happened – coincidentally – to be in the shapes of an O, an X and an O!

The Greater London Council (GLC) obtained the building in 1984 and later sold it to non-profit enterprise the Coin Street Community Builders. In the 1990s, the organisation had the building's interior redesigned to incorporate apartments, shops and restaurants. Despite the building winning many prestigious design awards since its redevelopment, and the fact that it's one of London's historical landmarks, it has yet to gain any sort of listed-building status. Floors 3–7 are private apartments, whilst the second floor can be hired for private functions and events. Floor 8 houses a separate bar and restaurant, both of which overlook the Thames, along with a small public viewing gallery that's open until 10pm. On the ground floor is *gallery@oxo*, which often hosts photography exhibitions.

## What to shoot and viewpoints

During the daytime, the building itself is actually quite hard to spot as it's concealed between Sea Containers House to the east and Gabriel's Wharf to the west. The building sits above the Thames Path and many people pass under the OXO tower building. It's therefore a good place to people-watch and capture some interesting street photography images – there are two paths (split by columns) that allow you to lurk and wait for the perfect shot of someone rushing past. A wooden pier, directly in line with the tower, leads out into the Thames and this is a perfect spot from which to shoot the city to the east, the OXO tower above and Gabriel's Wharf.

Around the rear of the building, you'll often find interesting sculptures dotted around the restaurants. The towering building makes an interesting location to take photographs; in summer, the area is often in shadow until later in the afternoon, when the sun finally makes an appearance.

*Top: Looking east from Gabriel's Wharf. Canon 5D II, 17–40mm at 24mm, ISO 100, 20s at f/7.1, tripod, LEE ND 0.9 grad. Sept. **Right**: Lamppost by OXO Tower Wharf. Canon 5D II, 70–200mm at 85mm, ISO 250, 1/180s at f/8. May.*

## How to get here

The OXO tower can be found by following the directions to Blackfriars Bridge (page 208) then take the Thames Path from the southwest corner of the bridge for about 500m. The 381 bus from London Bridge will stop on the A3200; from there you can proceed east on foot until you find Broadwall Road to your left – this leads to the rear of the OXO building.

**Location Lat/Long**:  51.50849, -0.1083
**Location Postcode**:  SE1 9PH
**Underground & Lines**:  Blackfriars, Southwark, Waterloo: *Bakerloo, Circle & District, Jubilee, Northern*
**Main Station**:  Blackfriars, Waterloo
**Riverboat**:  Blackfriars Pier, Festival Pier
**Bus**:  381, RV1
**Cycle Hire**:  Sea Containers

## Accessibility ♿

The tower sits on a fully accessible street with standard street-level access for wheelchair users and those with limited mobility. The lifts up to the restaurants and gallery are accessible from street level. Note however that the viewing gallery has very limited space and if your mobility is limited, you may find it hard to see over the balustrade and access the view. The walkways and the Thames Path are open 24-hours a day all year round.

## Best time of year/day

The time of year only really matters if you wish to see leaves on the trees on the opposite bank. During the winter months, when there is less daylight, you can visit the viewing gallery and see the city lights much earlier than in summer. The viewing gallery is open from 8am–10pm and the view can be shot during the day or in late evening when the city lights are on.

## Public Viewing Gallery ♿

Take the lift up to the eighth floor to visit the public viewing gallery. Exit the lift and turn to your right. Pass the restaurant desk, and head towards the Thames, which you'll see through the windows. The viewing gallery is quite small but you'll be left alone to enjoy the view and use whatever equipment you wish to get your pictures. You can also stay after dark to secure some striking views of London at night. While the field of view is a little limited, I think it's certainly worth a visit.

## The whole building at night ♿

The OXO tower comes into its own at night, when the windows in the tower are illuminated, revealing the classic red of the OXO brand set against the white light of the windows. This can be shot from the open hexagonal area next to Gabriel's Wharf, which allows you to incorporate the OXO tower into a wider shot of the distant city with the lights reflected in the Thames. Try to time your visit with a slow or slack tide. The other classic viewpoint is from the opposite bank of the Thames: shooting from Victoria Embankment enables you to incorporate the OXO tower, the blue illumination of Sea Containers House and the London Eye in the distance. Also consider shooting from the northern side of Blackfriars Bridge for a slightly different angle of the tower and other buildings lit up in the London skyline.

*Artwork in the courtyard – rear of OXO Tower Wharf. Canon 5D IV, 24–70mm at 24mm, ISO 200, 1/125s at f/8. June.*

*Top: Looking east from the 8th floor OXO Tower viewing gallery. Canon 5D IV, 24–70mm at 70mm, ISO 200, 190s at f8. Sept.*

*Above: Jewellery for sale in OXO Tower Wharf. NEX-C3, E 18–55mm at 18mm, ISO 1600, 1/60s at f/3.5. Jan.*

*Opposite top: Rear courtyard at night. Canon 5D IV, 24–70mm at 42mm, ISO 100, 2s at f/8, tripod. May. Bottom left: South Bank. Canon 5D IV, 24–70mm at 27mm, ISO 100, 1s at f/8, tripod. May. Right: Novelties for sale, OXO Tower Wharf. NEX-C3, E 18–55mm at 18mm, ISO 1600, 1/50s at f/3.5. Jan.*

Situated on the South Bank between the National Theatre and the OXO building is Gabriel's Wharf. This eclectic mix of artisan shops has been described as London's oldest pop-up. The space was designed by utilising a set of garages and adding a *trompe l'oeil* backdrop to increase the perception of the space. The bars and restaurants here are extremely popular – people often stop on their way past as they proceed along the Thames Path. The spacious, open area directly in front of the Wharf, known officially as the South Bank Observation Place, and Gabriel's Pier both offer some of the best views of the city skyline.

The Thames, being a tidal river, recedes quite a long way at low tide revealing a sandy beach directly in front of Gabriel's Wharf. You will often find artists, street performers and sand-sculptors working on the beach once the tide drops.

## What to shoot and viewpoints

### South Bank Observation Place ♿

The South Bank Observation Place – the open, paved area in front of the wharf building – is one of the best spots from which to capture dawn images of the city skyline, and there are no restrictions on equipment. With this viewpoint so close to water level, and if you're lucky enough to be there on a slack tide, you might well be able to capture a reflection of the OXO Tower and the entire city skyline.

*Opposite top: An evening crowd at Gabriel's Wharf. Canon 5D II, 17–40mm at 17mm, ISO 100, 13s at f/11, tripod. Sept. Bottom: A quiet Gabriel's Wharf. Sony A6000, 16–50mm at 16mm, ISO 100, 1/200s at f/5. Apr.*

*Looking east at sunrise from Gabriel's Wharf. Canon 5D IV, 24–70mm at 24mm, ISO 400, 1/45s at f/22. Apr.*

## Street photography &

In addition to the wonderful views, there is much to see here in terms of street photography. This is a 'pinch point', with many people passing as they walk along the Thames Path between the Tate Modern and Waterloo. Consequently, there are ample opportunities to capture people rushing past and the painted wharf building makes a superb backdrop to shoot the rush of London life.

## Evening and Gabriel's Pier &

At dusk and into the late evening, Gabriel's Pier offers a perfect vantage point. Positioned in front of the OXO building, it enables you to shoot the wonderful warm glow of the lights of Gabriel's Wharf; the packed restaurants and the bustle of the people adding life to a London night scene. The buildings of the wharf are low – they don't rise above a second storey – meaning the composition is easy to work with. There are no strong streetlights to cause flares and with no restrictions on tripods you couldn't ask for a better spot to shoot a slice of London nightlife.

*Above: Jogger on the South Bank. Sony A6000, 16–50mm at 16mm, ISO 100, 1/1000s at f/5. July. Above right: Rain on the South Bank. Sony A6000, 16–50mm at 19mm, ISO 100, 1/200s at f/5. July.*

## How to get here

The wharf is located next door to the OXO Tower, so follow the directions in the Blackfriars Bridge chapter (page 208). Proceed from the southwest corner of Blackfriars Bridge along the Thames Path, heading west, until you pass under the OXO Tower. Directly in front of you on the Thames Path you will find Gabriel's Wharf.

| | |
|---|---|
| **Location Lat/Long**: | 51.50845, -0.11064 |
| **Location Postcode**: | SE1 9PP |
| **Underground & Lines**: | Blackfriars, Southwark, Waterloo: *Bakerloo, Circle & District, Jubilee, Northern* |
| **Main Station**: | Blackfriars, Waterloo |
| **Riverboat**: | Blackfriars Pier, Festival Pier |
| **Bus**: | 381, RV1 |
| **Cycle Hire**: | Sea Containers |

## Accessibility &

The wharf is fully accessible with excellent service for wheelchair users and those with limited mobility. Some shops may have space restrictions and so may not be fully accessible to all.

## Best time of year/day

Any time of year works well for this location, though summer will enable you to catch foliage and blooms on the nearby trees. Early in the morning, when the shops are still closed, the area is very quiet, which allows time to capture the wharf devoid of people. Around midday, as the restaurants begin to open, it gets busier and this can add yet more life to your images. During the evening the area is illuminated and vibrant, with cosy shots to be had from the nearby Gabriel's Pier.

*Top*: Gabriel's Wharf after dark. Canon 5D IV, 24–70mm at 24mm, ISO 100, 15s at f/8, tripod, LEE ND 0.9 grad. May. **Above left**: Cruising along the South Bank. Sony A6000, 16–50mm at 42mm, ISO 100, 1/320s at f/5.6. July. **Above**: Winter on South Bank. Canon 5D IV, 24-70mm at 70mm, ISO 1600, 1/30s at f/6.7. Mar.

*Early morning looking east from Gabriel's Wharf. Sony A6000, 16–50mm at 16mm, ISO 100, 13s at f/16. Jan.*

The Royal National Theatre, to give it its full title, is a large, tiered, concrete building located along the South Bank between Gabriel's Wharf to the east and the Royal Festival Hall to the west. Debate about the need for a national theatre began in 1849, when a pamphlet lamenting the lack of somewhere to host serious theatre productions was produced. It wasn't until 1963 that the current National Theatre (NT) was finally finished, after countless objections from the government that it was a waste of money.

The Brutalist architecture of the NT has divided opinion: Prince Charles described the National Theatre as 'a clever way of building a nuclear power station in the centre of London without anyone objecting'. While Sir John Betjeman – not known for his love of concrete architecture – described the building as 'a lovely work and so good from so many angles'. And the building has had the distinction of simultaneously appearing in several annual top-ten lists of most beloved and most hated British buildings!

## What to shoot and viewpoints

For the photographer there are two distinct subjects to work with at the National Theatre.

### The Building ♿

The first is the building itself, where I'm inclined to side with Betjeman. The building is very much in the Brutalist concrete style but in bright light, this works to its advantage; severe contrast serves it well and you can shoot a great many interesting monochrome images simply by walking around the building, looking up, and aligning its strong lines. The stairwells that lead on to the South Bank Thames Path allow you to ascend to the rooftop terraces and from here you can take in sweeping views of the London skyline, although the mature trees along the South Bank do tend to obscure some of the scene. While walking around the building, keep an eye out for the interesting touches to the concrete; you will find wood-grain imprinted into it in many places and it's almost as if the designers of the building knew the grain would work well in monochrome photographs.

*Statue of Laurence Olivier outside the National Theatre, South Bank. Canon 5D IV, 24–70mm at 25mm, ISO 100, 10s at f/8, tripod. May.*

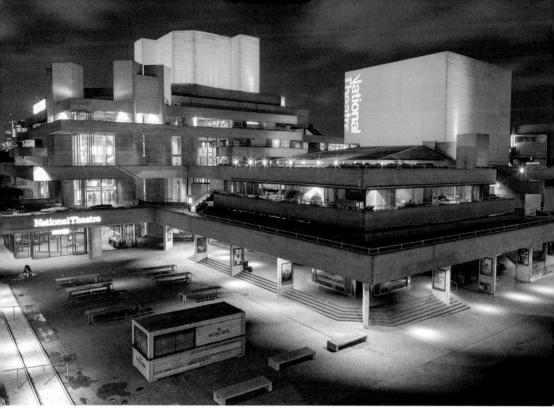

*Above*: National Theatre. Canon 5D IV, 24–70mm at 24mm, ISO 100, 10s at f/8, tripod, LEE ND 0.9 grad. May.

*Below*: Puddles on the South Bank. Sony A6000, 16–50mm at 16mm, ISO 100, 1/80s at f/4.5. Jan.

### The Thames Path ♿

The second area to concentrate on is the Thames Path directly in front of the National Theatre building, underneath the magnificent mature trees that line the edge of the river path. I have spent countless hours at this location, usually in the mornings, photographing people. As the light comes in from the east it moves between the trees lighting the scene and the people, bathing it all in a warm glow. The key to good compositions is to shoot from either end of the walkway making use of the curves of the path as the line of trees leads into the distance. Make sure to shoot between the trees and also along the lamp-lined railings at the edge of the river path. The curve of the path is at its strongest here and you can to use the trees to mask the buildings behind, capturing people or an empty scene – whatever your preference – with the Thames and the buildings of the Victoria Embankment opposite forming the perfect backdrop.

### Puddles ♿

We're not quite done with this location; it has one more secret to yield and this is only revealed on rainy days. The spot in front of the National Theatre building has to be, in my opinion, one of the best puddle-shooting locations in London! Something about the pavement slabs being constantly pushed down by the weight of the thousands who pass by every hour has caused them to sag every so slightly, forming dips that collect rainwater and create huge puddles. After about a week of solid downpours, it's almost impossible to pass through as the puddles are so huge. With puddles comes the opportunity to shoot reflections. I've lost countless hours and received many strange looks as I've squatted over the South Bank puddles! The second you see your first reflection of the tree-lined Thames Path, trust me, you'll be hooked. Be sure to capture the trees and, if possible, a blue sky with clouds. Use the benches as solid foreground objects to anchor image compositions. And once you've the mastered the knack of squatting over the puddles, experiment with capturing people; runners, joggers and cyclists make great subjects to capture in reflection against the backdrop of the Thames Path along the South Bank.

*Opposite top left: Stark lines outside the National Theatre. Sony A6000, 16–50mm at 32mm, ISO 160, 1/160s at f/5. May. Top right: Lone figure heading towards Waterloo Bridge. Canon 5D II, 70–200mm at 200mm, ISO 200, 1/20s at f/6.7. Nov.*

### How to get here

The National Theatre is next to Gabriel's Wharf so follow the directions in the Blackfriars chapter, then proceed from the southwest corner of Blackfriars Bridge along the Thames Path heading west until you pass Gabriel's Wharf. Where the line of trees begins, marks the start of the National Theatre. You can also walk here from the London Eye – just head east along the Thames Path.

| | |
|---|---|
| Location Lat/Long: | 51.50711, -0.11425 |
| Location Postcode: | SE1 9PX |
| Underground & Lines: | Southwark, Waterloo: Bakerloo, Jubilee, Northern, Waterloo & City |
| Main Station: | Waterloo |
| Riverboat: | Festival Pier |
| Bus: | 1, 59, 188, 381, RV1 |
| Cycle Hire: | Belvedere Road |

### Accessibility ♿

This location is fully accessible with excellent service for wheelchair users and those with limited ability.

### Best time of year/day

The best time of year to visit is during spring and summer when the area is greener and the flowers are in bloom. After heavy or prolonged rain, any time of year is rewarding when it comes to capturing reflections in the puddles. A daytime visit is generally best, when the most light is available and the exterior architecture of the NT has the most contrast.

*Opposite left: Puddles on the South Bank. Sony A6000, 16–50mm at 16mm, ISO 100, 1/100s at f/4.5. Jan. Right: Dawn sun on the South Bank benches. Sony A6000, 16–50mm at 16mm, ISO 100, 1/640s at f/4.5. May.*

The first Waterloo Bridge was constructed as a toll bridge at the beginning of the 19th century and by 1930 it was beginning to show serious signs of wear and tear. It was eventually rebuilt in 1945 after suffering damage during wartime raids over the city, and was, in fact, the only bridge to be hit in London. The bridge gets several cultural name-checks: *Waterloo Sunset* by The Kinks – a song about watching life go by – references it, and it makes an appearance in the final scene of *Trainspotting*.

Waterloo Bridge has superb city views up and down the Thames, bags of street life and, if you intend to shoot some night scenes, this location is a must.

## What to shoot and viewpoints

### From the bridge ♿

The bridge has a well-earned reputation as providing one of the best views along the Thames from ground level. It rises high above the river and its distance from other bridges affords it stunning views both up and downriver. Although it's a public highway, you're free to use a tripod on the walkways but, of course, please respect others by taking up the minimum space needed for your kit. It's better to visit when there's less foot traffic, during the golden hour and later into the evening as city lights take over darkening skies.

The bridge occupies a unique position on what is almost a right-angle bend in the river giving clear views to the east and taking in St Paul's, the Tate and the Shard amongst other key sights. Shoot from the south-west side and you'll have clear views of Jubilee Bridge, the London Eye and Westminster. During early morning, the sun rising in the east will light the buildings on the South Bank, and as it rises between the buildings, you'll have the opportunity to capture sun-rays. Once you're done, cross to the western viewpoint and start shooting to the south-west. You can capture the warm morning light illuminating Westminster and The Houses of Parliament.

*Looking south from Waterloo Bridge to the Houses of Parliament. Canon 5D II, 24–70mm at 52mm, ISO 100, 30s at f/8, tripod, LEE ND 0.9 grad. June.*

*Opposite: The South Bank from Waterloo Bridge. Canon 5D IV, 24–70mm at 24mm, ISO 100, 30s at f/8, tripod, LEE ND 0.6, grad. May.*

*View east from Waterloo Bridge. Canon 5D II, 24–70mm at 32mm, ISO 200, 15s at f/8, tripod, LEE ND 0.6 grad. June.*

### South Bank end of the Bridge ♿

During the day, especially in the summer months, there are some interesting scenes to be shot on the South Bank from just in front of the National Theatre using the lines of trees and river-facing benches as foreground interest. Often, people will rest for a short while on the benches that face the bridge and this type of composition – daily life in the city – is a must. A solitary figure relaxing; a couple – either creates an opportunity to capture the human side of city life. There are further opportunities to shoot directly under the South Bank arch during the day when the light is bright. The underside of Waterloo Bridge is constructed from a series of concrete slats, which offer an undulating and repeating pattern of lines that recede into the distance. This pattern can be shot as an abstract composition, or try pulling back and waiting a few seconds for someone to pass by; you can use their form and shape to disrupt the lines. There is often a book market set up under the South Bank arch of Waterloo Bridge, which offers the chance for some street photography of the sellers and patrons as they mill around the stalls.

### The Steps

If you find yourself on Victoria Embankment (north side) and passing under Waterloo Bridge, pause for a short while and capture the steps that lead from the Embankment

### How to get here

You can't miss Waterloo Bridge; for starters it has Waterloo Bridge in large letters on both sides! It's situated by the National Theatre so again, follow the directions in the Blackfriars chapter (page 208), then proceed from the southwest corner of Blackfriars Bridge along the Thames Path heading west until you pass Gabriel's Wharf and the National Theatre – the bridge is right next to it. You can also walk from the London Eye east along the Thames Path to the National Theatre. Alternatively, you can arrive via Temple Station on the Circle and District lines. Exit the station and walk west along Victoria Embankment until you reach Waterloo Bridge around 250m from Temple Station.

| | |
|---|---|
| **Location Lat/Long**: | 51.50739, -0.11579 |
| **Location Postcode**: | SE1 9PZ |
| **Underground & Lines**: | Southwark, Waterloo: *Bakerloo, Jubilee, Northern, Waterloo & City* |
| **Main Station**: | Waterloo |
| **Riverboat**: | Festival Pier |
| **Bus**: | 1, 59, 188, 381, RV1 |
| **Cycle Hire**: | Belvedere Road |

*Top*: City from Waterloo Bridge looking east. Canon 5D IV, 24–70mm at 48mm, ISO 100, 15s at f/11, tripod, LEE ND 0.9 grad. May.

up to the bridge pathway. The steps on the north bank are very steep and have featured in quite a number of urban photographic competitions over the years. They're especially effective when you include a single person in your shot as their presence breaks the solid lines of the steps' repeating pattern.

## From the Bridge at Night ♿

In the late evening and into the night, shooting to the southwest provides a stunning view of the lights along the Thames, largely because there's a mixture of tones: the violet lights of the Jubilee Bridge that resemble little flower heads; the stark red of the London Eye; the soft warm tones of Parliament and Big Ben and the bright yellow street lamps along the Embankment. Above all of this hangs the dark night sky. There is probably no better free-to-shoot sight in London than photographing the lights downriver. Use a mid-range 24–70mm lens to capture a wide vista and then switch to a zoom lens to pick up key details and isolate the parts of the scene that interest you most. Use a long exposure to capture the boats that cruise up and down the river, adding a sense of life and motion to a vibrant city scene.

## Accessibility ♿

The bridge is fully accessible with access for wheelchair users and those with limited mobility. Note the steps either side of the bridge may present some problems, so it may be advisable to take one of the side streets that lead back to the riverside on either end of the bridge.

## Best time of year/day

Any time of year is good for a visit, though spring and summer enables you to capture the green foliage of riverside trees. The best time of day is early morning when, with fewer people around, isolating individuals in shot is easier. In the afternoon more people take the river path between the sights. Evenings get very busy on the South Bank as the restaurants are in full swing, however shooting from the bridge is often very quiet. Many people cross but few stop for more than a few moments.

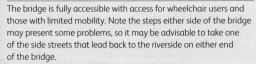

*Above left*: Late night yogurt stall, South Bank. Canon 5D II, 17–40mm at 17mm, ISO 100, 15s at f/11, tripod, LEE ND 0.6. Sept.
*Right*: Early morning sunlight on Waterloo Bridge. Sony A6000, 16–50mm at 16mm, ISO 100, 1/250s at f/5. Sept.

*Waterloo Bridge. Sony A6000, 16–50mm at 27mm,
ISO 100, 1/80s at f/5. July.*

*Working on Waterloo Bridge. Canon 5D IV, 24–70mm at
24mm, ISO 200, 1/1000s at f/8. June.*

*Opposite top left: Banksy homage, Waterloo Bridge southside
steps. Canon 5D IV, 24–70mm at 24mm, ISO 200, 1/45s at f/8.
June. Top right: Passer-by under Waterloo Bridge. Sony A6000,
16–50mm at 27mm, ISO 3200, 1/100s at f/4.5. July.*

*Opposite bottom left: Pausing by Waterloo Bridge. Sony A6000,
16–50mm at 32mm, ISO 125, 1/160s at f/5. June. Bottom right:
Book browsers at the Waterloo Bridge book market. Canon 5D IV,
70–200mm at 121mm, ISO 200, 1/90s at f/9.5. June.*

The Golden Jubilee Bridges are a pair of pedestrian bridges that flank Hungerford Bridge (a railway bridge). The original Hungerford Bridge was a suspension footbridge located between Waterloo and Westminster bridges that was designed and constructed by Isambard Kingdom Brunel in 1845. The bridge was later bought by the South Eastern Railway company and demolished and rebuilt as a railway bridge in 1864. The chains from the original bridge were reused in the construction of the Clifton Suspension Bridge in Bristol.

Various adjustments and alterations were made to the Hungerford Bridge including the addition of pedestrian walkways. These walkways became dilapidated and dangerous – there was a murder on one of them in 1999 – and plans were drawn up to completely replace them with modern, open, safe pedestrian footpaths. The improvements required some very complex engineering solutions, not least of which was the laying of the bridge foundations on the riverbed: the Bakerloo underground line lies just 15m below the river bend at Hungerford Bridge, and there was very strong evidence that there could still be bombs from the Second World War on the riverbed! Consequently, the work was carried out by hand and foundations were carefully dug overnight when both the Bakerloo line and Hungerford Bridge could be closed. Finally, to minimise impact on the trains using the Hungerford Bridge, the footbridges were built in sections, with each span slowly slotted into place as required. The Jubilee footbridges, opened in 2002, have won many awards for design and innovation and with nearly 9 million people using the bridges each year, they are now the busiest pedestrian bridges in London.

*Top: Waterloo Bridge looking east from Jubilee Bridge. Canon 5D IV, 24–70mm at 54mm, ISO 200, 1/45s at f/11. Apr.*

*Dawn sky looking east from Jubilee Bridge. Sony A6000, 16–50mm at 16mm, ISO 100, 6s at f/11, tripod, LEE ND 0.9 grad. Jan.*

*Dawn view towards Parliament from Jubilee Bridge. Sony A6000, 16–50mm at 29mm, ISO 100, 1/800s at f/5.6. May.*

*Snow on Jubilee Bridge. Canon 5D IV, 24–70mm at 24mm, ISO 800, 1/30s at f/8. Mar.*

## What to shoot and viewpoints

The Golden Jubilee Bridges are not just intriguing subjects to shoot, they are also useful platforms to shoot from – both up and down the River Thames.

### Close up on the bridges ♿

When shot at night the pylons supporting the walkways are illuminated with soft violet-coloured lights resembling flowers, adding interesting effects to images shot from Waterloo Bridge towards Westminster.

When shooting up close, the pylons work well in compositions as they form a receding set of arches over the walkways. The key is to shoot at quiet times, capturing a solitary figure crossing the walkways. I tend to find that the south-facing bridge (on the Westminster side) is often quieter than its northern counterpart.

*Early morning looking south from Jubilee Bridge. Canon 5D II, 17–40mm at 17mm, ISO 100, 30s at f/10, tripod, LEE ND 0.6 grad. Jan.*

**Top left**: *Heavy snowfall by Jubilee Bridge. Canon 5D IV, 24–70mm at 54mm, ISO 800, 1/30s at f/8. Mar.*

**Next spread left**: *Commuters passing between Waterloo and the City. Sony A6000, 16–50mm at 47mm, ISO 100, 1/800s at f/5.6. Apr.* **Right**: *Tattershall Castle floating restaurant, Victoria Embankment. Canon 5D II, 24–70mm at 64mm, ISO 200, 8s at f/11, tripod. Dec.*

## How to get here

There are many ways to reach the bridges: you can exit Embankment Station via Circle and District lines – exit via the riverside entrance and the bridges are directly above the station. You can also come in via Westminster Station and walk along Victoria Embankment heading east. If you're on the south side of the river, then the bridges are around 250m north of the London Eye.

**Location Lat/Long**: 51.50561, -0.11831
**Location Postcode**: SE1 8XX
**Underground & Lines**: Embankment, Waterloo: *Bakerloo, Circle & District, Jubilee, Waterloo & City*
**Main Station**: Waterloo
**Riverboat**: Festival Pier
**Bus**: 1, 59, 188, 381, RV1
**Cycle Hire**: Belvedere Road

## Accessibility ♿

There are lifts on either side of both bridges making them fully accessible to wheelchair users and those with limited mobility.

### Best time of year/day

A visit here is worthwhile any time of year but I urge you to visit at night or early in the morning, when isolating and capturing individuals is easier with fewer people around. In the afternoon more people will appear, taking the river path between the sights. The bridges' close proximity to the London Eye and Westminster makes them a hotspot for visitors. Because of this, care and consideration is necessary when setting up a tripod on the bridge during busy times.

*Red dawn sky looking east from Jubilee Bridge. Sony A6000, 16–50mm at 16mm, ISO 100, 0s at f/16. Jan.*

## Views from the bridges ♿

These two pedestrian bridges really come into their own at dawn and dusk, when they can be used as platforms to shoot up and downriver, capturing Waterloo to the north and Westminster to the south. The best angles are essentially at or near the ends of the bridges. So for shots of the London Eye, head out about 75m from the South Bank shore on the southern bridge – this will offer enough of the London Eye to ensure you can include the full wheel and the Houses of Parliament opposite. Moving to the southwest end of the bridge, you'll find it crosses the A3211 road below; this affords a magnificent view of the traffic leading up to Big Ben between the trees. Shot at night with a long exposure, you'll capture superb traffic streaks acting as the perfect lead lines to this London landmark. Shooting from the northern bridge affords a wonderful vista of the Thames that includes the Royal Festival Hall, Waterloo Bridge and the Victoria Embankment.

You can use tripods on the bridge walkways but please be conscious of other pedestrians. At peak times, especially during late evenings, the walkways are extremely busy with people vying to capture London's amazing night-time vistas. This footfall causes minor vibrations to tripods and monopods the further you head out and position yourself between pylons. Consider placing your tripod legs in a tight formation so you don't trip anyone and stay close to the pylons to minimise vibration at busy times.

*Opposite: Jubilee Bridge. Sony A6000, 16–50mm at 16mm, ISO 100, 1/250s at f/5. July.*

Situated in Lambeth and located directly below the London Eye, Jubilee Gardens is a public park opened by Queen Elizabeth II in 2012. The site was formally occupied by the Dome of Discovery, which was designed for the 1951 Festival of Britain exhibition. Whilst the park itself is of interest, this section of the Thames Path know as the Queen's Walk (a circular walk taking in Westminster Bridge via the Millennium Bridge) is very worthy of your attention.

## What to shoot and viewpoints

There are two key areas (within and next to the park) that present photographic opportunities.

### In the park &

The first location is at the far eastern side of the park. From here you'll find winding paths that lead directly to the London Eye. These lead lines work very well both during the daytime and at night when long exposures of the London Eye cause the red lights of the wheel to fuse into a giant red eclipse creating a captivating image. Please note the restrictions on tripod use.

### No tripods in the park

The park is patrolled by private security 24 hours a day and tripods are banned. If you do erect a tripod within the grounds, you'll be politely asked almost immediately to put it away by one of the patrols. Fortunately, there are plenty of benches and other street furniture, on which you can place a bag as a camera platform and shoot low light images, ideally long exposures of the London Eye. Note that this restriction only applies to the park and the land directly below the London Eye; the area to the northeast (along the Thames Path) has no such limits.

### The Queen's Walk &

The second location to shoot is immediately next to Jubilee Gardens along the Queen's Walk (part of the Thames Path) that lies directly to the western side of the park. During the day and early evening street performers draw in the crowds, and during the late evening, as the light fades and the city lights brighten, you'll have the opportunity to

*Watching the sunset from Jubilee Gardens. Canon 5D II, 17–40mm at 40mm, ISO 100, 0s at f/16, tripod, LEE ND 0.6 grad. Sept.*

capture shots of the crowds with the Houses of Parliament and Big Ben in the distance. This is also another prime location for 'puddle shots'. Wait for the rain to create puddles then – shooting hand-held – crouch down and shoot the reflections of passers-by as they hurry past with their umbrellas. If you position yourself over the right puddle at just the right elevation it's possible to capture Big Ben and the ornate street lamps in its reflection to add that extra sparkle to your compositions. »

*Opposite: Chasing bubbles by Jubilee Gardens. Canon 5D IV, 24–70mm at 70mm, ISO 400, 1/350s at f/4. July.*

*Living statue, South Bank. Canon 5D IV, 70–200mm at 200mm, ISO 200, 1/250s at f/8. Apr.*

This spot in front of the gardens is incredibly busy from midday until late evening most days and it's another of London's sweet street photography spots. It takes practice to duck and dive between the crowds but with so many people and so much going on, it won't be long until you fill your storage cards with lively images of people enjoying this superb London hotspot.

*Top right: Jubilee Gardens, South Bank. Sony A6000, 16–50mm at 37mm, ISO 800, 1/160s at f/5.6. Nov.*

*Opposite top: Looking towards Westminster from South Bank. Sony A6000, 16–50mm at 16mm, ISO 100, 1/80s at f/5. Nov.*
*Bottom left: Big Ben through sculpture, Jubilee Gardens. Sony A6000, 16–50mm at 21mm, ISO 100, 1/200s at f/4.5. Mar.*
*Right: Riding along Jubilee Gardens at dawn. Sony A6000, 16–50mm at 41mm, ISO 100, 1/400s at f/5.6. Apr.*

## How to get here

The gardens and walk are located directly below the London Eye; simply follow the instructions to the London Eye on the south bank of the River Thames.

| | |
|---|---|
| **Location Lat/Long**: | 51.50415, -0.119 |
| **Location Postcode**: | SE1 7JA |
| **Underground & Lines**: | Waterloo, Westminster: *Bakerloo, Circle & District, Jubilee, Northern, Waterloo & City* |
| **Main Station**: | Waterloo |
| **Riverboat**: | Festival Pier, London Eye Millennium Pier |
| **Bus**: | 211, 77, 381, RV1 |
| **Cycle Hire**: | Jubilee Gardens |

## Accessibility ♿

This location is fully accessible with excellent service for wheelchair users and those with limited mobility.

## Best time of year/day

The garden is open 24 hours a day but with it being so close to the London Eye and Westminster security is quite tight so if you visit during quiet times you may be reminded that tripods are not allowed in Jubilee Gardens. Shooting during the day offers images with plenty of people and street entertainers, whilst during the evening the city lights, especially those on the London Eye, offer some interesting opportunities.

The London Eye, originally called the Millennium Wheel, is one of the world's best-known Ferris wheels and currently Europe's tallest at 135 metres. It's the most popular paid tourist attraction in the UK and is visited by nearly 4 million people every year.

Originally opened on 31st December 1999 by the then Prime Minister Tony Blair as the British Airways London Eye, it has undergone several rebranding exercises and is currently owned by, and operated as, the Coca-Cola London Eye. Consequently, it has also changed colour to match the brand, morphing from blue to red.

## What to shoot and viewpoints

### Viewpoint 1 – Front Facing, across the River ♿

One of the best places from which to shoot the wheel is across the river on Victoria Embankment's north shore, by the Royal Air Force Memorial. If you're lucky enough to be there during a slack tide, just after sunrise (which usually happens only once or twice a year), you'll be treated to a stunning, almost perfect reflection.

*Opposite top*: Looking east from Westminster Bridge, early morning. Canon 5D II, 17–40mm at 17mm, ISO 100, 25s at f/11, tripod, LEE ND 0.9 hard grad. Dec.

### Viewpoint 2 – From Westminster Bridge ♿

Shooting from Westminster Bridge – again when the Thames settles between tides – you'll be able to shoot reflections of the London Eye and County Hall.

### Viewpoint 3 – The Avenue of Lights ♿

A popular location from which to shoot the wheel is on the avenue that leads from the Shell Oil building, up towards the Eye. If you position yourself just right, the wheel will appear to blend into the lights, very nearly forming the Omega symbol: Ω

### Viewpoint 4 – Underneath ♿

Shooting directly up in the gondolas and struts offers a unique and slightly abstract view of this iconic structure.

One thing to watch for when you visit: at night, when both the London Eye and County Hall (next door) are lit, on the hour the colours of County Hall change in time with the peals of Big Ben. Usually County Hall is illuminated blue but as the bells toll the hour, the colours may change to red or yellow for the sixty seconds it takes the bells to toll.

*Opposite bottom*: London Eye after the rain, early morning. Canon 5D II, 17–40mm at 17mm, ISO 100, 25s at f/11, tripod. Jan.

## How to get here

As one of London's largest and most recognisable landmarks it's very easy to find as it peeks above most buildings. The easiest way to find the Eye is to head to Westminster Station on the Circle or Jubilee line, exit the station and head towards Westminster Bridge. Once on the bridge, you can't miss the London Eye.

| | |
|---|---|
| **Location Lat/Long**: | 51.50338, -0.11954 |
| **Location Postcode**: | SE1 7PB |
| **Underground & Lines**: | Waterloo, Westminster: *Bakerloo, Circle & District, Jubilee, Northern, Waterloo & City* |
| **Main Station**: | Waterloo |
| **Riverboat**: | Festival Pier, London Eye Millennium Pier |
| **Bus**: | 211, 77, 381, RV1 |
| **Cycle Hire**: | Jubilee Gardens |

## Accessibility ♿

The London Eye is fully accessible with excellent service for wheelchair users and those with limited ability.

## Best time of year/day

During winter the trees will be bare, ensuring you can capture the illuminated wheel without any foliage blocking it. The site around the London Eye is open all year round but if you intend to shoot from inside the pods, then obviously you'll need to visit during opening times. Early morning before dawn is the best time to secure people-free shots of the London Eye illuminated. Shooting during the middle of the day is harder as the area directly below the wheel gets very busy indeed. Late evening, after the Eye closes, is also a reasonable time but there are usually still a lot of people about.

## Opening hours

Opening time 10am. Closing time between 6pm and 8.30pm. Times vary throughout the year so please check the website (*www.londoneye.com*) before your visit. You can also save on ticket prices when you book in advance online.

## Admission prices

Check the website for up-to-date prices and deals.

### Viewpoint 5 – On the Eye ♿

Whilst there are several great places to get an aerial view of central London, if you can stand the queue, the London Eye is one of the best. It opens from 10am and closes between 6.30pm and 8.30pm. It costs from £27 to around £37 per person. You get one revolution for your money and it lasts around thirty minutes. There are thirty-two passenger capsules, each holding twenty-five people and the views are spectacular.

As you board from the eastern side of the wheel, you'll see it travels anticlockwise, rising with views south and eastwards (looking toward the Shard and St Paul's). As it passes the halfway point it overlooks West London and Westminster, so don't rush to shoot the Houses of Parliament the moment you board – you'll have 10–15 minutes before you reach the highest point. Take time instead to shoot the east of the city as you ascend. As the capsule begins to cross the halfway point, start shooting to the west; the Thames riverbank opposite Parliament shot in portrait makes a bold composition. About 2–3 minutes after you begin to descend, the view will clear of other pods, offering an unobstructed view of west London.

Be aware that on bright days any light-coloured clothing will reflect in the pod's glass so try to wear dark clothing to minimise reflection.

It's well worth buying a fast-track ticket, especially if you have young children, as the queues can be long. Wheelchair users are required to go online and book a time slot. Health and safety means only two wheelchair users per capsule are permitted and eight on the London Eye at any one time.

Save time by booking tickets online at:
*www.londoneye.com*

*Top: London Eye at night. Canon 5D II, 24–70mm at 24mm, ISO 50, 30s at f/14, tripod. Jan. **Left**: Pods and structure from below. Canon 550D, –S15–85mm at 22mm, ISO 100, 1/800s at f/6.3. May.*

***Next spread**: Slack tide on the Thames, early morning. Canon 5D II, 17–40mm at 17mm, ISO 200, 1/60s at f/8. May.*

*Above*: View from pod looking east over the city. Canon 5D IV, 17–40mm at 17mm, ISO 200, 1/90s at f/11. July.

*Below*: Looking west. Canon 5D IV, 17–40mm at 17mm, ISO 200, 1/125s at f/11. July.

- **Houses of Parliament • Parliament Square**
- **Westminster Abbey • Westminster Bridge**

**Westminster is one of the liveliest tourist hotspots in London. Millions of people from all over the world visit the area around the Houses of Parliament and it has one of the highest concentrations of historic landmarks in all of London.**

In this chapter we restrict our activities to the Palace of Westminster – home of the Houses of Parliament – and the surrounding area: Parliament Square, Westminster Abbey and Westminster Bridge – all collectively known as Westminster, which lies within the City of Westminster. Unsurprisingly, the name Westminster is derived from 'a minster, west of the city', however these days the name is mostly used as shorthand to refer to the Houses of Parliament – the seat of government, much as Whitehall refers to the Civil Service. The larger City of Westminster (covering 21km sq.) includes locations such as Hyde Park, Buckingham Palace, Westminster Cathedral and Covent Garden, all of which have their own chapters.

The area of Westminster was already established prior to the Norman invasion of 1066, when Edward the Confessor began the construction of an abbey at the site now occupied by the Palace of Westminster. For over 600 years Westminster and the City of London were distinct with no formal relationship and it was only in the mid-16th century when the areas around Westminster began to be settled that the two areas began to join up. It took until the mid-20th century for various acts and administrative legalities to finally establish Westminster as the formal seat of government and to establish the City of Westminster's true boundary.

*Next spread (large image): VP7. The Houses of Parliament at night from Lambeth. Canon 550D, at 20mm, ISO 100, 10s at f/6.3, tripod. Nov.*

## What to shoot and viewpoints

Being as it is, the seat of UK political power, security is very tight; there are barriers, armed police and security patrols in constant evidence. However, despite this presence and perhaps because so many tourists visit this famous location, security is generally very tolerant of people taking photos. There are restrictions on tripod use but these will be noted where appropriate.

We start at locations east of the Thames at Parliament Square then make our way south to Victoria Tower Gardens. After heading over the Thames via Lambeth Bridge, we take a left to follow the Albert Embankment by the river to Westminster Bridge.

*Opposite: Crossing Westminster Bridge in the fog. Sony A6000, 16–50mm at 16mm, ISO 200, 1/160s at f/4. Nov.*

## How to get here
### Westminster – general
Start your exploration of Westminster by alighting at Westminster Station, where you'll find yourself at Westminster Bridge (west side).

| | |
|---|---|
| **Location Lat/Long:** | 51.50083, -0.12685 |
| **Location Postcode:** | SW1A 0AA |
| **Underground & Lines:** | St James's Park, Westminster: Bakerloo, Circle and District, Jubilee, Northern, Waterloo & City |
| **Main Station:** | Victoria, Waterloo |
| **Riverboat:** | Westminster Pier |
| **Bus:** | 3, 11, 12, 24, 87, 88, 148, 211, N3, N11, N44, N87 |
| **Cycle Hire:** | Storey's Gate, Abingdon Green |

### Accessibility ♿
Most areas within Westminster are standard streets. Some are cobbled but most are flat with no steps and, where required, ramps are in place to ensure full accessibility for wheelchairs. The only exception is the arch under Westminster Bridge (VP6); because steps offer the the only direct route down, you'll need to go to the western end of Westminster Bridge and turn left into Belvedere Road. Head north for around 200m, then turn and go towards the rear of the London Eye. Turn left again on to the Thames Path and head back to the underpass that heads under Westminster Bridge to reach the arch and Lambeth Walk.

### Best time of year/day
This location can be shot all year round.

*VP7. Westminster Bridge and Big Ben at dusk. Canon 5D II, 24–70mm at 24mm, ISO 100, 20s at f/16, tripod, LEE ND 0.6 grad. June.*

*VP7 Early morning looking west over Westminster Bridge during slack tide. Canon 5D II, 17–40mm at 17mm, ISO 100, 10s at f/8. Jan.*

### Viewpoint 1 – Parliament Square ♿

The official name for the building that constitutes the Houses of Parliament is The Palace of Westminster. This Gothic-style building, designed by Charles Barry in the 19th century, was classified as Grade I listed in 1970 and is now a UNESCO World Heritage site. Although generally referred to as Big Ben, the building's clock tower is actually called the Elizabeth Tower; Big Ben is the main bell within it. At the southern most end of the site is the Victoria Tower – a fireproof repository for books and documents – which, when first constructed, was the tallest secular building in the world. Parliament Square, located to the west and directly next to the site of the main Parliament building, is often used as a political meeting point for a wide range of protests. South of Parliament Square lies Westminster Abbey and south from here, along Abingdon Street, are the Abingdon Street Gardens. This particular area is most well known for being the site at which TV news crews conduct interviews with MPs. During fine weather there will often be at least one or two film crews at work there.

There is much of interest for the photographer here at all times of the day and in all weather. The area can be extremely busy during the day with thousands of other visitors passing through, so if you wish to shoot images with far fewer people, early morning is best. There's a high security presence but the staff are very tolerant of people wishing to take photographs and rarely intervene. Tripods are permitted in Parliament Square but use with discretion as the area can be very busy, meaning you may be asked to remove it for safety reasons. I've taken photographs in the Square in the early hours of the morning and at dawn and have had no issues.

### Phone boxes

There are three red phone boxes located on the northern side of the square, which can make a great image when aligned or used as foreground interest. The classic shot of the red phone box below Big Ben can also be shot here but come early – this is probably one of the busiest spots in Westminster as numerous visitors like to have their picture taken emerging from a phone box.

*VP1. Reflection of Big Ben in Parliament Square. Sony A6000, 16–50mm at 23mm, ISO 100, 1/250s at f/5. Oct.*

### Winston Churchill and Lloyd George Statues

Crossing on to the traffic island that is Parliament Square you can shoot an image of the Churchill statue in front of Big Ben. Arrive during or after it has been raining and the

### How to get here

#### VP 1 – Parliament Square

Leave Westminster Underground station and turn to your right. You may wish to pause to get a photo of the giant underground roundel in front of Big Ben (you'll see the green grass of Parliament Square directly to your right) – it's essentially a square roundabout. Proceed to the crossing at the start of Whitehall.

#### Best time of year/day

It can be shot all year round but early mornings just after sunrise and late evenings are the quietest times, when there are fewer people around. Note that protests sometimes take place in the Square and this can lead to the area being busier than normal or completely closed, if the police deem it necessary.

Parliament Square. Sony A6000, E 55–210mm at 71mm, ISO 1000, 1/160s at f/5. Nov.

VP1. Night in Parliament Square. Canon 5D II, 17–40mm at 24mm, ISO 100, 30s at f/20, tripod, LEE ND 0.9 grad. May.

path leading to Big Ben will offer a superb reflection of the tower and statue. Visit after dark and the statues provide dominant (some might say eerie) foreground interest when set against the trees under which they stand. In all, there are twelve statues of statesmen and other notable individuals in the square, the most recent three being Millicent Fawcett, the campaigner for women's suffrage, Mahatma Gandhi and Nelson Mandela.

## Reporting from Westminster

Heading south along Abingdon Street, past the Jewel Tower, you will find Abingdon Street Gardens, where TV news crews often film. There's a path leading through the gardens and using a very wide-angle lens creates an unusual, almost distorted view of Victoria Tower as the path's dominant shape leads back towards Parliament Square.

There are many locations around Parliament Square that afford spectacular views of the clock tower, some of which are directly under the Underground sign next to Westminster Station. Head down the steps next to the Boudicca's chariot statue (next to Westminster Bridge) and, if you shoot from the eastern side of the square facing Big Ben, you can also incorporate the London Eye in your photographs.

VP1. Parliament Square signage. Canon 5D II, 70–200mm at 138mm, ISO 400, 1/125s at f/9.5. Mar.

## Viewpoint 2 – Westminster Abbey ♿

Westminster Abbey (formally known as Collegiate Church of St Peter of Westminster) is located to the south side of Parliament Square. The abbey consists of the main abbey building and a large set of buildings to the south. During the day the public are allowed to walk through the courtyards but there is an admission charge to enter the abbey. Its exterior, designed in the Gothic style, is an interesting building to shoot; you'll find you need a very wide-angle lens to encompass a shot of the larger entrances, especially the famous Western Facade entrance. Personally I would advise looking for details around the exterior of the main abbey building. The most interesting features are the stone carvings of the 20th-century martyrs mounted on the western facade above the entrance. Here you'll find statues of illustrious names including Dr Martin Luther King Jr and Esther John. There is also a tradition of creating a temporary Garden of Remembrance during Remembrance Sunday (the second Sunday in November), which consists of thousands of crosses and other commemorations to the war dead and remains open to the public from dawn to dusk for approximately two weeks after the Remembrance services. A classic shot of the abbey can be taken from across the road, outside the Queen Elizabeth II Centre. Avoid standing on the raised grass area – it's private land. Instead use the cobbled area adjacent to the grass and shoot from under the tree, where you can use the curvature of the raised grass as a good lead line.

*Opposite left. VP2. Infrared image of Westminster Abbey. Canon 5D II, 17–40mm at 24mm, ISO 200, 1/90s at f/8. May. **Right**: VP2. Outside Westminster Abbey. Canon 5D IV, 70–200mm at 106mm, ISO 200, 1/45s at f/8. May. **Middle**: VP2. Remembrance at Westminster Abbey. Sony A6000, 16–50mm at 16mm, ISO 100, 1/100s at f/4.5. Nov. **Bottom left**: VP2. Exterior, Westminster Abbey entrance. Canon 5D II, 24–70mm at 70mm, ISO 200, 1/100s at f/6.3. Oct. **Bottom right**: VP2. Wooden door into Westminster Abbey. Canon 5D II, 24–70mm at 24mm, ISO 800, 1/8s at f/6.3. Oct.*

*VP2. Westminster Abbey. Canon 5D IV, 17–40mm at 17mm, ISO 400, 1/500s at f/8. Oct.*

## VP 2 – Westminster Abbey

Having reached Parliament Square you will see Westminster Abbey on the south side of the Square. Simply head in that direction and cross the road at the crossing situated in the south-western corner.

### Best time of year/day

The best time of year to shoot the exterior of the Abbey is in the summer months between April and September. At this time of year the sun rises and casts light across the north side of the building allowing you to shoot in the morning before it opens and gets busy. This time of year also allows you to shoot in the evening when the sun goes down late enough to catch the warm evening light on the western end of the building, where the statues are located. At other times of the year the light rises directly over the inaccessible southern side of the building making it harder to shoot as the bright light will blow out the sky.

**Location Lat/Long:** 51.49936, -0.12733
**Location Postcode:** SW1P 3PA

### Opening hours

Mon to Sat 9.30am–4.30pm. Closed Sun.
Wednesday lates 4.30–6pm.

### Admission prices (2019)

| | | Wednesday lates ticket offer |
|---|---|---|
| **Adults:** | £23.00 | £11.00 |
| **Children** (aged 6–16): | £10.00 | £5.00 |
| **Students** (with ID): | £20.00 | £11.00 |
| **Seniors** (aged 60+): | £20.00 | £11.00 |

*VP3. Victoria Park Gardens, looking north in autumn. Sony A6000, 16–50mm at 16mm, ISO 100, 1/250s at f/4.5. Oct.*

## Viewpoint 3 – Victoria Tower Gardens ♿

Located south of the Palace of Westminster and adjacent to the Victoria Tower is Victoria Tower Gardens. This small park was commissioned and designed by Sir Joseph Bazalgette, the chief engineer of the Metropolitan Board of Works, whose major achievement was to create the London sewer system, all but stopping the cholera epidemics that plagued 19th-century London.

The garden is only open between dawn and dusk but has some interesting features worthy of closer attention. The park's most famous feature is the Buxton Memorial Fountain, which commemorates the abolition of slavery throughout the Commonwealth. There are also memorials to the famous suffragette Emmeline Pankhurst and the Burghers of Calais.

## VP 3 – Victoria Tower Gardens

You can simply walk east back through Parliament Square and turn right into Abingdon Street by the statue of Oliver Cromwell and proceed until you pass the Victoria Tower – there you will find the park. However, I would advise a slightly more interesting route: head west towards Victoria Street and turn left into Great Smith Street. Proceed for around 200m until you find Little Smith Street on your left, then take this road. When you reach the junction with Tufton Street, turn left and then right into Great College Street, which leads directly to Victoria Park, or turn right at Tufton Street (from Little Smith Street) and then left into Great Peter Street, which will again lead you to Victoria Park. This small area to the south of the Abbey is a wonderful little place and often quiet as it's away from the crowds. It also allows access midweek to the Dean's Yard – part of Westminster Abbey and School.

### Best time of year/day

The park is only open dawn to dusk but it's open all year round. My favourite time to visit is in the mornings when it's quiet and easier to isolate subjects. During summer and autumn the trees are in leaf, making more interesting compositions.

| | |
|---|---|
| **Location Lat/Long**: | 51.49675, -0.12466 |
| **Location Postcode**: | SW1P 3JA |

### Opening hours

Victoria Tower Gardens is open from dawn till dusk.

*VP3. Victoria Park Gardens, looking north in autumn. Sony A6000, E 55–210mm at 55mm, ISO 400, 1/40s at f/5. Oct.*

*VP3. Anti-slavery memorial, Victoria Park Gardens. Canon 5D IV, 24–70mm at 24mm, ISO 200, 1/750s at f/6.7. May.*

The three viewpoints that are worthy of consideration are:

**A.** Enter the park at the southern entrance (by Lambeth Bridge) and head to your right by the embankment wall (next to the river). Using a telephoto lens, make use of the line of trees and benches to create a receding motif; this is most effective on a bright morning with rich shadows. It's worth trying to capture a single commuter enjoying the quiet before heading off to work, as this can break up the composition and give the receding lines a sense of scale.

**B.** Place the Buxton Memorial in the foreground. Shot with a very wide-angle lens, the memorial can make a striking point of interest as its array of colours come to life when the bright morning sun strikes it. Try to shoot wide enough to encompass the entire construction and situate the Victoria Tower in the background. Including some foliage softens the scene and forms a natural frame when combined with the trees to the western side of the park.

**C.** Finally, stand directly to the left of the Buxton Memorial and shoot directly towards the Victoria Tower. Visit during the middle of the day in the spring and summer months, when there are people using the park – they'll add some much-needed foreground interest. City workers and students often play ball games in the wide open spaces and really bring the scene alive.

*VP3. Infrared anti-slavery memorial. Canon 5D II, 17–40mm at 17mm, ISO 200, 1/250s at f/8. May.*

*VP4. From Lambeth Bridge towards Houses of Parliament. Canon 5D II, 24–70mm at 30mm, ISO 100, 30s at f/11, tripod, LEE ND 0.9 grad. June.*

### Viewpoint 4 – View from Lambeth Bridge ♿

From Victoria Tower Gardens, walk south to Lambeth Bridge and cross over it. As you reach the end of the bridge there is an elevated viewpoint from the steps leading down on to the walkway of the Albert Promenade. This is my personal favourite viewpoint of the Houses of Parliament and Westminster Bridge and best regarded as a dawn or dusk cityscape photo opportunity.

Ideally, try using a tripod, deep f-stop of f/11 or above and find a position that allows you to capture the balance of natural light from the sky, the lights from the lamps of the Albert Promenade and the warmth of the soft orange light from Westminster. You'll be shooting long exposures and at this time of day there will be few people around so they'll simply blur to almost nothing in shot. During foggy mornings this viewpoint is simply one of the best places to be in London.

There is another image opportunity: if you position yourself on Albert Promenade and use a zoom lens, seek to capture the line of lamps illuminated along the promenade. Shot with a fast enough shutter speed, you'll be able to capture people as they pass behind the lamps, adding a little more motion and life to your image.

### Viewpoint 5 – The Albert Promenade ♿

The Thames Path runs in a straight line between Lambeth Bridge and Westminster Bridge. On dusk and dawn shoots look to capture the view with the pathway as a lead line through the image but including the entire east-facing side of the Palace of Westminster. At dawn the path will fall into shadow while the buildings will capture the morning

### VP 4 – View from Lambeth Bridge

Head to the southern end of Victoria Park and this will lead up steps to the western side of Lambeth Bridge. Alternatively, leave the western side of the park and proceed along the roadside (around to the bridge footpath) if you're not able to use the steps. The Palace of Westminster and Westminster Bridge can both be shot from Lambeth Bridge. Proceed over the bridge to the eastern side.

### Best time of year/day

I find evenings and into the late evening at any time of year the best time to visit this particular location. Plan to arrive just before sunset and you'll be treated to a wonderful sky over Parliament. You should be able to capture the lamps along Albert Embankment as they come on.

**Location Lat/Long**: 51.49464, -0.12431
**Location Postcode**: SE1 7SG

*Opposite: VP5. On Albert Promenade by Westminster Bridge. Canon 5D II, 70–200mm at 200mm, ISO 200, 1/125s at f/4. Nov.*

VP5. Misty night along the Thames by Parliament. Canon 5D II, 24–70mm at 43mm, ISO 50, 30s at f/10, tripod. Jan.

sunlight. At dusk the opposite is available; the buildings will fall into silhouette and the path will glow with the warmth of the setting sun, with the stone walls and benches fully lit. People tend to sit and take in the late afternoon sun on the benches here, making perfect foreground subjects for your London-based compositions. Also, watch for people simply pausing to take in the view. With the overhanging trees and the many ornate lamps lining the wall next to the river, my favourite type of shot is taken using a long lens and short f-stop to isolate a single figure or couple. Place them in such a way that the trees and lamps recede out of focus behind them. The best time of year to visit this spot is late autumn. Rain or shine, the rich red and orange hues of the trees along Albert Promenade are hard to resist.

## VP 5 – Albert Embankment
Simply proceed down the steps to the river path from the eastern end of Lambeth Bridge; this is the Albert Embankment. For those with limited mobility, take the roadside footpath and from there you will find a ramp leading on to Albert Embankment.

### Best time of year/day
The best time of year for Albert Embankment has to be autumn, when the glorious rich tones of the golden leaves and the chance of rain make this one of the hotspots for autumnal London. Autumn also increases the chance of getting a foggy morning on the Thames and there's no greater treat than shooting the Houses of Parliament in mist just before dawn. It can, of course, be shot all year round but autumn takes some beating. If you wish to isolate people as they come along the path, then shoot in the morning and late evenings when there are fewer people around. If you don't want any people in shot, shoot late in the evening, overnight or in the early hours.

**Location Lat/Long**: 51.49821, -0.12046
**Location Postcode**: SE1 7LB

## Viewpoint 6 – View through the arch towards Big Ben

This is another classic location and adorns the cover of this very book. This wonderfully simple shot is very easy to obtain: ideally you'll need to arrive late morning on a sunny day with a few clouds for maximum effect. While it can be shot in any condition, I find it works best on bright sunny days as this ensures there is plenty of light and you won't lose highlight or shadow details.

This arch stands at the end of the Albert Promenade by the east end of Westminster Bridge. If you're coming from the direction of the London Eye along the Thames Path, don't climb the steps to the bridge – instead take the path that leads under the bridge; you'll emerge at the perfect spot on the other side. If crossing from the west, cross to the southern pathway, head down the steps to the Albert Promenade you see stretching south. As you get to the bottom, turn right and begin taking the walkway under the bridge, then turn around as you go under the bridge. I find it best shot with a fairly wide-angle lens – something between 16mm and 24mm. This will ensure you capture enough of the arch stonework as well as Big Ben framed in the arch. Any wider and you'll push Big Ben back in the perspective, making it too small; any narrower and you'll not be able to capture the arch. You may find it helpful to squat down if you can and lean against the wall, as this will offer the widest viewpoint.

## Viewpoint 7 – Westminster Bridge ♿

As with many London bridges, Westminster Bridge was originally a private venture, funded by merchant capital and built originally in 1739, despite strong opposition from the Corporation of London. The current bridge was built and opened in 1863, after its predecessor started to show signs of severe subsidence. Once again a Gothic style was employed to ensure it was in keeping with the Parliament building. This section will include the most famous viewpoint of Parliament, viewing the building over the Thames using Westminster Bridge and other viewpoints along Albert Promenade, which runs from Westminster Bridge to Lambeth Bridge further south. A little known fact: the bridge is painted green – the same colour as the seating in the House of Commons. Lambeth Bridge, by contrast, is painted red – to match the colour of the seating in the House of Lords.

## Albert Promenade next to Westminster Bridge

Probably the most famous viewpoint of all is from Albert Promenade (VP5) directly to the south of Westminster Bridge. Here you'll find an uninterrupted view of the entire east-facing side of the Parliament building – the perfect place to capture the building, especially when the Thames is at slack tide. The best time is usually during golden hour but after dark can also offer some spectacular results as the Parliament building is illuminated at night. You can opt for a narrow viewpoint using the bridge as a lead line, although take care with the exposure as the shadows

### VP 6 – View through the arch towards Big Ben

Proceed along Albert Embankment by the side of the Thames until you reach Westminster Bridge. Head under the bridge by taking the small walkway to the left of the steps that ascend or access the viewpoint from Westminster Bridge on the east side.

### Best time of year/day

While the view next to the river path can be very busy, the view through the arch looking to Big Ben is often fairly quiet at most times of the day. The shot is very limited, so many simply get their image and move on. Any time of year works well here, as there's no foliage to worry about. The best time of day is late morning, about two or three hours after sunrise on a sunny day with a little cloud. This ensures the bridge and tower are well lit when you take the shot.

| | |
|---|---|
| **Location Lat/Long**: | 51.500670, -0.119948 |
| **Location Postcode**: | SE1 7GA |

### VP 7 – Westminster Bridge – Albert Promenade

Proceed over the bridge from Westminster Underground station then take the steps at either side of the eastern end of the bridge. Those with limited mobility will need to go via Belvedere Road, along to the London Eye and then south along the river path to the bridge (see also VP5).

### Best time of year/day

This spot is a Mecca for photographers looking for that classic 'Westminster Bridge leading to Big Ben' shot so at the golden hour you may find yourself hemmed in or without a spot. If you really want this shot, you'll need to arrive at least an hour before sunset or sunrise, especially on foggy mornings. I have seen upwards of fifteen photographers standing tripod to tripod at this spot on evenings when unusual weather is forecast. In winter, it is generally less busy.

| | |
|---|---|
| **Location Lat/Long**: | 51.50086, -0.12196 |
| **Location Postcode**: | SW1A 2JH |

*VP6. Big Ben through Westminster Bridge arch, southside. NEX-C3, E 18–55mm at 18mm, ISO 320, 1/160s at f/4. Dec.*

*VP7. Westminster Bridge at sunset. Canon 5D II, 24–70mm at 28mm, ISO 100, 1/10s at f/22, tripod, HiTech 3 stop reverse LEE ND. Sept.*

under the arches can lead to large dark areas and attendant noise in images. A wider view offers the entire length of the building, which looks spectacular when the Thames is calm enough to throw up a reflection. If the Thames is in full flow, I suggest going for a very long exposure that will smooth the water and add a nice, natural, dynamic foreground. If shooting at sunset, once again take care with the exposure; the sun will set behind the building putting the east-facing side in shadow. Pause a while and wait for the sun to set enough to start bringing the light back into balance. Your patience will be rewarded as the sun will set and paint colours on to the clouds – a great balance with the building's harsh architecture. A long exposure at sunset can also offer an opportunity to capture cloud streaks, which add drama. Be warned that this is a very popular spot, especially when a good sunset is in the offing so arrive early to ensure a good spot. I've been there many times and can confirm it's not unusual to find two dozen photographers lined up with tripods ready to shoot.

*VP7. By Westminster Bridge. Canon 5D II, 24–70mm at 38mm, ISO 800, 1/60s at f/4.5. June.*

*Long-exposure trails – Westminster Bridge. Canon 5D II, 17–40mm at 17mm, ISO 200, 15s at f/11, tripod, LEE ND 0.9 hard grad. Dec.*

*Foggy morning on Westminster Bridge. Canon 5D II, 24–70mm at 45mm, ISO 1600, 1/8s at f/8. Oct.*

## View along Westminster Bridge and traffic streaks

A popular composition is traffic streaks across Westminster Bridge. To achieve this classic shot, arrive late evening or before dawn and position yourself about a third of the way over the bridge from the eastern shore, on the southern path. You'll need an exposure time of around 5–10 seconds, then wait for a bus to start to cross the bridge, heading west. When the bus is about 10–15 metres behind you, begin the exposure. The bus will then take about 5–10 seconds to reach Big Ben and this should provide the classic traffic streaks. As an alternative, try the same shot on the opposite side of the bridge.

## Foggy Mornings

There are opportunities to shoot images along the bridge during the daytime, something not many consider when they see the scene. Early on foggy mornings I've captured solitary figures crossing the bridge with Big Ben in the background, barely visible through the fog. One of my most popular photographs is just such an image (see page 246). I wanted to shoot the classic location (just below the bridge), using the lead line of the bridge into the fog. However, with so many photographers already *in situ* I couldn't find a space I liked. I left that spot and started walking over the bridge,

*Top: VP7. Westminster Bridge and Big Ben in the fog. Canon 5D II, 24–70mm at 28mm, ISO 50, 15s at f/8, tripod. Jan. **Above**: Snow along Queen's Walk looking towards Parliament. Sony A6000, 16–50mm at 22mm, ISO 250, 1/160s at f/4. Feb.*

where I snapped an image of an individual making his way to work; it has since become one of my most popular images ever! Such is photography. We can't always get what we planned but with luck on our side we may be offered something infinitely better and you may be the only person to have obtained that special image. Don't always follow the crowd – do something different and see what happens.

### County Hall

It is possible to shoot Parliament from the north side of Westminster Bridge in front of County Hall but note that this area is private land and tripods are not allowed for safety reasons. You're welcome to shoot using the wall as a resting place for your camera (use a beanbag or jumper to nestle the camera during long exposures). The wall is quite substantial and wide but be careful as there is no ledge and if you knock your camera it will drop into the Thames never to be seen again!

### Viewpoint 8 – St Thomas Hospital Fountain ♿

Note that the fountain is a private location within the hospital grounds. You're free to walk in and enjoy the gardens – even take some pictures – but if you erect a tripod or take too long, the hospital security may ask you to leave. The garden is there for the enjoyment of everyone, including patients of the hospital, who may not wish to be in your photos, so please be respectful while at this location.

The garden contains a large pool and at its centre there is a very unusual sculpture that resembles a strange alien-like creature and acts as a fountain. Shoot the sculpture to one side of Big Ben (in the distance) or position yourself in

*VP8. Fountain of St Thomas's Hospital. Canon 5D II, 24–70mm at 24mm, ISO 200, 30s at f/11, tripod. Dec.*

such a way as to place the clock face of the tower within the 'head' of the sculpture. For extra sparkle, if the fountain is not active, try to capture the reflection in the pool.

### Viewpoint 9 – Boudicca Rebellion Statue ♿

The statue of Boudicca and her daughters riding on a chariot pulled by two raging horses is located on the north western corner of Westminster Bridge, a stone's throw from Big Ben, and is easy to find. There are two really effective ways to take photos of this iconic statue: firstly, stand on the opposite side of the road from the statue, so as to position the London Eye's huge spokes directly behind it. Shoot with the statue in full sharp focus but the spokes of the London Eye slightly out of focus; this works best with a blue sky and some light cloud. Secondly, arrive early in the morning and shoot from the bottom of the stairs that lead down from the bridge to the north river path past the boats and cruises. Shoot upwards capturing the statue and Big Ben behind it. Both should be sharp to make best use of this viewpoint. It can be shot later in the day but you'll inevitably find it harder as flocks of visitors make it hard to isolate the subjects. I think it works best with the stairs adding lead-in foreground interest and when processed with a monochrome treatment to really bring out the two key subjects.

*VP8. Fountain at St Thomas Hospital. Sony A6000, 16–50mm at 44mm, ISO 100, 1/200s at f/5.6. May.*

*VP9. Boudicca statue in front of the London Eye. Canon 5D IV, 70–200mm at 150mm, ISO 200, 1/2000s at f/4. Oct.*

### VP 8 – St Thomas Hospital Fountain

Proceed to the southern footpath on Westminster Bridge and walk east. At the bus stops take the path into St Thomas and you will see the park to your right. Proceed south and turn right to find the path in.

#### Best time of year/day

I find the sculpture in the pond works well both day and night and particularly so when the fountain is operational. The garden may on occasion be closed for repair work but is usually open 24 hours a day all year round.

Location Lat/Long:   51.50036, -0.11936
Location Postcode:   SE1 7GA

*Opposite: VP9. Boudicca and Big Ben. Sony A6000, 16–50mm at 16mm, ISO 100, 1/60s at f/4. Nov.*

### VP 9 – Boudicca Rebellion Statue

The statue is immediately outside the Westminster Underground station on the northwest corner of the bridge.

#### Best time of year/day

During the day Westminster Bridge is incredibly busy; thousands of visitors cross back and forth so I would advise you only shoot handheld during these times. Shooting upwards from the bottom of the steps is harder during the day due to the number of people moving through so the best time is early mornings before 8 or 9am – most visitors won't venture out before then, especially at weekends. During the week you'll find it busy with commuters but they will usually be passing through and will rarely trouble you on the steps by the statue.

Location Lat/Long:   51.50111, -0.1237
Location Postcode:   SW1A 2JH

Situated on Victoria Embankment just north of the Houses of Parliament, the Battle of Britain Monument commemorates those, known as 'the Few', who gave their lives during one of the most famous air battles of modern history. The Battle of Britain took place between 10th July and 31st October 1940 over the skies of the English Channel, London and southern England where the RAF Fighter Command fought and eventually overcame the Luftwaffe, forcing the Germans to postpone and eventually cancel their invasion plans.

The monument was sculpted by artist Paul Day, (who also designed the statue of the couple in St Pancras station) and was cast by the Morris Singer foundry – the same company that forged the lions in Trafalgar Square. It was unveiled by Prince Charles on 18th September 2005. The monument has many reliefs illustrating civilian and military scenes, as well as almost 3,000 names of pilots inscribed in it, from over fourteen countries that participated in the Battle of Britain.

*Battle of Britain Memorial, Westminster. Sony A6000, Fisheye 8mm at 8mm, ISO 100, 1/800s at f/8. Apr.*

## What to shoot and viewpoints

It's a tricky subject to shoot as there are so many interesting aspects to it. The best way to approach this monument is to shoot small sections. The central piece is the almost life-size sculpture of the pilots running towards their planes making ready for battle. Use a wide-angle lens to exaggerate their size and scale; if you have a fisheye lens, this works very well to make the memorial seem even more imposing. Take a step back to shoot a wider scene with the clear blue sky and the London Eye peeking over the top of the memorial. Just after the memorial services during early November, poppy blooms and crosses adorn the monument and hopefully ensure we never forget those immortal words: "Never was so much owed by so many to so few."

*Opposite top: Close up of Battle of Britain Memorial. NEX-C3, E 18–55mm at 18mm, ISO 1600, 1/50s at f/3.5. Nov.*
*Middle left: The memorial on a sunny morning. Sony A6000, 16–50mm at 16mm, ISO 100, 1/160s at f/4.5. Nov.*
*Right: Battle of Britain Memorial. Sony A6000, 16–50mm at 16mm, ISO 100, 1/160s at f/4.5. Jan. Bottom left: Close up of the memorial. NEX-C3, E 18–55mm at 25mm, ISO 800, 1/160s at f/5.6. Dec. Right: Close up of the memorial. NEX-C3, E 18–55mm at 18mm, ISO 1600, 1/50s at f/3.5. Nov.*

## How to get here

Make your way towards Westminster Station on the Circle or Jubilee lines, then exit the station towards the Thames and proceed north along Victoria Embankment until you find the memorial, directly opposite the London Eye.

| | |
|---|---|
| **Location Lat/Long:** | 51.50306, -0.12343 |
| **Location Postcode:** | SW1A 2NS |
| **Underground & Lines:** | Charing Cross, Embankment, Westminster: *Bakerloo, Circle & District, Jubilee, Northern* |
| **Main Station:** | Charing Cross |
| **Riverboat:** | Westminster Pier |
| **Bus:** | 12, 53, 148, 453 |
| **Cycle Hire:** | Northumberland Avenue, Whitehall Place |

## Accessibility ♿

The monument lies along the Victoria Embankment on a wide, flat footpath that is accessible to all.

## Best time of year/day

The memorial is not fenced off so it can be photographed any time of year. It is lit during the night but with minimal lighting so the best time is during daylight hours. Just after sunrise and before sunset, warm light is sometimes cast over the monument.

# ST JAMES'S
# & VICTORIA

Once the location of St James the Less – a 12th-century leper hospital – the area of St James's developed into one of the most exclusive residential areas in London during the 17th century. The elite of the day took up residence here and many gentlemen's clubs were opened to cater for a wealthy clientele. The area subsequently earned the nickname 'Clubland'. To this day, Mayfair and St James's remain London's most affluent areas, home to exclusive shopping streets New Bond Street and Jermyn Street and the beautiful arcades around Piccadilly.

Several monarchs left their mark on the area: Henry VIII used the parks for deer hunting; these parks were later remodelled as private sanctuaries during the Stewart dynasty, and the Victorian era saw many of the city parks opened to the public for recreation. This Victorian legacy continues to this day. Green Park and St James's Park offer welcome refuge from the city. Flora and fauna abound in the parks, now under the dedicated stewardship of The Royal Parks Foundation – a charity that manages the eight largest open areas within London.

This section begins right in the heart of Mayfair and St James's, where the architecture of opulence was funded by money from the Industrial Revolution, when Great British engineers and entrepreneurs quite literally changed the world. We pass through some stunning city parks that are always a joy to experience, and on to the seat of royal authority for the last 150 years: the magnificent Buckingham Palace. Finally, we proceed through Victoria and bohemian Pimlico, before arriving at Tate Britain and the River Thames.

*Previous spread*: Buckingham Palace frontage on a sunny day.
Sony A6000, 16–50mm at 17mm, ISO 100, 1/1000s at f/5. Jul.

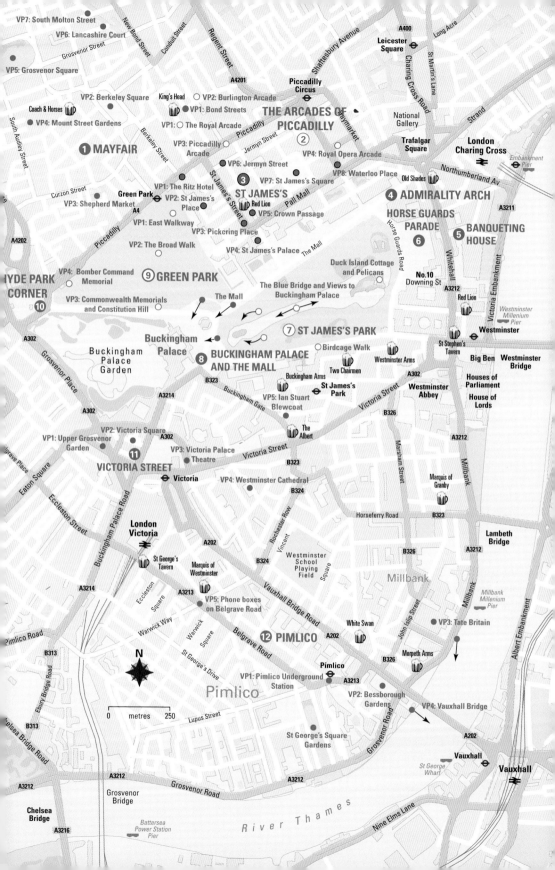

**Mayfair is one of the most affluent areas in the world, packed with exclusive shops, hotels, restaurants, art galleries, clubs, prestigious London addresses and foreign embassies.**

The area was originally fields and home to an annual fair, the May Fair, for many years until 1764. The Grosvenor family acquired the area in the 17th century and invested heavily, transforming it into the expensive borough it is today. The family built open squares such as Hanover Square, Berkeley Square and Grosvenor Square, surrounded by costly high-quality houses (including several owned by the Rothschild family). The First World War witnessed a decline of the aristocracy and a reduced servant workforce but Mayfair retained its status as companies were invited to set up headquarters and foreign countries to site their embassies in the area.

Mayfair is still an exclusive area and has the honour of being the most expensive property on the Monopoly board. It has retained its grand architecture, and its squares, streets, gardens and alleyways are rich in photographic opportunity, especially in the summer. It is probably one of the best places to visit during Christmastime, when the street decoration and shop fronts are extremely lavish and sure to delight.

## What to shoot and viewpoints

### Viewpoint 1 – Old Bond Street and New Bond Street ♿

If you have very deep pockets and you're looking for that special gift, you'll find no better place than Old Bond Street and New Bond Street. New Bond Street leads south from Oxford Street until it reaches Clifford Street where Burlington Arcade begins. There is a short pedestrian area, then New Bond Street continues for another 100m before it changes to Old Bond Street, which connects to Piccadilly. Situated in the small pedestrian area, sits the sculpture *Allies*. This bronzework depicts Roosevelt and Churchill seated on a wooden park bench with enough room for one person to sit between them – a great spot for a photo opportunity. Old Bond Street plays host to couture fashion including Chanel, Prada and Gucci, while New Bond Street

(to the south) is populated by jewellers such as Tiffany and Cartier. At its northern end, as it reaches Oxford Street, are a wider variety of shops. It's a superb place to go people spotting and dabble in street photography; who knows, you might even spot a celebrity or two out shopping.

*Opposite top left: VP1, New Bond Street, Mayfair. Canon 5D IV, 17–40mm at 17mm, ISO 1600, 1/30s at f/4. Dec.*
*Top right: VP1. New Bond Street. Canon 5D IV, 70–200mm at 70mm, ISO 400, 1/30s at f/8. May.*

*Middle left: VP1. Churchill and Roosevelt statue, New Bond Street. Canon 5D IV, 24–70mm at 58mm, ISO 400, 1/30s at f/5.6. May.*
*Middle right: VP1 New Bond Street. Canon 5D IV, 70–200mm at 70mm, ISO 400, 1/20s at f/8. May.*

*Bottom left: VP1. Shops in New Bond Street. Canon 5D IV, 70–200mm at 121mm, ISO 400, 1/45s at f/8. May.*
*Bottom right: VP1. New Bond Street. Canon 5D IV, 70–200mm at 78mm, ISO 400, 1/20s at f/8. May.*

## How to get here

Mayfair is essentially in a rectangle of four Tube stations: Green Park and Piccadilly on the south side, Bond Street and Marble Arch to the north. To tour the key locations in this area it's probably best starting from Piccadilly, which can be reached by bus or Tube.

**Underground & Lines:** Bond Street, Green Park: *Central, Jubilee, Piccadilly, Victoria*

### Accessibility

All locations and viewpoints are on ordinary city streets and should present no accessibility issues.

### Best time of year/day

You can shoot here all year round, day and night, though some of the parks and gardens may be closed at night or have restricted access. The best times of the year are summer for blooms and foliage, and autumn for colourful parks and gardens. Christmas, when the decorations are in place, is one of the best times of the year to visit.

### VP 1 – Old Bond Street and New Bond Street

Old Bond Street and New Bond Street can be found about halfway along Piccadilly (the road) between Piccadilly Circus and Green Park, leading north from Piccadilly (the road). Walk north along Old Bond Street until you reach the *Allies* statue on the pedestrian area that joins the two halves of Old and New Bond Street. Proceed north about 100m until you find the junction with Bruton Street and turn left.

**Location Lat/Long:** 51.50955, -0.14145
**Location Postcode:** W1S 4QB
**Bus:** 94, 139, 159, N113
**Cycle Hire:** Grafton Street

*VP2. Coach and Horses pub, Mayfair. Canon 5D IV, 24–70mm at 45mm, ISO 400, 1/45s at f/8. May.*

*VP2. Lansdowne Row, Berkeley Square, Mayfair. Canon 5D IV, 17–40mm at 30mm, ISO 1600, 1/45s at f/4. Dec.*

## Viewpoint 2 – Berkeley Square &

A location made famous by the song *A Nightingale Sang in Berkeley Square*, this small public space is located right at the heart of Mayfair. The park in the square's centre is often used to display huge pieces of contemporary sculpture and these alone are worth the visit. Annabel's restaurant has a reputation for putting on one of the best Christmas displays, covering the front of the three-storey building with traffic-stopping decorations.

## Viewpoint 3 – Shepherd Market &

Located just off busy Piccadilly is Shepherd Market, once home to the original May Fair. This quiet little area is chiefly populated by small restaurants and shops, mostly to service the lunchtime office crowd. Shepherdess Walk and the surrounding streets offer some interesting opportunities both night and day. On summer days you'll find people nipping out to the cafes and bistros. This location offers a chance to capture a slightly more relaxed city atmosphere, and in spring and summer some of the houses are decorated with wonderful floral displays. During the evening the lights of the street cafes offer a more intimate city ambience.

### VP 2 – Berkeley Square

To reach Berkeley Square, go west along Bruton Street, pass the Coach and Horses pub on your left and Berkeley Square Gardens is directly ahead at the end of the street.

| | |
|---|---|
| **Location Lat/Long**: | 51.50958, -0.14576 |
| **Location Postcode**: | W1J 6BE |
| **Bus**: | 22, N22 |
| **Cycle Hire**: | Farm Street, Bruton Street |

### VP 3 – Shepherd Market

Shepherd Market lies primarily on Curzon Street. Leave Berkeley Square at its southwest corner and follow Fitzmaurice Place. Turn right at the end on to Curzon Street and proceed west until you reach the entrance to Shepherd Market; you'll see a large London street sign with Shepherd Market on it above a small alleyway lined with restaurants (the entrance is on the opposite side of the street to a large church building). You can also reach Shepherd Market by way of Piccadilly: walk along Piccadilly towards Hyde Park Corner until you begin to pass Green Park. To the north side of Piccadilly you'll find White Horse Street; this leads directly into the heart of Shepherd Market.

| | |
|---|---|
| **Location Lat/Long**: | 51.50647, -0.14683 |
| **Location Postcode**: | W1J 7PN |
| **Bus**: | 6, 14, 19,38, N19, N38, N97 |
| **Cycle Hire**: | Clarges Street, Curzon Street |

*Top middle*: VP2. Annabel's private club – Christmas display, Berkeley Square. Canon 5D IV, 17–40mm at 26mm, ISO 200, 30s at f/22, tripod. Dec. **Right**: VP3. Shepherd Market diners. Sony A6000, 16–50mm at 16mm, ISO 100, 1/640s at f/4.5. July.

*Middle left*: VP3. Shepherd Market early morning after rain. Canon 5D II, 17–40mm at 17mm, ISO 400, 1s at f/11. Oct. **Middle right**: VP3. Charles Street, Mayfair in autumn. Canon 5D IV, 70–200mm at 93mm, ISO 400, 1/125s at f/6.7. Nov.

VP3. The Kings Arms pub in Shepherd Market. Sony A6000, 16–50mm at 16mm, ISO 100, 1/500s at f/4. July.

*VP4. Mount Street Gardens, western entrance. Sony A6000, Fisheye 8mm at 8mm, ISO 400, 1/160s at f/8. Nov.*

*VP4. Mount Street Gardens, Mayfair. Canon 5D IV, 24–70mm at 70mm, ISO 400, 1/45s at f/8. May.*

## Viewpoint 4 – Mount Street Gardens ♿

Of all the open spaces in Mayfair this is possibly the smallest and probably one of the nicest. Located close to the Thomas Goode shop on South Audley Street, the western entrance to the garden is quite unusual with two traditional red telephone boxes by the gate. The park has two other entrances – one to the south by St George's Primary School that often has a superb floral display. The other is to the north and emerges by the Connaught Hotel and Mount Street. The park, like so many in London, is a haven of tranquility after the bustle of the street. The floral displays and benches positioned in leafy groves offer a small slice of peace before you head back out into the city.

## Viewpoint 5 – Grosvenor Square ♿

Grosvenor Square, named after the Grosvenor family (now the very wealthy property-owning family, the Dukes of Westminster), is located in the northern part of Mayfair. Until recently it was the home of the United States of America Embassy – a huge concrete building designed in a stark 1960s style. Grosvenor Square is similar in style to the other large squares in Mayfair: a wide, open space surrounded on all sides by large townhouses and hotels but the square has several memorials and monuments

## VP 4 – Mount Street Gardens

Mount Street Gardens are tricky to locate as all the entrances are quite well hidden. Make your way to Curzon Street to the north of Shepherd Market – there are two alleys that lead from Shepherd Market directly on to Curzon Street. Head north along Hertford Street and proceed east along Curzon Street until you find the two alleys. Proceed north along Queen Street and turn left into Charles Street, past the tree on the traffic island. Immediately take a right north along Chesterfield Street. Keep moving until you reach a junction with South Street at the far end. Turn left and to your right you will see St George's Primary School – the garden entrance runs directly to the right of the school. Another entrance to Mount Street Gardens can be found on South Audley Street to the western side of the park, and this is where the telephone boxes are located.

| | |
|---|---|
| **Location Lat/Long**: | 51.50912, -0.1507 |
| **Location Postcode**: | W1K 2TH |
| **Bus**: | 22, N22 |
| **Cycle Hire**: | Farm Street, Bruton Street |

## VP 5 – Grosvenor Square

Grosvenor Square can be reached from Mount Street Gardens by leaving the gardens via the South Audley Street entrance to the western side of the park. Pass the Thomas Goode shop to your left and as you reach South Audley Street proper, turn right and head north. Grosvenor Square is directly at the top of South Audley Street, around 500m from the entrance you just left.

| | |
|---|---|
| **Location Lat/Long**: | 51.51147, -0.15137 |
| **Location Postcode**: | W1K 2HP |
| **Bus**: | 7, 94, 98, 133, 139, 390, N7, N98 |
| **Cycle Hire**: | Grosvenor Square, Millennium Hotel |

*VP5. Infrared image of Grosvenor Park with Roosevelt statue. Canon 5D II, 17–40mm at 17mm, ISO 200, 1/90s at f/6.7. May.*

*VP5. The victims of 9/11 attacks memorial, Grosvenor Square. Canon 5D IV, 17–40mm at 17mm, ISO 400, 1/60s at f/8. May.*

*VP5. RAF memorial Grosvenor Square. Canon 5D IV, 24–70mm at 27mm, ISO 200, 1/180s at f/8. May.*

that make intriguing photographic subjects. As you enter from the south, an RAF memorial with a large eagle perched atop it rears up; to the north is the statue of Roosevelt (who brokered peace at the end of World War II) and to the eastern side is the memorial to those who lost their lives in the 9/11 attacks. It's a modest garden with a wooden cabana bearing an inscription.

*VP6. Lancashire Court, Mayfair. Canon 5D IV, 70–200mm at 180mm, ISO 400, 1/180s at f/5.6. Sept.*

*VP6. Scooter in Lancashire Court. NEX-C3, E 18–55mm at 20mm, ISO 1600, 1/20s at f/3.5. Dec.*

## Viewpoint 6 – Lancashire Court &#9855;

Tucked at the end of South Molton Street and running behind New Bond Street is Lancashire Court. This unusual location has a quaint charm of its own with cobbled walkways that line narrow alleys leading to the central courtyard – it's a joy to shoot day and night. The light behaves in odd ways as it strains to get into the tight spaces, and at night the closeness of the alleys and the lights of the restaurant (located in the central courtyard) offer more cosy evening images.

## Viewpoint 7 – South Molton Street &#9855;

Located just off Oxford Street and leading in a diagonal direction back to New Bond Street, South Molton Street is one place not to miss when visiting London at Christmas, when several large, brightly lit arches are displayed. Usually illuminated by thousands of small blue lights they make for a unique photograph, especially if you build a composition around the arch nearest to you. When it rains the light is scattered in all directions and, in heavy rain, stunning reflections are on offer.

## VP 6 – Lancashire Court

For Lancashire Court, leave Grosvenor Square via Grosvenor Street, which lies in the far southeast corner of the square, then head directly east along Grosvenor Street until you reach the pedestrian thoroughfare of Avery Row, which lies to your left. Proceed along Avery Row for around 100m and you'll find Lancashire Court to your right. Take the next left and this will lead you into the main open square in Lancashire Court. You may wish to partake of refreshments here at the restaurant located in the square.

| | |
|---|---|
| **Location Lat/Long**: | 51.51282, -0.14603 |
| **Location Postcode**: | W1K 4AR |
| **Bus**: | 7, 98, 159, N7, N98 |
| **Cycle Hire**: | Marylebone Lane, Woodstock Street |

## VP 7 – South Molton Street

Exit Lancashire Court to the north, via Avery Row or any of the alleys that lead to Brook Street, then turn to your left and start moving east – you will find South Molton Street to your right. It's a very wide, open pedestrian street during the day. The northern end of South Molton Street emerges directly on to Oxford Street.

| | |
|---|---|
| **Location Lat/Long**: | 51.51309, -0.14663 |
| **Location Postcode**: | W1K 5DN |
| **Bus**: | 7, 98, 159, N7, N98 |
| **Cycle Hire**: | Marylebone Lane, Woodstock Street |

*VP6. Lancashire Court, Mayfair. Sony A6000, 16–50mm at 16mm, ISO 500, 1/160s at f/4. July.*

*VP6. Lancashire Court. Sony A6000, 16–50mm at 32mm, ISO 200, 1/60s at f/5. Aug.*

*VP7. Christmas arches on South Molton Street. NEX-C3, E 18–55mm at 18mm, ISO 1600, 1/60s at f/4, tripod. Dec.*

The first shopping centres or malls were covered arcades and there are none better than the Arcades of Piccadilly. The name Piccadilly came from Robert Baker, a tailor and local landowner who sold lace collars or 'piccadills' in the early 1600s. The arcades provide unusual photographic opportunities with ornate facades, arches, sculptures and shoppers, as well as some very upmarket shopping.

The original arcade is Burlington Arcade built in 1819 by the Earl of Burlington so that his wife could shop without her braving the crime-ridden streets of London. The arcade is patrolled by doormen – 'beadles' – in traditional dress, who ensure the arcade maintains its regency decorum by discouraging 'singing, humming and hurrying'. It has seen its share of drama: in 1964 six masked men drove a car straight into the arcade and robbed one of the jewellers. They made off with £30,000 of goods and were never caught; they are the reason gates were installed and are now locked at night.

Royal Arcade, built in 1879 as a shopping arcade for the public, was one of the first of its kind. Originally called The Arcade it acquired its royal name when Queen Victoria visited a shirtmaker there in 1880. Its Victorian style with a high-saddled roof and decorated stucco arches has changed little in the last 140 years, making it a striking location.

By far the youngest of the four arcades is Piccadilly Arcade, built in 1909 and linking Piccadilly with Jermyn Street. Its ornate interior was designed by George Thrale Jell, and it houses some of the more bespoke shops you will find in St James's.

Royal Opera Arcade is the last surviving piece of John Nash's Opera House, which burned down in 1867. During the 19th century the shops here sold clothes, music scores and opera glasses but also operated a number of high-class brothels at night, serving clientele from the local gentlemen's clubs.

## What to shoot and viewpoints

The best way to see all four arcades is by way of a walking tour starting from Green Park Underground Station.

### Photographic Tip

The two most common ways to capture tunnel-shape arcades is to either offset yourself to one side of the arcade, so the nearest shops opposite you appear to be very large in the frame but recede rapidly towards the vanishing point. The other, more traditional approach is to simply shoot directly in the centre, ensuring perfect symmetry of the shops and arches. Take care with symmetrical forms like these though; if you're even slightly off-centre, it can look obvious so take your time while shooting, check the edges of the frame (top and bottom) to ensure the image is symmetrical.

### Viewpoint 1 – Royal Arcade ♿

This arcade is only around 50m long but very tall. While a wide-angle lens does the most justice when capturing this beautiful arcade, midrange lenses of 24–70mm will work well too. Because of the high-saddled glass roof, during the day, light simply pours in so there won't be any ISO issues. As this is one of the few arcades left in London with its original Victorian decoration, be sure to capture the amazing stucco arches and, as a bonus if you have a fisheye or wide-angle lens, shoot looking directly up at the roof. This is a key location to visit as Christmastime, when decorations add a special touch to photographs.

### Viewpoint 2 – Burlington Arcade ♿

Stretching for almost 200m, this arcade is so long it appears to vanish at its far end. This is one of the most popular of the arcades and during the day it can be very busy. Arrive just before opening time, while the gates are still locked, and during the summer months, when the sun has had time to rise. The arcade will be flooded with light, so shoot through the gates – you can even use them to steady your hand. Then enter the arcade just as it opens and immediately begin shooting before visitors enter from the other end and fill the shot. One of my preferred techniques when shooting at Christmastime is to arrive about an hour before opening on a Sunday morning. The shop staff will be arriving one or two at a time and this offers you the chance to capture a single person

*Above*: VP1. Royal Arcade lamps. Canon 5D IV, 70–200mm at 85mm, ISO 400, 1/45s at f/8. May **Below**: VP2. Burlington Arcade. Canon 5D IV, 70–200mm at 97mm, ISO 800, 1/180s at f/4.5. Nov.

*Above*: VP1. Royal Arcade. Sony A6000, Fisheye 8mm at 8mm, ISO 100, 1/160s at f/8. July. **Below**: VP2. Burlington Arcade. Canon 5D IV, 24–70mm at 35mm, ISO 800, 1/250s at f/8. June.

heading up the arcade, surrounded by ornate Christmas lights and decorations – a very rare photographic opportunity. Use a zoom lens while shooting to compress the long arcade or use a wide-angle lens and really exaggerate the perception of depth in the scene.

## Viewpoint 3 – Piccadilly Arcade ♿

This is a slightly harder location in which to take photos because of the mostly artificial light so a high ISO will be required. Additionally, due to the fact this arcade conveniently joins Piccadilly and Jermyn Street, it is a very popular cut-through and so obtaining clear shots of the whole arcade will be slightly harder during the middle of the day when it's busy. Just like Royal Arcade, Piccadilly Arcade is quite short, but very tall and narrow, so a wide-angle lens will serve you well. Features that makes this location special are the wonderful curved glass shop fronts; they catch the light and reflections, providing this arcade with its unique character. If you're looking to shoot the details here, aligning the small circular skylights with the electric lanterns suspended from the ceiling gives an unusual repeating pattern. And like the other locations around the West End, Christmastime adds extra spice to images taken in Piccadilly Arcade. Note the arcade is closed at night and the gates locked.

Exit Piccadilly Arcade via Jermyn Street, where you should take your time. Make a point to visit the world-famous Fortnum and Mason store – their chocolate counter is a particular favourite of mine. You will also find the Paxton and Whitfield cheese emporium located on Jermyn Street, offering a vast selection of cheeses you're unlikely to find anywhere else.

## Viewpoint 4 – Royal Opera Arcade ♿

The final arcade feels quite closed with its very low ceiling and narrow width – it's about 3m wide. The best photos can be taken from the southern entrance (located on Pall Mall) – shoot from just outside on the steps. This is a relatively quiet arcade, home mostly to cafes and restaurants rather than shops. The ceiling is constructed from a series of circular skylights with lanterns in between. If you have a zoom lens, isolating just a small section of the ceiling with its repeat pattern of lamp-skylight-lamp-skylight is very effective, especially on bright days when the skylights light up. Using a standard midrange 24–70mm lens you can drop down low to the ground and easily capture the whole length of the arcade including the ceiling with its repeating pattern.

## How to get here

**Underground & Lines:** Green Park, Piccadilly Circus: *Bakerloo, Jubilee, Piccadilly, Victoria*
**Main Station:** Charing Cross
**Bus:** 6, 14, 19, 38, N19, N38, N97
**Cycle Hire:** St James's Square

## Accessibility ♿

All locations and viewpoints are on ordinary city streets and should present no accessibility issues.

## Best time of year/day

Can be shot all year round during the day. All the arcades are closed at night or have restricted access at times outside normal business hours. Summer provides strong lighting during the middle of the day, casting shadows and offering interesting lighting conditions as well the ability to shoot at lower ISO. Christmas is one of the best times of the year for a visit as the decorations are in place.

## VP 1 – Royal Arcade

Follow directions to Old Bond Street located halfway along Piccadilly. The nearest Tube station is Green Park. Proceed north along Old Bond Street and you'll see the grand entrance to the arcade to your left, around 250m from Piccadilly.

**Location Lat/Long:** 51.50893, -0.14178
**Location Postcode:** W1S 4DR

## Opening hours

Mon to Sat 9am–6pm.
Sun 10am–6pm

Burlington Arcade and Piccadilly Arcade are situated directly opposite one another, about halfway along Piccadilly. Simply proceed along Piccadilly, heading west from Piccadilly Circus to Green Park (or east from Green Park to Piccadilly Circus). You'll see the grand entrances to both arcades to your left and right.

*Opposite: VP3. Beau Brummell statue looking into Piccadilly Arcade. Canon 5D IV, 24–70mm at 45mm, ISO 400, 1/20s at f/8. June.*

*VP3. Piccadilly Arcade after hours, shot through gates with tripod. Canon 5D II, 17–40mm at 17mm, ISO 100, 6s at f/22 Dec.*

## VP 2 – Burlington Arcade

**Location Lat/Long:**   51.50972, -0.14095
**Location Postcode:**   W1J 0QJ

### Opening hours

Mon to Sat 9am–7.30pm
Sun 11am–6pm

## VP 3 – Piccadilly Arcade

**Location Lat/Long:**   51.50826, -0.13918
**Location Postcode:**   SW1Y 6NH

### Opening hours

Mon to Sat 9am–7.30pm
Sun 11am–6pm

## VP 4 – Royal Opera Arcade

Royal Opera Arcade is best reached by first making your way to Piccadilly Circus, then heading south along Regent Street St James's towards Waterloo Place. As you reach the bottom of Waterloo Place, turn left into Pall Mall at the Crimea statue (featuring Florence Nightingale) and head east towards Trafalgar Square. Stay on the left side of the street and keep a careful eye out for the entrance to the Royal Opera Arcade on your left. It's very small and easily missed and lies directly opposite the grand Institute of Directors (IoD) building.

**Location Lat/Long:**   51.50822, -0.13246
**Location Postcode:**   SW1Y 4AN

### Opening hours

Mon to Sat 7am–5pm
Sun 11am–5pm

*Opposite: VP4. Royal Opera Arcade. Canon 5D IV, 24–70mm at 24mm, ISO 200, 1/30s at f/8. June.*

The area of St James's in the West End of London was once famed as the most desirable and exclusive residential area of London. It was named after the 12th-century leper hospital St James the Less, which occupied the site where St James's Palace now stands. By the 18th and 19th century the area became known as Clubland, due to the large number of gentlemen's clubs, the most well known being White's on St James's Street. After the Second World War corporations and private investment companies began to buy up properties in the area. Located so close to the thriving heart of London's West End, St James's, with its quieter streets and close proximity to London parks, offers the visitor somewhere to slow down and escape the pace of the West End.

St James's Palace is located to the southern side of the St James's area. Built by Henry VIII in 1536 and once the main royal palace in the city of London, it was displaced by Buckingham Palace in the 19th century. Clarence House next door is now the residence of the Prince of Wales. The palace is now mainly used to house the administrative centre for the Royal Family and is often used to host visiting heads of state.

## What to shoot and viewpoints

### Viewpoint 1 – The Ritz Hotel ♿

Located along Piccadilly just next door to Green Park is the world famous Ritz Hotel. Of most interest to the photographer is the long covered walkway that makes up the pavement on the south side of Piccadilly. This walkway with its perfect repeating pattern of stone arches makes for interesting images. It works best when there are few people, so you may have to visit early in the morning or late evening. Shoot using a long lens from one end to the other to capture the wonderful receding lines of the walkway's interior – the arches to the left or right of the composition – leading the eye to a solitary figure at the far end. Be sure to capture the Ritz Hotel signage located at either end of the walkway; this is constructed from around fifty bulbs and in the twenty years I've been walking past the hotel, I've yet to see a single bulb out of service! Shoot the sign with a very tight aperture to force the blades in your lens to star these wonderfully bright lamps adding that spark, literally, to the shot. This is another West End location that has a character all its own at Christmastime, when the various lamps that hang the length of the walkway are linked by long fir wreaths and baubles. Along the front of the hotel more wreaths are hung between the arches.

VP1. The Ritz hotel at Christmas. Canon 5D II, 17–40mm at 24mm, ISO 100, 4s at f/8, tripod. Dec.

VP1. Commuters near the Ritz. NEX-C3, E 18–55mm at 39mm, ISO 1600, 1/60s at f/4.5. Jan.

## How to get here

**Underground & Lines**: Green Park, Piccadilly Circus: *Bakerloo, Jubilee, Piccadilly, Victoria*
**Main Station**: Charing Cross
**Bus**: 6, 9, 14, 19, 38, N9, N19, N38, N97
**Cycle Hire**: St James's Square, Waterloo Place

## Accessibility

All locations and viewpoints are on ordinary city streets and should present no accessibility issues.

## Best time of year/day

Can be shot all year round, day and night. St James's Square Garden is closed at night. Best times of the year are summer for blooms and foliage and autumn in the parks and gardens for the colours. Night shooting is worthwhile at many of these locations and offers some unusual photographic opportunities. Christmas is one of the best times of the year for many of the urban locations as the decorations will be in place.

## VP 1 – The Ritz Hotel

Arrive via Green Park station, exit via the park then loop back on yourself and head to Piccadilly. Turn right on Piccadilly and you will immediately head under the walkway in front of the Ritz Hotel.

**Location Lat/Long**: 51.50722, -0.14169
**Location Postcode**: W1J 9BR

*Opposite*: A Rolls Royce parked on St James's Street. Sony A6000, E 55–210mm at 55mm, ISO 1250, 1/160s at f/4.5. Nov.

VP1. The Ritz hotel at Christmas. Canon 5D IV, 24–70mm at 66mm, ISO 100, 15s at f/19, tripod. Dec.

*VP2. St James's Place early morning. Canon 5D II, 24–70mm at 62mm, ISO 100, 4s at f/11, tripod. Jan.*

### Viewpoint 2 – St James's Place ♿

Opposite Pickering Place on St James's Street is an L-shaped lane called St James's Place – a quiet little street often used by the local office crowd as a cut-through to Green Park. Head to the end of St James's Place, follow it to the right, and opposite the Stafford Hotel is a tiny passage, which between 6am and 10pm allows direct access into Green Park. If you take this route through to the park, be sure to pause a while in St James's Place, where you'll find some interesting photographic opportunities. No 4 is where Chopin resided prior to his last public performance and the house is often festooned with blooms in summer. Spencer House, one of the finest 18th century aristocratic townhouses open to the public, is located at the far corner of St James's Place. The ornate interior is incredible and well worth a visit. The main entrance to the Stafford Hotel is also located here. Constructed from gorgeous red brick, the hotel is a riot of colour during summer, when blooms are hung on its railings. At Christmastime their exterior light display is worth the visit alone; it covers the entire front of the building and is a spectacular sight to capture.

### Viewpoint 3 – Pickering Place ♿

This is one of those blink-and-you-miss-it locations. This tiny little square is located along a small alleyway at the southern end of St James's Street next to Berry Bros and Rudd wine merchants. The square has just one restaurant but the architecture and design make it a great little stop for another piece of London's history. Pickering Place was the location for the Texas Legation – a diplomatic mission in the mid-19th century, when Texas was establishing international ties with Britain and France to protect itself from Mexico and alert the United States to its plight. When Texas joined the US in 1845, the Legations in London and Paris were shut down, however a plaque in Pickering Place still marks its presence.

*Opposite top left: VP2. St James's Hotel. Canon 5D IV, 24–70mm at 24mm, ISO 100, 8s at f/11. Dec.*

## VP 2 – St James's Place

Keep walking east along Piccadilly until you reach the junction with St James's Street leading away to the south. Head south down St James's Street and you will pass the entrance to St James's Place to your right, around 100m before St James's Palace, which you'll see directly in front of you.

An alternative and shorter route to St James's Place is through Green Park. Take the eastern walkway south through Green Park for around 400 yards. You'll see a little alley leading from the park through and under the buildings that line its eastern side. During the day this is very busy with the office crowd using it as a cut-through into the park, and it leads directly to the Stafford Hotel in St James's Place.

**Location Lat/Long**: 51.50555, -0.14015
**Location Postcode**: SW1A 1NP

## VP 3 – Pickering Place

Leaving St James's Place, cross over St James's Street and directly to the left of the wine merchants is a little alley, which leads into Pickering Place.

**Location Lat/Long**: 51.505438, -0.13793468
**Location Postcode**: SW1A 1EF

*Top*: VP2. Snow in St James's Place. Sony A6000, 16–50mm at 35mm, ISO 100, 1/200s at f/5.6. Feb.

*Middle*: VP2. St James's Place. Sony A6000, 16–50mm at 16mm, ISO 250, 1/160s at f/4. Aug.

*Bottom*: VP3. Pickering Place courtyard. Canon 5D IV, 17–40mm at 17mm, ISO 400, 1/60s at f/4. Oct.

*VP3. Entrance to Pickering Place. Canon 5D II, 17–40mm at 22mm, ISO 400, 1/60s at f/4. Sept.*

*VP3. Pickering Place, St James. Canon 5D IV, 70–200mm at 70mm, ISO 800, 1/60s at f/4. Oct.*

### Viewpoint 4 – St James's Palace ♿

St James's Palace, home to minor royals, is a red brick Tudor palace that has much to offer the visiting photographer. In the main courtyard adjacent to Marlborough Road, you will often find guardsmen protecting the palace dressed in the traditional red tunic and Buzby bearskin helmets. You can get around 75m away so a medium sized zoom lens of around 100mm will be needed to capture close-up details, especially when they loosen up during their guard duty roster. Each day around midday the marching band arrives from Buckingham Palace, they parade in the courtyard and this can be observed from the other side of the road. Visitors will often follow the marching band from Buckingham Palace to St James's Palace so it can become very crowded at the viewing spot during the parade. At other times there are one or two key spots I've found: early on bright sunny days the sun will cast wonderful shadows under the arches of the walkway at the top of Marlborough Road. Standing among the arches you can capture a wonderful image with superb contrast, which can be made more effective by the presence of a single person passing through this spot. This same location can be shot at night from the opposite side of Marlborough Road, when the extremely bright security lights around the courtyard cast shadows back into the road and there's a spot where you can include the old gas lamps to the left of the shot and capture the palace building in all its glory. Opposite the palace, still on Marlborough Road, is the Queen's Chapel, a large cream-coloured building.

### Viewpoint 5 – Crown Passage ♿

Located at the far end of Pall Mall is a tiny little passage that has one pub and a few shops. During the week this spot comes alive with the office crowd. I love shooting pictures here due to the passage's very tight confines;

*Top*: VP4. St James's Palace at night. Canon 5D IV, 24–70mm at 38mm, ISO 100, 30s at f/8, tripod. Dec.

## VP 4 – St James's Palace

As you exit Pickering Place, turn left and St James's Palace is directly ahead. The arched walkway is at the northern end of Marlborough Road and to the east side of the palace building. Marlborough Road is easy to spot as it has distinctive red tarmac leading towards St James's Park.

**Location Lat/Long**: 51.50498, -0.13722
**Location Postcode**: SW1A 1BQ

## VP 5 – Crown Passage

Opposite St James's Palace on the north side of Pall Mall is Crown Passage, a small pedestrian alleyway that leads directly north, you will see the Red Lion pub at the entrance as you walk in. This passage can be very busy at lunchtimes with the office crowd picking up their lunch.

**Location Lat/Long**: 51.50572, -0.13766
**Location Postcode**: SW1Y 6PP

*Above*: VP4. Guards marching away from St James's Palace. Canon 5D IV, 24–70mm at 38mm, ISO 200, 1/180s at f/8. June.

*Top*: VP4. Guards on duty at St James's Palace. Sony A6000, 16–50mm at 50mm, ISO 125, 1/160s at f/5.6. June. *Above*: VP4. Patterns of light by St James's Palace. Canon 5D II, 24–70mm at 24mm, ISO 200, 1/80s at f/11. Jan.

it has an almost medieval feel. As it swells with people at midday it's hard work to capture the mood but worth it when you get that perfect 'busy' image, especially when it rains and the passage fills with umbrellas. During weekends the area is quiet and if you arrive before dawn you can shoot a quiet shot of the passage using the Red Lion with its old frontage caught in the gas lamps as the perfect foreground.

*Top*: Teatime bus, St James. Canon 5D IV, 24–70mm at 35mm, ISO 1600, 1/3000s at f/4. Jul.

*Above*: VP6. Jermyn Street, West End. Sony A6000, 16–50mm at 41mm, ISO 500, 1/160s at f/5.6. May.

*Top*: VP 6. Looking east along Jermyn Street from St James's St. Sony A6000, 16–50mm at 37mm, ISO 100, 1/250s at f/5.6. June.

*Above*: VP7. Spring in St James's Square. Sony A6000, 16–50mm at 16mm, ISO 100, 1/400s at f/5. Apr.

*Top left*: VP7. Daffodils in St James's Square. Sony A6000, 16–50mm at 25mm, ISO 100, 1/250s at f/5. Apr.

*Top Middle*: VP7. The Slender Man, St James's Square. Sony A6000, 16–50mm at 16mm, ISO 100, 1/200s at f/4.5. June.

*Top right*: VP6. Fortnum and Mason doormen, St James's. Canon 5D II, 17–40mm at 26mm, ISO 200, 1/350s at f/8. Jul.

*Above*: VP8. Waterloo Place at dawn during Christmas. Canon 5D II, 24–70mm at 24mm, ISO 100, 6s at f/11, tripod. Dec.

*VP5. Crown Passage before dawn. NEX-C3, E 18–55mm at 24mm, ISO 1600, 1/5s at f/4. Jan.*

*VP8. Florence Nightingale statue Waterloo Place. Canon 5D IV, 70–200mm at 97mm, ISO 200, 1/90s at f/8. Nov.*

### Viewpoint 6 – Jermyn Street ♿

Of all the streets in London, Jermyn Street has to be one of my favourite places to go for street photography. City streets all over London offer such opportunities but I've yet to come across another street like Jermyn Street; a huge variety of people visit the area, window-shopping or simply passing through to St James's. Rain or shine, this street always seems to offer two or three really interesting people to photograph.

### Viewpoint 7 – St James's Square ♿

The area of St James's is centred around this wonderful little park square. So many of London's small parks are dominated by just one aspect but St James's Square, like its larger namesake St James's Park, has a few. There are always a number of flowerbeds during the spring and summer, and as the trees take on their rich foliage, they offer some great photographic opportunities. Pieces of contemporary art are often on display on the greens and are changed quite regularly, which encourages people to

visit time and time again. The park is almost enclosed by the trees, ensuring there's a feeling of sanctuary from the manic pace of the nearby West End. All these elements make this spot a must see. Buy some food at one of the local shops in Piccadilly or Regent Street then make your way to this little haven of peace and quiet.

### Viewpoint 8 – Waterloo Place ♿

Waterloo Place, which crosses Pall Mall, is a square adorned with memorials and statues and is located at the southern end of what is now known as Regent Street St James's, close to St James's Square.

If coming from Piccadilly Circus head directly south towards Parliament, which you will see in the distance. As you reach the end of the street it will open out into a large area – Waterloo Place – which is dominated by The Guards Crimean War Memorial at the centre of the traffic island. You will notice a pile of disused cannon to the northern side of the memorial; these are broken Russian cannon recovered from

*VP5. A milliner's shop in St James's. Sony A6000, 16–50mm at 21mm, ISO 800, 1/160s at f/4. Sept.*

## VP 6 – Jermyn Street

Emerging at the northern end of Crown Passage onto King Street, cross over heading north then cut diagonally and take Bury Street north for around 400 yards until you reach Jermyn Street.

**Location Lat/Long**: 51.50755, -0.13933
**Location Postcode**: SW1Y 6LX

## VP 7 – St James's Square

From Jermyn Street turn right and head east past Fortnum and Mason. When you reach the church St James's Piccadilly to your right, take a right down Duke of York Street; you'll see St James's Square directly ahead of you.

**Location Lat/Long**: 51.50721, -0.13534
**Location Postcode**: SW1Y 4LE

## VP 8 – Waterloo Place

Leave St James's Square via the eastern exit on to Charles II Street then continue until you emerge on to Regent Street St James's. Turn to your right to arrive at Waterloo Place.

**Location Lat/Long**: 51.50755, -0.13282
**Location Postcode**: SW1Y 4BN

the Siege of Sevastopol during the Crimean War. Using a zoom lens, shoot the statue at top of the war memorial aligned with the statue of the Duke of York (atop a huge pillar in the background). This is very effective at dawn or dusk during the blue hour. A wider shot of the entire space looking south works well but take a position slightly off centre and to the northwest side of the square, then wait for the light to balance between the bright lights of the hotel on the eastern side and the sky to the south. If possible visit during December – the Christmas tree erected in Waterloo Place has to be the best in London bar none! If you enjoy shooting traffic-streak images, then take up a position facing north on one of the traffic islands north of the Crimean memorial. Here you can shoot the traffic as it makes its way to and from Piccadilly Circus. Finally, for a truly fantastic image in the late evening, walk to the Duke of York statue – the huge column you see just south of Waterloo Place – and shoot back towards Waterloo Place. This will include the statues, the brightly lit buildings and the traffic leading towards Piccadilly.

Admiralty Arch is located on the southwest side of Trafalgar Square, linking the square to The Mall that leads to Buckingham Palace. The arch is quite a recent addition to London's landmarks and was completed in 1912, designed as a memorial to Queen Victoria by her son Edward VII. Originally a residence for the First Sea Lord, it later became a government office until the lease expired in 2012 and it was sold to a private development company to be turned into a hotel and conference building.

## What to shoot and viewpoints

This is an interesting building to shoot, especially when flags are flown from it to mark state occasions such as the Trooping of the Colour. Of the three archways only two are open to traffic so with a quick dash across the road you can stand in the centre of the road in front of the gates and shoot in both directions. One of the most common shots is a long exposure image of traffic moving through the arch, although this takes some practice as the traffic often slows or stops at the traffic lights just beyond. Like many of London's sights it's not somewhere you may wish to visit specifically but it's certainly one of the more interesting minor landmarks and worth shooting if you happen to be in the area seeing sights such as Buckingham Palace or Trafalgar Square.

If you do visit, see if you can find the Duke of Wellington's nose … along the side of one of the two traffic arches is a life-size nose set at a height of two metres. Legend has it the nose was placed there so the mounted military could touch it and pay respect to the Iron Duke, who is held in high esteem by the cavalry. In fact, it was placed there by artist Rick Buckley to highlight the rise of the 'Big Brother' society. Personally, I prefer the myth.

*Opposite top left*: Wellington's Nose, Admiralty Arch. Sony A6000, 16–50mm at 50mm, ISO 320, 1/160s at f/5.6. Oct.
*Top right*: Master and Commander at Admiralty Arch. Sony A6000, 16–50mm at 29mm, ISO 100, 1/160s at f/5.6. Sept.

*Opposite bottom*: Admiralty Arch. Sony A6000, 16–50mm at 18mm, ISO 100, 1/640s at f/4.5. June.

Admiralty Arch from The Mall. Canon 5D IV, 24–70mm at 45mm, ISO 100, 10s at f/16, tripod. Nov.

## How to get here

The nearest Tube station is Charing Cross and many buses stop at Trafalgar Square, which is adjacent to Admiralty Arch. Make your way to Trafalgar Square then exit the square by The Mall, which begins in the farthest southwest corner of Trafalgar Square.

| | |
|---|---|
| **Location Lat/Long**: | 51.50679, -0.12865 |
| **Location Postcode**: | SW1A 2WH |
| **Underground & Lines**: | Charing Cross, Embankment: *Bakerloo, Circle & District, Northern* |
| **Main Station**: | Charing Cross |
| **Riverboat**: | Embankment Pier |
| **Bus**: | 9, 11, 24, 87, 88, N9, N11, N87 |
| **Cycle Hire**: | Waterloo Place |

## Accessibility

This is a flat road with ramps at suitable spots for crossing the road. It should present no issues for anyone with limited mobility.

## Best time of year/day

Just after sunrise during the summer the sun will rise behind Admiralty Arch casting a warm rich light over the trees along The Mall, while the sky remains blue. This works particularly well when combined with lush green trees and the rich hues of flags, when they are present. Towards the end of the day, shoot from the Buckingham Palace end towards Admiralty Arch, as the sun will be lighting the trees in the opposite direction. At sunset, again shoot towards Buckingham Palace to catch any colour in the clouds. At night, it's possible to shoot traffic streaks on The Mall although traffic is limited and traffics lights mean it can be tricky to get the timing just right for exposures.

Designed by famous architect Inigo Jones and built in 1622, this incredible building is the last remaining component of the Palace of Whitehall, where English monarchs lived in the 16th and 17th centuries. The original Banqueting House burned down in 1619 when workmen clearing up after a New Year's party decided to set fire to rubbish inside the building and razed it to the ground! James I had the current building built and just 27 years later, in 1649, his son, Charles I was beheaded in front of it. Rumour has it the clock atop the Household Cavalry Museum building (on the opposite side of the road) has a black dot on its face that indicates the exact time Charles I was executed on 30th January 1649.

The design was a revelation at the time; Inigo Jones was heavily influenced by Italian design and prior to this English architecture had been based on the rather outdated medieval style of forts and castles. When Cromwell ousted the monarchy, Jones's career was over as he was regarded as an ardent royalist. He died in 1652 never having seen his work receive the acclaim it later garnered.

William of Orange took the throne in the late 17th Century and hated the Whitehall area (not surprising considering his mother had died of smallpox at Whitehall Palace when William was just 10 years old). Banqueting House was left unused for a long time then turned into a military museum during the first half of the 20th century, when it housed the skeleton of Napoleon's horse. Now a major visitor attraction, it is owned and run by the Historic Royal Palaces charity, which also maintains Hampton Court and the Tower of London. An interior shot of Banqueting House features on the Electric Light Orchestra's debut album cover.

## What to shoot and viewpoints

### The Main Hall &

The building is split into two floors: the undercroft and the two-storey double-cube room on the first floor. A double-cube is where the dimensions of the room equate to two cubes.

Mathematical precision in design is a major tenet of Palladianism (an Italian style of classical Greek architecture). When you first enter the main hall on the first floor, it's breathtaking – the room is so open and full of light and the ceiling (painted by Peter Paul Rubens) is stunning. It's such a huge space, you won't easily capture its beauty without a wide-angle lens. The key shots are captured from the corners of the room, where you'll be able to pull in the hall's full grandeur. If you're quick and careful, stand in the entrance and shoot the full length of the room to capture the perfect symmetry of the hall.

### Using the Mirrors &

Interesting photos can be gained from kit kindly supplied by the Historic Royal Palaces: to allow more comfortable viewing of the ceiling, two large mirrors are located on moving pedestals in the middle of the room. Simply lean over and you'll see a perfect reflection of the ceiling. Position your camera on the edge of one these mirror-pedestals and you'll be able to capture it. The mirror is angled at around 30 degrees, so move around it with your lens close to edge of the frame to shoot some intriguing images. If you have a fisheye lens, use it here to emphasise the magnificence of the scene. Position yourself close to the centre of the room, crouch down and shoot directly upwards – you should be able to capture the entire ceiling in a single image.

### The Undercroft &

After enjoying the splendour of the Main Hall, spend some time in the Undercroft below. It's very much a low-light, high ISO situation but with a steady hand, there are some interesting images of candle stands and whitewashed arches to be shot here.

I find the building is little known and having visited several times during my lunch hour there were never any queues, although there were always visitors admiring the Main Hall. It's an incredible building and if you've bought a pass for all the Historic Royal Palaces buildings, I would urge you to visit this unique piece of British history.

*Opposite top left: Banqueting House, Whitehall. Canon 5D II, 17–40mm at 17mm, ISO 400, 1/60s at f/4.5. Mar.*
*Top right: Undercroft within the Banqueting Hall. Canon 5D II, 17–40mm at 17mm, ISO 800, 1/60s at f/4. Mar.*

## How to get here

The nearest Tube station is Charing Cross and many buses stop at Trafalgar Square, which is at the top of Whitehall where Banqueting House is located. Make your way to Trafalgar Square then exit the square by Whitehall, which begins directly south of Trafalgar Square (you should see Big Ben at its far end). Alternatively, alight at Westminster Tube station and proceed north up Whitehall. Banqueting House is located directly opposite Horse Guards Parade.

| | |
|---|---|
| **Location Lat/Long**: | 51.50459, -0.126 |
| **Location Postcode**: | SW1A 2ER |
| **Underground & Lines**: | Charing Cross, Embankment, Westminster: *Bakerloo, Circle and District, Jubilee, Northern* |
| **Main Station**: | Charing Cross |
| **Riverboat**: | Embankment Pier, Westminster Pier |
| **Bus**: | 3,11,12, 24, 53, 87, 88, 159, N3, N11, N53, N87 |
| **Cycle Hire**: | Northumberland Avenue, Embankment Place |

## Accessibility

The Main Hall of Banqueting House is accessible to wheelchair users via a lift in an adjoining property. The lift is available from Monday to Friday. A ramp down to the Undercroft is available.

## Best time of year/day

The building is only open during visiting hours so it can only be shot during the day. Bright sunny days ensure the light penetrates into the Main Hall, casting shadows and keeping the ISO requirement down.

## Opening hours

Mon to Sun: 10am–5pm (Last admission: 4.30pm)

## Admission prices (2019)

Please note that payment is by cash only.

| | |
|---|---|
| **Members**: | Free |
| **Adults**: | £6.30 |
| **Children** (aged 5–15): | Free |

*Middle: The ceiling of Banqueting House, Whitehall. Sony A6000, Fisheye 8mm at 8mm, ISO 200, 1/13s at f/8. May.*

*Left: The throne at Banqueting House. Sony A6000, Fisheye 8mm at 8mm, ISO 320, 1/10s at f/8. May.*

**If you want photographs of mounted cavalry officers or guardsmen, this is the place to visit.**

During the time of Henry VIII (the 1500s) this parade ground was a tiltyard – a site used for jousting and other ceremonial occasions. It later became the headquarters for the British Army when the Duke of Wellington was commander-in-chief; his office is located in one of the buildings and is still, along with the Iron Duke's original desk, in use by the Army's General Officer.

During the 20th century the parade ground was used as a 500-space car park for civil servants working in the nearby government offices – a benefit known as 'the great perk'. After a failed mortar attack on 10 Downing Street in 1991 (which was carried out from Horse Guards Avenue) it was requested the car park be converted to a public open space due to security concerns. Members of the civil service strongly objected to losing their 'great perk' but their objections were in vain: the car park was resurfaced in 1997 and opened as a public space and parade ground.

*Heading out of Horse Guards Parade. Canon 5D IV, 70–200mm at 200mm, ISO 400, 1/2000s at f/4.5. July.*

The ground is open to the west side and people are free to walk across it, through the arches under the Household Cavalry building and to gain access to Whitehall. To its southern side there is an armed police presence, as the boundary here is the garden wall of 10 Downing Street.

## What to shoot and viewpoints

### The Changing of the Queen's Life Guard ♿

The Changing of the Queen's Life Guard takes place daily. The Life Guard leaves Hyde Park Barracks at 10.28am on weekdays (9.28am Sundays) and rides to Horse Guards Parade via Hyde Park Corner, Constitution Hill and The Mall. The ceremony of changing the Life Guard takes place on Horse Guards Parade at 11am weekdays. This is a great opportunity to take photographs as there are no barriers and you can get quite close.

*Opposite top left: Guard on duty, Horse Guards Parade. Canon 5D II, 70–200mm at 200mm, ISO 400, 1/250s at f/16. Sept. Right: Life Guard from the Household Cavalry, Whitehall. Sony A6000, 16–50mm at 16mm, ISO 100, 1/400s at f/5. Sept.*

*Opposite bottom left: Mounted Life Guard outside Horse Guards Parade. Sony A6000, E 35mm at 35mm, ISO 100, 1/60s at f/4. Oct. Right: East entrance to Horse Guards Parade. Sony A6000, 16–50mm at 16mm, ISO 100, 1/250s at f/5. Nov.*

### Anytime ♿

At any other time there is one good reason to visit Horse Guards Parade: to get the classic shot of a mounted cavalry officer. The main building to the east of the parade ground is the Household Cavalry Museum and Dover House. A public walkway leads through three arches under the main building that leads towards Whitehall and you will often find troops dressed in the full red, white and gold regalia of the Household Cavalry. The entrance from Whitehall to the buildings is where you will often find two mounted cavalry officers on their horses. They are an obvious draw for visitors to London and it can get very busy indeed as people try to pose for selfies in front of the guards and their mounts. It takes patience but you can get relatively clear images of the mounted officers. Position yourself about two metres directly in front of the horse and don't try to shoot too wide as you'll capture too many people in shot. Instead, look to keep a narrow field of view and wait patiently for a gap to appear. It's a classic image and well worth the wait.

While there you will often see guards wearing their full ceremonial uniform and holding their swords posted in courtyard alcoves. If you're there early in the morning (around 8am at weekends), you'll find guards on foot already in position and you'll have plenty of time to capture some detailed shots as very few visitors venture there before 10am. You can get as close as a metre from each guard. Any closer and they will bark at you to stand back – it's quite amusing to witness a visitor taken aback by it! Wait for 10–15 minutes and you should be able to see the captain of the guard make the guard changeover. The captain and two replacement guards emerge from the main museum building and the existing guards are replaced, accompanied by a lot of loudly barked orders. Sometimes armed police ask people to stand back for safety as the guards hold their swords while they march across the courtyard. It's a superb chance to capture some close-up shots of this spectacle. The police are usually very tolerant of people taking photos and I've always found them good company while you wait for your shot.

## How to get here

Follow the same directions for Banqueting House. Horse Guards Parade lies directly opposite.

**Location Lat/Long**: 51.50463, -0.12828
**Location Postcode**: SW1A 2AX
**Underground & Lines**: Charing Cross, Westminster: *Bakerloo, Circle and District, Jubilee, Northern*
**Main Station**: Charing Cross
**Riverboat**: Embankment Pier, Westminster Pier
**Bus**: 3,11,12,24,53,87,88,159, N3, N11, N53, N87
**Cycle Hire**: Northumberland Avenue, Whitehall Place

## Accessibility ♿

All locations and viewpoints are on ordinary city streets and should present no accessibility issues.

## Best time of year/day

Horse Guards Parade can be shot all year round, day and night although the gates around the main buildings are closed at night. On certain occasions the police and armed forces may close the main buildings and parade ground. The best time of day to capture the soldiers on parade is first thing in the morning, around 9 or 10am, just as the visitor crowds begin to build. If you wish to catch a parade in progress, most occur in summer and autumn, Trooping the Colour takes place in early June.

## The Household Cavalry Museum

The Household Cavalry Museum is situated at Horse Guards Parade and is worth a visit to learn more about the cavalry's history.

## Opening hours

Open daily. 10am–6pm (Apr to Oct). 10am–5pm (Nov to Mar). Closed for the Marathon, Easter Friday and Christmas Eve to Boxing Day.

## Admission prices (2019)

Please note that payment is by cash only.

| | |
|---|---|
| **Adults**: | £8.50 |
| **Children** (aged 5–15): | £6.50 |
| **Family** (2 Adults 3 children): | £22.50 |
| **Students** (with ID): | £6.50 |
| **Seniors** (aged 60+): | £6.50 |
| **Serving Military Personnel** (with ID): | £4.25 |

*Opposite: Looking south into Horse Guards Parade ground at dawn. Sony A6000, 16–50mm at 16mm, ISO 100, 1/250s at f/4.5. Sept.*

*Above: Guards Memorial seen through Horse Guards Parade archway. Canon 5D IV, 70–200mm at 150mm, ISO 400, 1/1000s at f/4. Oct.*

# EVENTS

### The Trooping of the Colour – Once A Year ♿

The Trooping of the Colour is celebrated on the Queen's official birthday, on the second Saturday of June at 11am. Over a thousand guardsmen, two hundred horses, cannons and six bands march from Buckingham Palace along The Mall to Horse Guards Parade, Whitehall and back again.

### Beating Retreat ♿

Beating Retreat takes place on the Wednesday and Thursday evenings preceding Trooping the Colour. Beating Retreat dates from the 16th century when a cannon was fired at sunset so any nearby army patrols would return to the castle. It is now marked by parading troops, bands, rifle and cannon fire and fireworks.

Both events require tickets. For more information about this and other events, visit: *householddivision.org.uk*

If you don't have a ticket, you will have to stand on the other side of Horse Guards Road behind barriers and you'll need a zoom to capture details. However as the troops arrive and depart, they can be photographed right in front of you.

St James's Park is situated between Horse Guards Parade and Buckingham Palace, with The Mall to the north and Birdcage Walk to the south. Once a swampy marsh, it is now one of London's stunning open spaces owned and operated by the Royal Parks (*royalparks.org.uk*). Covering nearly sixty acres, it originally had a formal canal running through it (built by Charles II in the 17th century) but remodelling by famous landscape gardener John Nash in the 19th century saw the canal turned into a long slender lake. The views of Buckingham Palace from the park are very special and a visit is a must – repeatedly, if you are a local-to-London photographer, as there is much to photograph as the seasons change. Early mornings from spring to autumn can be particularly rewarding.

## What to shoot and viewpoints

As one of the chain of parks from Kensington to the heart of London, St James's Park, with its lake, trees and flowers, waterfowl and views of the surrounding city, is a wonderful place to go all year around. Enter the park from any direction and you can circle the lake; my advice is use the central Blue Bridge at the park's centre to ensure your walk takes a figure-of-eight route that will include the best parts of the lake. I have described some key viewpoints but beyond these, the best approach is to go for a wander.

### Duck Island Cottage and Pelicans ♿

To the eastern end of the park sits Duck Island Cottage (built in 1841 and restored in 1982), the HQ of the London Historic Parks and Gardens Trust. It's a lovely sight at any time of day – its wonderfully quaint appearance quite at odds with the city around it. As you pass the modern lakeside cafe, you'll come across the famous pelicans, originally gifts from the Russian Ambassador in the 17th century. Apparently pelicans are not averse to eating anything they consider food; this is perfectly true: a friend and I once saw one eat a live pigeon, much to visitors' horror. You will also see coots, moorhens, ducks, geese and many others species.

*Opposite*: *Wildflowers bloom in St James's Park. Canon 5D II, 24–70mm at 48mm, ISO 200, 1/250s at f/8. June.*

*Cottage by the lake in St James's Park. Sony A6000, 16–50mm at 16mm, ISO 100, 1/400s at f/5. July.*

*Buckingham Palace from the bridge in St James's Park. Canon 5D IV, 24–70mm at 70mm, ISO 200, 1/250s at f/9.5. June.*

## The Blue Bridge and Views to Buckingham Palace &

Continue along the north side and you'll come to the central Blue Bridge – a good place to get great views along the lake: to the west towards Buckingham Palace; to the east towards Horse Guards Parade, Big Ben and the London Eye. You'll also be surrounded by waterfowl. On a calm morning this is a great place to capture a reflection of the palace in the lake's water, as sun bathes the area in warm light. Head east, closer to Buckingham Palace, and on the path either side of the lake, near the small island, and close to The Mall, are several superb viewpoints of Buckingham Palace to discover, with flowerbeds and paths providing the foreground.

## How to get here

The easiest option is to arrive on the District/Circle line at St James's Park station. Exit the station on the north side and walk to the eastern side of the imposing Ministry of Justice building, along Queen Anne's Gate. Head straight on through the alley until you arrive on Birdcage Walk, then cross over the road into the park. The path will lead you to the Blue Bridge and the circular pathway. If coming from the north, head to the southern side of Green Park, cross over The Mall and into St James's Park. Alternatively, if you're coming from Trafalgar Square, you can walk through Admiralty Arch in its southwest corner and begin walking along the south side of The Mall until you come to the northeast corner of St James's Park.

| | |
|---|---|
| **Location Lat/Long**: | 51.50276, -0.13458 |
| **Location Postcode**: | SW1A 2BJ |
| **Underground & Lines**: | Charing Cross, Embankment, St James's Park, Westminster: *Bakerloo, Circle and District, Jubilee, Northern* |
| **Main Station**: | Charing Cross |
| **Riverboat**: | Embankment Pier, Westminster Pier |
| **Bus**: | 3, 11, 12, 24, 53, 87, 88, 159, N3, N11, N53, N87 |
| **Cycle Hire**: | Northumberland Avenue, Whitehall Place |

### Duck Island Cottage and Pelicans
| | |
|---|---|
| **Location Lat/Long**: | 51.50299, -0.13003 |
| **Location Postcode**: | SW1A 2BJ |

### The Blue Bridge
| | |
|---|---|
| **Location Lat/Long**: | 51.50231, -0.13521 |
| **Location Postcode**: | SW1A 2BJ |

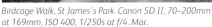

*Birdcage Walk, St James's Park. Canon 5D II, 70–200mm at 169mm, ISO 400, 1/250s at f/4. Mar.*

## View to Buckingham Palace

**Location Lat/Long**:   51.50255, -0.13834
**Location Postcode**:   SW1A 2BJ

## Birdcage Walk

**Location Lat/Long**:   51.50121, -0.13187
**Location Postcode**:   SW1A 2BJ

## Accessibility  ♿

All locations and viewpoints are on level ground with no steps or steep gradients and should present no accessibility issues.

## Best time of year/day

My advice would be to visit early morning or late evening as the park, and in particular the Blue Bridge with its superb view of Buckingham Palace, is a visitor magnet on sunny days. The north side of the park catches the light and its many trees offer shade so that's another draw in summer. The south side of the park is more densely populated with shady trees, making it the perfect place to sit down for a rest with a packed lunch before moving on to your next location.

**Safety Warning**: London is statistically a very safe city; crime in the centre is quite rare but do exercise caution. Please be careful if you are in any of the Royal Parks during the hours of darkness. Police patrols are frequent but the parks are often lit by gas lamps and can be very dark at night with some areas not covered by CCTV. On rare occasions there have been incidents of violent crime so be cautious: go in pairs or groups if you intend to visit the parks after midnight and always inform someone where you're going and what time you intend to be back.

## Birdcage Walk ♿

Cross the Blue Bridge and head along the south side of the lake or up Birdcage Walk's long tree-lined boulevard towards the far western end of the park. Birdcage Walk is a wonderful place to visit early in the morning at weekends, when it's hard to resist the perfect shot of a solitary figure walking along the tree-lined path. Turn at the far western end of the park then head back along the north side of the lake (heading east) and you will find yet more waterfowl. In autumn and winter this part of the park is one of my favourites; the evergreens here, combined with deciduous trees shedding their leaves make it the perfect place to capture end-of-year scenes in the capital.

*Top left: Spring in the park. Canon 5D II, 24–70mm at 35mm, ISO 200, 1/160s at f/14. Apr.*

Buckingham Palace was originally Buckingham House, a townhouse built in 1703 for the Duke of Buckingham. In 1761 George III bought the house as a private residence for Queen Charlotte and it was known as Queen's House. During the 19th century the architects John Nash and Edward Blore added three wings to the main building creating a central courtyard and Queen Victoria took residence 1837. Since then it has become the home and administrative headquarters of the reigning monarch.

There have been some interesting developments on the site throughout the years: originally Marble Arch stood as the entrance to Buckingham House until the main building was remodelled in the 19th century and Marble Arch was moved to its current location at the end of Oxford Street. When Prince Albert died, Queen Victoria couldn't bear living at the palace any longer and it began to fall into disrepair. A note was pinned to the palace fence in 1864, advertising that the building was to be put up for sale. The design we see today was not in fact the one Blore had built; it was major remodelling work in 1913 that created the now iconic building.

The palace has been the scene of many protests and events: in 1914 over 20,000 suffragettes led by Emeline Pankhurst marched on the palace in an attempt deliver a petition to the King. Pankhurst was subsequently arrested and taken to Holloway Prison. It was the gathering place for the VE (Victory in Europe) celebrations in 1945, when Winston Churchill joined the royal family on the balcony. The balcony itself has become famous as the location where every royal couple makes an appearance alongside the royal family after marrying, to the delight of cheering crowds. At 8am on 10th March 1977 at the height of punk rock, Malcolm Maclaren set up a trestle table outside the palace and the Sex Pistols signed a record contract with A&M Records to release their single *God Save the Queen*.

## THE MALL

The Mall (the 'all' is pronounced as in the name Alan) is the wide road that connects Buckingham Palace in the west with Trafalgar Square (through Admiralty Arch) to the east. The name comes from the original purpose of this long promenade – a playing field for the game pall-mall (a game very similar to croquet) during the 17th century. The road was redesigned at the turn of the 20th century as a major ceremonial route and to this

*Snow on The Mall outside Buckingham Palace . Sony A6000, 16–50mm at 16mm, ISO 100, 1/250s at f/5. Feb.*

end the tarmac was coloured red to give the illusion of a red carpet leading to Buckingham Palace. The road itself is exactly 0.5 nautical miles long. Buses are not permitted on The Mall or in front of Buckingham Palace without the express permission of the monarch and it is closed to traffic on Saturdays, Sundays, public holidays and on ceremonial occasions. The Mall is used for many events, when the road and surrounding streets are closed to traffic. These include the annual Trooping of the Colour and the London Marathon, which has its finish line on The Mall.

***Next spread**: Buckingham Palace flowerbeds in Summer. Sony A6000, 16–50mm at 23mm, ISO 100, 1/800s at f/5. Apr.*

*Christmas Day at the palace. Canon 5D II, 24–70mm at 27mm, ISO 100, 20s at f/8, tripod. Dec.*

## What to shoot and viewpoints

### Buckingham Palace ♿

Buckingham Palace is a classic London landmark that draws visitors from all over the world. Its stunning facade, remodelled in 1913, is world famous. The site is not very big at all, consisting of the two large flowerbeds in front of the palace and the Victoria Memorial. During spring and summer the flowerbeds are a joy to see – a beautiful mix of colour and variety, especially the tulips that are a regular feature. A wide-angle lens is most useful as you take the quarter-circle paths around the beds. Seek to capture the colour of the flowers in the foreground, the Victoria memorial offset slightly and a blue sky behind the main palace building – this is the most common shot of the palace.

Once complete, and if you do have a zoom lens, look to take some interesting close-up and isolated shots of interesting features: the top of the Victoria Memorial, the flag on top of the palace – assuming it is flying and thus signalling the Queen is at home. There are also interesting views to be had a little further back such as

shots looking down The Mall (often decked with flags) to the palace. Alternatively, head into Green Park or St James's park (previous chapter) to capture the palace between the trees.

During autumn and winter the palace can be seen from Green Park, which lies to the north. In autumn there is a wonderful image to be had of rich golden leaves in the foreground, leading to the palace in the background. In winter, when the trees are bare, the palace can be seen more clearly from the park, enabling you to form more interesting compositions.

### Fewer People

For images with fewer people in (or none), visit just after sunrise or at night.

*Opposite left: Statue atop the Victoria Memorial in front of Buckingham Palace. Canon 5D IV, 70–200mm at 200mm, ISO 200, 1/1000s at f/8. July.*

## How to get here

The two easiest ways to get to Buckingham Palace are either to head to Trafalgar Square, leave via Admiralty Arch and simply walk down The Mall until you reach the palace. If you prefer a slightly shorter walk, then head to Green Park and walk directly south through the park towards the palace. You'll find most people here are going to or coming from the palace, so you won't find it difficult to find your way there.

| | |
|---|---|
| **Location Lat/Long**: | 51.50153, -0.14188 |
| **Location Postcode**: | SW1A 1AA |
| **Underground & Lines**: | Green Park, Hyde Park Corner, St James's Park: *Circle and District, Jubilee, Piccadilly, Victoria* |
| **Bus**: | 13, 16, 38, 52, 390, N16, N38 |
| **Cycle Hire**: | Buckingham Gate, Storey's Gate |

## Accessibility ♿

This is a flat road with ramps for crossing at appropriate locations and should present no issues for those with limited mobility.

## Best time of year/day

During the summer the sun will rise behind Admiralty Arch casting a warm, rich light over the trees along The Mall and also ensuring the sky remains blue. This works very well when set behind the green trees and rich colours of flags when they are present. Towards the end of the day, shoot from the Buckingham Palace end towards Admiralty Arch as the sun will light the trees in the opposite direction. At sunset shoot towards Buckingham Palace once again to catch any colour in the clouds. Alternatively, visit at night when it's possible to shoot traffic streaks on The Mall, although traffic is limited and with the traffic lights it can be tricky to get the timing just right for exposures.

## Opening hours

The State Rooms of Buckingham Palace are open for visitors throughout the Annual Summer Opening in Aug and Sept.

20th July to 31st Aug 9.30am–7.30pm (Last Admission 5.15pm)
1st to 29th Sept 9.30am–6.30pm (Last Admission 4.15pm)

## Admission prices (2019)

**The State Rooms.**

| | |
|---|---|
| **Adults**: | £25.00 |
| **Under 5s**: | Free |
| **Children** (aged 5–17): | £14.00 |
| **Students** (with ID): | £22.80 |
| **Seniors** (aged 60+): | £22.80 |
| **Family** (2 Adults and 3 Children): | £64.00 |

**Royal Day Out (The State Rooms, the Royal Mews and The Queen's Gallery.**

| | |
|---|---|
| **Adults**: | £45.00 |
| **Under 5s**: | Free |
| **Children** (aged 5–17): | £24.50 |
| **Students** (with ID): | £40.00 |
| **Seniors** (aged 60+): | £40.00 |
| **Family** (2 Adults and 3 Children): | £114.50 |

More details can be found at: *buckinghampalace.co.uk*

**Above**: *Buckingham Palace in autumn from Green Park. Canon 5D IV, 24–70mm at 40mm, ISO 200, 1/125s at f/8. Nov.*

*Snow in Green Park, looking towards the palace. Sony A6000, 16–50mm at 29mm, ISO 100, 1/200s at f/5. Feb.*

*The flag-lined Mall leading to Buckingham Palace. Canon 5D II, 70–200mm at 70mm, ISO 200, 1/250s at f/11. May.*

## The Mall ♿

There are two key spots on The Mall from which to shoot images, the first of which is from just in front of Admiralty Arch: the centre arch is only opened on ceremonial occasions so it's an ideal place to set up your tripod for a shot along The Mall. The second spot is at the junction of The Mall and Horse Guards Parade; there is a crossing here that you can safely stand by to get shots towards Buckingham Palace. You can use a zoom lens to compress the view down The Mall and still be able to capture Buckingham Palace in the centre of the image, ensuring it's large enough to be recognisable.

Most of the year no flags line The Mall but on state occasions the flags of the attending head of state will be raised alternately with the Union Jack. During the summer months you'll find flags raised more than during the winter months. The best time to shoot this classic location is early morning, when a ceremonial occasion is scheduled for the following days. This often results in Union Jack flags being raised all the way along The Mall. In the morning, if shooting from Admiralty Arch, the sun will rise behind you, leading to a rich blue sky overhead. If you get there early on the day of an event, you may find The Mall completely empty and it's an opportunity not to be missed.

On days when there is traffic along The Mall, pick a time before or after the main 8–9am rush hour; at this time you're more likely to be able to isolate a single London cab heading towards you.

Once you have the classic shot down The Mall consider isolating the flags to make interesting compositions with London cabs or the occasional horse-drawn carriage that may be on the move along The Mall. The army and those responsible for maintaining the royal carriages will sometimes use The Mall to transfer vehicles between locations for repair or cleaning so keep an ear out for the clattering of hooves when you're there.

## Changing of The Guard on The Mall ♿

At midday Monday to Friday during summer a marching band will proceed from Buckingham Palace to St James's Palace to change the guard. This is a prime time to catch an interesting image of the band marching along the western end of The Mall, before they turn north towards St James's Palace.

*Opposite top: Autumn fog on The Mall. Sony A6000, 16–50mm at 50mm, ISO 640, 1/20s at f/8. Nov. **Bottom**: Taxi passing along The Mall. Sony A6000, 16–50mm at 31mm, ISO 100, 1/400s at f/5.6. Apr.*

Green Park lies to the north of Buckingham Palace and is one of the three main Royal Parks in central London. The triangular-shaped park covers forty-seven acres, has no lakes and, unlike the other parks, no flowerbed arrangements either. The park in fact has a grisly past: it's believed the area was originally a swamp used to dispose of those who died of leprosy in the city. It's regarded as one of the more sedate parks, consisting as it does of trees growing in grassy areas, apart from the two central walkways leading from Piccadilly to Buckingham Palace. The rest of it feels more natural and less regimented than other parks.

*Frozen leaves in Green Park. NEX-C3, E 18–55mm at 32mm, ISO 500, 1/160s at f/4. Dec.*

The far western end sees the park rise slightly and this is a great spot to shoot images of the park's landscape. A few squirrels live in the park but they're not as tame or abundant as those in St James's Park to the southeast.

Located at the far western end of Green Park is the Royal Airforce Bomber Command Memorial. It was erected in 2012 and funded mostly by donations from the public, with a campaign spearheaded by Bee Gees member Robin Gibb. Made from Portland stone, the aluminium roof was part constructed from metal salvaged from a Canadian Halifax bomber that crashed into a Belgian swamp in 1944. The Halifax was pulled from the swamp, the bodies of the crew interred with full military honours, and the remains of the aircraft sent to Canada for the restoration of another Halifax aircraft. The rest was used to construct the memorial's roof. At the centre of the memorial stands a 9-foot high representation of a returning bomber crew fresh from their plane.

*The eastern walkway, Green Park. Canon 5D II, 70–200mm at 180mm, ISO 200, 1/30s at f/8. Oct.*

## What to shoot and viewpoints

### Viewpoint 1 – East Walkway ♿

Approach from Green Park Underground station at the northern tip of the park and you'll emerge up along the ramp that leads south from the ticket hall. This will lead you straight to the fountain of the Goddess Diana, located at the furthest northern point of the park. Take the short path east towards the buildings past the concession stand. You'll find yourself on a wide downward-sloping path with buildings to your left and a lamp-lined railing to your right. Follow the path downward and it will begin to curve away to the left. During summer and autumn this spot makes for a wonderful tree-lined image with old-style gas-lamps (they are genuine gas-powered lamps) peeking through the foliage. Look for a couple walking hand-in-hand ahead of you – the colourful foliage will add a superb backdrop, especially in autumn. The natural lead line of the black painted railing helps to constrain the viewer's eye and lead it through the image. As you reach the bottom of the short hill, the path leads in a straight line to The Mall and here once again the black railing offers a very strong lead line through any photograph you take.

*Heavy snowfall in Green Park. Sony A6000, 16–50mm at 36mm, ISO 100, 1/250s at f/5.6. Feb.*

*Green Park in autumn, looking south down the eastern walkway. Canon 5D II, 70–200mm at 200mm, ISO 200, 1/45s at f/8. Oct.*

*Looking south in the park to Buckingham Palace. Canon 5D II. 70–200mm at 70mm, ISO 200, 1/60s at f/8. Oct.*

## Viewpoint 2 – The Broad Walk ♿

Bisecting the park at a slight angle from Piccadilly to Buckingham Palace are two tree-lined walkways. The trees are very mature and set equidistant from one another, forming the classic repeating pattern photographers love so much. During bright summer days the play of light and shadow created by the trees along the two pathways offers some great photographic opportunities. During autumn the walkways will fill with thousands of leaves shed by the trees lining the routes and it's impossible to resist a shot of a lone person or a couple strolling up the path from the bottom towards Piccadilly. Try a midrange lens to capture people or a zoom lens to compress the perspective and pull the trees tighter together, emphasising the repeating pattern of the tree trunks. The western pathway leads downhill into a thick copse of trees at the bottom and during summer and autumn, as the sun rises in the east, it casts light through the closely set trees by Buckingham Palace ensnaring the warm morning glow before the sun heads skywards.

*Autumn walk in Green Park. Canon 5D II, 70–200mm at 97mm, ISO 200, 1/15s at f/8. Oct.*

## Viewpoint 3 – Commonwealth Memorials and Constitution Hill ♿

The main road that runs from Wellington Arch along the southern side of Green Park towards Buckingham Palace is known as Constitution Hill. Located at the western end by Wellington Arch are the Commonwealth war memorials to those from countries including South Africa, Australia and Indonesia, who gave their lives in service of the Allies during World War II. These memorials are quite impressive and on bright sunny days they can soak up sunlight and stand in stark contrast to the surrounding greenery.

Shoot east along the cycle track that runs alongside Constitution Hill, using a zoom lens; it's a must-have shot and works especially well on later autumn mornings when a slight mist may appear. At night there are traffic streak shots to be had shooting west uphill from Buckingham Palace along Constitution Hill road.

## How to get here

The best option is to arrive by Tube at Green Park Underground station. This has an exit that leads from the ticket hall into the far northwest corner of the park next to the eastern walkway. If coming from Piccadilly Circus, simply walk along Piccadilly, to the entrance of Green Park just past the Ritz hotel. If coming from St James's Park, walk towards Buckingham Palace and cross over in front of the Victoria statue. Directly to the north lies Green Park.

| | |
|---|---|
| **Location Lat/Long**: | 51.50398, -0.14357 |
| **Location Postcode**: | SW1A 1AA |
| **Underground & Lines**: | Green Park, Hyde Park Corner: *Jubilee, Piccadilly, Victoria* |
| **Bus**: | 9, 14, 19, 22, 38, N9, N19, N22, N38 |
| **Cycle Hire**: | Green Park Station, Wellington Arch |

## Accessibility ♿

All locations and viewpoints are on paved paths and walkways and should present few accessibility issues. Note that the east walkway gradient is a little steep and stretches for some distance from top to bottom. It's accessible to most but should be avoided if your mobility is severely restricted.

## Best time of year/day

Green Park is open all year, day and night. The best time is early morning to early evening – especially if you wish to capture images of the gas lamps in balance with the park's surrounding landscape. The best time of year is definitely in autumn, much like St James's Park. Should London see a winter snowfall, it's not to be missed.

**Safety Warning**: London is a very safe city; crime in the city centre is quite rare but do exercise caution and care. Please be extremely careful if you are in any of the Royal Parks during the hours of darkness. There are police patrols but the parks are often lit by gas lamps and can be very dark indeed at night, with some areas not always covered by CCTV. On occasion there have been rare incidents of violent crime reported so please be sensible and go in pairs or groups if you intend to visit the parks after midnight.

## VP 1 – East Walkway
| | |
|---|---|
| **Location Lat/Long**: | 51.50583, -0.14159 |
| **Location Postcode**: | SW1A 1AA |

## VP 2 – The Broad Walk
| | |
|---|---|
| **Location Lat/Long**: | 51.50438, -0.14328 |
| **Location Postcode**: | SW1A 1AA |

## VP 3 – Commonwealth Memorials and Constitution Hill
| | |
|---|---|
| **Location Lat/Long**: | 51.50239, -0.14368 |
| **Location Postcode**: | SW1A 1AA |

## VP 4 – Bomber Command Memorial
| | |
|---|---|
| **Location Lat/Long**: | 51.50335, -0.14894 |
| **Location Postcode**: | SW1A 1AA |

## VP 5 – Royal Gun Salutes
| | |
|---|---|
| **Location Lat/Long**: | 51.50284, -0.14495 |
| **Location Postcode**: | SW1A 1AA |

*Snowfall in the park. Sony A6000, 16–50mm at 24mm, ISO 100, 1/400s at f/5. Feb.*

*Couple kissing in Green Park. Canon 5D II, 70–200mm at 200mm, ISO 200, 1/180s at f/4. Oct.*

*Top*: The Bomber Command memorial, Green Park. Sony A6000, Fisheye 8mm at 8mm, ISO 200, 1/160s at f/8. Nov.

*Middle*: Pilot on the Bomber Command Memorial. NEX-C3, E 18–55mm at 27mm, ISO 200, 1/200s at f/4.5. Dec.

*Above*: Firing of the gun salute during Trooping the Colour. Canon 5D II, 70–200mm at 200mm, ISO 200, 1/350s at f/6.7. June.

*Top*: Bomber Command Memorial. Sony A6000, 16–50mm at 33mm, ISO 160, 1/60s at f/5. Nov.

*Above*: Cavalry assembling for the gun salute in Green Park. Canon 5D II, 70–200mm at 81mm, ISO 400, 1/250s at f/6.7. June.

*Opposite top left*: Light trails leading up Constitution Hill. Canon 5D IV, 70–200mm at 100mm, ISO 200, 30s at f/16. Dec.
*Top right*: Constitution Hill, Green Park. Canon 5D IV, 70–200mm at 150mm, ISO 200, 1/15s at f/11. Feb.
*Bottom*: Constitution Hill memorial. Sony A6000, Fisheye 8mm at 8mm, ISO 100, 1/200s at f/8. July.

*Cavalry assembling on Constitution Hill. Sony A6000, 16–50mm at 41mm, ISO 125, 1/80s at f/5.6. June.*

### Viewpoint 4 – Bomber Command Memorial ♿

While in Green Park don't miss the opportunity to see the Bomber Command Memorial at the far western end. It's a magnificent memorial to the 55,000 who gave their lives in service of the bombing raids during World War II. There are quite a few photographic opportunities offered by this huge monument. Using a wide-angle lens on a bright day enables you to capture the entire interior of the memorial with the crew at the centre looking out into the light.

### Viewpoint 5 – Royal Gun Salutes ♿

During special state occasions such as Coronation Day (3rd June), The Queen's Official Birthday (the second Saturday in June) or state visits, Green Park is used to host the cavalry and their cannon salutes. A 21-gun salute will be fired, usually around 12pm (but not on Sundays). Spectators will be held back around 250m from the gun positions so a zoom lens is a must for detail shots of

the cannon as they fire. The best position is on the path that leads from the western corner and along the northern side of the open space directly adjacent to Constitution Hill. Careful timing is required to capture a cannon blast and the smoke leaving the barrel but you'll have several chances as there are usually five or six guns. Aim to shoot the guns and crew of the nearest two cannon if you have a 200mm lens. As the cavalry arrives and departs there are some great chances to capture the commanders on their mounts. See the notice boards around the park or the website (*www.royalparks.org.uk*) for a full list of events and dates.

*Opposite: Mounted cavalry officer, Trooping the Colour. Canon 5D II, 70–200mm at 155mm, ISO 200, 1/180s at f/6.7. June.*

**Situated at south-east corner of Hyde Park, where six streets converge, is Hyde Park Corner, the main features of which are the Wellington Arch and the Ionic Screen. They were both designed by Decimus Barton during a renovation of the area beginning in 1825 to make the area rival the splendour of European capital cities.**

The Duke of Wellington's residence Apsley House is located nearby and several monuments around the area pay tribute to the Duke and his service to the nation. The arch was originally the gateway arch into Green Park and Buckingham Palace but was moved after serious traffic congestion. It now sits at the top of Constitution Hill. When it was first constructed, this victory arch had a statue of the Duke of Wellington on top, proclaiming the defeat of Napoleon, but complaints about how ridiculous the statue looked in relation to the arch led to the latter's removal. The statue remained initially, however, when the arch was moved to its present location in 1883, a Quadriga statue – an Angel of Peace riding in a horse-drawn chariot – was placed on top instead. The statue of the Duke of Wellington was quietly relocated to Aldershot.

## What to shoot and viewpoints

The two main points of interest here are Wellington's Arch and the Ionic Screen. The arch, being so large and made from white stone, reflects colours and tones wonderfully at sunrise and sunset. The statue atop makes a very imposing subject to shoot from the front or rear, using either a mid-range lens or focussing on details with a zoom lens. During summer, when the surrounding trees have foliage, they make a superb way to block empty sky and give a sense of depth to any composition, using the arch as the main subject. While you're there, consider the details of the arch – the stark contours of the stone caught in harsh sunlight make for interesting high-contrast images suitable for wall-hung prints.

If you have a zoom lens, you can use it to isolate details. Move across the southern road crossing and you can shoot a close up of the statue atop the arch, directly facing into

a deep blue or cloud-strewn sky. When processed with strong contrast, the heroic posture of the statue really comes into its own.

The Ionic Screen to the north of the arch is the perfect place to view the cavalry arriving from the barracks in Kensington. Around 11am each day they pass through the arch on their way through Hyde Park Corner and down Constitution Hill. Shoot them in front of the screen or the arch.

Finally, as you make your way into Hyde Park, make a quick detour to the ornate Queen Elizabeth Gate with its Act of Union emblems of the lion and the unicorn.

For a peek into the Queen's back gardens, you can visit the balconies of Wellington Arch, and historic exhibits are frequently held at the arch. Go to: *english-heritage.org.uk* for opening times and tickets.

## How to get here

Use the Piccadilly line to get to Hyde Park Corner station. Exit the station and you'll arrive directly at this location. Alternatively, a more pleasant route is via Green Park: make your way to Green Park via Tube or bus. If you arrive via Green Park Station, or come along Piccadilly from Piccadilly Circus, keep walking west along Piccadilly until you reach Wellington Arch at Hyde Park Corner. If you do walk along Piccadilly, I would advise nipping into Green Park and taking the pathway on the north side of the park. It's away from the traffic and while the noise won't vanish, it's a much more pleasant way to get there than along the roadside.

| | |
|---|---|
| **Location Lat/Long**: | 51.50203, -0.15129 |
| **Location Postcode**: | W1J 7JZ |
| **Underground & Lines**: | Hyde Park Corner: *Piccadilly* |
| **Bus**: | 6, 14, 19, 38, 74, N19, N38, N97 |
| **Cycle Hire**: | Hyde Park Corner, Wellington Arch |

### Accessibility ♿

All locations and viewpoints are on ordinary city streets and should present no accessibility issues.

### Best time of year/day

Access to Hyde Park Corner and the Wellington Arch are available 24 hours a day all year round. While it can get busy during the day, people are mostly passing through to other places and won't stop long. The best time for people-free images is first thing in the morning as the sun rises behind the arch. At night it's illuminated, creating a highly recommended viewpoint. Summer and autumn offer colourful foliage that can add foreground interest.

***Above***: *Wellington Arch statue, Hyde Park Corner. Canon 5D II, 70–200mm at 121mm, ISO 200, 1/180s at f/8. Oct.*

***Below***: *Wellington Arch at night. Canon 5D IV, 24–70mm at 24mm, ISO 200, 20s at f/8, tripod. Nov.*

Victoria Street links Victoria Station to the Palace of Westminster in the east. The area is the main commercial centre of the borough of the City of Westminster.

Most people visit the area by way of passing through Victoria Station on their way to somewhere or to reach the Palace of Westminster. There are however, several notable landmarks in this small and often overlooked part of London that is named after Queen Victoria.

The Victoria Palace Theatre, originally built in 1832, has a large golden statue of the Russian prima ballerina Anna Pavlova atop its highest dome. The statue was removed in 1939 for cleaning, promptly lost and subsequently replaced by a replica. Little Ben clock stands opposite the theatre on a traffic island. Erected in 1892 as a gesture of Franco-British friendship by the French oil company Elf Aquitaine Ltd, it mimics its much larger cousin, Big Ben.

Westminster Cathedral, situated close to Victoria Station, is one of the more unusual church buildings in London. Designed and built by John Bentley in 1903, it has a Neo-Byzantine design made entirely from brick with no steel reinforcements – quite remarkable considering it was built in 1903 when the new steel and concrete materials were being used so prevalently. Its unusual red- and white-striped brickwork is a sight to see.

The Blewcoat School building is situated on Caxton Street. It was built in 1709 as a schoolhouse for the poor and operated until 1926. It was subsequently used by the National Trust, first as their headquarters and later as a gift shop, until 2013 when it was sold to bridal gown designer Ian Stewart. The square building still retains many of the exterior designs that reveal its original purpose as a schoolhouse, including the distinctive blue-coated statue above the entrance.

*Windows on Lewisham Street close to Victoria Street. NEX-C3, E 18–55mm at 20mm, ISO 1000, 1/160s at f/4. Dec.*

## What to shoot and viewpoints

### Viewpoint 1 – Upper Grosvenor Garden ♿

This small triangular-shaped garden, located precariously on a traffic island, is small but features a rather dramatic bronze statue of a lioness chasing down a gazelle and makes a very interesting image to take home. Also located in the garden is the Rifle Brigade Monument. It can be shot from the front but I feel that with the large open space directly opposite the gardens (the rear garden of Buckingham Palace!) you can position the lone soldier against this backdrop, creating a forlorn image of the figure staring out into a vast open sky.

### Viewpoint 2 – Victoria Square ♿

A tiny garden that can be measured in feet and inches rather than yards, Victoria Square offers the unique opportunity to shoot a statue of a very young Queen Victoria. Most statues of the formidable royal are based on her later years, but this particular statue is of a young, innocent princess about to take the world by storm. In summer the foliage and blooms bring this little square alive and offer different ways to shoot the statue, using the trees, bushes and flowers to frame it. The garden itself is locked so poke your lens through the bars.

*Opposite top: VP1. Statue in Grosvenor Gardens, Victoria. Canon 5D IV, 24–70mm at 40mm, ISO 400, 1/250s at f/8. June. Left: VP2. Statue of young Queen Victoria. Canon 5D IV, 24–70mm at 63mm, ISO 200, 1/250s at f/8. June. Right: Window bars and shadows, Chelsea. Canon 5D IV, 24–70mm at 70mm, ISO 200, 1/500s at f/8. July. Bottom right: VP2. Victoria Square. Canon 5D IV, 24–70mm at 70mm, ISO 200, 1/350s at f/4. June.*

*VP3. Gold statue atop the Victoria Palace Theatre. Canon 5D II, 70–200mm at 200mm, ISO 200, 1/750s at f/8. June.*

## Viewpoint 3 – Victoria Palace Theatre ♿

The Victoria Palace Theatre, a gleaming white stone building located directly opposite Victoria Station, is hard to miss. There are two interesting viewpoints: one with Little Ben in the foreground; the other is found east along Victoria Street, where you can shoot the building on its corner. The first viewpoint is easy to shoot and works well on a bright sunny day, which will illuminate both subjects and make the building look brilliant white. The traffic island also functions as a crossing so it can be tricky to shoot during busy periods but patience will be rewarded. Moving east along Victoria Street opens up the opportunity to shoot the corner of the theatre and also get a clear shot of the gold statue of Pavlova. Even using a midrange lens of 24–70mm you'll be able to capture the building and its statue. Use a 200mm or greater zoom lens to isolate the statue.

*Opposite top left: VP3. Little Ben clock tower, Victoria Street. Canon 5D IV, 24–70mm at 46mm, ISO 200, 1/750s at f/8. July.*

## How to get here

### VP 1 – Lower Grosvenor Garden
Exit Victoria Station to the north straight on to Victoria Street and turn immediately left towards the parks. Follow Victoria Street to the west as it curves to the right, heading past Lower and Upper Grosvenor gardens.

| | |
|---|---|
| **Location Lat/Long**: | 51.49762, -0.14685 |
| **Location Postcode**: | SW1W 0DH |
| **Bus**: | 2, 13, 16, 36, 38, 52, 148, 390, N2, N16, N38 |
| **Cycle Hire**: | Allington Street, Eaton Square |

### VP 2 – Victoria Square
Exit Upper Grosvenor Garden, using the nearest crossing, then head to the eastern side of Victoria Street at the intersection where the two pointed ends of Lower and Upper Grosvenor gardens meet. From here, head into Beeston Place. Walk about 100m past the Goring hotel and Victoria Square is first on your right. Take the lane into Victoria Square, where you'll find the statue of Queen Victoria.

| | |
|---|---|
| **Location Lat/Long**: | 51.49772, -0.14491 |
| **Location Postcode**: | SW1W 0QY |
| **Bus**: | 2, 13, 16, 36, 38, 52, 148, 390, N2, N16, N38 |
| **Cycle Hire**: | Allington Street, Eaton Square |

## VP 3 – Victoria Palace Theatre

Leave Victoria Square via the southeast exit, turn left into Buckingham Palace Road and proceed north for about 50m, until you come to the main road, Bressenden Place. Follow this road to your right, heading south until you come to the fork in the road. Victoria Palace Theatre is to your right-hand side. It's best to cross over Victoria Street for a clearer view.

| | |
|---|---|
| **Location Lat/Long:** | 51.49693, -0.1418 |
| **Location Postcode:** | SW1E 5EA |
| **Bus:** | 11, 24, 148, 211, 507, 211, N11, N136 |
| **Cycle Hire:** | Allington Street |

## VP 4 – Westminster Cathedral

Proceed east along Victoria Street for around 100m. Westminster Cathedral is to your right, set back from Victoria Street.

| | |
|---|---|
| **Location Lat/Long:** | 51.49563, -0.1387 |
| **Location Postcode:** | SW1P 1LT |
| **Bus:** | 11, 24, 148, 211, 507, 211, N11, N136 |
| **Cycle Hire:** | Ashley Place |

### Opening hours

Mon to Sat 10am–4pm. Sun 10am–3pm.

### Admission prices (2019)

| | |
|---|---|
| **Adults:** | £4.50 |
| **Children** (aged 5–15): | £2.30 |
| **Students** (with ID): | £3.00 |
| **Seniors** (aged 60+): | £3.00 |

## VP 5 – Ian Stuart Blewcoat

For the Blewcoat School, proceed along Victoria Street for around 500m until you reach the major junction with the B323 and The Albert pub on the opposite corner. Head north up the B323 and, as it begins to curve to the left (after about 250m), you'll see the rear of the Blewcoat School in the open area to your right.

| | |
|---|---|
| **Location Lat/Long:** | 51.49853, -0.13604 |
| **Location Postcode:** | SW1H 0PY |
| **Underground & Lines:** | St James's Park: *Circle and District* |
| **Bus:** | 24, 148, 211, N44, N136 |
| **Cycle Hire:** | Buckingham Gate |

### Accessibility

All locations and viewpoints are on ordinary city streets and should present no accessibility issues. If shooting from a restricted height, such as from a wheelchair, you may find the view of the Queen Victoria statue in Victoria Square partly obscured by the gates.

### Best time of year/day

Can be shot all year round, day and night. Some of the gardens and parks may be closed at night or have restricted access. The best times of the year are summer, for blooms and foliage, and autumn (in the parks and gardens) for seasonal colour.

*Above: VP4. Unusual brickwork patterns of Westminster Cathedral on Victoria Street. Canon 5D IV, 24–70mm at 24mm, ISO 200, 1/500s at f/8. July.*

*Above*: VP4. Detail of the mosaic, Westminster Cathedral. Canon 5D IV, 24–70mm at 43mm, ISO 100, 1/45s at f/4. May.

*Below*: VP5. Blewcoat Building, Victoria. Canon 5D IV, 24–70mm at 70mm, ISO 200, 1/45s at f/5.6. May.

## Viewpoint 4 – Westminster Cathedral ♿

Walk east along Victoria Street and you'll find the cathedral to your right next to a large piazza-style space. The viewpoints to capture the entire building are limited and work by shooting with a standard lens from the side of Victoria Street. As you get closer to the cathedral, look to isolate some of the wonderful details and be sure to capture the image and inscription above the main entrance. The cathedral is open during service times and you're free to walk in and enjoy its impressive interior.

## Viewpoint 5 – Ian Stuart Blewcoat ♿

Blewcoat School is a very small building but the key to shooting this interesting little landmark is to shoot the details, especially the blue-coated statue above the main entrance. Be sure to capture the flower displays on the front of the building.

*Opposite*: VP5. Blewcoat House, Victoria. Sony A6000, 16–50mm at 16mm, ISO 100, 1/320s at f/5. June.

Pimlico is an affluent area just south of Victoria, its southern boundary formed by the River Thames. The area was primarily designed by 19th-century town planner Thomas Cubitt and it is known for its parks, squares and Regency architecture, much of which is protected; Pimlico, despite its small size, has over 350 Grade II listed buildings. The area was home to Winston Churchill, designer Laura Ashley and the actor Laurence Olivier.

## What to shoot and viewpoints

### Viewpoint 1 – Pimlico Underground Station

If visiting Tate Britain, you'll most likely arrive via Pimlico underground station, one of the last few stations to be completed on the Victoria line. The station's key features are the wonderful prints of famous pieces of art that adorn the tiles in the entrance tunnels. Tate Britain has housed la crème de la crème of British art and Pimlico station celebrates this. As you exit the ticket hall you will immediately see the decorated tiles at the top of the stairs that lead into the exit tunnels. This is a very low light situation, a high ISO works best, and space is tight, so bring a wide-angle lens.

### Viewpoint 2 – Bessborough and St George's Square Gardens ♿

The area around Pimlico and Victoria is built up with few green spaces, however there is respite and sanctuary from the purely urban: located to the east of Pimlico station is a small green square known as Bessborough Gardens, and to the south of the station is St George's Square Gardens – both are worth a visit. They are quite similar – both are tree-lined with open green spaces and each has a fountain in the grounds. Bessborough, the smaller of the two has houses directly adjacent to it and is only open during the daytime. St George's Square, as suggested by the name, is located at the centre of a rectangle of Georgian townhouses. Again, it's only open during the daytime but its open spaces are much larger and it has more facilities than Bessborough.

## How to get here

### Accessibility ♿

With the exception of Pimlico station, all locations and viewpoints are on ordinary city streets and should present no accessibility issues. The vast majority of sections within the Tate Britain gallery are fully accessible. Pimlico station however, does not have step-free access or platform-to-entrance lifts. The art displays in the entrance tunnel are on a ramp so they are accessible to wheelchair users. If you wish to see these, I advise travelling by bus or heading to Victoria and proceeding from there at street level.

### Best time of year/day

Can be shot all year round, day and night. Some of the gardens and parks may be closed or have restricted access at night. Tate Britain is only open during normal visiting hours. Pimlico station may be closed late at night on weekdays.

### VP 1 – Pimlico Underground Station

Take the Victoria Line Tube to Pimlico station and exit via Bessborough Street in order to see the artworks adorning the tunnel walls.

| | |
|---|---|
| **Location Lat/Long**: | 51.48922, -0.13342 |
| **Location Postcode**: | SW1V 2JA |
| **Bus**: | 24, 360, C10 |
| **Cycle Hire**: | Rampayne Street, St George's Square |

### VP 2 – Bessborough Gardens

Leaving the station, take Bessborough Street and walk around the curve in the road heading east. You will arrive at Vauxhall Bridge Road. Stay on the south side of the road and turn to your right: you'll see Bessborough Gardens.

| | |
|---|---|
| **Location Lat/Long**: | 51.48863, -0.1305 |
| **Location Postcode**: | SW1V 1HJ |
| **Bus**: | 2, 36, 88, 185, N2, N136 |
| **Cycle Hire**: | Vauxhall Bridge |

### St George's Square Gardens

Leave Vauxhall Bridge and head back to the junction of Vauxhall Bridge Road and Grosvenor Road leading to the west. Stay on the south side of Grosvenor Road for about 250 yards until you find access to the Thames Path. Use this to head back to Vauxhall Bridge for step-free access to the southwest river path. By way of interest, this is the outfall for the Tyburn river that flows under London streets all the way from Belsize Park in north London. Continue for another 250m west along Grosvenor Road until you reach a small park to your left by the river – this is the Pimlico Garden and Shrubbery. Cross Grosvenor Road and head north to reach St George's Square Garden. Enter where you see the small circular fountain.

| | |
|---|---|
| **Location Lat/Long**: | 51.48747, -0.13481 |
| **Location Postcode**: | SW1V 3RD |
| **Bus**: | 2, 36, 88, 185, 360, N2, N136 |
| **Cycle Hire**: | St George's Square |

*Top left*: VP1. Pimlico Station. Canon 5D IV, 17–40mm at 17mm, ISO 800, 1/45s at f/4. June. **Right**: VP1. Pimlico Station. Canon 5D IV, 17–40mm at 17mm, ISO 800, 1/30s at f/4. June.

*Above left*: VP2. Bessborough Gardens. Canon 5D IV, 24–70mm at 70mm, ISO 100, 1/250s at f/8. June. **Middle**: VP2. Bessborough Gardens fountain. Canon 5D IV, 24–70mm at 59mm, ISO 200, 1/60s at f/8. June. **Right**: VP2. Bessborough Gardens. Canon 5D IV, 24–70mm at 38mm, ISO 200, 1/30s at f/8. June.

*Far left*: VP2. Bessborough Gardens fountain. Canon 5D IV, 24–70mm at 38mm, ISO 200, 1/45s at f/8. June. *Left*: VP2. Pimlico townhouse. Canon 5D IV, 24–70mm at 24mm, ISO 200, 1/30s at f/8. June.

*Above*: VP3. Tate Britain main entrance. Canon 5D II, 17–40mm at 17mm, ISO 125, 1/200s at f/5.6. May.

### Viewpoint 3 – Tate Britain ♿

Tate Britain, formally the National Gallery of British Art, is the oldest of the Tate galleries of England alongside Tate Modern, Tate Liverpool and Tate St Ives. Situated on Millbank close to Vauxhall Bridge, the gallery opened in 1897 and houses some of the most precious and valuable pieces of art in the UK, including the entire J.W. Turner collection. Prior to 2000, and the opening of the Tate Modern along South Bank, Tate Britain housed both classical and modern collections. A renovation in 2012 saw the opening of nine new galleries and a reinforced floor to accommodate larger, heavier pieces of sculpture. It is one of the largest museums in the country.

The Tate has no issues with people taking photographs of the displays and art, although flash photography and tripods are not permitted, so use a high ISO. I have concentrated here on exploring the architecture of the building – its interior and exterior – and exhibits in the grounds.

From the moment you enter the classic portico entrance, you can't help but feel inspired. The entrance hall is a joy; situated right underneath the glass dome, during bright days the hall lights up and with a very wide-angle or fisheye lens, you can capture the entire area. There are some wonderful plays of light, from the lower hallways (close to the cafeteria in the basement) to the enormous central hall.

The large central gallery sometimes hosts performances and dance displays and I often find a great challenge in shooting images of the performers and the audience, trying to capture the expressions on their faces.

### VP 3 – Tate Britain

Leave Bessborough Gardens by the same exit onto Vauxhall Bridge Road and cross over at the nearest crossing. Head towards the bridge and take Millbank, which leads towards the river around the large tall apartment block by the bridge. Head east along Millbank for around 500m until you see Tate Britain on the west side of Millbank; its grand facade is hard to miss.

| | |
|---|---|
| **Location Lat/Long**: | 51.4907, -0.12663 |
| **Location Postcode**: | SW1P 4RG |
| **Riverboat**: | Millbank Pier – **Tate to Tate Tours** – The Tate Boat runs every 40 minutes during gallery opening times between Tate Britain and Tate Modern. The Tate Boat is operated by MBNA Thames Clippers. |
| **Bus**: | 2, 36, 87, 88, 185, 436, C10 |
| **Cycle Hire**: | Millbank House, Rampayne Street, Regency Street, Vauxhall Bridge |

### Opening hours

Mon to Sun 10am–6pm. Closed 24–26 Dec.

### Admission price (2019)

Free.

*VP3. Lower ground floor of Tate Britain. Sony A6000, Fisheye 8mm at 8mm, ISO 200, 1/100s at f/8. May.*

The museum itself is huge and, much like its counterpart, the Tate Modern, you will find so many interesting things to shoot as you explore – it's a composition playground! Be sure to head down the spiral staircase to the cafeteria and shoot the curves and lines of the marble staircase as it ascends to ground level. Patience is a must as it does get busy but you'll be well rewarded. I urge you to explore the whole museum.

*VP3. Staircase in the entrance hall of Tate Britain. Sony A6000, Fisheye 8mm at 8mm, ISO 200, 1/125s at f/8. May.*

**Left**: *VP3. Staircase inside Tate Britain. Sony A6000, Fisheye 8mm at 8mm, ISO 200, 1/60s at f/8. May.*

**Top right**: *VP3. Tower block by Vauxhall Bridge. Canon 5D IV, 24–70mm at 28mm, ISO 200, 1/250s at f/8. July.*

**Opposite right**: *VP3. Love, Aluminium by Lorenzo Quinn by Vauxhall Bridge. Sony A6000, Fisheye 8mm at 8mm, ISO 200, 1/2500s at f/8. May.*

*VP4. Vauxhall Bridge and buildings. Canon 5D II, 24–70mm at 24mm, ISO 100, 30s at f/7.1, tripod, LEE ND 0.9 grad. May.*

### Viewpoint 4 – Vauxhall Bridge &

Vauxhall Bridge was built in 1906 and has remained largely unchanged. Its construction was delayed by five years after the foundations and piers were in place as it was discovered the soft river clay wouldn't support the planned concrete bridge. Steel was used instead.

The bridge features eight statues located at the span points on the bridge. Frederick Pomeroy designed the four statues on the upstream piers: *Agriculture, Architecture, Engineering* and *Pottery* and Alfred Drury the four on their downstream counterparts: *Science, Fine Arts, Local Government* and *Education*. The statues are not visible from the bridge and go largely unnoticed, but from either side they are easy to photograph with a telephoto lens.

Located to the southwest side of the bridge is a building that looks as if it were built by the Aztecs. This is St George Wharf and Tower, built between 2010 and 2012 – a mixed-use riverside development of offices, retail units and restaurants. To the north of the bridge on the Vauxhall side is another striking building, and probably one of London's worst kept secrets: it's believed to be the headquarters of the SIS and MI6, the UK's primary intelligence service … although if you ask, no one will confirm or deny it.

A great viewpoint lies riverside here on the Thames Path in front of Tate Britain, where there is a stunning view of Vauxhall Bridge and the south bank of the Thames. This cityscape offers something all year round: shot during the winter months, the sun rises directly over the southern end of the bridge; on summer evenings the bridge is bathed in the glowing sun. Moving to the south of the bridge on the Tate side of the Thames, again on the Thames Path, allows you to photograph the bridge and the St George Wharf and Tower straight on. The buildings are quite low profile with the tower being the only tall building on the horizon, so think in terms of a 16:9 'long and wide' formatted image during editing to create a panoramic feel.

### Viewpoint 5 – Phone boxes on Belgrave Road &

Situated on Belgrave Road at the junction with Warwick Way are four equidistant, free-standing, classic red telephone boxes. There are several places in London where you can find similar collections but they're often tucked out of sight; this particular collection stands out in the open and as they're facing east, they're exposed to direct morning sunlight, making them easy to shoot.

*Opposite top right: VP4. Apartment blocks. NEX-C3, E 18–55mm at 18mm, ISO 200, 1/160s at f/4, tripod, LEE ND 0.9 grad. Dec.*

## VP 4 – Vauxhall Bridge

As you exit the Tate Britain building, cross over Millbank towards the riverside and head towards Vauxhall Bridge, which will be to you right in a westerly direction. A walk along the riverside offers the chance to capture details, and the spot at Riverside Walk Gardens is the best place to shoot the vista of the MI6 building, the bridge and the buildings on the far side of the bridge. Head along the riverside path, up the steps (or go around the apartment block via Millbank, if you prefer), crossing over Vauxhall Bridge Road. You'll find some steps that descend to the south side of Vauxhall Bridge. If you're unable to manage the steps, keep heading for the step-free way to reach the southwest side of Vauxhall Bridge river path.

| | |
|---|---|
| **Location Lat/Long**: | 51.4878, -0.1275 |
| **Location Postcode**: | SW8 2LQ |
| **Riverboat**: | Millbank Pier |
| **Bus**: | 2, 36, 88, 185, 360, N2, N136 |
| **Cycle Hire**: | Millbank House, Rampayne Street, Regency Street, Vauxhall Bridge |

*VP4. Vauxhall Bridge statues. Canon 5D IV, 70–200mm at 200mm, ISO 200, 1/125s at f/6.7. June.*

## VP 5 – Telephone Boxes on Belgrave Road

The four phone boxes stand at the southwest corner of the junction of Belgrave Road and Warwick Way.

| | |
|---|---|
| **Location Lat/Long**: | 51.49175, -0.14128 |
| **Location Postcode**: | SW1V 1RQ |
| **Bus**: | 24 |
| **Cycle Hire**: | Gloucester Street |

*VP5. Four-in-a-row phone boxes, Gloucester Road, Pimlico. Canon 5D IV, 24–70mm at 24mm, ISO 200, 1/250s at f/8. July.*

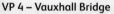

# BATTERSEA, BELGRAVIA & CHELSEA

Battersea, Belgravia and Chelsea are all quieter, more affluent parts of London. Similar to Mayfair, Belgravia and Chelsea were developed during the 17th century by the great and the good as places to escape the hectic city whilst remaining close enough to conduct business daily. Belgravia is well known for its embassies, while Chelsea was an enclave for many renowned artists and writers of the 19th and 20th centuries.

If you have an interest in vexillology (the study of flags) then Belgravia is the place to come; many countries, both large and small, have their embassies in Belgravia and each country's crest and flag adorn these grand buildings.

South of Belgravia lie Chelsea and Kensington. Unlike the City, which is brash and unapologetic about its wealth, Chelsea is more restrained, preferring instead to offer small boutiques and bistros, quiet, stylish residential streets and some interesting photographic opportunities you won't find in other parts of London.

At its southern boundary is the Royal Hospital Chelsea, a unique institution. This armed forces retirement home was designed by Sir Christopher Wren and is home to residents who, on formal occasions, don distinctive red dress uniforms. It's free to enter and it's one of the friendliest places you'll find in London. I highly recommend a visit.

Finally, cross the river into Battersea Park – 200 acres of stunning beauty located just on the edge of the bustling metropolis. Here are yet more gems for the photographer, including the ornate Peace Pagoda, the boating lake and Festival of Britain water gardens.

*Previous spread*: *VP5. Battersea Park boating lake. Canon 5D IV, 24–70mm at 24mm, ISO 200, 1/60s at f/8. June.*

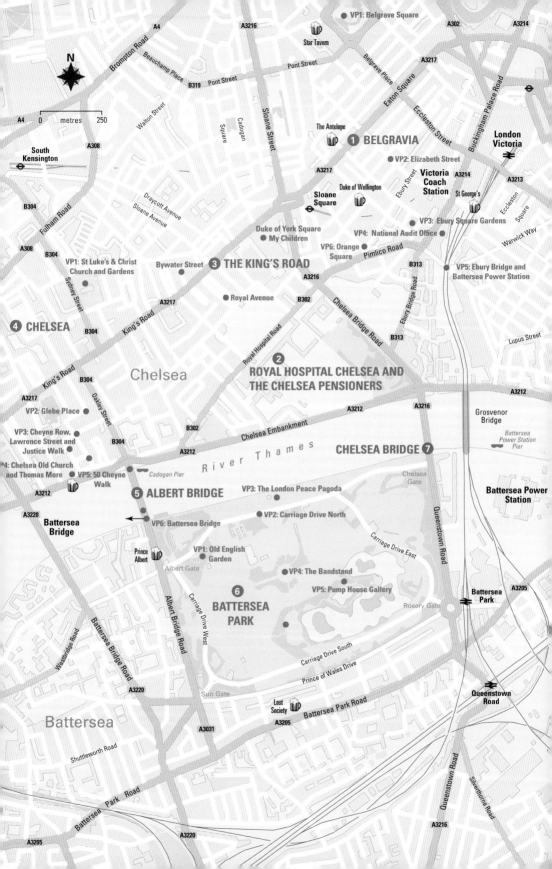

N

A4  0  metres  250

**VP1: Belgrave Square**

Star Tavern

A4    A3216    A302    A3214

Brompton Road    Beauchamp Place    B319    Pont Street    Pont Street    Belgrave Place    Eaton Square    Eccleston Street    Buckingham Palace Road    A3217

Walton Street    Cadogan Square    Sloane Street

The Antelope

**① BELGRAVIA**

South Kensington    A308

A3217    VP2: Elizabeth Street    Ebury Street    Elizabeth Street

**London Victoria**

Draycott Avenue    Sloane Avenue

Duke of Wellington    **Victoria Coach Station**    A3214    A3213    Eccleston Square    St George's

B304

Fulham Road    A308    B304    Sloane Square    Duke of York Square    VP4: National Audit Office    VP3: Ebury Square Gardens    Warwick Way

My Children    VP6: Orange Square    Pimlico Road    B313

VP1: St Luke's & Christ Church and Gardens    Bywater Street    **③ THE KING'S ROAD**    A3216    VP5: Ebury Bridge and Battersea Power Station    Ebury Bridge Road    Lupus Street

Sydney Street

Royal Avenue    B302    Chelsea Bridge Road    B313

**④ CHELSEA**    B304    King's Road    A3217    Royal Hospital Road    A3212    A3216    A3212

Chelsea    **② ROYAL HOSPITAL CHELSEA AND THE CHELSEA PENSIONERS**    Grosvenor Bridge    Battersea Power Station Pier

King's Road    B304    Oakley Street    B302    A3212    Chelsea Embankment    A3212

VP2: Glebe Place    A3217    **CHELSEA BRIDGE ⑦**    **Battersea Power Station**

VP3: Cheyne Row, Lawrence Street and Justice Walk    B304    River Thames    Chelsea Gate    Queenstown Road    A3205

VP4: Chelsea Old Church and Thomas More    VP5: 50 Cheyne Walk    Cadogan Pier    VP3: The London Peace Pagoda    Chelsea Bridge

A3212    **⑤ ALBERT BRIDGE**    VP2: Carriage Drive North

A3220    VP6: Battersea Bridge    Carriage Drive East    **Battersea Park**    A3205

**Battersea Bridge**    Prince Albert    VP1: Old English Garden    Albert Bridge Road    Carriage Drive West    VP4: The Bandstand    VP5: Pump House Gallery    Rosery Gate

Albert Gate    **⑥ BATTERSEA PARK**    **Queenstown Road**

Westbridge Road    Battersea Bridge Road    A3220    Carriage Drive South    Prince of Wales Drive    Queenstown Road    Silverthorne Road

Sun Gate    Lost Society    Battersea Park Road    A3216

**Battersea**    Shuttleworth Road    A3031    A3205

Battersea Park Road    A3205    A3220    A3216

**Belgravia was once a dangerous place at night due to highwaymen and robbers, and there are grisly tales of murder. But despite its reputation for crime, it was noted, its market gardens made the area a very pleasant place to visit... presumably during the daytime!**

In the Middle Ages the area was known as Five Fields and in the 19th century the affluent Grosvenor family – the Dukes of Westminster – developed it with grand stucco houses and squares in an attempt to rival Mayfair as *the* place for the wealthy to live. The area was renamed Belgravia after the village of Belgravia in Cheshire, which is close to the Grosvenor family's country residence, Eaton Hall. After World War II the area changed from mostly wealthy residential properties to business premises and a number of foreign embassies. Recently however, many wealthy companies have moved from Belgravia to the City or to the Docklands – areas that are closer to the hub of London's financial business – and Belgravia is once again becoming the place for the super wealthy to reside. As well as grand architecture, shops and cafes, Belgravia is home to one of the best viewpoints of Battersea Power Station.

## What to shoot and viewpoints

### Viewpoint 1 – Belgrave Square &#9855;

At the heart of Belgravia sits Belgrave Square with its impressive five-acre private garden. Surrounding the square are fifty properties, many of which are embassies. If you're seeking to take pictures of national flags *in situ*, then this is the place to come. Some of the embassies are patrolled by guards so use your discretion while taking photos. At the centre of the square is the private garden. It's only open to residents of the square, but it is possible to photograph its three key statues: Christopher Columbus, Prince Henry and *The Vitruvian Man* – an homage to Leonardo Da Vinci.

*Opposite left: VP2. Tea shop in Chelsea. Canon 5D IV, 24–70mm at 24mm, ISO 200, 1/500s at f/8. June. **Right**: VP2. Old farriers signage by a Chelsea mews. Canon 5D IV, 24–70mm at 30mm, ISO 200, 1/500s at f/8. June.*

### Viewpoint 2 – Elizabeth Street &#9855;

Situated just south of the large Eaton Square Gardens is Elizabeth Street – a treasure trove of shops (including a branch of Peggy Porschen – a striking pink cake shop at the far southern end) adorned with beautiful floral decorations during the summer months. There are also some superb bijou mews that are the hallmark of affluent west London, such as Eaton Mews West with its old farriers signage still painted on the side of an adjacent townhouse. This little street is great to photograph on busy summer days. Use discretion and avoid using a tripod if possible; hand held here is better.

*Opposite: VP1. Embassy flags on display in Belgravia Square. Canon 5D IV, 24–70mm at 70mm, ISO 200, 1/500s at f/8. June.*

## How to get here

The easiest way to start your journey through Belgravia is from Hyde Park Corner. Begin by walking to the south side of the old hospital building then along Grosvenor Crescent. This will take you to Belgrave Square.

| | |
|---|---|
| **Underground & Lines:** | Hyde Park Corner, Sloane Square, Victoria: *Circle and District, Piccadilly, Victoria* |
| **Main Station:** | Victoria |
| **Bus:** | 11, 170, 211, C10, N11 |
| **Cycle Hire:** | Belgravia Square, Eaton Square, Ebury Bridge, Elizabeth Street |

### Accessibility &#9855;

These are flat city streets with good crossings. Some roads are very busy so using the pedestrian crossings is a must. The side roads are much quieter and crossing them should present no issues.

### Best time of year/day

This area is best in spring, summer and autumn for the foliage and flowers, and when the cafes are open and busy with people during the day and early evening. Strong summer light works well with the striking architecture of the area. Elizabeth Street is great both day and night, and during Christmastime the shops here put on some beautiful displays.

### VP 1 – Belgrave Square

Leave Hyde Park Corner and walk west towards St George's Hospital, which lies directly adjacent to Hyde Park Corner. Head south for about 100m until you find Grosvenor Crescent to your right; it's easy to spot as its curved line of townhouses lead left into Belgrave Square.

| | |
|---|---|
| **Location Lat/Long:** | 51.49921, -0.15485 |
| **Location Postcode:** | SW1X 8PZ |

*Below*: VP2. The Alfred Tennyson pub, Belgravia. Canon 5D IV, 24–70mm at 27mm, ISO 100, 20s at f/9.5, tripod, LEE ND 0.9 grad. Nov.

*Above*: VP1. Belgravia houses. Canon 5D IV, 24–70mm at 46mm, ISO 200, 1/45s at f/11. June.

### Viewpoint 3 – Ebury Square Gardens ♿

In keeping with the small-is-beautiful motif of the area, Ebury Square Gardens (not to be confused with Eaton Square Gardens) is a tiny park located on the borders of Belgravia, Chelsea and Victoria. It's worthwhile stopping here for the great little central fountain, park keepers hut, flowerbeds and tall trees.

### Viewpoint 4 – National Audit Office ♿

Built in the 1930s, when air travel was in its infancy and only for the wealthy, this stunning building was originally the Empire Air Terminal for Imperial Airways (later BOAC). Passengers would check in here, then they and their luggage would be ferried to Croydon Airport just south of London or to catch the flying-boats from Southampton. Photographing this building conjures images of Fritz Lang's *Metropolis*; the *moderne* and its striking architecture just begs to be shot in high contrast monochrome. It's best photographed when there is strong light against the east and west sides – this heightens the contrast making the monochrome processing so much more effective. Look to stand on the opposite side of Buckingham Palace Road and shoot upwards. A small traffic island next to the rear of the coach station is a good place to position yourself but be careful as coaches pass by all the time.

*Above: VP3. Ebury Square Gardens, Victoria. Canon 5D IV, 24–70mm at 24mm, ISO 200, 1/60s at f/8. June.*

### Viewpoint 5 – Ebury Bridge and Battersea Power Station ♿

An inner city train junction and depot doesn't sound much of a draw for taking photographs but this location is one of my all time favourites. Just a short walk from Victoria Station is Ebury Bridge on Sutherland Street, where an open walkway leads down a ramp to a British Transport Police office. Stand at the top of the ramp and you'll be granted a wonderful view of dozens of snaking train lines leading into Victoria Station (around quarter of a mile north of the bridge) with an unobstructed view of Battersea Power Station as the backdrop.

The best time to shoot is late evening, just as the blue hour fades. Having located the entrance to the walkway, place your tripod on the barrier directly by the wall and look to shoot around a 24–40mm focal length with an f/11 or greater aperture to ensure good depth. The key to shooting good light streaks is to watch the timing of the trains. Dusk falls earlier in winter and as rush hour begins just as dusk arrives, you should be able to capture more trains. (In summer it's later so far fewer trains will be on offer.) Look to get your exposures to around 20–30 seconds and press the shutter when trains begin their approach from the south beyond the bend or as they leave Victoria, as they pick up speed. It'll take a few practice shots to get it right but you'll soon have the timing down and a very special image to take home.

## VP 2 – Elizabeth Street

Leave Belgrave Square by Chesham Place located in the far southwest corner of the square between the Spanish and German embassies. Proceed west for about 250m until you reach a small triangular garden on your right then proceed to the left of this until you see a fork in the road – you should see the Diplomat Hotel. Take the left hand road and head along Lyall Street for about five minutes. As you pass between Eaton Square Gardens (either side of you), you will enter Elizabeth Street, which adjoins the end of Lyall Street.

**Location Lat/Long**: 51.493396, -0.15134
**Location Postcode**: SW1W 9PJ

## VP 3 – Ebury Square Gardens

As you leave the southern end of Elizabeth Street take Ebury Street heading west. Turn left at the garage on the corner and head south along Semley Place. Walk on the west side of the street until you reach Ebury Square Gardens to your right – it's approximately 300m along the road.

**Location Lat/Long**: 51.49173, -0.15019
**Location Postcode**: SW1W 9QJ

## VP 4 – National Audit Office

Leave the southern exit of Ebury Square Gardens and proceed along a small street called Avery Farm Row. On the corner you will find a small memorial fountain to the Marquess of Westminster. Turn left and head towards the major junction about 50m in front of you. Turn left here and head east along Buckingham Palace Road for about 200m until you see the imposing structure of the National Audit Office with its ten-storey-high clock tower.

**Location Lat/Long**: 51.49163, -0.1484
**Location Postcode**: SW1W 9SP

## VP 5 – Ebury Bridge

From the National Audit Office on Buckingham Palace Road head west around 200m to the junction with Ebury Bridge Road. Take an immediate left and head up a small incline to the bridge. You will see the entrance to the train depot to your right.

**Location Lat/Long**: 51.4902, -0.14855
**Location Postcode**: SW1W 9TB

## VP 6 – Orange Square

Leave the junction of Buckingham Palace Road and Ebury Bridge Road to head northwest along the curved Pimlico Road for around 500m. Orange Square is to your right, directly opposite The Orange Public House and Hotel.

**Location Lat/Long**: 51.49069, -0.15288
**Location Postcode**: SW1W 8UN

## Viewpoint 6 – Orange Square ♿

Orange Square is located along a short stretch of Pimlico Road. On Saturday mornings in the summer it hosts an organic farmers market. At the centre of the square, also known locally as Mozart's Square, stands a statue of a very young Mozart, who lived on Ebury Street for a short time, staring down at anyone brave enough to approach. This is a colourful location to photograph on market day, and also to enjoy an early breakfast at The Orange Public House and Hotel opposite.

*Top*: *VP4. Empire Airways Building, Victoria. Canon 5D IV, 24–70mm at 58mm, ISO 200, 1/750s at f/8. June.*

*VP6. Orange Square Market, Chelsea. Canon 5D IV, 24–70mm at 24mm, ISO 200, 1/90s at f/8. June.*

*VP5. Ebury Bridge train depot looking towards Battersea Power Station. Canon 5D IV, 24–70mm at 70mm, ISO 200, 30s at f/16, tripod resting on bridge. Nov.*

The Royal Hospital Chelsea, designed originally by Sir Christopher Wren, has been a retirement and nursing home for British Army veterans for over 300 years. Founded by Charles II in 1682, the requirements for residency are that you are over 65, of good character and free of any financial obligation to support a spouse or family. Chelsea Pensioners, as the residents are called, was once the term to describe all war veterans who had an army pension as these were administered and paid by the Royal Hospital Chelsea.

The residents are required to wear 'blues' – a mix of blue trousers, blue shirt and dark blue cap while in the grounds. Off campus they wear civilian clothes, and at ceremonial events they wear the traditional red frock coat and ribbons earned during their time in the services.

The hospital is split into distinct areas: Light Horse Court and College Court, Figure Court (which lies at the centre of the hospital), the beautiful Ranelagh Gardens and the large event area that hosts the famous annual Chelsea Flower Show to the south. All areas are open to the public with the exception of the residents' private quarters; the event area is only open when an event is taking place.

The Royal Hospital Chelsea is run by a charitable trust, so please purchase something from the on site gift shop or make a donation to help the upkeep of this wonderful place. Not only are the hospital and grounds beautiful places to photograph but this location is one of the friendliest I've had the pleasure to visit.

## What to shoot and viewpoints

Enter the hospital via the London Gate located on Royal Hospital Road. To the left of the gate is an old graveyard, which is worth a look for its 18th-century gravestones.

### The Great Hall and Chapel &

The main building, Light Horse Court, is located 50m south along East Road on the right. Its central courtyard is home to a gilded statue of Charles II, dressed in the attire of a Roman leader. To the north of the main courtyard is the main entrance, which leads into the vestibule. Turn left for the Great Hall or right for the chapel. A guide will accompany you, (this prevents crowds and preserves the peaceful atmosphere of the chapel) and there are usually several available so you won't be kept waiting long. »

*Opposite: Royal Chelsea Hospital chapel. Canon 5D IV, 24–70mm at 24mm, ISO 400, 1/20s at f/8. June.*

*Figure Square, Royal Chelsea Hospital. Canon 5D IV, 24–70mm at 24mm, ISO 200, 1/500s at f/8. June.*

*Figure Square, Royal Chelsea Hospital. Canon 5D IV, 24–70mm at 24mm, ISO 200, 1/250s at f/9.5. June.*

There are some wonderful photographs to be had in the main courtyard, especially shooting along the colonnade at the north side on bright sunny days. Arrive at opening time and the sun will still be low enough to cast stunning shadows of the columns across the plaques; the contrast of bright stone and dark shadows is not to be missed. Just after opening time the hospital is very quiet, so it's possible to obtain shots with no people or perhaps just one of the residents passing between buildings. The addition of a single person to a harsh stone composition softens the image. Moving out into the courtyard, don't miss the chance to take a wide shot of the impressive brilliant-white entrance that connects the Great Hall and chapel. This can be shot in isolation directly head-on or move further south into the courtyard and, from an angle, place the golden statue of Charles II in your shot to add strong foreground interest.

## The Pensioner Statue ♿

Pass the entrances to the Great Hall and chapel and you'll arrive at the front of the main building by the statue of the Chelsea Pensioner with his stick raised in the air. Photographing the statue at the front of the hospital is tricky on bright days, as you'll be shooting directly into the sun. Exposure blend, shoot towards the west and watch for sun flare or wait for shade.

## College Court ♿

You can reach College Court from north of the main courtyard: proceed west from where you entered and leave via the entrance at the far western end of the colonnade – this will bring you out into College Court. To its far western side is the National Army Museum.

College Court is quieter than Light Horse Court and you're free to walk around the square. The buildings to the north are the private recreation rooms and clubs for the residents and the original signs over the doorways are worthy subjects, with traditional lampposts providing both foreground subjects and leading lines. Shoot from the far side of College Court to capture a grand vista of the original main building, using trees as foreground interest.

## Infirmary, Cafe and Ranelagh Gardens ♿

Starting from East Road (the main avenue that leads south from the entrance at London Gate) the Infirmary is on the left next to the gift shop and museum. Head through the entrance and past the flower garden on your right. You'll see a cafe; from here, head south (past tennis courts) into Ranelagh Gardens.

As you pass the flower garden, there are items of interest in place, such as the four-column pottery stands to commemorate the fallen. The artworks are produced by the residents and some of the pieces are very touching. Pause as you enter the cafe area and look to your right: there's a superb shot through the colonnade with the rear of the old infirmary building framed in the distance. Use the flowerbeds in the foreground and you'll have a compelling image. The gardens are a place to unwind; walk the paths looking to use them as lead lines into the foliage and flowerbeds. There are some interesting man-made objects in the garden too, such as the brick shade to the north and a second statue of a pensioner, this time seated. It's the perfect place for contemplation before heading back to the museum and gift shop.

## How to get here

The easiest route is to arrive at Sloane Square Tube station and walk or take the bus south to the hospital.

**Location Lat/Long**: 51.48747, -0.15828
**Location Postcode**: SW3 4SR
**Underground & Lines**: Sloane Square, Victoria: *Circle and District, Piccadilly, Victoria*
**Main Station**: Victoria
**Bus**: 11, 137, 170, 211, 360, 452
**Cycle Hire**: Ormonde Gate

## Accessibility ♿

With so many elderly residents living in the hospital, many of whom have restricted mobility, all accessibility requirements are fully catered for in the public areas, including stair lifts to the Great Hall and chapel.

## Best time of year/day

The hospital is open seven days a week between 10am and 5pm and entrance is free. You can visit all year round but the summer months are best for good light and the best images of architecture.

King's Road is a bustling, beautiful street, full of shops, galleries, markets, pubs and restaurants. It's also synonymous with designers Mary Quant and Vivienne Westwood, the model Twiggy, the Swinging Sixties and punk – Malcolm McLaren and Vivienne Westwood established their punk fashion boutique SEX here. The hippy chicks and the punks may have gone but the street is still fashionable.

King's Road was originally a private road, built in the 1600s for King Charles II to enable him to travel from St James's Palace to Fulham. The road itself stretches quite some distance and is split into two parts: King's Road and New King's Road. For the purposes of this location we will concern ourselves with the eastern section (which is around 1.5km long) that leads from Sloane Square to the area just north of Battersea Bridge.

## What to shoot and viewpoints

There is so much to photograph along the old King's Road, but here are three of my favourite subjects; I'll leave the rest for you to explore.

### *Two Pupils* by Allister Bowtell ♿

Leave Sloane Square by King's Road at the southwest exit and after 100m (and tucked just out of sight) is the entrance to Duke of York Square and two sculptures called *Two Pupils* – a boy and a girl wearing the uniform of the Royal Military Asylum, circa 1814. They're quite different from the formal statues that are common in London. Try getting down low to photograph this playful pair, or treat as portrait.

*Opposite: Two Pupils statue, Sloane Square. Canon 5D IV, 24–70mm at 38mm, ISO 200, 1/180s at f/4.5. July.*

*Boy from Two Pupils statue by Sloane Square. Canon 5D II, 70–200mm at 200mm, ISO 200, 1/180s at f/8. June.*

*Girl from Two Pupils statue by Sloane Square. Canon 5D II, 70–200mm at 169mm, ISO 400, 1/90s at f/4. May.*

*Royal Avenue looking towards Royal Chelsea Hospital. Canon 5D IV, 24–70mm at 70mm, ISO 400, 1/250s at f/8. July.*

## Royal Avenue ♿

Head 300m further west from the sculptures along King's Road and to your left is the tree-flanked Royal Avenue, which was designed by Sir Christopher Wren during the reign of William III (1690s) to connect Kensington Palace with the Royal Chelsea Hospital. The full avenue never came to fruition, but ended at the King's Road and its presence is quite incongruous – a wide, open green-flanked space adjacent to a densely packed shopping street. The light can be challenging when shooting this avenue: on sunny days there will be huge dynamic range – you may need to take multiple exposures and blend the shots. Walk to the end of the avenue, turn right and on to N°. 19 St Leonard's Terrace; this is where Bram Stoker, author of *Dracula*, once lived.

## Bywater Street, Painted Houses ♿

Proceed 100m west along King's Road from the Royal Avenue and to your right is Bywater Street, one of several famous painted-house streets. These pastel-coloured houses are best photographed from the southern end looking north with a midrange (24–70mm) lens on good light days midweek, when there are fewer cars.

## More Locations

I find Tryon Street intriguing with its mesmerising curve. In the summer many shop fronts are decorated with floral displays. Halfway down the old King's Road is The Ivy Chelsea Garden, one of the most incredible floral displays of any shop in London, and a popular spot for taking selfies. Opposite sits Dovehouse Green, a small city square great for street photography. Behind Dovehouse Green is the rear entrance to the Chelsea Farmers Market – home to bespoke shops that sell anything from jewellery to fresh produce; it's well worth having a wander here.

***Opposite top**: Painted houses, Bywater Street, Chelsea. Canon 5D IV, 24–70mm at 24mm, ISO 200, 1/125s at f/8. July.*

***Opposite bottom left**: Flower bedecked restaurant on King's Road, Chelsea. Canon 5D IV, 24–70mm at 42mm, ISO 200, 1/30s at f/8. June. **Right**: Flower bedecked tea shop on King's Road. Canon 5D IV, 24–70mm at 24mm, ISO 400, 1/250s at f/8. June.*

## How to get here

Take the District line to Sloane Square and proceed east out of Sloane Square and along King's Road.

| | |
|---|---|
| **Location Lat/Long**: | 51.48984, -0.16368 (Bywater Street, painted houses) |
| **Location Postcode**: | SW3 4XB |
| **Underground & Lines**: | Sloane Square, Victoria: *Circle and District, Victoria* |
| **Main Station**: | Victoria |
| **Bus**: | 11, 19, 22, 211, 319, N11, N19, N22 |
| **Cycle Hire**: | Royal Avenue 1, Royal Avenue 2 |

## Accessibility

This is a standard city street that should present no issues for those with limited mobility.

## Best time of year/day

King's Road is vibrant during the summer months, when warm weather encourages the shops to put on wonderful displays and the street cafes are abuzz. It's more quiet and subdued during the winter months but still well worth visiting. Midday to evening is best, when there is good light and more people around.

There has been a settlement at Chelsea since before the Middle Ages and even then it was a wealthy place. With the River Thames marking its southern border, the area was known as the 'riverside landing place for chalk' or 'Chelchith' in Old English and later as 'a village of palaces'. The area has strong royal connections: Henry VIII once owned the manor of Chelsea, but it is better known, along with its main artery, King's Road (see page 360) as a centre for fashion, music and youth-driven cultural revolutions such as the Swinging Sixties and punk. As punk burned out in the early 1980s, bohemian artists and musicians moved out of Chelsea and up to Notting Hill. This accelerated the growth of Chelsea as an exclusive residential area inhabited by 'Sloane Rangers' – a term first coined by *Harpers & Queen* magazine and used to refer to affluent upper-middle and upper class twenty-somethings with a fashionable lifestyle. This way of life is further documented in the structured-reality TV series *Made in Chelsea*, which chronicles the lives of affluent young people in Belgravia, King's Road, Chelsea and Knightsbridge.

Today, almost ten per cent of Chelsea residents were born in the US and it's now home to financiers, media stars and musicians. And although there are many exclusive shops and boutiques, Chelsea has a much more 'urban-village' feel than the West End.

## What to shoot and viewpoints

Chelsea has many unique sights and hidden details to photograph, so a wander around with a camera is always interesting. To help you on your way here are some of my favourite places:

### Viewpoint 1: St Luke's & Christ Church and Gardens ♿
Nineteenth-century St Luke's is one of the earliest examples of the Gothic Revival churches in London, its construction funded by the government's Church Building Act of 1824. In 1836 Charles Dickens and Catherine Hogarth were married here, a few days after Dickens' first huge success *Pickwick Papers* was published. The church and its beautiful gardens are a joy to photograph in the summer, when there is a riot of colour. Use trees to frame compositions of the church.

### Viewpoint 2: Glebe Place ♿
Turn into the quiet streets of south Chelsea and the noise and bustle of King's Road just melts away. Glebe Place offers sanctuary; at its end is a country cottage – now Chelsea Open Air Nursery School, which is surrounded by Georgian houses. The cottage is best photographed at weekends or during holidays, along with the foliage-covered houses nearby.

*VP2. Chelsea school. Canon 5D IV, 24–70mm at 28mm, ISO 200, 1/250s at f/8. June.*

*Opposite left: VP2. Chelsea resident taking it easy. Canon 5D IV, 24–70mm at 45mm, ISO 200, 1/500s at f/6.7. June.*
*Middle: VP1. Church of St Luke's Gardens. Canon 5D IV, 24–70mm at 24mm, ISO 100, 1/60s at f/8. June.*
*Right: VP4. Quiet street in Chelsea. Canon 5D IV, 24–70mm at 24mm, ISO 200, 1/500s at f/8. June.*

*White house with flowers, Kensington. Canon 5D IV, 24–70mm at 27mm, ISO 200, 1/60s at f/8. July.*

## Viewpoint 3: Cheyne Row, Lawrence Street and Justice Walk &

Follow Glebe Place towards the river to Upper Cheyne Row, turn left and, at number 33, proceed west. This area – Cheyne Row, Lawrence Street and Justice Walk are wonderfully quaint streets that have remained largely unaltered since they were built. Cheyne Row was the home to several china-producing workshops, both manufacture and decoration. Josiah Wedgewood would produce pottery in Stoke-on-Trent then dispatch it to his workshop in Cheyne Row, where it would be decorated and sent to local shops for purchase by the affluent residents. Don't miss Nº. Fifty Cheyne Row, a bright blue public house that is bedecked in flowers in the summer.

## Viewpoint 4: Chelsea Old Church and Thomas More &

If you walk down Justice Walk (through an alley) and turn left on to Old Church Street, you'll reach Chelsea Old Church by the river. Built in 1157 this parish church was here when Chelsea was just a village. Aside from beautiful gardens, the most striking subject here is the statue of Sir Thomas More. Despite being counsellor to Henry VIII, More was executed as a traitor by Henry after refusing to acknowledge the king as head of the church during the Reformation. More had a private chapel built here in 1528 and the statue acknowledges his martyrdom.

## How to get here

The easiest way to begin your exploration of south Chelsea is to start from King's Road at Sydney Street, opposite Chelsea Old Town Hall and about ten minutes' walk from Sloane Square.

**Underground & Lines:** Sloane Square, Victoria: Circle and District, Piccadilly, Victoria
**Main Station:** Victoria
**Bus:** 19, 49, 319, 345, 170, N19, N31

## Accessibility &

All locations are on level city streets and should present no issues. The church buildings have ramps to aid anyone with limited mobility.

## Best time of year/day

The best time to visit is daytime in the spring and summer for floral displays, foliage and great light. The locations in this section are described in a 'walk and shoot' style; while you can easily use a tripod in all the places detailed, they're not really landscape locations so you may find it easier to shoot handheld.

## VP 1 – St Luke's & Christ Church and Gardens

Having reached Sydney Street junction from King's Road, head north to St Luke's, which you'll find about 200m from King's Road and on your right.

**Location Lat/Long:** 51.4894, -0.16968
**Location Postcode:** SW3 6NH

## VP 2 – Glebe Place

Glebe Place is south of King's Road at around Nº. 219. Turn south off King's Road and head to the far end of Glebe Place as it enters a bend.

**Location Lat/Long:** 51.48541, -0.16964
**Location Postcode:** SW3 5JE

## VP 3 – Cheyne Row, Lawrence Street and Justice Walk, and Nº. Fifty Cheyne Pub

Starting from the nursery school on Glebe Place, continue to Upper Cheyne Row and the Church of the Holy Redeemer at the junction then take a right into Cheyne Row at Nº. 33. At the bend at the far western end of Cheyne Row (where it turns into Lawrence Street) head south until you find the turning into Justice Walk to your right at Nº. 11 Lawrence Street. Nº. Fifty Cheyne Pub is at the end of Cheyne Row.

**Location Lat/Long:** 51.48403, -0.16986
**Location Postcode:** SW3 5HL

## VP 4 – Chelsea Old Church and Sir Thomas More

From the far western end of Justice Walk (as it emerges from a narrow alley into Old Church Street), turn left to the Chelsea Embankment. Chelsea Old Church is next to the river.

**Location Lat/Long:** 51.48294, -0.17077
**Location Postcode:** SW3 5LT

*Above*: VP6. Fifty Cheyne, Chelsea. Canon 5D IV, 24–70mm at 25mm, ISO 200, 1/350s at f/8. June.

*Below*: House in Chelsea. Canon 5D IV, 24–70mm at 25mm, ISO 200, 1/90s at f/8. June.

Albert Bridge is a striking landmark, especially at night when illuminated by the 4000 LED bulbs attached to it. Situated at the western end of Battersea Park, it links Chelsea with Battersea, much like Chelsea Bridge. Due to some dodgy engineering it can vibrate when traffic is heavy and it's been nicknamed 'The Trembling Lady', in fact there are warnings at each end that states troops must 'break step' before crossing! Originally it was a toll bridge, but like many toll bridges it didn't make any money and was soon brought into public ownership when passage across it became free. The toll booths remain today and night or day it makes a great photographic subject.

## What to shoot and viewpoints

Take care if shooting the bridge at night: it is brightly lit so you have to be careful not to blow the highlights when taking long exposures. This is one subject when shooting at the Golden Hour (before and just after sunset) is vital to achieve a good shot.

The bridge can be shot from all four corners and each will offer something different. From the south side, either enter Battersea Park and approximately 20m in you can shoot over the railings, or walk to the south-west side; from there you'll have a very clear view, allowing you to determine how wide you wish to make the bridge appear within your frame.

Head over the bridge to the north side and you can shoot the entire structure. Other subjects here include a red phone box and an illuminated passage under the bridge. Boats moored on the north side provide some foreground interest.

Shooting whilst standing on the bridge enables you to capture one set of the pillars and lights. Alternatively, use a zoom lens to align the street lamps on the bridge, making them disappear as they retreat. It's even better still if you manage to capture someone walking under them. And of course this is a great place for traffic streaks.

*Albert Bridge at sunrise from the north shore. Canon 5D II, 17–40mm at 17mm, ISO 100, 4s at f/8, tripod, LEE ND 0.6 grad. Oct.*

*Opposite top: Albert Bridge at sunrise from the north shore. Canon 5D II, 17–40mm at 17mm, ISO 100, 2s at f/16, tripod, LEE ND 0.6 grad. Oct. Middle: Albert Bridge illuminated at dusk. Canon 5D II, 17–40mm at 40mm, ISO 100, 20s at f/11, tripod, LEE ND 0.9 grad. Oct. Bottom: Looking north over Albert Bridge at night. Canon 5D II, 17–40mm at 19mm, ISO 100, 25s at f/14, tripod. Oct.*

## How to get here

Follow the instructions to reach Chelsea Bridge and then proceed either along the north side of the Thames or via the path through Battersea Park, next to the south bank of the Thames.

| | |
|---|---|
| **Location Lat/Long:** | 51.48235, -0.1667 |
| **Location Postcode:** | SW11 4PL |
| **Underground & Lines:** | Sloane Square: Circle and District |
| **Main Station:** | Battersea Park, LSWR Queens Road Station |
| **Riverboat:** | Cadogan Pier |
| **Bus:** | 170 |
| **Cycle Hire:** | Ethelburga Estate, Phene Street |

## Accessibility &#9855;

Travelling to and around Albert Bridge is fully accessible and should present no problems.

### Best time of year/day

There are three times of the day that provide the best opportunities for photographs: late evening just as the bridge is illuminated; early morning looking from the northwest across the bridge – there is a good chance of an illuminated sky as background to the structure – and finally, at midday looking from within Battersea Park, which lies at the bridge's southeast corner.

The area where Battersea Park is situated was once a famous spot for duelling – the Duke of Wellington attended a duel here in 1829. This 200-acre park, situated by the south bank of the Thames, opened in 1858, and in 1864 hosted the very first game of football using the new Football Association rulebook. The park has much variety and interest for keen photographers, including a nature reserve, the London Peace Pagoda – a commemorative peace monument – many statues, a boating lake, gardens, a bandstand, an art gallery and avenues of trees and old fashioned street lights.

## What to shoot and viewpoints

### Viewpoint 1 – Old English Garden ♿

At the northwest corner of Battersea Park, by the Carriage Drive North close to the river, is the Old English Garden. Planted in 1900, it fell into disrepair until health charity, Thrive and fragrance company, Jo Malone worked to restore the garden and re-invigorate it. This is a paved garden and bursts with life in the summer, when all kinds of traditional English garden flowers and a variety of insects including butterflies, bees and dragonflies make it home. There are so many opportunities for images both full, wide-angle landscapes encompassing the colours of the blooms, and macro photography of the insects that thrive amongst the flowers.

### Viewpoint 2: Carriage Drive North ♿

Carriage Drive North by the river is a tree- and lamp-lined avenue, well used by pedestrians and cyclists. It's a great spot to capture images of people as they travel down the avenue and through the trees, especially in autumn.

*Opposite: VP3. Battersea Park Peace Pagoda at dawn. Canon 5D II, 17–40mm at 17mm, ISO 100, 1/13s at f/8, tripod, LEE ND 0.9 grad. Oct.*

### Viewpoint 3: The London Peace Pagoda ♿

Situated by the Thames just above Carriage Drive North, the London Peace Pagoda is a wonderful subject to photograph. It's impressive and beautiful at any time: at night it's illuminated, and at dawn and dusk golden light is cast on its surface. The Peace Pagoda was presented to Londoners by the Venerable Nichidatsu Fuji, founder of the Japanese Buddhist movement, Nipponzan Myohoji, and is one of many worldwide peace pagodas, designed to promote peace after the atomic bombing of Hiroshima and Nagasaki.

### Viewpoint 4: The Bandstand ♿

At the center of the park is a bandstand that is often used in the summer for concerts. It has a circle of trees around it, and avenues branching from it. The possibilities for framing the bandstand using the trees and the avenues are numerous.

## How to get here

Situated between Albert and Chelsea Bridges, there are four entrances to the park. Follow the directions for the Chelsea Bridge location, using Sloane Square station as a starting point, then cross Chelsea Bridge to the park. If you prefer not to walk, there are many bus routes to the park. The easiest is the 344, which can be caught from London Bridge, Monument or Liverpool Street Station and will drop you outside the park.

| | |
|---|---|
| **Location Lat/Long:** | 51.47925, -0.1567 |
| **Location Postcode:** | SW11 4NJ |
| **Main Station:** | Battersea Park, LSWR Queens Road Station |
| **Riverboat:** | Battersea Power Station Pier |
| **Bus:** | 156, 344, 436 |
| **Cycle Hire:** | Albert Bridge Road, Ethelburga Estate, Prince of Wales Drive, Queens Circus, Sopwith Way |
| **Car Park:** | There is one large pay-and-display car park at the northeast corner of the park. It has around 200 spaces but when the weather is fine, the car park fills early. |

### Accessibility ♿

The park is flat with tarmac paths leading to all locations, meaning there should be no accessibility issues.

### Best time of year/day

Spring through to autumn is the best time to visit, though the park is open all year round and most parts open 24/7.

*Above*: VP1. Wild garden, Battersea Park. Canon 5D IV, 70–200mm at 70mm, ISO 200, 1/125s at f/8. June.

*Above*: VP2. Looking east along the Carriage Drive North. Sony A6000, 16–50mm at 32mm, ISO 100, 1/100s at f/5.6. June.

*Albert Bridge from Battersea Park. Canon 5D IV, 24–70mm at 24mm, ISO 200, 1/180s at f/8. June.*

*VP4. Infrared image of Battersea Park bandstand. Canon 5D II, 17–40mm at 26mm, ISO 100, 1/60s at f/11. June.*

### Viewpoint 5: Pump House Gallery ♿

The gallery is located in the four-storey Victorian building that stands by the side of the boating lake and was a former pump house for the park's fountains. This area is also home to a gazebo and flowerbeds, which, along with the lake, make great compositions, especially on windless days when reflections in the water are clear.

### Viewpoint 6: Battersea Bridge ♿

Close to Battersea Park, Battersea Bridge can be found to the west of Albert Bridge, 500m upriver. The best views of Battersea Bridge are found shooting from Albert Bridge or standing by the riverside at the southeast corner of Battersea Bridge. Shooting at night from Albert Bridge, when the River Thames is quite still will offer an amazing vista of Battersea Bridge in the foreground with Lots Road

Power Station behind, the lights from the far buildings reflected in the water. Shooting from Battersea Bridge itself (looking east) offers a similar view but, of course, without the bridge. Shoot from the side of Battersea Bridge looking north and you'll have a classic bridge-as-lead-line composition – in this case leading to the low-profile skyline on the north shoreline of the Thames.

**Safety**: London is a very safe city but do exercise caution when in parks during the hours of darkness. Although patrolled and for the most well lit, it is wise to go with a friend.

*Above*: VP5. Battersea Park boating lake. Canon 5D IV, 24–70mm at 24mm, ISO 200, 1/60s at f/8. June.

*Below*: VP6. Battersea Bridge at night. Canon 5D II, 24–70mm at 34mm, ISO 50, 30s at f/8, tripod. Jan.

*Chelsea Bridge, Battersea Park. Canon 5D IV, 24–70mm at 28mm, ISO 200, 1/500s at f/8. June.*

Connecting Battersea Park to Chelsea in the north is the beautiful Chelsea Bridge. Built in 1934 as a means of bringing employment to the area during the Great Depression, all materials were sourced from within the British Empire. Due to its proximity to Chelsea Football club there was uproar when the bridge was painted red (red being the colour of London rivals, Arsenal) and so it was repainted red, white and blue. It was one of the world's first self-anchored suspension bridges and is now Grade II listed.

## What to shoot and viewpoints

The bridge is illuminated at night and makes a great subject to shoot during the golden hour as dusk begins to fall. There are no clear viewpoints from the north shore so any photography below the bridge must be done from the south (Battersea Park side). On the bridge itself you can shoot traffic streaks in either direction and if you do visit, I would recommend shooting Albert Bridge the same evening, as both can be reached via Battersea Park with just a ten-minute walk between them. Daytime is best to photograph the bridge's plaques, the golden ships that sit atop the pillars at each end and the painted suspension cables and rivets.

*Opposite: Chelsea Bridge at dusk. Canon 5D II, 17–40mm at 17mm, ISO 100, 20s at f/16, tripod, LEE ND 0.9 grad. Oct.*

**Battersea Footbridge**, located directly under the southern end of the bridge, carries the Thames Path walkway and allows you a very low viewpoint looking northwards along the bridge's span . The walkway is curved and provides a wonderful lead line with its polished steel handrail.

## How to get here

The easiest route to Chelsea Bridge is to make your way to Sloane Square Tube station. Exit the station and head south along Sloane Gardens – this will lead you to Chelsea Bridge Road. Follow this road south until you reach the bridge.

| | |
|---|---|
| **Location Lat/Long**: | 51.48376, -0.14967 |
| **Location Postcode**: | SW8 4PF |
| **Underground & Lines**: | Sloane Square: *Circle and District* |
| **Main Station**: | Battersea Park, LSWR Queens Road Station |
| **Riverboat**: | Battersea Power Station Pier |
| **Bus**: | 44, 137, 360, 452, N44, N137 |
| **Cycle Hire**: | Chelsea Bridge |

## Accessibility &#9855;

Both the bridge and the walkway that runs under it are fully accessible.

### Best time of year/day

Chelsea Bridge can be shot at any time of year or day, although shooting at dawn or dusk can offer the opportunity to have a sunrise or sunset sky in the background. Shooting from within Battersea Park (through the trees) is possible all year round but spring to autumn is preferable, when foliage provides natural framing.

*Above*: Chelsea Bridge lights. Canon 5D IV, 24–70mm at 70mm, ISO 200, 1/500s at f/8. July.

*Above*: Chelsea Bridge at dusk. Canon 5D II, 17–40mm at 32mm, ISO 100, 15s at f/20, tripod, LEE ND 0.9 grad. Oct.

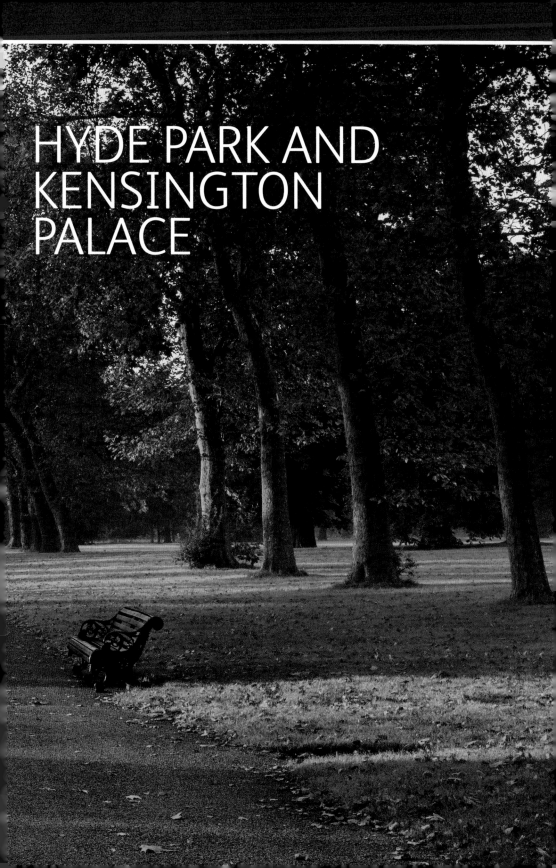

# HYDE PARK AND KENSINGTON PALACE

**Hyde Park, the splendid jewel among London's Royal Parks. This world-famous 350-acre open space right in the heart of the city draws over 12 million visitors a year. And with its variety of landscapes, stunning wide-open spaces and the Serpentine – the largest single body of water in Greater London after the River Thames – it's easy to see why. I consider Hyde Park so important, I've devoted an entire section to it and when you visit, I hope you'll agree that somewhere so magnificent deserves this attention.**

Hyde Park is actually two parks joined together: Kensington Gardens to west and Hyde Park to the east, bisected by a main road that crosses right through the park and over the Serpentine, which, incidentally, is also technically two lakes in one: the Long Water to the west and the Serpentine to the east.

Like so many of London's parks it began as farming land, enclosed as a hunting ground by Henry VIII. Charles I remodelled the areas as garden during the 17th century and opened it to the general public. To the east in Hyde Park you'll find ornamental rose gardens and flowerbeds that are tended all year round; the wide open space that hosts major concerts and other events, and the Serpentine with its bathing area and boating sections. To the west, in Kensington Gardens, lie dense wooded areas, which blaze with rich colour in autumn as the leaves turn, and wild meadow areas that encourage wildlife to flourish.

All across the park are a variety fountains, monuments, memorials, a water garden designed by Prince Albert, and Kensington Palace, former home of the late Diana, Princess of Wales.

*Previous spread*: Low early morning sun, looking south to the Royal Albert Hall. Canon 5D II, 24–70mm at 50mm, ISO 100, 0s at f/18, tripod, LEE ND 0.9 grad. Sept.

*VP6. Foggy dawn in Hyde Park by the Serpentine Bridge. Canon 5D II, 17–40mm at 17mm, ISO 400, 30s at f/8, tripod, LEE ND 0.9 grad. Sept.*

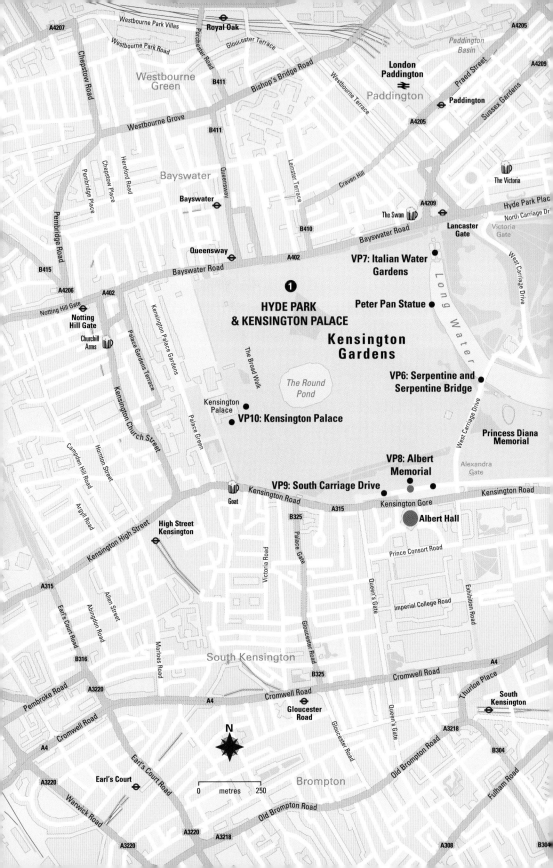

Hyde Park is the largest of the four Royal Parks – Kensington Gardens, Hyde Park, Green Park, and St James's Park – all of which form a continuous 'green lung' in Central London.

It was originally a hunting ground and deer park used by Henry VIII, who seized the land from the monks of Westminster Abbey. In the 1600s, Charles I developed the park and employed a ranger. It was opened to the public in 1637 and has been a popular public space ever since. The Great Exhibition was held here in 1851 and the Crystal Palace, a huge glass building, was erected here as an event space where exhibitors showcased technology from the Industrial Revolution. The park has been used for outdoor concerts including the Rolling Stones free concert in 1969 and Queen's free concert in 1976. Sadly, the park has also witnessed tragedy, when in 1982 the IRA detonated bombs killing eleven members of the armed forces and seven horses.

Today the park is well used by Londoners and visitors alike as a place to wander and relax, and through the year there are regular events such as military parades and gun salutes, and an annual Winter Wonderland.

As well as exploring the highlights of this 350-acre park, we will also visit Kensington Gardens and Palace, which merges with Hyde Park in the west. Kensington Palace is the official residence of the Duke and Duchess of Cambridge (Prince William and Catherine Middleton) and other royals. And it was, of course, home to Diana, Princess of Wales.

## What to shoot and viewpoints

At over 350 acres there are so many things to see: more than twenty monuments, various styles of landscaped garden, wide open spaces, wooded areas, the open-air swimming facilities on the Serpentine and historical buildings. There is no specific best time of day or year to visit as the park is always in a state of change in line with the seasons. Early morning during spring and autumn can offer some great opportunities as the Serpentine creates mist (and sometimes fog) to engulf the park – this is always a treat to shoot. I personally like to shoot in the south-west side of the park; the more densely wooded areas make for more pleasing compositions and the wildlife seems to prefer that area of the park.

The park has two main road or carriage drives: South Carriage Drive, which leads from Hyde Park Corner to the West Carriage Drive, just south of Serpentine Bridge. The other is West Carriage Drive, which crosses the park from north to south over Serpentine Bridge, exiting by the Royal Geographic Society building.

We will start at the northeast corner of the park.

### Viewpoint 1 – Marble Arch ♿

Marble Arch was designed by John Nash in 1827 and was originally the entrance to Buckingham Palace. Queen Victoria found the palace too small for her growing family, so in 1851 it was expanded and the arch was dismantled and moved to its isolated location at the corner of Hyde Park at the junction of Oxford Street, Park Lane and Edgware Road.

Due to the volume of traffic (and people), getting clear shots of the arch during the day is tricky so visit early in the morning or at night when it is less busy. Although a large structure it appears small in relation to its surroundings so finding a suitable composition can sometimes be difficult. Standing isolated on a traffic island does allow all-round viewpoints and the arch's white marble facade catches the colours at dawn and dusk. When shooting night compositions, fast-moving traffic can be used to add a dynamic feel in long exposure shots. To best capture these effectively I recommend positioning yourself to the southeast of the arch, where Cumberland Gate and the A4202 meet.

*Opposite top: VP1. Long exposure of the Christmas wheel at Marble Arch. Canon 5D II, 17–40mm at 17mm, ISO 100, 30s at f/18, tripod, LEE ND 0.9 grad. Aug.*
*Right: VP1. **Still Water** by Nic Fiddian-Green Marble Arch, Hyde Park. Canon 5D IV, 24–70mm at 35mm, ISO 200, 1/500s at f/6.7. July.*

*Previous spread: Blossom in Kensington Gardens, Albert Memorial. Canon 5D IV, 24–70mm at 24mm, ISO 200, 1/125s at f/11. Apr.*

## How to get here

There are several Tube stations and many bus stops located around Hyde Park, which means you can pretty much find your way there from anywhere in London. The two key Tube stations are Marble Arch to the northwest corner and Hyde Park Corner to the southwest corner of the park.

**Location Lat/Long:** 51.50847, -0.17273
**Location Postcode:** W2 2UH
**Underground & Lines:** Hyde Park Corner, Knightsbridge, Lancaster Gate, Marble Arch: *Central, Piccadilly*
**Bus:** 2, 6, 7, 9, 10, 14, 15, 19, 22, 23, 30, 36, 52, 72, 82, 98, 113, 137, 148, 159, 274, 390, 414, C2

## Accessibility &

The park is fully accessible with paths to all the main attractions, though a few (such as Queen Caroline's Retreat) are located in dense grassy areas and may not be fully accessible.

## Best time of year/day

Any time of year and day are great for photographing Hyde Park and Kensington Palace, although summer for the flowers and foliage is not be missed. In spring and autumn, after a warm day and a clear cold night, mist sometimes hangs over the Serpentine. Spring provides cherry blossom, whilst autumn often brings clear light and rich colours. The park will be quieter at dawn, and sunrise sees atmospheric rays of light through the trees.

**Safety**: London is a very safe city but do exercise caution when in Royal Parks during the hours of darkness. Although patrolled, and for the most well lit, it is wise to go with a friend.

*VP2. Flowers by the Animals in War Memorial, Park Lane. Canon 5D IV, 24–70mm at 27mm, ISO 200, 1/180s at f/8. July.*

## Viewpoint 2 – Animals in War Memorial ♿

This memorial was inspired by Jilly Cooper's book *Animals in War* and the author helped raise funds for the design and building of the monument. Designed by David Backhouse and erected in 2004, the memorial commemorates all the animals conscripted to fight under military command. Try standing on the eastern side of the monument and allowing the entire memorial to fill the frame; it will reduce the number of exterior distractions. The second viewpoint is through the monument: position yourself in front of the horse and look back towards the memorial.

## Viewpoint 3 – *The Joy of Life* Fountain ♿

*The Joy of Life Fountain*, sculpted in 1963 by T.B. Huxley-Jones, is located close to the eastern edge of the park by Park Lane. The fountain can be shot from almost any angle and direction – wide or close with a zoom – and is great to photograph with people around.

## Hyde Park

Most places in Hyde Park are very well signposted; signs are located all over the park and should help you find your way. If you ever get lost, just follow the path until you find the Serpentine – all paths lead from the Serpentine to the locations described.

### Opening hours

Hyde Park is open from 5am until midnight all year round.

### VP 1 – Marble Arch

Take the central line to Marble Arch Tube station or take one of the many buses that go from Victoria or Oxford Street to Marble Arch.

**Location Lat/Long**: 51.51315, -0.15892
**Location Postcode**: W1H 7EJ

### VP 2 – Animals in War Memorial

Head south away from Marble Arch along Park Lane, then walk along the left side of Park Lane until you reach the pedestrian crossing to the memorial. Park Lane is a six-lane road with fast-moving traffic, so please don't take chances – use the crossings.

**Location Lat/Long**: 51.51111, -0.15751

### VP 3 – *The Joy of Life* Fountain

Take the pedestrian path closest to the Park Lane through Hyde Park, heading away from Marble Arch. The fountain is around 500 yards south of the Marble Arch entrance.

**Location Lat/Long**: 51.50851, -0.15588

VP2. *Animals in War Memorial, Park Lane. Canon 5D IV, 24–70mm at 34mm, ISO 200, 1/90s at f/8. July.*

VP3. ***The Joy of Life*** *fountain, Hyde Park. Canon 5D II, 70–200mm at 160mm, ISO 200, 1/90s at f/6.7. Oct.*

VP3. *Lazy afternoon by **The Joy of Life** fountain. Canon 5D IV, 70–200mm at 70mm, ISO 400, 1/2000s at f/4. July.*

VP3. ***The Joy of Life*** *fountain. Canon 5D IV, 70–200mm at 200mm, ISO 400, 1/750s at f/4. July.*

*VP4. Achilles Statue, Hyde Park. Canon 5D IV, 24–70mm at 30mm, ISO 200, 1/180s at f/8. July.*

## Viewpoint 4 – Achilles Statue ♿

The Statue of Achilles, or Wellington Monument, is an 18ft statue of the Greek hero commemorating the soldier and politician, Arthur Wellesley, first Duke of Wellington (1769–1852). It caused quite a stir when it was unveiled, despite the statue's modesty having been concealed with a fig leaf! Interestingly, the funds for the statue were raised by an upper class society, known as Ladies of England. Try composing the statue directly head-on as you enter the park gates, and try wide and zoomed detail shots. It can be shot both night and day and reveals interesting textures as the light comes up just before sunrise.

## Viewpoint 5 – Rose Gardens ♿

Found in the south-eastern corner of the park, across the road from the Hyde Park Corner station entrance, is the Rose Garden. Created in 1994 and laid out in the shape of a horn, there are formal flowerbeds and wildflower sections; two fountains: *Boy and Dolphin*, and *Diana the Huntress*; a metal pergola – with its strong compositional arches – and several park benches. Sunny summer days are best to explore this garden, and the fountains make great compositions surrounded by flowers. There is a lot to go at so it's great to spend an hour or so here.

### VP 4 – Achilles Statue

Exit Hyde Park Corner station then follow the signs to enter Hyde Park through the Apsley Gate entrance located next to Apsley House. The statue is around 150 yards to north of Apsley House.

**Location Lat/Long:**     51.50451, -0.1527

### VP 5 – Rose Gardens

Exit Hyde Park Corner station and head west away from the station along South Carriage Drive; you will see the gardens to your right.

**Location Lat/Long:**     51.50389, -0.15559

### VP 6 – Serpentine and Long Water

Follow the directions to the Rose Gardens then pass through the gardens heading west away from Hyde Park Corner Tube station. The lake is 250 yards west of the Rose Gardens.

**Location Lat/Long:**     51.50621, -0.17255

### VP 7 – Italian Water Gardens

Starting from the Serpentine, head towards the bridge. Proceed north from the bridge following the paths to the western side of the lake.

**Location Lat/Long:**     51.51072, -0.17558

### VP 8 – Albert Memorial

Start from the water gardens, heading west away from the water towards Kensington House. As you reach the *Physical Energy* statue of the figure on the horse, turn left and head south along the wide tree-lined path towards the gilded statue of Prince Albert at the end of Lancaster Walk.

**Location Lat/Long:**     51.50235, -0.1777

*VP6. Rose Garden, Hyde Park. Canon 5D II, 70–200mm at 106mm, ISO 200, 1/350s at f/8. June.*

## VP 9 – South Carriage Drive

Exit Hyde Park Corner station and follow signs into Hyde Park. The first road inside the park is South Carriage Drive.

**Location Lat/Long:** 51.50178, -0.18027

## VP 10 – Kensington Palace

Follow directions to the Serpentine then head past the bridge, taking the left-hand-side path towards the Italian Water Gardens. When you see the statue of the figure on horseback (across the open area), you should spot Kensington Palace in the distance.

**Location Lat/Long:** 51.50583, -0.18772
**Location Postcode:** W8 4PX

### Opening hours

Kensington Palace is open Mon to Sun 10am–6pm.
Last Admission: 5pm.

### Admission prices (2019)

**Adults:** £17.50
**Children:** £8.70

***Opposite right**: VP5. Summer among the flowers in Hyde Park. Canon 5D IV, 24–70mm at 70mm, ISO 200, 1/250s at f/8. Apr.*

## Viewpoint 6 – Serpentine & Serpentine Bridge ♿

The Serpentine is Hyde Park's lake, divided by Serpentine Bridge with Long Water to the north of the bridge. It was originally fed by two rivers, the Westbourne and the Tyburn, but is now fed by three boreholes. The bridge and the lake with its curved shape are great to work with from the lakeside footpaths, and there is plenty of waterfowl, including swans to work into your compositions. Close to the Peter Pan statue (on the west side of Long Water) a line of posts crosses the water; you'll often find a mixture of birds using these to perch on. The Peter Pan statue was commissioned by JM Barrie, the author of *Peter Pan*, who was inspired to create his famous character by visits to the park. There is only a front-on viewpoint of Peter, but note the intricate decorations of the story's characters which adorn the statue's plinth.

After a warm day in spring or autumn, a clear cold night can often follow and a low mist sometimes forms over the Serpentine. This is worth getting up early for. The *Serenity* statue is situated along the south side of the Serpentine water about 100m east of the Serpentine Bridge. At the far eastern end of the Serpentine is the Serpentine waterfall. It's situated in an area called The Dell, which is closed to the public, but it can be photographed over the fence that surrounds it.

*VP7. Italian Water Garden, Kensington Gardens. Canon 5D II, 17–40mm at 20mm, ISO 200, 1/90s at f/11. Oct.*

## Viewpoint 7 – Italian Water Gardens &

The Italian Water Gardens are located at the far northern end of Long Water, above Serpentine Bridge. Built in the 1860s and restored in 2011 they have four main basins with central rosette fountains carved out of marble; a Portland stone and white marble Tazza Fountain and a collection of stone statues and urns. The original design for the water garden comes from Osborne House on the Isle of Wight, where Queen Victoria and Prince Albert took many of their summer holidays. Early morning or late evening is ideal to shoot this area, when there is glowing low light. At dawn, as the sun rises and lights any cloud that may be present, you have an uninterrupted view of the sky to the south. This is a great place for reflections and for street photography.

*Opposite top left: VP7. Taking time out in the Italian Water Garden. Canon 5D II, 70–200mm at 106mm, ISO 200, 1/90s at f/16. Oct. **Top middle**: VP7. Italian Water Garden. Canon 5D IV, 24–70mm at 30mm, ISO 200, 1/350s at f/8. June. **Top right**: VP7. Albert Memorial in front of The Royal Albert Hall. Canon 5D II, 70–200mm at 106mm, ISO 200, 1/500s at f/8. May.*

*Opposite main: VP8. Albert Memorial. Canon 5D II, 70–200mm at 70mm, ISO 200, 1/750s at f/8. June. **Middle far right**: VP8. Wildflowers in Kensington Gardens by the Albert Memorial. Canon 5D IV, 24–70mm at 60mm, ISO 200, 1/90s at f/16. July.*

## Viewpoint 8 – Albert Memorial &

In 1867 Queen Victoria was devastated by the loss of her beloved husband, Prince Albert at just 42 years old and she wanted a grand memorial created. Built in a classical Gothic style, a gilded statue of Albert sits under the canopy gazing south towards another memorial in his honour: the Royal Albert Hall. I'm very proud to be the owner of photographs of the memorial and hall taken by my great-great-grandfather; the images were used as postcards for the Francis Frith Company in 1890.

A wide-angle lens is best to capture this large monument with the Royal Albert Hall as a background from the tree-lined boulevard, Lancaster Walk, which lies behind the monument. People in your shot will add scale. Another pleasing shot can be taken from across Albert Lawn – the open area between West Carriage Drive and the statue; isolate the memorial in profile against the sky. The monument was repainted in 2012 and the stunning colours and motifs make wonderful pictures when using a zoom lens to capture the details.

*Above*: VP8. Detail of the Albert Memorial. Canon 5D IV, 70–200mm at 200mm, ISO 200, 1/180s at f/16. July.

*VP8. Hyde Park in autumn. Canon 5D IV, 70–200mm at 100mm, ISO 200, 1/125s at f/8. Nov.*

## Viewpoint 9 – South Carriage Drive &

South Carriage Drive runs along the southern edge of Hyde Park and into Kensington Gardens. In Hyde Park the drive is a road used by vehicles and the cavalry as they pass from Kensington Barracks to Buckingham Palace and Horseguards Parade to the east. To capture the Household Cavalry as they go to Constitution Hill, aim to be on the drive by 11.30am. Shooting South Carriage Drive in Kensington Gardens is a more laid-back affair; with no vehicles or processions, it's all about people watching and street photography.

## Viewpoint 10 – Kensington Palace &

Kensington Palace was originally a Jacobean mansion built in the 17th Century in what was then the village of Kensington. King William III and Queen Mary II bought the property in 1689, it was extended and improved by Sir Christopher Wren, and has been a royal residence ever since. The public areas of the house were opened in 1899, when the palace took on the dual role of royal household and royal museum. Its most famous resident was Diana Princess of Wales, and when she was tragically killed in Paris in 1997, the palace became the focus of mourning with over a million bouquets placed outside.

It's a very easy subject to shoot, and the east and south sides of the house can be photographed night and day; the grounds are open during the middle of the day. Morning light works wonderfully against the building's exterior and the grounds in front of the main house, particularly in summer when the flowers bloom. There are many paths and borders to use as leading lines.

*Opposite top: VP9. Life Guards returning to barracks via Hyde Park. Canon 5D II, 70–200mm at 70mm, ISO 200, 1/500s at f/6.7. June.*
*Middle left: VP9. Mounted Life Guard by Hyde Park. Canon 5D II, 70–200mm at 70mm, ISO 400, 1/500s at f/8. June.*
*Middle right: VP10. Kensington Palace, Kensington Gardens. Canon 5D IV, 24–70mm at 24mm, ISO 200, 1/250s at f/8. June.*

*Opposite left: VP9. Bicycle fans during a cycling event in Hyde Park. Canon 5D II, 70–200mm at 70mm, ISO 250, 1/125s at f/5.6. May.*
*Middle: VP10. Kensington Palace. Canon 5D IV, 70–200mm at 127mm, ISO 200, 1/60s at f/8. June. Right: VP10. Round Pond, Kensington Gardens. Canon 5D IV, 70–200mm at 93mm, ISO 200, 1/250s at f/8. June.*

# SOUTH KENSINGTON

**Kensington and Knightsbridge cover a vast area and offer a terrific variety of fascinating sights for the photographer.**

The section begins with a visit to a pub (always a crowd pleaser!) – the Churchill Arms is famous for its incredible all-year-round floral displays. The proprietor of this pub has garnered countless horticultural awards, so images of this amazing building are bound to be sure-fire winners when posted on social media.

If London excels at one thing, it's making sure no two city parks are the same. Holland Park has the unique Kyoto Garden – an incredibly beautiful, traditional Japanese water garden complete with waterfall. In addition, there are densely wooded areas in the north of the park, as well as the remains of Holland House, and some wonderful flower displays. My favourite spot – the eastern walkway – is somewhere not to be missed in autumn.

At the southerly side is Brompton Cemetery. I have a fondness for shooting images in city cemeteries and Brompton is one of the most rewarding with its rich variety of wildlife, stunning buildings and a tree-lined central avenue that offers yet more terrific photographic opportunities.

Turning east and heading south of Hyde Park, you'll pass the Natural History Museum with its stunning interior and vast array of specimens; the Royal Albert Hall – another masterpiece of Victorian design, and unique architectural delights such as South Kensington Station and Bibendum.

It's a large area to cover but Kensington and Knightsbridge offer some unforgettable sights and certainly won't disappoint.

*Previous spread*: *Albert Memorial and The Royal Albert Hall, bright sunny morning. Canon 5D II, 17–40mm at 17mm, ISO 100, 1/80s at f/11, tripod, LEE ND 0.9 grad. Sept.*

*Extreme fisheye view of the Natural History Museum ceiling. Sony A6000, Fisheye 8mm at 8mm, ISO 200, 1/160s at f/8. June.*

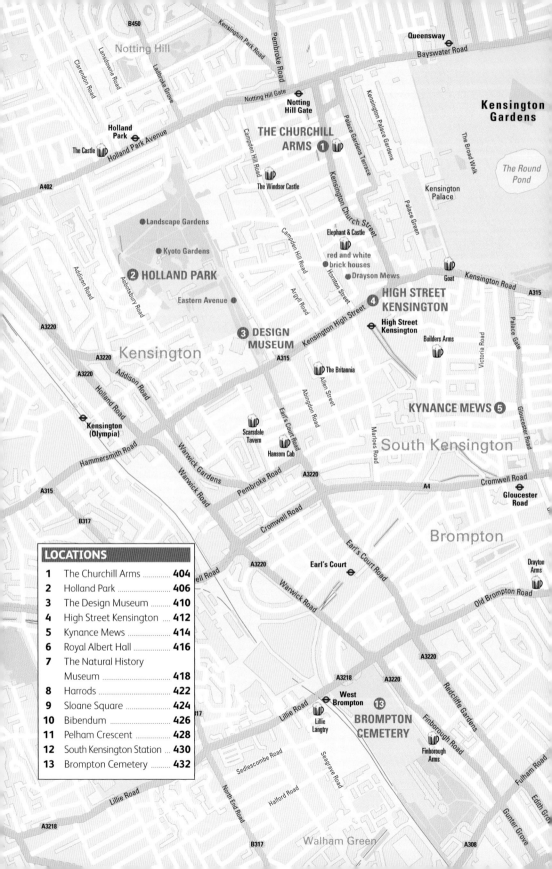

**Notting Hill**

**Kensington Gardens**

**The Round Pond**

**THE CHURCHILL ARMS** ❶

The Windsor Castle

Holland Park

The Castle

● Landscape Gardens

● Kyoto Gardens

❷ **HOLLAND PARK**

Eastern Avenue ●

Kensington

❸ **DESIGN MUSEUM**

Elephant & Castle
red and white
● brick houses
● Drayson Mews

Goat

**HIGH STREET KENSINGTON** ❹

Kensington Palace

High Street Kensington

Builders Arms

● The Britannia

**KYNANCE MEWS** ❺

Kensington (Olympia)

Scarsdale Tavern

Hansom Cab

**South Kensington**

Gloucester Road

**Brompton**

Earl's Court

Drayton Arms

West Brompton

Lillie Langtry

❶❸ **BROMPTON CEMETERY**

Finborough Arms

**Walham Green**

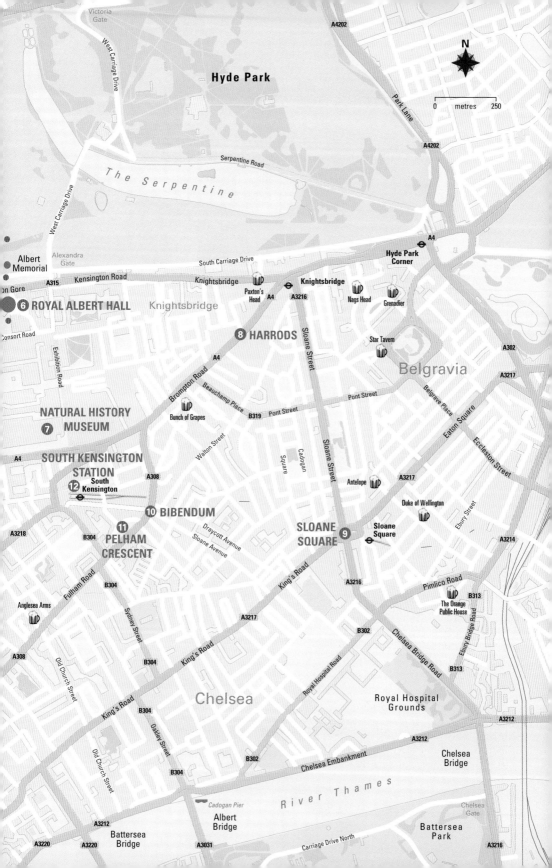

The Churchill Arms is one of the most recognisable pubs in London; the pub's website describes it as 'dripping in flowers' and this is no exaggeration; the display includes over two hundred flower baskets and window boxes and costs the brewery around £25,000 a year. It's money well spent. The Churchill Arms was originally built in 1750, and in the 1800s Winston Churchill's grandparents were regular visitors, hence the name. The ale and food are excellent, and Churchill memorabilia adorns the walls.

## What to shoot and viewpoints

The best time to visit is from around 10am onwards, when the sun lights the east-facing side of the pub. If you shoot with a midrange lens (24–70mm) from the opposite side of the road, you'll need a little patience as you wait for traffic and people to move out of shot. If you have an ultra-wide-angle or fisheye lens, shoot from the corner of Campden Street – cars are often parked on the corner so a little work is required to get these out of shot. Finally, use your zoom and move around the building to pick up details such as the pub signage amongst the flowers and the arches of flowers over doors and windows.

*Churchill Arms, Notting Hill. Canon 5D IV, 24–70mm at 43mm, ISO 200, 1/90s at f/8. Sept.*

*Opposite top: Churchill Arms, Notting Hill. Canon 5D IV, 24–70mm at 24mm, ISO 400, 1/90s at f/8. July.*

*Opposite bottom: Churchill Arms in summer, Notting Hill. Canon 5D IV, 24–70mm at 62mm, ISO 200, 1/90s at f/8. Sept.*

## How to get here

Leave Notting Hill Gate underground station or bus stops E and H on Notting Hill Gate road. Head east for about 50m and take Kensington Church Street (A4204) to your right heading south. The pub is on your right after about 500m. You can catch a bus from stop P (opposite the pub) to Victoria and South Kensington.

| | |
|---|---|
| **Location Lat/Long**: | 51.50692, -0.1948 |
| **Location Postcode**: | 119 Kensington Church Street, W8 7LN |
| **Underground & Lines**: | Notting Hill Gate: *Central, Circle and District* |
| **Bus**: | 31, 94, 148, 27, 28, 52, 70, 328 |

*Previous spread: Kynance Mews West. Canon 5D IV, 24–70mm at 38mm, ISO 200, 1/180s at f/8. June.*

## Accessibility   ♿

The exterior of the pub is fully accessible as is the ground floor of the pub itself.

### Best time of year/day

It can be shot all year round. The best times of day are morning for the sunlight, and evenings. The best days to visit are the weekend when there will be less traffic and people in your shots. The pub has a spectacular floral summer display and a special Christmas one, which in 2018 featured ninety-seven Christmas trees and 21,500 lights!

For more information visit: *www.churchillarmskensington.co.uk*

Holland Park is the name given to the fifty-four acres of Royal Park and the surrounding district. The public park once served as the grounds of the private Holland House, but the building was badly damaged in 1940 during bombing raids over London. The house and grounds were purchased by the local council in 1952 and opened to the public. The ruins of Holland House play host to an open-air theatre and is the home of Opera Holland Park, which gives performances during the summer months. The park is divided into three unique sections: semi-woodland to the north, landscape gardens including the Kyoto and Fukushima gardens at the centre, and sports grounds to the south.

The jewel in the Holland Park crown is the Kyoto Garden. Designed in the style of a Japanese water garden, it was donated by the Chamber of Commerce of Kyoto in 1992.

## What to shoot and viewpoints

There are three distinct areas of interest to the photographer: the Japanese gardens, the landscape gardens by the house and the eastern avenue.

In autumn the walkway to the far eastern side of the park is worth visiting – its golden brown foliage combining with the long walkway leading to a vanishing point. Walk to the top of the path and shoot back towards the south, where the Design Museum is located. Include people in shot and use a 70mm+ lens to compress perspective. Aim to arrive about ninety minutes after sunrise and at a weekend, when it's generally quieter. During spring and autumn there's often a chance of light mist and crepuscular rays through the trees.

Make your way to the Kyoto Garden, following signs from the top of the eastern pathway. Try to obtain photos without people in; I always feel the serenity of the garden works best without human distraction but you'll need patience to wait for clear shots. Begin taking photos at the point you enter the garden to the south. Shooting across the pond offers reflections of the plants and ornaments that decorate the pond, and birds such as herons and coots will enhance the natural feel. Shooting from the western side means you can capture the waterfall on the eastern side. For maximum impact, seek to include reflections. The narrow bridge that crosses in front of the waterfall is a popular spot for visitors so arrive early and be patient. »

*Opposite top*: *Japanese Kyoto Garden, Holland Park. Canon 5D II, 24–70mm at 45mm, ISO 250, 1/30s at f/16. May.*

## How to get here

Holland Park Tube station is north of the park. Leave the station and turn left. Walk for about 100m then take Holland Park road to your right. Follow it as it curves to the right and after approximately 500m, you'll see the entrance and the park's name in large letters on the wall.

| | |
|---|---|
| **Location Lat/Long**: | 51.5032, -0.20365 |
| **Location Postcode**: | W8 6LU |
| **Underground & Lines**: | High Street Kensington, Holland Park: *Central, Circle and District* |
| **Mainline Station**: | Kensington Olympia Station |
| **Bus**: | 31, 94, 148, 228, N207 |
| **Cycle Hire**: | Abbotsbury Road, Holland Park, Ilchester Place |

## Accessibility ♿

Some areas in the densely wooded parts of the park are harder to access for those with limited mobility due to steep inclines but the southern areas of the park and the Kyoto Garden are fully accessible.

### Best time of year/day

Spring right through to autumn are the best seasons to visit. The park is open dawn to dusk with the Kyoto Garden open from 10am to 5pm.

*Opposite*: *Holland Park. Canon 5D IV, 24–70mm at 24mm, ISO 400, 1/350s at f/8. July.*

Holland Park Walk in autumn. Canon 5D II, 70–200mm at 100mm, ISO 400, 1/60s at f/8. Oct.

*Holland Park Walk in autumn. Canon 5D II, 17–40mm at 23mm, ISO 800, 1/45s at f/19. Oct.*

The woodlands to the north of the park are managed but have a natural look, with winding paths that meander through the dense trees. During summer, when foliage is thick, low light will require a higher ISO.

Complete your visit by touring the flower gardens by the main buildings. You'll find all manner of sculptures and areas of the original Holland House. Explore the maze of garden paths that surround the house and you'll discover fountains, rose gardens, painted frescos and even peacocks. And after midday in summer months, you'll have the chance to include people in these shots, enlivening your photographs.

**Top**: *Waterfall in the Kyoto Garden. Canon 5D IV, 24–70mm at 34mm, ISO 200, 1/6s at f/19. July.*

**Above**: *Holland Park. Canon 5D IV, 24–70mm at 24mm, ISO 200, 1/90s at f/8. July.*

**Opposite**: *Heron in the Kyoto Garden. Canon 5D II, 70–200mm at 200mm, ISO 250, 1/180s at f/11. May.*

Entrepreneur Sir Terence Conran founded the Design Museum in 1989 as a place to display the heritage of design in four key areas: industrial, fashion, graphic and architectural design. Originally the Design Museum was located at Shad Thames but the place became too cramped. Conran invested £20 million of his own money to buy a new space in Kensington that was three times bigger, and the museum moved there in 2016. There are three floors of exhibits: paid-for exhibitions on the ground floor; workshops on the second floor, and public galleries on the third. The museum won the European Museum of the Year in 2018.

## What to shoot and viewpoints

In keeping with the principles of good design, the interior of the museum is functional, with clean lines that make perfect subject matter for abstract images. Look to isolate the beams that support the parabolic roof with its curves and twists, and the interplay between light and shadow. Including people in such vast interior spaces adds emotional weight and helps bring images into balance, softening them and making them more interesting for viewers. The museum is not only educational but a wonderful place to practise composition skills.

*Design Museum, Holland Park. Canon 5D IV, 24–70mm at 24mm, ISO 1600, 1/15s at f/6.7. July.*

***Opposite top***: *Design Museum. Canon 5D IV, 24–70mm at 24mm, ISO 800, 1/15s at f/5.6. July.*

***Opposite***: *Abstract of the ceiling, Design Museum. Canon 5D IV, 24–70mm at 46mm, ISO 1600, 1/15s at f/6.7. July.*

## How to get here

Travel to High Street Kensington on the District Line, exit the station and turn left at the main entrance on Kensington High Street, heading east. After about 250m you'll see the entrance to Holland Park with the Design Museum on the left.

| | |
|---|---|
| **Location Lat/Long**: | 51.49989, -0.20024 |
| **Location Postcode**: | W8 6AG |
| **Underground & Lines**: | High Street Kensington, Holland Park: *Central, Circle and District* |
| **Mainline Station**: | Kensington Olympia Station |
| **Bus**: | 31, 94, 148, 228, N207 |
| **Cycle Hire**: | Abbotsbury Road, Holland Park, Ilchester Place |

## Accessibility ♿

The museum is fully accessible to all.

## Best time of year/day

This interior location requires no special time of year or day, however to minimise the number of people in your shots, arrive at opening time midweek.

## Opening hours

10am–6pm. The museum is open until 8pm on the first Friday of every month. It is closed on Christmas Eve, Christmas Day and Boxing Day. Visit *www.designmuseum.org* for more information.

***Opposite right***: *Design Museum. Canon 5D IV, 24–70mm at 43mm, ISO 1600, 1/15s at f/6.7. July.*

Centered around High Street Kensington Tube station, this small area just west of Hyde Park has a few interesting side streets that are worth exploring.

## What to shoot and viewpoints

Leaving the ticket hall of the Tube station you'll enter the station shopping arcade. Walk to the street entrance and shoot back towards the ticket hall to capture the symmetry of the arcade. This is best shot early in the morning before the crowds arrive. Leave the station entrance and take Hornton Street, which is on the other side of Kensington High Street, opposite the station entrance. Head north for about 250m until you reach the crossroads with Holland Street. Here you'll find unusual red- and white-brick houses only found in this part of London. These are best shot with a tight composition and a zoom lens to isolate the houses and remove distractions. Take a right along Holland Street, and after 50m you'll find Drayson Mews and its wonderful, curved, cobbled street – aim to make the curve the most important part of your image. Continue east along Holland Street for around 10m. With Gordon Place to your right, you can make a wonderful composition using the green lamppost at the centre of foliage and the red- and white-brick townhouses in the background. Again, head east along Holland Street for around 50m, until you find Kensington Church Walk – a small alley. Take this, heading south and this quiet path will lead you through the churchyard of St Mary Abbots and back to Kensington High Street opposite the Tube station. The Barkers building can be found 100m east of High Street Kensington station, directly opposite Kensington Church Street junction.

*Unusual house design in Holland Park. Canon 5D II, 70–200mm at 78mm, ISO 250, 1/350s at f/8. May.*

*Lamppost, Kensington. Canon 5D IV, 17–40mm at 17mm, ISO 200, 1/45s at f/8. July.*

## How to get here

Take the Circle or District line to Kensington High Street station, or take the number 9 bus from Piccadilly Circus to Hammersmith.

| | |
|---|---|
| **Location Lat/Long**: | 51.50097, -0.19269 |
| **Location Postcode**: | W8 5SA |
| **Underground & Lines**: | South Kensington, Sloane Square: *Circle and District, Piccadilly* |
| **Bus**: | 9, 23, 28, 49, 328, N9, N28 |
| **Cycle Hire**: | Argyll Road, Derry Street, Wrights Lane |

## Accessibility ♿

These are all street-level locations and should present no issues.

### Best time of year/day

The best time is during the day from spring through to autumn.

*Opposite: Entrance hall, High St Kensington Underground station. Sony A6000, Fisheye 8mm at 8mm, ISO 200, 1/60s at f/8. May.*

*Barkers building, Kensington. Canon 5D IV, 24–70mm at 42mm, ISO 200, 1/750s at f/5.6. July.*

*Autumn on Kensington Church Walk. Canon 5D II, 70–200mm at 70mm, ISO 200, 1/20s at f/8. Oct.*

*Drayson Mews, Kensington. Canon 5D II, 70–200mm at 70mm, ISO 200, 1/125s at f/9.5. Oct.*

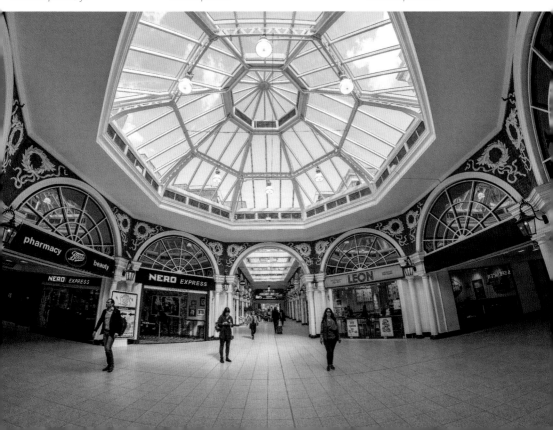

Originally used as stables for horses, Kynance Mews was called Cornwall Mews until 1924. The mews, described as 'sheer rustic rose-petal-perfect-pretty' by guidebook author David Tucker, have appeared in several films and are Insta-famous. They are also a highly sought after location to live; in 1970 you could buy a house in the mews for around £9,000, today the average price is over £2 million.

There are three arches here, all with Grade II listed status. This mews holds a secret: during autumn the Virginia creeper that adorns the eastern arch on Launceston Place turns blood red and it's hard to resist photographing.

## What to shoot and viewpoints

The first viewpoint is the mews entrance arch on the eastern side of Launceston Place. Visit during autumn when the Virginia creeper leaves turn blood red; the combination of bright red leaves and the quaint houses seen through the arch make the image stunning.

The second viewpoint is found by crossing Launceton Place to the west mews. Shoot looking away from the road – the house closest to the arch is festooned with wisteria in spring and a wide-angle lens is useful to capture the arch and the houses in the foreground.

The third viewpoint is Kynance Place. Walk north, leaving the arches behind you and, after about 75m, a pedestrian alleyway to your right leads into Kynance Place. Here you'll find the green lampposts that are unique to Chelsea. Compose images with the lampposts against the bright white walls and wooden-framed windows. Including passers-by will lend your images a lively feel.

The fourth and final spot is to proceed west along Kynance Mews' western section until you find a set of steps to your right around half way along. These steps lead to Christ Church on Eldon Street. During spring and summer mornings the small grounds to the northern side of the church catch the warm tones of sunlight.

Please be aware that although the mews are public roads, people live there and expect visitors to respect their privacy. Try to keep noise to a minimum while taking photos.

*Opposite top left: Kynance Mews West. Canon 5D IV, 24–70mm at 38mm, ISO 200, 1/180s at f/8. June. **Top right**: Kynance Mews in spring, Kensington. Canon 5D IV, 24–70mm at 50mm, ISO 400, 1/90s at f/11. July.*

***Middle**: Kensington lamppost, Kynance Place. Canon 5D IV, 24–70mm at 40mm, ISO 200, 1/45s at f/8. Sept.*

## How to get here

Take the Piccadilly line to Gloucester Road underground station, exit the station and head west along Cromwell Road towards the Holiday Inn. Opposite the hotel is Grenville Place – follow this north for 200m until you reach a mini roundabout, where the road becomes Launceston Place. After 50m you'll see Kynance Mews.

| | |
|---|---|
| **Location Lat/Long**: | 51.497430, -0.185877 |
| **Location Postcode**: | SW7 4QR |
| **Underground & Lines**: | Gloucester Road: *Circle and District, Piccadilly* |
| **Main Station**: | London Bridge |
| **Bus**: | 49, 74, N74 |
| **Cycle Hire**: | Gloucester Road |

## Accessibility ♿

The mews are at street level so shooting the entrances should present no issues. If steps pose a problem, you may wish to take the long way round to Christ Church by heading north away from the mews and taking the first left, pass Launceston Place Restaurant. Then take the next left, continue for 250m and you'll see the church.

## Best time of year/day

The best time of year is autumn when the Virginia creeper is in all its crimson glory. The best time of day is just before midday to avoid whiteout skies.

***Opposite left**: Christ Church Kensington. Canon 5D IV, 24–70mm at 24mm, ISO 200, 1/60s at f/8. July. **Right**: Kynance Mews in autumn. Canon 5D IV, 24–70mm at 50mm, ISO 200, 1/45s at f/5.6. Oct.*

There isn't a more distinctive building in London than the Grade I listed Royal Albert Hall. First proposed in 1851 by Prince Albert as a permanent place of enlightenment for the public, the hall was eventually opened by Queen Victoria in 1871. Sadly Albert died in 1861 and never saw the hall completed. The first concerts were a disaster: the architecture destroyed the acoustics and people remarked that it was the only concert hall where a composer could hear their work played twice! It wasn't until 1969 when sound-baffling 'mushrooms' were installed in the ceiling and the echo problem was solved.

The Hall is primarily a premier concert venue – it hosts the BBC Sir Henry Wood Promenade Concerts, known as 'The Proms', an annual eight-week summer season of daily classical music concerts – but it also hosts speakers, graduation ceremonies, ballet and even sporting events. The array of events means the hall is true to Prince Albert's original vision and, as this majestic building is a joy to photograph, it should be high on your list of locations.

## What to shoot and viewpoints

There are two key viewpoints from which to photograph the Royal Albert Hall.

### The Front: From the Albert Memorial ♿

The first is at the base of the Albert Memorial in Hyde Park (opposite the concert hall), from where you can include the statue in your composition. You'll be shooting south into the sun's path during summer so visit after midday or when cloud obscures the sun to prevent lens flare or exposure issues.

### The Rear: From Prince Consort Road ♿

For the other main viewpoint head to the rear of the building and photograph from Prince Consort Road. This spot offers the chance for compositions with no traffic and you can use the steps as a lead line to the building. Additionally, the rear of the building offers the chance of a longer shot using a shorter focal length.

## Triumph of the Arts and Sciences

Once you have completed your front and rear images, consider using your zoom lens to begin isolating the 'Triumph of the Arts and Sciences' frieze that is wrapped around the entire structure. Isolate sections, include the curvature of the structure and use blue sky as a background. This works well when shooting the rear of the building with sunlight providing warm yet strong contrasting light.

*Opposite top left: Albert Memorial and Royal Albert Hall. Canon 5D IV, 24–70mm at 58mm, ISO 100, 1/15s at f/16, tripod. July.* ***Top right****: Albert Memorial and The Royal Albert Hall. Canon 5D II, 70–200mm at 106mm, ISO 200, 1/500s at f/8. May.* ***Middle left****: Royal Albert Hall at night. Canon 5D IV, 24–70mm at 27mm, ISO 100, 30s at f/13, tripod, LEE ND 0.9 grad. July.* ***Bottom left****: Royal Albert Hall, rear entrance. Canon 5D IV, 70–200mm at 97mm, ISO 200, 1/60s at f/8. Nov.* ***Bottom right****: Detail of the Royal Albert Hall. Canon 5D IV, 70–200mm at 165mm, ISO 200, 1/90s at f/16. July.*

## How to get here

The easiest underground route is by taking the Piccadilly line to Knightsbridge. Turn left out of the station and head west along Kensington Road with Hyde Park on your right. The Hall is around half-a-mile from the station. A better option is to catch bus number 9 from Piccadilly Circus to bus stop (RC) directly outside the hall.

| | |
|---|---|
| **Location Lat/Long**: | 51.50104, -0.1775 |
| **Location Postcode**: | SW7 2AP |
| **Underground & Lines**: | Gloucester Road, Knightsbridge, South Kensington: *Circle and District, Piccadilly* |
| **Main Station**: | Paddington |
| **Bus**: | 9, 23, 52, 70, 360, 452, 702, N9, N52 |
| **Cycle Hire**: | Kensington Gore |

## Accessibility ♿

The exterior of the hall is fully accessible and should present no problems though the steps from Prince Consort Road will present issues for wheelchair users.

## Best time of year/day

You can visit the hall any time of year but the best time of day is morning when the sun lights the rear of the hall (for close-ups of the exterior). Midday is ideal for the front-facing shots and it's worth visiting late in the evening to see the exterior lit up.

## Admission prices (2019)

Interior tours run daily from 10am–4pm, when personal photography is allowed. For more infoormation go to: *www.royalalberthall.com*

| | |
|---|---|
| **Adults**: | £13.75 |
| **Children**: | £6.75 |
| **Students**: | £11.75 |

The Natural History Museum is one of three museums in South Kensington, along with the Science Museum and the Victoria and Albert Museum. Work on the Natural History Museum began in 1873 and it opened ten years later. Prior to this, the natural history collection – plant and animal specimens – were housed at the British Museum. The government purchased the original collection (71,000 items) from Dr Hans Sloane – an Irish physician, naturalist and collector. However, because of an almost comedic disregard for the specimens and infighting between collectors, many specimens were sold, destroyed and mislabelled.

Palaeontologist Richard Owen was given the job of sorting out the British Museum natural history department and he redefined what a museum should be. Owen requested a new building for the natural history collection and in 1886 the move from the British Museum to the current location was complete.

*Stonework at the National History Museum. Canon 5D II, 24–70mm at 27mm, ISO 1600, 1/30s at f/3.2. May.*

The exterior of the building is a joy to photograph and, once you step inside (photography is allowed), the interior architecture and the exhibits, from dinosaurs to moon exploration, is a wonderful voyage of discovery.

## What to shoot and viewpoints

### Outside ♿

The exterior of the building is adorned with carvings of flora and fauna, and a zoom lens is best to capture and isolate these terracotta mouldings. The gates, even when closed, allow you to capture the building. With a wide-angle lens, use the curved ramps at the entrance as lead lines. Try a visit at night as the building is usually illuminated.

### Inside ♿

To ensure you can enter the building at opening time, queue at the corner of Cromwell Road and Exhibition Road. Doors open at exactly 10am, so start queuing at around 9.30am to get in quickly. Most days see around 500 people queuing by opening time. »

*Natural History Museum. Sony A6000, Fisheye 8mm at 8mm, ISO 800, 1/6s at f/8. May.*

*Natural History Museum shot through the gates. Canon 5D IV, 24–70mm at 32mm, ISO 100, 30s at f/6.7, tripod. July.*

*Natural History Museum stairs. Sony A6000, Fisheye 8mm at 8mm, ISO 800, 1/160s at f/8. June.*

*Charles Darwin statue. Canon 5D IV, 24–70mm at 34mm, ISO 400, 1/60s at f/9.5. June.*

***Opposite***: *Main hall. Sony A6000, Fisheye 8mm at 8mm, ISO 100, 1/200s at f/8. June.*

There is much to photograph as you explore the museum – be drawn by whatever interests you most. My stand-out composition of choice is where the main entrance leads into the main hall; head to the end of the hall, up the steps past Darwin's statue, then double back along the upper balcony. Finally, ascend the steps to the top floor. You'll find yourself by a balcony overlooking the main hall, where the whale is suspended. This wide balcony is useful to rest your camera on to get a steady shot without using a high ISO. If you have a very wide-angle or fisheye lens then this is the place to use it. Opening time is ideal for an image with the whale in the centre of your shot, especially on a bright sunny day, as the sun will enter the main hall through the skylights, casting strong bands of light across the rear of the hall. Another great image can be found at the rear of the building: go up the stairs to the cross-section of the tree trunk, then turn around to shoot, using the brass handrail as a lead line into the hall, along with the curvature of the ceiling.

## How to get here

Take the Piccadilly line to South Kensington Tube station, leave via the above-ground exit and make your way at street level towards Exhibition Road. Alternatively, use the underground tunnel that runs directly from the ticket hall to the museum entrance – the tunnel is perfect for getting children to the museum safely as there are no roads to cross.

| | |
|---|---|
| **Location Lat/Long**: | 51.49674, -0.17637 |
| **Location Postcode**: | SW7 5BD |
| **Underground & Lines**: | Gloucester Road, South Kensington: *Circle and District, Piccadilly* |
| **Bus**: | 14, 49, 70, 74, 345, 360, 414, 430, C1 |
| **Cycle Hire**: | Exhibition Road, Thurloe Place |

## Accessibility

The museum is fully accessible. The wheelchair-accessible entrance is located on Exhibition Road, and you can hire wheelchairs in the museum. There are twelve disabled parking bays on Exhibition Road, if you wish to arrive early and park close to the museum. Assistance dogs are welcome in the museum with outside facilities to exercise your dog after your visit. Large-print maps are available on request and induction loops are fitted to the audio/visual displays. The museum also runs specimen-handling events for the blind.

## Best time of year/day

The museum is open all year round but the best time of day is early in the morning at opening time. The sun will illuminate the front of the main building and the interior of the great hall will be well lit. At Christmastime, an ice rink is installed in the grounds and you can observe the skaters from Exhibition Road. The museum grounds are only open during the day.

## Opening hours

Open daily 10am–5.50pm (Last entry 5.30pm).
Closed 24–26th Dec.

## Admission price (2019)

**Free**.

The museum is run by a charitable trust and entry is free so please consider making a small donation at the entrance or buying something from the gift shop. Attractions like the Natural History Museum are only able to offer free entry due to donations, so it's important we do all we can to keep these wonderful places open for all. Visit: *www.nhm.ac.uk* for more information.

*Harrods at night. Canon 5D II, 17–40mm at 25mm, ISO 100, 8s at f/18, tripod. Oct.*

**Shop owner Charles Henry Harrod – draper, mercer, and haberdasher – wanted to catch the trade from The Great Exhibition when it was situated in Hyde Park, so he set up a small shop at Harrods' current Knightsbridge location in 1834. His store eventually became one of the most prestigious shops in the world and the largest single department store in Europe.**

Harrods has its own postcode and was the first store in England to have a 'moving staircase' – an escalator. Nervous customers were offered brandy at the top to revive them after their 'ordeal'! The store has a strict dress code and staff have declined entry to many celebrities considered not properly attired. Harrods is now owned by the state of Qatar through its sovereign wealth fund, the Qatar Investment Authority.

## What to shoot and viewpoints

The Harrods building is famous for its incredible light display, which is switched on at dusk. The entire building is covered with thousands of bulbs and illuminated signs. Due to its uniform shape and design, the store can be shot from either side. Shooting from the opposite side of the road will allow you to capture the building in its entirety with a wide-angle lens and also to include traffic streaks from the road in shot.

*Flags outside Harrods. Canon 5D II, 70–200mm at 200mm, ISO 200, 1/125s at f/8. June.*

*Harrods fully illuminated. Canon 5D II, 17–40mm at 17mm, ISO 100, 8s at f/18, tripod. Oct.*

## How to get here

Take the Piccadilly line to Knightsbridge station. As you exit the station, turn left and head east for 500m to Harrods.

**Location Lat/Long**:  51.49965, -0.16361
**Location Postcode**:  SW1X 7XL
**Underground & Lines**:  Knightsbridge: *Piccadilly*
**Bus**:  14, 74, 414, C1
**Cycle Hire**:  Montpelier Street

## Accessibility &

The store is a street-level location and should present no issues.

## Best time of year/day

Visit all year round and try to shoot in the evening, just after dusk.

*Harrods signage. Canon 5D IV, 70–200mm at 138mm, ISO 200, 1/60s at f/8. Oct.*

*Buses meeting in Sloane Square. Sony A6000, Fisheye 8mm at 8mm, ISO 400, 1/500s at f/8. June.*

**Marking the boundaries between Belgravia, Chelsea and Knightsbridge, Sloane Square was named after Sir Hans Sloane and was formally known as Hans Town; signs in some streets north of the square still display the original name. The location was made famous in the 1980s as of haunt of the 'Sloane Rangers' and later by the TV show *Made in Chelsea*, which details the lives of young, wealthy residents.**

## What to shoot and viewpoints

This is an easy location to shoot. It's a busy square with lots of people, shops and buses – a typical London scene in fact. The key subjects are people resting on the benches, the fountain and the pigeons bathing in it. The square itself is not very large so a wide-angle lens will stretch perspective and help draw attention to the subjects in the foreground, whilst removing the less interesting shops and offices that line the square. As the sun enters the space, its beams of light will be useful as lead lines to people on the benches. A zoom lens will isolate details such as birds in the fountain. Buses use the square to turn around, so when shooting short depth-of-field shots, pay attention to large swathes of red in the background. The canopy of trees provides shade in the summer and autumn and also reduces the chance of highlight blowouts as strong midday sun fills the square. Early in the morning the nearby cafes offer street photography opportunities as people linger over coffee and newspapers; these shots work best on quiet Sunday mornings.

*Opposite: Sloane Square fountain. Canon 5D II, 70–200mm at 200mm, ISO 200, 1/30s at f/8. June.*

*Pigeon in the Sloane Square fountain. Canon 5D II, 70–200mm at 200mm, ISO 200, 1/60s at f/8. June.*

*Labradors in Sloane Sqaure. Canon 5D II, 70–200mm at 155mm, ISO 200, 1/30s at f/6.7. May.*

## How to get here

Take the District or Circle line to Sloane Square Tube station or take the number 22 from Oxford Circus to Sloane Square.

**Location Lat/Long:** 51.49235, -0.15643
**Location Postcode:** SW1W 8BB
**Underground & Lines:** South Kensington, Sloane Square: *Circle and District, Piccadilly*
**Bus:** 11, 19, 21, 22, 211, C1, N11, N19, N22
**Cycle Hire:** Sedding Street

## Accessibility ♿

This is a street-level location that should present no issues.

## Best time of year/day

During the daytime, sunny days work best as the trees hold back just the right amount of light, and beams of light can be used in compositions. On overcast days the square will darken a little and you'll need to increase ISO and exposure to compensate.

*Exterior of Bibendem. Canon 5D II, 17–40mm at 37mm, ISO 100, 1/30s at f/10. May.*

A five-minute walk from South Kensington Tube station is Bibendum, or Michelin House. Bibendum is the French name for the character we know as the Michelin Man – mascot of the Michelin tyre company – and this Grade II listed building was first built as a garage in 1911. It served two functions in fact: garage and the UK headquarters of Michelin, until it was sold to restaurateur Sir Terence Conran and publisher Paul Hamlyn in 1985. It's now known as the Bibendum Oyster Bar but because Conran loved the building, he retained all its original features during the building's interior redesign. Bibendum looks quite incongruous considering its postcode, as it was designed and built at the end of the Art-Nouveau period.

## What to shoot and viewpoints

Both night and day Bibendum is a superb building to photograph. Its true beauty lies in the brightly coloured decorations that adorn the exterior; a mix of tiles and glass are used to create colours and shapes. Viewpoints from which to shoot the building are limited as it's situated on a busy junction – it was, after all, originally a working garage – so use the traffic islands in the middle of the junction to gain a clear line of sight. From here, you can see the front and east-facing side of the building. If you have a wide-angle lens, use the crossing just in front of the building to capture a clear shot.

During the day use a standard midrange lens to pick out details in the decor, especially the wonderful friezes that adorn the sides of the building, depicting classic motor racing scenes from the early 20th century. The restaurant opens just before lunchtime and the main entrance houses flower stalls that add a burst of colour. In the evening and at night, when the building's illuminations are switched on, is when Bibendum really shines.

## How to get here

Take the Piccadilly or District line to South Kensington Tube station, exit the station on the south side and follow Pelham Road (with the brick wall to your left) for about 450m and it will lead directly to Bibendum.

**Location Lat/Long:** 51.49333, -0.16893
**Location Postcode:** 81 Fulham road, SW3 6RD
**Underground & Lines:** South Kensington: *Circle and District, Piccadilly*
**Bus:** 360
**Cycle Hire:** Sloane Avenue

*Opposite: Stained glass window, Bibendum. Canon 5D II, 70–200mm at 160mm, ISO 200, 1/125s at f/8. June.*

## Accessibility ♿

This is a street location and should present no problems.

## Best time of year/day

It can be shot at any time of year and any time of day.

*Above: Bibendum at night. Canon 5D II, 17–40mm at 17mm, ISO 100, 4s at f/9, tripod. Oct.*

*Solitary bicycle on Pelham Crescent, Chelsea. Sony A6000, 16–50mm at 16mm, ISO 100, 1/200s at f/5. May.*

If you find yourself in Kensington, I recommend making time to stop at Pelham Crescent. Situated very close to Bibendum (page 426), Pelham Crescent is one of the most sought after areas in London, with an average house price in 2019 of around £9 million. This wonderful crescent with its Georgian townhouses was constructed in 1825 and it's a delight to photograph.

## What to shoot and viewpoints

You will need a midrange or zoom lens to isolate and compress the houses. Stand on the edge of the road and shoot at an angle that captures the curvature of the crescent. Using a zoom lens will compress the perspective and draw the houses closer together offering a more intimate image. Lampposts are situated around the crescent and offer an additional component for your compositions. This is a residential street so discretion should be taken while taking pictures; please be mindful that you're taking photographs of people's houses and show due consideration.

## How to get here

Make your way to Bibendum (page 426) then proceed west along Fulham Road for about 100m until you see the crescent on the north side of the road.

**Location Lat/Long**:    51.493153, -0.17057592
**Location Postcode**:   SW3 6SN
**Underground & Lines**:  South Kensington: *Circle and District,*
                                  *Piccadilly*
**Bus**:                         360
**Cycle Hire**:          Sloane Avenue

## Accessibility ♿

This is a residential street and should present no issues.

### Best time of year/day

Any time of year is good for a visit. The best time of day is morning to midday, when the sun lights the houses and brings out the wonderful contrast of the architecture.

*Above*: Houses on Pelham Crescent. Canon 5D II, 70–200mm at 70mm, ISO 200, 1/125s at f/8. June.

*Opposite*: Pelham Crescent on a sunny morning. Canon 5D II, 70–200mm at 111mm, ISO 200, 1/350s at f/8. June.

South Kensington station is best known as the gateway to the Natural History Museum, so most visitors arrive and simply take the underground tunnel to the museum. However, this west London station has some wonderful aspects that deserve more attention. The station is a labyrinth and has the feel of a place that has grown organically, with bits bolted on as it has grown, giving it a unique charm.

## What to shoot and viewpoints

The District and Circle lines arrive at the upper platforms, and here you'll find a small wildflower garden located at the far eastern end of the platforms – the end farthest from the exit. A standard midrange lens should suffice for shooting here and mornings are best on sunny days to capture the summer mood. After exiting the gates in the ticket hall, head down the tunnel that leads all the way to the museum entrances. The tunnel is quite dark so a high ISO works best, and use a short depth of field to isolate individuals walking ahead of you, or buskers playing. If you leave the ticket hall at street level, you'll enter a small shopping arcade. On bright days the shadow lines cast by sunlight can be used in strong compositions; use a wide-angle

*Garden at the eastern end of South Kensington Station platform. Canon 5D II, 24–70mm at 24mm, ISO 200, 1/45s at f/8. May.*

lens to capture the scene and increase the sense of space by extending the perspective. Outside the station you'll find cafes – take a seat and keep your camera close to capture the people around you – and to the southwest, a distinctive bronze statue of Hungarian composer Béla Bartók.

*Statue of Bartok outside South Kensington Station. Canon 5D II, 24–70mm at 28mm, ISO 200, 1/90s at f/8. June.*

## How to get here

Take the Piccadilly, Circle or District lines to the station.

| | |
|---|---|
| **Location Lat/Long**: | 51.49416, -0.17395 |
| **Location Postcode**: | SW7 2NB |
| **Underground & Lines**: | South Kensington, Sloane Square: *Circle and District, Piccadilly* |
| **Bus**: | 14, 70, 74, 430, 360, 414, C1, N74, N97 |
| **Cycle Hire**: | South Kensington Station |

## Accessibility &#9855;

South Kensington station is accessible to all.

## Best time of year/day

The platform, flower garden and cafes around the station are best shot in spring and summer. The tunnel can be shot any time of year.

**One of 'Magnificent Seven' cemeteries of London, Brompton is perhaps the most beautiful. Consecrated in 1839 and still in use today with over 35,000 gravestones and monuments, it is one of the largest central London cemeteries. There is a large variety of wildlife for the inner city – it's home to bats, foxes, macaws and owls and more than two hundred species of moth. There are also sixty-odd species of tree.**

During the 19th century, Buffalo Bill's Wild West show visited the nearby Earl's Court Exhibition Grounds and sadly several Sioux tribe members died while working in the show. They were buried in Brompton Cemetery. During the late 20th century some of the bodies were exhumed and sent home to their tribal burial grounds in America. The writer Beatrix Potter lived close by and apparently often enjoyed walking in the cemetery. It's believed that she used some of the names on gravestones for characters in her books.

## What to shoot and viewpoints

For the key viewpoints start at the north end of the cemetery and walk along the central avenue that leads to the chapel in the distance. This avenue is the perfect place to take long shots of solitary figures; a 150–200mm lens works incredibly well here, as it will compress the perspective and help isolate figures. Keep an eye out for flowers around the plots and for wildlife – robins and squirrels perched atop headstones make for good images. If you have an infrared camera, the central walkway works well later in the morning as the sun's light hits the canopy of trees. >>

*Brompton Cemetery central avenue in autumn. Canon 5D IV, 70–200mm at 111mm, ISO 400, 1/125s at f/6.7. Oct.*

*Chapel, Brompton Cemetery. Canon 5D IV, 24–70mm at 50mm, ISO 200, 1/180s at f/11. June.*

*An early morning dog walker in Brompton Cemetery. Canon 5D IV, 70–200mm at 138mm, ISO 400, 1/350s at f/4.5. June.*

## How to get here

Take the District Line to West Brompton station. Exit the station and turn right, then walk for around 100m. The cemetery entrance is on your right.

**Location Lat/Long:**   51.48481, -0.19067
**Location Postcode:**   SW5 9JE
**Underground & Lines:**   Earl's Court, West Brompton: *District and Piccadilly*
**Bus:**   14, 74, 190, 211, 328, 414, 430, C1, C3
**Cycle Hire:**   Harcourt Terrace, Hortensia Road

## Accessibility

Most of the cemetery is fully accessible but there are some sections such as the colonnades that have some steps. Also note that if you have limited mobility, you'll need to arrive via the eastbound platform or by bus, as the station's westbound platform is not fully accessible.

## Best time of year/day

The best time of year is from spring through to autumn, when the colours are most vibrant. The cemetery is open during the day, from dawn to dusk and mornings are generally the quietest time to visit.

*Chapel, Brompton Cemetery. Canon 5D IV, 24–70mm at 24mm, ISO 200, 1/350s at f/11. June.*

As you break cover from the central avenue, take the right path into the curve of the colonnade tunnel. On bright mornings the stark lines from the columns cast shadows against the back wall, making excellent monochrome images, and the presence of a figure among the shadow lines makes a compelling one. Looking out to where the main chapel is situated, use the arches as frames for angels on top of the tombs. As you exit the tunnel and arrive at the front of the chapel, head round the back to get pictures of this domed building. Take the eastern path from the chapel, back along the far edge of the cemetery among the dense foliage – this will bring you back to your starting position at the north entrance.

Amongst the trees, and worth searching out, are memorials and mausoleums to artists, actors, activists and industrialists, as well as soldiers, scientists, sports people and socialites. You'll find the grave of suffragette Emmeline Pankhurst here. For an interactive map of people buried in the cemetery visit: ***www.royalparks.org.uk***

*Top right: Brompton Cemetery. Canon 5D IV, 70–200mm at 200mm, ISO 400, 1/1500s at f/4. June. Middle: Graves in Brompton Cemetery. Canon 5D IV, 70–200mm at 200mm, ISO 200, 1/350s at f/4.5. June. Bottom: Flowers in Brompton Cemetery. Canon 5D IV, 70–200mm at 150mm, ISO 200, 1/350s at f/8. June.*

*Opposite: Brompton Cemetery walkways. Canon 5D IV, 70–200mm at 144mm, ISO 200, 1/90s at f/5.6. Oct.*

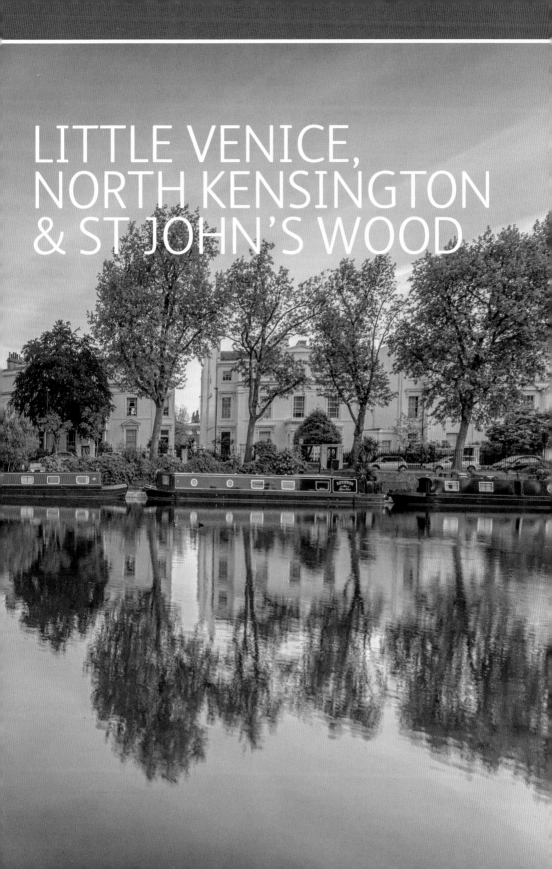

# LITTLE VENICE, NORTH KENSINGTON & ST JOHN'S WOOD

**And now on to one of the shorter sections of the book: Little Venice, North Kensington and St John's Wood which all lie along the Grand Union Canal.**

We begin with a location that is truly world famous: Abbey Road – the street where the Fab Four (the Beatles) were photographed on the pelican crossing. The iconic image featured on the cover of their eleventh studio album, *Abbey Road*. You can visit that very same crossing (now a protected historical landmark), pose as one of the band and have your photo taken by a friend. If you're on a solo trip, the famous Abbey Road Studios operates a 24-hour web-cam, where you'll be able to see yourself on the crossing and download your own keepsake image of your visit.

Little Venice is next and this well-known canal junction is a great place to shoot reflections of boats, trees by the canal and the surrounding houses. As you walk west along the Grand Union Canal, see what river wildlife you can spot before looking out for one of London's most iconic examples of Brutalist architecture: Ernő Goldfinger's Trellick Tower, which makes a striking statement as it rears up against the London skyline. It's even more impressive up close, conjuring images of *Brave New World* with its minimalist compositions and harsh architecture. Close to Trellick Tower you'll find London's most famous market: Portobello Road. It's not a place you generally go to buy anything specific but, trust me, with so many unusual items on offer, you're bound to come away with something!

Finally, the section ends with a visit to another of my favourite London cemeteries, Kensal Green. This magnificent Victorian resting place offers some of the best examples of tombs and mausoleums in London. While perhaps not as varied as the more well known Highgate to the far north, Kensal Green offers some sights you won't find in any other of London's 'Magnificent Seven' cemeteries.

*Pathway, Kensal Green Cemetery. Canon 5D II, 70–200mm at 51mm, ISO 200, 1/20s at f/11. Oct.*

*Previous spread: Looking across Little Venice on a bright, still morning. Canon 5D II, 17–40mm at 17mm, ISO 100, 1/8s at f/11, tripod, LEE ND 0.9 grad. May.*

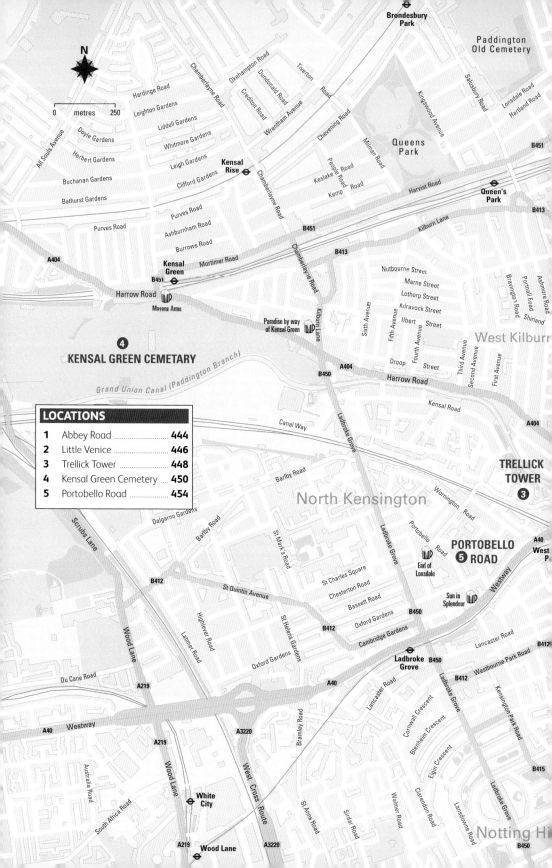

N

0 metres 250

Hardinge Road
Leighton Gardens
Liddell Gardens
Doyle Gardens
Whitmore Gardens
Herbert Gardens
Leigh Gardens
Buchanan Gardens
Clifford Gardens
Bathurst Gardens
Purves Road
Purves Road
Ashburnham Road
Burrows Road

All Souls Avenue

Chamberlayne Road
Okehampton Road
Dundonald Road
Crediton Road
Wrentham Avenue
Tiverton Road

Brondesbury Park

Paddington Old Cemetery

Queens Park

Chevening Road
Milman Road
People Road
Keslake Road
Kemp Road
Harvist Road

Kingswood Avenue
Salusbury Road
Lonsdale Road
Hartland Road

Kensal Rise

Queen's Park

B451

B413

Chamberlayne Road

B451

B413

Kilburn Lane

Nutbourne Street
Marne Street
Lothorp Street
Kilravock Street
Ilbert Street

Bravington Road
Portnall Road
Ashmore Road
Shirland

A404

Kensal Green
B451

Mortimer Road

Harrow Road

Masons Arms

Paradise by way of Kensal Green

Kilburn Lane

Sixth Avenue
Fifth Avenue
Fourth Avenue
Third Avenue
Second Avenue
First Avenue

West Kilburn

**KENSAL GREEN CEMETARY**  4

Droop Street
B450
A404
Harrow Road

Kensal Road

A404

Grand Union Canal (Paddington Branch)

Canal Way

Ladbroke Grove

**TRELLICK TOWER**  3

Scrubs Lane

Dalgarno Gardens

Barlby Road

North Kensington

Wornington Road

Portobello Road

**PORTOBELLO ROAD**  5

A40 West P

Barlby Road
St Mark's Road
St Charles Square
Chesterton Road
Bassett Road
Oxford Gardens

Ladbroke Grove

Earl of Lonsdale

Sun in Splendour

Westway

B412

Highlever Road
Latimer Road
St Quintin Avenue
St Helens Gardens

Oxford Gardens

B412

B450

Cambridge Gardens

Lancaster Road

A40

Du Cane Road

Wood Lane

A219

Westway

A219

A3220

A40

Ladbroke Grove

Cornwall Crescent
Blenheim Crescent
Elgin Crescent
Clarendon Road

Lancaster Road
Westbourne Park Road
Kensington Park Road

B412

B412

Ladbroke Grove

B415

Australia Road
South Africa Road

Wood Lane

West Cross Route

A3220

St Anns Road
Bramley Road
Sirdar Road
Walmer Road
Lansdowne Road

White City

B450

Wood Lane

A219

Notting Hi

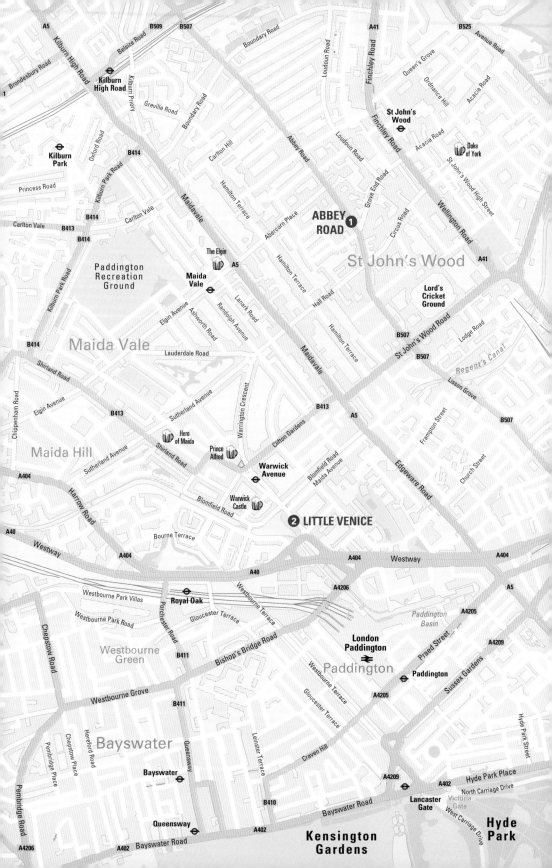

Abbey Road (the B507) runs through St John's Wood, close to Lord's Cricket Ground and if it wasn't for four Liverpudlian musicians who had their photograph taken by Iain Macmillan for an album cover in 1969, it would be just another leafy London road. The Beatles recorded most of their albums at Abbey Road Studios then named their 11th album, *Abbey Road*. Its famous album cover features John, Paul, George and Ringo walking across the zebra crossing next to the studios.

*Abbey Road sign. Canon 5D II, 70–200mm at 200mm, ISO 100, 1/1600s at f/4. May.*

It can be busy here – walking across the zebra crossing is a much sought after image – but it's worth the trip. Just make sure you go early. The studio is now a listed building and is protected from development. The roster of famous albums recorded here is long, stretching from classical music to the birth of rock and roll to contemporary albums.

*Opposite: Abbey Road crossing. Canon 5D II, 17–40mm at 17mm, ISO 100, 1/320s at f/4. May.*

## What to shoot and viewpoints

The famous image is an easy shot to take: simply wait for a gap in the traffic, move to the centre of the road and take the picture. While there, you can also shoot diagonally from the corner of the crossing to get an interesting angle. Make sure you visit the front gate of Abbey Road Studio as the graffiti adorning the front wall can provide interesting images (and you can add your own, if you so wish).

*Apt graffiti on the Abbey Road Studio wall. Canon 5D II, 70–200mm at 200mm, ISO 100, 1/1000s at f/4. May.*

## How to get here

Take the Jubilee line to St John's Wood Tube station, exit the station and head west along Grove End Road. As it veers slightly to the left, you'll reach the junction of Abbey Road. The crossing lies to your right and the studio itself is about 20m further on. If you drive there, it's best to park in one of the area's side roads and walk back to the crossing as Abbey Road itself has double yellow lines.

A webcam on Abbey Road Studios' website stores images for 24 hours after your visit. They can be shared via social media. *www.abbeyroad.com/crossing*

| | |
|---|---|
| **Location Lat/Long**: | 51.5322, -0.17783 |
| **Location Postcode**: | NW8 9AY |
| **Underground & Lines**: | St John's Wood: *Jubilee* |
| **Bus**: | 46, 139, 187, 189 |
| **Cycle Hire**: | Grove End Road |

## Accessibility ♿

This is a street-level attraction that should present no issues.

## Best time of year/day

The best time to visit is in the morning. You'll be able to get a clear shot of the crossing, there will be fewer people, less traffic and the sun will be at your back, lighting the crossing and the road.

*Previous spread: World famous Abbey Road crossing. Canon 5D IV, 24–70mm at 40mm, ISO 200, 1/20s at f/8. Aug.*

Little Venice, also known as Browning's Pool, is a canal junction where the Grand Union Canal and Regents Canal meet just west of Regent's Park. There's some dispute as to how the area gained the name Little Venice but it's believed Lord Byron coined the term by jokingly comparing the locale to Venice. Its nickname, Browning's Pool is a nod to poet Robert Browning, who lived in the area in the 19th century.

## What to shoot and viewpoints

The triangular lagoon allows long canal boats to turn and pass each other. The public towpaths stretch to the north and south, and the areas to the east side are for private mooring. This is a great spot to shoot sunrise and sunset, as soft warm light hits the water, the boats and buildings. Most of the boats are permanently moored here but some are passing through. Not only is there a wide view of the lagoon to shoot, there are also interesting details to be isolated on the boats and the blue bridge that carries Westbourne Terrace Road to the west. The wide-open area of the lagoon ensures that the sky is included in your shots, and this works very well at dawn and dusk, adding atmosphere to your images. Shooting from the western side of the lagoon offers the best morning shots; look towards the bridge where the Waterside Cafe is moored. There are no issues with using tripods in this location but if it's busy, try to avoid getting in the way of other visitors.

The surrounding area is really worth exploring as it offers Regency architecture, great pubs, cafes and restaurants.

*Opposite: Little Venice, looking west. Canon 5D II, 17–40mm at 17mm, ISO 100, 0s at f/11, tripod, LEE ND 0.9 grad. May.*

*Little Venice, looking east. Canon 5D II, 17–40mm at 17mm, ISO 100, 1/6s at f/11, tripod, LEE ND 0.9 grad. May.*

*Little Venice, looking west. Canon 5D II, 17–40mm at 17mm, ISO 100, 1/6s at f/11, tripod, LEE ND 0.6 grad. May.*

## How to get here

Take the Bakerloo line to Warwick Avenue station. Exit the station and follow Warwick Avenue directly south away from the roundabout. About 250m south of the station you'll see the bridge. Take the towpath down to water level and walk around the lagoon.

| | |
|---|---|
| **Location Lat/Long**: | 51.52154, -0.18321 |
| **Location Postcode**: | W9 2PF |
| **Underground & Lines**: | Paddington, Warwick Avenue: *Bakerloo, Circle and District, Hammersmith & City* |
| **Mainline Station**: | Paddington |
| **Bus**: | 6, 18, 46, 187, N18 |
| **Cycle Hire**: | Warwick Avenue Station |

## Accessibility ♿

Access is at street level, even on the towpath, so this location should present no issues.

### Best time of year/day

The towpath is open and accessible all year round. Dawn and dusk will provide atmospheric images. Autumn colours on days with still water will offer wonderful reflections.

*Opposite: Reflections in Little Venice. Canon 5D II, 17–40mm at 17mm, ISO 100, 1/8s at f/8, tripod, LEE ND 0.6 grad. May.*

# [3] TRELLICK TOWER

Architect Erno Goldfinger designed both the Trellick and Belfron towers. The thinking behind high-rise design in the 1960s was that it was intended to offer an almost utopian style of living, superb views and community living in a compact space. The stark lines and Brutalist design aesthetic is of keen interest to those who appreciate all forms of city architecture. While the dream of high-rise utopian living didn't materialise, the architecture does provide rich photographic images.

## What to shoot and viewpoints

The building is very large so a wide-angle lens is a must if you wish to capture the building as whole. Set against a cloudy sky with lots of texture, it makes for superb monochrome images. Shoot from the concrete walkways next to Elkstone Road to the south. Get down low and shoot upwards at an extreme angle to exaggerate the scale of the tower. Try standing on Elkstone Road and perpendicular to the south-facing side of the tower, then use a zoom lens to isolate several of the apartments. Each living space has personal touches put there by their residents and when you capture a section in detail it makes a compelling composition, especially as an A2 print. Use a midrange lens to isolate the top of the building and the observation deck against the sky.

*Apartment balconies at Trellick Tower. Canon 5D II, 70–200mm at 70mm, ISO 200, 1/60s at f/8. July.*

## How to get here

Take the Circle line to Westbourne Park station. Exit the station and turn left, then walk about 200m to the bridge that crosses the river. Take the river path to your left, leading away from the flyover. Follow the river path west towards the tower – you should be able to see it about 500m ahead of you.

| | |
|---|---|
| Location Lat/Long: | 51.523666, -0.20527 |
| Location Postcode: | W10 5UR |
| Underground & Lines: | Westbourne Park: *Circle, Hammersmith & City* |
| Bus: | 23 |
| Cycle Hire: | Bevington Road, Bevington Road West |

## Accessibility ♿

The viewpoints are at street level and there are ramps available so should present no issues.

### Best time of year/day

I find the best time to visit is on dull, overcast or stormy days when the sky behind the building can be incorporated to create foreboding, moody images.

*Opposite: The stark Trellick Tower, Westbourne Park. Canon 5D II, 17–40mm at 40mm, ISO 200, 1/180s at f/8. July.*

Consecrated in 1833, Kensal Green Cemetery is located to the northwest side of central London and is split in two – the more modern and active St Mary's Catholic cemetery to the west, and the historic (and more interesting) Gothic Victorian cemetery with its ornate mausoleums to the east.

This cemetery is the resting place of many famous celebrities: Ingrid Bergman was cremated here before her ashes were scattered in Sweden; Freddie Mercury is commemorated here by a plaque revealing his real name, Farrokh Bulsara, and actor Alan Rickman (of Harry Potter fame) and Christine Keeler (who nearly brought down the British government) were both cremated here. Of all the London cemeteries, this is the one in which I have spent the most time, just walking and taking photographs.

## What to shoot and viewpoints

While the newer western side has some interesting parts to photograph, better still is the historic eastern side; the further east you venture, the more interesting the discoveries. Make your way to the central chapel – on bright sunny days the strong light in and around this building will provide interplay of light and shadow offering the chance for compelling compositions. Proceed to the eastern side of the chapel to see the avenue of ornate mausoleums – each tomb has its own character. Take time to observe the details on each one, as well as using trees and shrubs to add scale. If you have a wide-angle lens, look to incorporate the sky in some shots; a cloudy textured sky can be used to great effect. Halfway along the main avenue is a curved path that leads south. On autumn mornings the sun cuts through and lights the golden-brown foliage creating contrast. If I had to pick one tomb to photograph it would be the grave of Thea Canonero Altieri (in the eastern section, just northwest of the chapel), upon whose tomb rests a replica of the famous *Spirit of Ecstasy* statue that adorns Rolls Royce cars.

*Infrared image of mausoleum in Kensal Green Cemetery. Canon 5D II, 24–70mm at 24mm, ISO 200, 1/125s at f/8. Jan.*

## How to get here

Kensal Green Tube station on the Bakerloo line is just opposite the main entrance. The number 18 bus from Euston and Baker Street stations also stops directly outside the cemetery gates.

| | |
|---|---|
| **Location Lat/Long**: | 51.52859, -0.22575 |
| **Location Postcode**: | W10 4RA |
| **Underground & Lines**: | Kensal Green: *Bakerloo* |
| **Mainline Station**: | Kensal Green |
| **Bus**: | 18, 52 |

## Accessibility &#9855;

Most of the cemetery is paved so should present no issues, however in winter and after heavy rainfall some paths may be muddy.

## Best time of year/day

The cemetery is only open during the day so to shoot the morning sunlight close to dawn and visit between autumn and spring when sunrise is later. During summer, the harsh light after opening time provides strong contrast and penetrates the foliage to better light the mausoleums.

## Opening times

| | |
|---|---|
| **British Summer Time**: | Mon to Sat 9am–6pm, Sun 10am–6pm |
| **Greenwich Mean Time**: | Mon to Sat 9am–5pm, Sun 10am–5pm |
| **Bank Holidays**: | 10am–1.30pm |

Please make sure you leave enough time for your visit as gates are locked at the times stated above. The cemetery opening times provided are for the West Gate opposite Hazel Road. The East Gate, for pedestrian access only (near Ladbroke Grove), is locked at 4.30pm during the week and at the times stated above at weekends and on Bank Holidays.

*Opposite*: *The Spirit of Ecstasy, Kensal Green Cemetery. Canon 5D II, 24–70mm at 43mm, ISO 200, 1/90s at f/6.7. Jan.*

*Top*: Main avenue in the old section of Kensal Green Cemetery. Canon 5D II, 70–200mm at 121mm, ISO 200, 1/30s at f/13. Oct.

*Above*: Iron crucifix in Kensal Green Cemetery. Canon 5D II, 70–200mm at 144mm, ISO 200, 1/125s at f/4.5. Oct.

*Top*: Memorial in Kensal Green Cemetery. Canon 5D II, 70–200mm at 89mm, ISO 200, 1/250s at f/8. Oct.

*Above*: Chapel in the old section of Kensal Green Cemetery. Sony A6000, Fisheye 8mm at 8mm, ISO 100, 1/800s at f/8. Oct.

*Top*: Statue in the church in Kensal Green Cemetery. Sony A6000, Fisheye 8mm at 8mm, ISO 800, 1/160s at f/8. Oct.

Infrared image of Kensal Green Cemetery. Canon 5D II, 24–70mm at 55mm, ISO 200, 1/30s at f/8. Jan.

*Above*: Tombs in Kensal Green Cemetery. Canon 5D II, 24–70mm at 25mm, ISO 200, 1/60s at f/8. Jan.

*Items for sale at Alice's on Portobello Road. Canon 5D II, 70–200mm at 85mm, ISO 200, 1/250s at f/8. May.*

Situated in the heart of Notting Hill and running almost the entire length of the area, Portobello Road is vibrant and bohemian. The antique market is open on Saturdays, with the shops and stalls also open throughout the week. The Friends of Portobello Road's main aim is to maintain the unique character of the place, striving to keep big business chains out of the road as much as possible, and to this end they have been quite successful. The road also houses the Electric Cinema – one of the country's only two purpose-built buildings designed to show motion pictures.

## What to shoot and viewpoints

This is a great place to shoot some interesting people, shops and stalls. Start with the open-air market under the Westway flyover to the north and wind down the road until you reach the crossroads with Chepstow Villas. Take time to observe the characters there – visitors and locals. And be sure to shoot the world famous Alice's with its vibrant red front. This quaint-looking shop sells an eclectic assortment of antiques, curios and toys. At the top of Portobello Road, and if you have a zoom, use it to capture the wonderful line of shop fronts and signs that lead and curve away

down the road. Note that some stalls request you make a donation towards a chosen charity in order to take pictures, so please respect their wishes.

## How to get here

Depart at Ladbroke Grove station on the Circle and Hammersmith & City line, then exit the station and turn right, leaving the Tube line behind you. Walk about 50m until you reach Lancaster Road on your left. Take this road for about 100m and you'll arrive in Portobello Road. The number 7 bus from Oxford Circus station will take you to Westbourne Park Road, which is adjacent to Portobello Road.

| | |
|---|---|
| **Location Lat/Long**: | 51.52003, -0.20816 |
| **Location Postcode**: | W10 5TD |
| **Underground & Lines**: | Ladbroke Grove: *Circle, Hammersmith & City* |
| **Bus**: | 7, 23, 52, 452, 70, N7 |
| **Cycle Hire**: | All Saints Church, Blenheim Crescent |

## Accessibility &#x267F;

This locaion is all at street level and should present no issues.

## Best time of year/day

The best time of year to visit is summer, when fine weather and long days offer the best light. The market is open six days a week: Monday to Saturday. Friday afternoons and Saturdays are the busiest times, so arrive around lunchtime to have room to shoot without distractions.

*Opposite: A painted door in Portobello Road. Sony A6000, 16–50mm at 16mm, ISO 100, 1/160s at f/4. Oct.*

# CAMDEN & REGENT'S PARK

**Just north of the central London is Regent's Park – land that was seized by Henry VIII and turned into yet another hunting ground. Later monarchs remodelled and landscaped the park, as was the fashion, and finally, as fresh air and open spaces were needed for London's increasing population, it was opened to the public in the Victorian era.**

The park contains a huge rose garden and several lakes and ponds, each with their own character and charm. There are wide-open spaces and shady tree-lined areas to escape from the city on hot summer days. Be sure to begin your exploration of the park by arriving via Baker Street, home of Sherlock Holmes. The fictional detective's silhouette adorns station tiles, local shops and bars incorporate his name into theirs, and a large statue of Holmes greets travellers at the front of the station. Regent's Canal too should not be missed. It arcs around the entire northwest side of the park between Little Venice in the south and Camden Town to the north.

To the north of Regent's Park you'll find Primrose Hill with its incredible view of the London skyline. This is somewhere I urge you to visit at least once for a dawn shoot – nothing can beat capturing an image of the city as it wakes up to a glorious sunrise. Also located in the Primrose Hill area are the vibrant painted houses of Chalcot Square.

Next door to Primrose Hill is its outrageous and bohemian cousin, Camden Town. The glorious market with its narrow alleys offers trinkets and clothes you won't find anywhere else, whilst food vendors serve up delicious cuisine from all over the world. Side streets feature street art and, in the evening, the area is vibrant with people visiting Camden's bars, clubs, music venues and restaurants.

*Previous spread*: Inner circle pond on a bright sunny summer morning in Regent's Park. Canon 5D II, 70–200mm at 70mm, ISO 200, 1/50s at f/9, tripod. May.

*Next spread*: Sunlight path along the Boardwalk in Regent's Park. Canon 5D II, 70–200mm at 97mm, ISO 200, 1/14s at f/16, tripod. May.

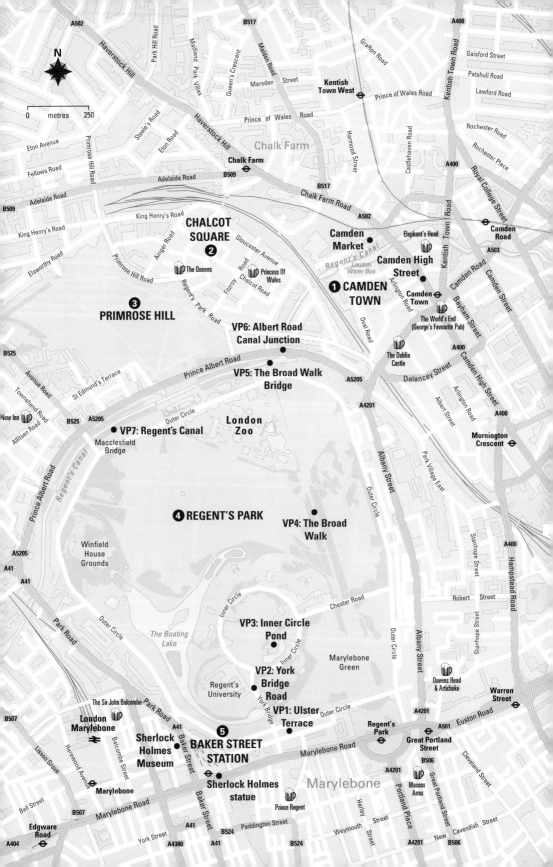

Camden Town is situated at the northeast corner of Regent's Park, alongside Regent's Canal. Once an area of industry, Camden Town, or just Camden, is now a bohemian place with bars, cafes, street markets and club venues; the area has been a centre of alternative culture in London for many years – especially for music. Pink Floyd played their first gig in Camden's Roundhouse and punk rock got a kick-start here in 1976, when the Stranglers and American punk band, the Ramones played together.

Arrive by Tube and you'll exit the station next to my favourite London pub, the World's End. The Underworld club under the pub has played host to some very famous heavy metal and hard rock names, and I should warn you that the World's End only plays hard rock on their sound system! For photography, Camden is all about the street life, colourful shops, the canal and the famous Camden Market.

## What to shoot and viewpoints

### Camden High Street

As you head north along Camden High Street you'll see the decorated shop entrances, including almost-naked Gothic angels, dragons and elephants. At such a sharp angle these can be tricky to frame, so reduce the effect by shooting from the opposite side of the street. During busy periods shoot using a zoom lens to isolate and compress the view, and try to include Camden signage in the background to give the images the stamp of authenticity. The alternative to distance shooting is close up, in-your-face street shooting. This takes a little more courage but don't worry – the place is packed with people too busy to care; many folk love the attention and some will pose without being asked!

### Camden Market

Once you reach the canal you'll see the famous Camden Market, which is more Persian bazaar with its labyrinthine alleyways, aroma of street food and colourful traders. Photography in the market is allowed, in fact it's actively encouraged, although a small number of stalls have

no photography signs (see page 466). Head through the main courtyard and shoot the food sellers hard at work, then make your way underground to the Stables. Here several horse statues offer a clue to the location's original purpose, and the statues are packed into such a tight space, you'll need a wide-angle lens to expand the area. As you emerge from the Stables, head around the back to the south side of the market with its long avenue of designer stalls, selling jewellery and clothing. Finally, to balance the manic nature of the market, head back to the High Street and take a walk down some of the side streets, where a lot of street artists work, decorating the walls along the alleyways. Take a left down Hawley Mews and turn left again back along Hartley Street, where you'll also find painted houses. Use a zoom lens to compress and isolate the colours.

## How to get here

Take the Northern line to Camden Town station – all Northern Line trains pass through Camden Town. Exit the station on either side. Looking north, to your right is the World's End pub on Kentish Town Road, and to your left is Camden High Street with Camden Market 250m directly ahead.

| | |
|---|---|
| **Location Lat/Long**: | 51.54119, -0.14487 |
| **Location Postcode**: | NW1 8QL |
| **Underground & Lines**: | Camden Town: *Northern* |
| **Main Station**: | Camden Road |
| **Riverboat**: | London Waterbus Company operate a service (*www.londonwaterbus.com*). **Regent's Canal Waterbus** between Little Venice and Camden Lock. One-way journey time approximately 55 minutes. |
| **Bus**: | 24, 214, 274, 393 |
| **Cycle Hire**: | Arlington Road, Castlehaven Road, Greenland Road |

## Accessibility &

Some parts of Camden Market are cobbled and some lower areas of the Stables are not accessible for wheelchairs or for those with limited mobility, however the vast majority of Camden Market is at ground level and fully accessible.

## Best time of year/day

I can suggest two ways to approach shooting in Camden and the market: arrive before 10am to (almost) have the place to yourself, though your images may feel empty and cold, or visit on busy afternoons from spring through to autumn when there will be dense crowds. Your images will require a bit of work but they'll convey a real sense of life and activity.

*Camden Lock Bridge with light trials. Canon 5D IV, 24–70mm at 28mm, ISO 100, 30s at f/16, tripod, LEE ND 0.9 grad. July.*

**Please note**: The *No Photography* signs are not in place to be difficult; stall owners say they put the signs up to keep their offerings off the internet, where they can be copied and sold far more cheaply, impacting on their livelihoods.

## Night Shooting

The railway bridge by the market can be shot from either side – the paintwork is different on each side. From the north looking south, shoot from about 50m from the bridge. This will give enough time to shoot the traffic streaks leading to the bridge. With the traffic lights timing can be tricky to keep the cars moving though the scene: look to shoot 2–3 seconds after the lights change and don't shoot if there are buses (their light trails dominate the image) – just use cars. When shooting from the south to the north, you'll sometimes find traffic parked in front of the market. Try to avoid including large white vans or brightly coloured cars; the focus should be the light trails to the bridge. Don't forget to head along the southside of the canal to shoot the Dingwalls building, the live music and comedy venue adjacent to Camden Lock. Head up on to the arching canal bridge, where there's a superb view of the canal and buildings below.

**Warning**: Camden is a great place and usually very safe, but because it's so busy, it's a prime spot for pickpockets. There are security guards and CCTV but people distracted by their next purchase make easy targets. Stay vigilant and don't let opportunistic crime spoil your visit.

*__Top right__: Town Crier working the avenues of Camden Market. Canon 5D IV, 24–70mm at 24mm, ISO 800, 1/125s at f/5.6. July. __Middle__: Italian Avenue, Camden Market. Canon 5D IV, 70–200mm at 106mm, ISO 800, 1/45s at f/6.7. July. __Bottom__: Food samples at Camden Market. Canon 5D IV, 70–200mm at 93mm, ISO 800, 1/90s at f/6.7. July.*

***Above***: *Camden Market from the canal bridge. Canon 5D IV, 24–70mm at 24mm, ISO 100, 90s at f/16, tripod, LEE ND 0.9 grad. July.*

***Below***: *Light trails from traffic. Canon 5D IV, 24–70mm at 27mm, ISO 100, 15s at f/13, tripod, LEE ND 0.9 grad. July.*

Built in 1850 and called St George's Square until 1937, Chalcot Square is a painted-house location in Primrose Hill and an exclusive area, home to many celebrities. The poets Ted Hughes and Sylvia Plath lived here, (at 3 Chalcot Square) and the philosopher Frederick Engels, a friend of Karl Marx lived at 122 Regent's Park Road. All have blue plaques – historic markers – indicating the houses they lived in. Whilst photographing these stunning pastel-coloured terraces, please respect the privacy of those who live there.

## What to shoot and viewpoints

The best houses lie on the north and east sides of the square – the sides that catch the sunlight in the morning. During the spring and summer, shoot with your back to the park railings and use a wide-angle lens. Also consider the viewpoint through the square's central garden, capturing the houses in the background and blue sky at the top of the frame.

*Painted houses in Chalcot Square Gardens, Primrose Hill. Canon 5D IV, 24–70mm at 59mm, ISO 200, 1/6000s at f/2.8. June.*

## How to get here

Take the Northern line to Chalk Farm station. Exit the station and cross the road, before turning to your right. Look for Bridge Approach Road to your left then follow this over the bridge. About 250m from the bridge you'll see Berkeley Road to your left; follow this for about 150m until you reach Chalcot Square.

**Location Lat/Long**: 51.54106, -0.15518
**Location Postcode**: NW1 8YA
**Underground & Lines**: Chalk Farm: *Northern*
**Bus**: 274

## Accessibility ♿

This location is on street level and should present no issues.

## Best time of year/day

The best time is during spring and summer around mid-morning, when the sun is high. This ensures no shadows fall on the houses to the north side of the square.

*Chalcot Square Gardens. Canon 5D IV, 24–70mm at 70mm, ISO 200, 1/1500s at f/5.6. June.*

*Opposite: Painted house in Chalcot Square Gardens. Canon 5D IV, 24–70mm at 51mm, ISO 200, 1/250s at f/8. June.*

**Primrose Hill (213ft or 65m) is one of the top three open-air locations that have great views of the London skyline. The other two spots are Greenwich Park and Parliament Hill in Hampstead (Photographing London – Vol 2). You'll decide which is the best when you've visited all three but Primrose Hill takes some beating: the trees are kept low so as not to obscure the view.**

At the summit of grassy Primrose Hill is an almost-180-degree view of the London skyline with most of London's prominent landmarks in sight. The land here was purchased as open space for all by an Act of Parliament in 1842 but the surrounding area is one of the most exclusive and expensive residential areas in London. Primrose Hill village is, and has been, home to famous poets, writers, artists and stars of the film and the music industry. Poets Sylvia Plath and WB Yeats lived there, as well as famous photographer Roger Fenton.

The village of Primrose Hill is a wonderful place to take a stroll on a quiet Sunday morning. The winding streets and Victorian townhouses make it an interesting location to explore and photograph. Who knows – you may even get a selfie with someone famous on their way to collect the Sunday papers!

## What to shoot and viewpoints

Primrose Hill's 213ft (65m) summit offers an unparalleled view over London. A shoot early morning or late evening when the skies turn red or orange is not to be missed. I prefer to shoot early morning, as there are fewer people around. And arriving early allows you to shoot the scene as it becomes illuminated; each of the skyline landmarks catches the light in their own special way. Just as the changes in light begin to reach their apex, I generally stop and change tack, preferring to shoot images of the people watching the sunrise – for example, silhouettes of couples huddling together on the benches, with city landmarks in the background. Stand around 30m back from those on the edge of the viewpoint and, using a 100mm+ zoom, focus on the people. Arrange the composition to place a distinctive landmark out of focus – this will make your image an authentic London shot. When you're done at the top of the hill, I suggest making time to visit the shops and cafes in Regent's Park Road to the northeast of the park.

*Primrose Hill cafe. Canon 5D IV, 24–70mm at 42mm, ISO 200, 1/3000s at f/2.8. June.*

*Primrose Hill cafe. Canon 5D IV, 24–70mm at 28mm, ISO 200, 1/350s at f/8. June.*

*Cafe in Primrose Hill. Canon 5D II, 24–70mm at 27mm, ISO 200, 1/125s at f/8. Oct.*

## How to get here

You can take the number 274 bus from Baker Street, which stops south of the park at the bottom of the hill. The alternative is to follow directions to Chalcot Square (page 468) only don't turn off Regent's Park Road. Instead, follow it past the Queens pub at the northeast corner of the park and walk through the park to the viewpoint.

**Location Lat/Long**: 51.53956, -0.1608
**Location Postcode**: NW3 3AX
**Underground & Lines**: Mornington Crescent, St John's Wood: Bakerloo, Northern
**Bus**: 274
**Cycle Hire**: Prince Albert Road

## Accessibility

There is level access to the viewpoint, however the hill itself is quite steep on the south side. Follow Regent's Park Road and make your way up the hill from the northeast corner of the park.

*Next spread: Dawn on Primrose Hill. Canon 5D II, 70–200mm at 111mm, ISO 100, 1/8s at f/16. Oct.*

## Best time of year/day

This wonderful view can be shot anytime of year and any time of day, however with the London skyline being so wide and flat it is best paired with an interesting sky, so dawn and dusk are the best times to shoot. Blue sky or cloudy days offer an alternative option if you're not an early riser.

*Sunrise on Primrose Hill. Canon 5D II, 70–200mm at 200mm, ISO 100, 1/6s at f/8, tripod, LEE ND 0.9 grad. Oct.*

Regent's Park, like Hyde Park, was a monastery ground appropriated during the Reformation by Henry VIII and turned into his private hunting ground. In the 19th century, the parkland as we see it today and the terraces and villas surrounding it were designed and built based on an idea of the Prince Regent – George IV, after whom the park is named.

The park is circular and consists of two rings, the Inner and Outer circles. The Inner Circle is the most developed area, with the lake and wetland area, cafes, Regent's College, an open-air theatre and the famous rose gardens – the Queen Mary Gardens, which have over 400 varieties of roses. The Outer Circle is home to London Zoo, the famous walk-through Snowdon Aviary by the canal, sport pitches and a road – the Outer Circle Road, which encircles the park.

## What to shoot and viewpoints

There is much to photograph in and around the park but here are a few key areas:

### Viewpoint 1 – Ulster Terrace ♿
Ulster Terrace is part of the Outer Circle Road and lies to the south of the park. Shoot at sunrise using a zoom lens to capture the beautiful old-style street lamps lining the terrace. Autumn or spring are best, and try including a London cab or a person to add a focal point to your composition.

VP3. Black swan on the Regent's Park lake. Canon 5D II, 17–40mm at 17mm, ISO 200, 1/20s at f/16, tripod, LEE ND 0.6 grad. May.

VP1. Lampposts on Ulster Terrace. Canon 5D II, 70–200mm at 144mm, ISO 200, 1/200s at f/9. May.

**Opposite**: VP1. Taxi on autumn morning, Ulster Terrace. Canon 5D II, 70–200mm at 200mm, ISO 200, 1/320s at f/9. May.

## Viewpoint 2 – York Bridge Road ♿

Get here early when there is very little traffic on the road over the bridge and use the road's curve in your composition. A midrange lens zoomed in will compress perspective and ensure the curves in the road to the bridge are in frame, as well as making the lamps appear closer to the bridge than they are. Alternatively, frame your shot over the bridge towards St Marylebone Parish Church.

## Viewpoint 3 – The Inner Circle Pond ♿

At the pond you'll find heron, swans, coots and various other birds. They are very tame and easy to shoot with a midrange 24–70mm lens. To the north of the pond is the waterfall, which can be reached by walking around the lake or simply by crossing the wooden bridge over the reed beds. Stand to the northeast of the lake and wait for sunlight to warm the scene. The wooden bridge shot through the reed beds also provides a strong image: use the path and benches to create a lead line in your composition.

*Opposite top: VP2. York Road leading out of Regent's Park. Canon 5D II, 70–200mm at 127mm, ISO 200, 1/25s at f/9. May. **Middle**: VP3. Wisteria-covered bridge in Regent's Park. Canon 5D II, 24–70mm at 24mm, ISO 100, 1/4s at f/16. May. **Bottom**: VP3. Heron fishing in the Regent's Park lake. Canon 5D II, 70–200mm at 100mm, ISO 200, 1/40s at f/8. May.*

## How to get here

Take Bakerloo line to Regent's Park station and exit directly into the park. Alternatively, take the number 205 bus from King's Cross Station. See the Regent's Park map for the specific locations.

| | |
|---|---|
| **Location Lat/Long**: | 51.528704, -0.15071869 |
| **Location Postcode**: | NW1 4NR |
| **Underground & Lines**: | Baker Street, Camden Town, Great Portland Street, Regent's Park, St John's Wood: *Bakerloo, Circle & Metropolitan, Hammersmith & City, Jubilee, Northern* |
| **Riverboat**: | London Waterbus Company operate a service (*www.londonwaterbus.com*). **Regent's Canal Waterbus** between Little Venice and Camden Lock. One-way journey time approximately 55 minutes |
| **Bus**: | 2, 13, 18, 27, 30, 74, 88, 113, 139, 189, 274, 453 |
| **Cycle Hire**: | Albany Street, London Zoo Car Park, Prince Albert Road, The Tennis Courts |
| **Car Park**: | Pay and display parking is available in Regents Park every day from 9am–6.30pm. The postcode for electronic device users is NW1 4NR, but please note this is for guidance only as the park covers a large area. Charges for pay and display parking are: Mon to Sat – £2.40 per hour (4 hours maximum stay), Sun and Public Holidays – £1.40 per hour (no maximum stay). Disabled badge holders and motorcyclists can park free of charge, but are subject to 4 hours maximum stay Mon to Sat. |

## Accessibility ♿

All locations and viewpoints are on paved paths and walkways and should present no accessibility issues. Do note that the east walkway gradient is a little steep and stretches for some distance.

## Best time of year/day

The park can be shot all year round and any time of day. The best time of year for flowers and colour is most certainly spring through to autumn.

**Safety Warning**: London is a very safe city; crime in the city centre is quite rare but do exercise caution. Please be extremely careful if you are in any of the Royal Parks during the hours of darkness. Police patrol the parks often but the parks are often lit by gas lamps and can be very dark at night, with some areas not covered by CCTV. On occasion there have been rare incidents of violent crime reported so please be sensible and go in pairs or groups if you intend to visit the parks after midnight. Always inform someone where you're going and what time you intend to be back.

*VP3. Black swans on the lake in Regent's Park. Canon 5D II, 17–40mm at 35mm, ISO 200, 1/40s at f/16, tripod, LEE ND 0.6 grad. May.*

*VP4. Regent's Park central avenue. Canon 5D II, 70–200mm at 165mm, ISO 400, 1/30s at f/11. May.*

### Viewpoint 4 – The Broad Walk
### (Tree-lined avenue) &

The Broad Walk is a very long tree-lined avenue that runs from the northeast park entrance by St Mark's Church, past London Zoo, all the way to Regent's Park station on the south side of the park. The far northern end adjoining London Zoo has a slight incline; use a zoom lens to shoot the benches as they ascend the hill. This works well on early mornings with a strong directional light. The highest part of the path is at the Ready Money Drinking Fountain, a four-sided granite and marble Gothic drinking fountain. From here, the path descends and there are multiple opportunities to photograph the long path, isolating single figures or couples in your composition.

### Viewpoint 5 – The Broad Walk Bridge &

The Broad Walk Bridge is a cast-iron bridge that leads directly from the north of the park by London Zoo out to Prince Albert Road and St Mark's Church. Early morning or late afternoon is best with the sun to your right and left respectively. A wide-angle lens will stretch perspective and increase perception of the bridge's size, and the church in the background makes a good focal point.

### Viewpoint 6 – Albert Road Canal Junction &

The view from the Broad Walk Bridge looking east over the canal junction towards where the boats and the Feng Shang Princess floating restaurant are moored is a beautiful scene any time of year or day, though it's great for reflections when there's no wind, and particularly attractive at night. After dark you will need to shoot using the bulb mode, with a 2–3 minute exposure at f/8; this will ensure colours and reflections are captured perfectly.

*Opposite top: VP5. Bridge over Regent's Canal from the north entrance of Regent's Park. Canon 5D IV, 24–70mm at 24mm, ISO 200, 30s at f/8, tripod. July.*

*Opposite: VP6. Feng Chang restaurant on Regent's Canal. Canon 5D IV, 24–70mm at 40mm, ISO 100, 120s at f/6.7, tripod, LEE ND 0.6 grad. July.*

*VP7. Canal boats along Regent's Canal. Canon 5D II, 70–200mm at 173mm, ISO 200, 1/40s at f/16. Apr.*

### Viewpoint 7 – Regent's Canal ♿

Regent's Canal is nine miles long, stretching from Paddington in the west to Limehouse in the east. The canal was created in 1820 to link the Grand Union Canal to the cargo ports on the River Thames in East London. It was used commercially until the 1970s but is now solely for pleasure craft. The canal wraps around the west and north of Regent's Park. Exit the park by the London Central Mosque to reach the canal at the far western side and take the towpath on the northern side. Walk until you reach the distinctive red Feng Shang Princess floating restaurant – it's just after London Zoo.

Think about taking long shots along the canal, seeking out interesting reflections of the many bridges. During the day canal boats will pass by roughly every 10–15 minutes so aim to capture one of the boats in the distance as it passes under a bridge. Spring and autumn bring the prospect of mist on the canal, as the sun's warmth touches the morning dew, and this will offer a misty haze as background to your images. As you reach the northern arc of the canal around the park, look to use the spire of St Mark's Church in the distance to add depth to your images. An evening shot of Feng Shang restaurant at the junction near St Mark's completes this location. The canal carries on to Camden and beyond

to King's Cross, all the way to East London. If you're up to the task, walking from Paddington Basin to Limehouse Basin is a great way to spend a long summer day.

*Opposite: VP7. Jogger along Regent's Canal. Sony A6000, 16–50mm at 16mm, ISO 100, 1/320s at f/5. Apr.*

*VP7. Bench along Regent's Canal. Sony A6000, 16–50mm at 30mm, ISO 100, 1/250s at f/5.6. May.*

Baker Street's most famous fictional resident lived at 221B: Sherlock Holmes. The street was also name-checked in Gerry Rafferty's song of the same name. Baker Street station was one of the original stations on the Metropolitan line, which in 1863 formed the world's first underground railway with steam trains running under London streets. The merging of three stations and the joining of five rail lines means that Baker Street station is a bit of a maze.

## What to shoot and viewpoints

The classic shot of the lone passenger standing among the shadowed arches can be achieved by taking the Circle line Tube to Baker Street station. The light is very dim indeed and tripods are not allowed on the platform. I've found that the trick to this shot is to position yourself on a bench opposite the section of platform you wish to shoot, place the camera on a jumper or bag next to you on the bench, then use the camera's timer to take the shot. This will allow you to use ISO 100 or 200 with a tight aperture setting of f/11. Obviously this means you'll slow the shutter but this can offer an interesting creative approach as you catch people motion-blurring as they move along the platform. The classic composition is to shoot three or four alcoves lined up in a shot with a single person sitting or standing in one of them. The lighting from within the alcoves casts a glow from above and helps to highlight their shape within the dingy light. A life-size statue of Sherlock Holmes is

*Sherlock Holmes statue, Baker Street Station. Canon 5D IV, 24–70mm at 32mm, ISO 100, 1/350s at f/2.8. May.*

situated at the station entrance, and there are many other references to Conan-Doyle's fictional detective around the station's interior. Look out for the Holmes ceramic tiles.

## How to get here

Take the Bakerloo or Circle line direct to Baker Street station. The Sherlock Holmes statue is situated outside Baker Street Tube station, on Marylebone Road. The Sherlock Holmes Museum is situated on Baker Street and bears the number 221B by permission of the City of Westminster, although it actually lies between numbers 237 and 241. It is at the north end of Baker Street, close to Regent's Park.

| | |
|---|---|
| **Location Lat/Long**: | 51.52316, -0.15686 |
| **Location Postcode**: | NW1 5LJ |
| **Underground & Lines**: | Baker Street Station: *Bakerloo, Circle, Hammersmith & City, Jubilee, Metropolitan* |
| **Bus**: | 13, 113, 139, 189, 274, N113 |
| **Cycle Hire**: | Westminster University |

## Accessibility &

The station itself has limited accessibility facilities, however disembarking from the Circle line and shooting the Baker Street platform should present no issues. You may require assistance to exit the station.

## Best time of year/day

The station interior can be shot any time of day and any time of year, however at weekends the station will have fewer passengers and therefore allow simpler compositions. The Sherlock Holmes statue is on the south side of the station; shoot west in the morning and east in the afternoon to avoid lens flare and blown highlights.

*Above*: Baker Street Station. Canon 5D II, 24–70mm at 32mm, ISO 200, 1/6s at f/2.8. July.

*Below*: The Sherlock Holmes Museum, Baker Street. Canon 5D II, 70–200mm at 70mm, ISO 400, 1/100s at f/13. May.

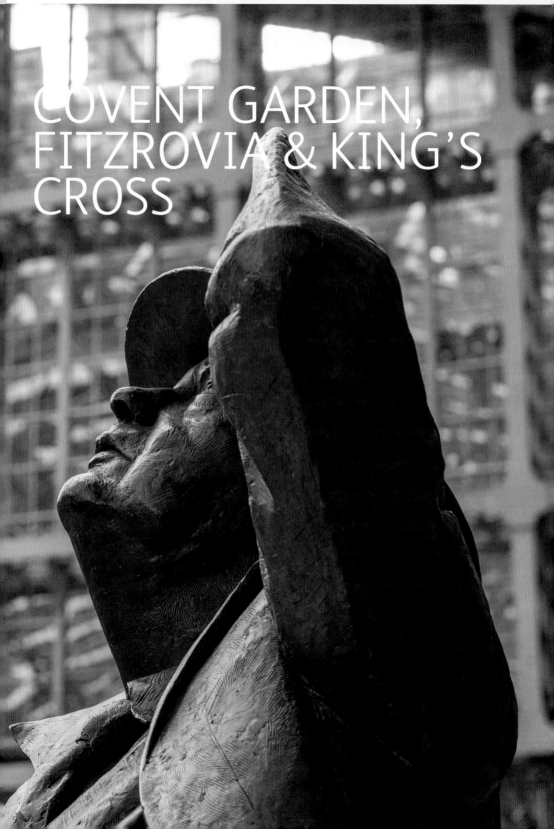

# COVENT GARDEN, FITZROVIA & KING'S CROSS

In this and the next section we visit some key central London locations. It's going to be a whirlwind treat for the senses, so buckle up. We start at King's Cross Station with an incredible artwork that has featured in images all over the world: the Light Tunnel is always a draw when images are posted on social media. Crossing into Bloomsbury we'll discover the British Museum with its magnificent Grand Court and check out the streets around the museum.

Fitzrovia is not well known by most visitors to London but I hope to put it on the photographic map. Key features include the stunning Warren Mews, the delightful modern Charlotte Street Hotel and Brewer Staircase, located inside Heal's department store.

Then we head along Oxford Street, Regent Street and Carnaby Street, with visits to Covent Garden, Leicester Square and Chinatown. All these locations will be awash with activity – there's always something that demands to be photographed, be it the performers in Covent Garden, the restaurants and shops of Chinatown, or the bustle of Oxford Street, Regent Street and Carnaby Street. It's safe to say this is the beating heart of the metropolis.

As we leave these places behind, London won't let you rest. We come to Piccadilly Circus and its famous statue, before moving on to Trafalgar Square and the monument built in honour of the greatest naval commander Britain ever produced, Lord Horatio Nelson.

Finally, we visit the River Thames embankment and the flower gardens and characters along Victoria Embankment.

*Previous spread*: Sir John Betjemen statue staring at the clock, St Pancras Station. Canon 5D II, 70–200mm at 70mm, ISO 200, 1/20s at f/8. May.

*Next spread*: VP1. Warren Mews during spring. Canon 5D IV, 24–70mm at 35mm, ISO 200, 1/20s at f/8. July.

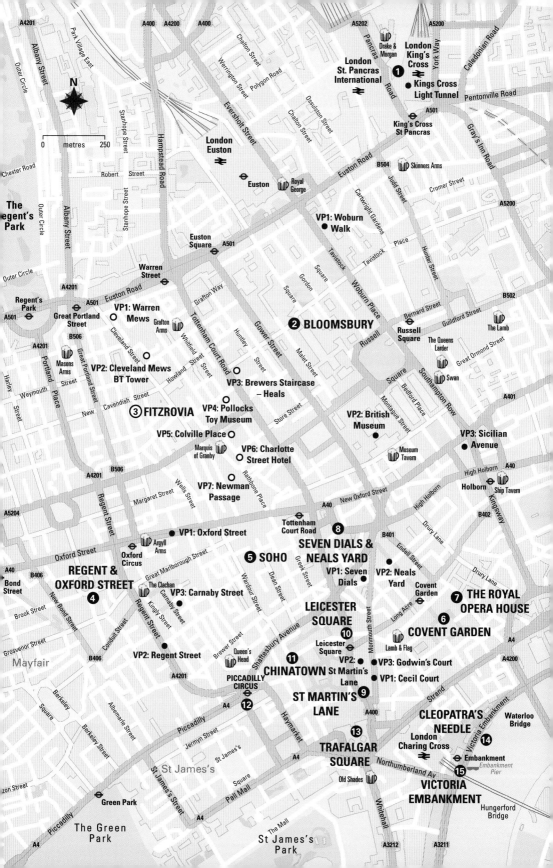

**N**

0 metres 250

A4201
A400 A4200 A400
A5202
A5200

Park Village East

Albany Street

Outer Circle

Chester Road

Chalton Street
Werrington Street
Polygon Road
Ossulston Street
Chalton Street

Pancras Road
York Way
Caledonian Road

Drake & Morgan

**London King's Cross**

**London St. Pancras International**  ①

**Kings Cross Light Tunnel**

Pentonville Road

A5200

**London Euston**

A501

**King's Cross St Pancras**

Gray's Inn Road

Euston Road

B504  Skinners Arms

Cromer Street

A5200

Euston  Royal George

Cartwright Gardens

Judd Street

Hunter Street

Hampstead Road
Stanhope Street

Robert Street

Everholt Street

**VP1: Woburn Walk**

Tavistock Place

Tavistock Square

Gordon Square

Woburn Place

Bernard Street

Guildford Street

B502

The Lamb

**Russell Square**

The Queens Larder

Great Ormond Street

Swan

Euston Square
A501

Warren Street

A4201

Euston Road

**VP1: Warren Mews**

Grafton Way

Gower Street

Malet Street

Russell Square

Southampton Row

A401

**Regent's Park**

A501  A501

**Great Portland Street**

B506

**VP2: Cleveland Mews BT Tower**

Grafton Arms

Cleveland Street

Whitfield Street

Huntley Street

Store Street

Montague Street

Bedford Place

**VP2: British Museum**

Museum Tavern

**VP3: Sicilian Avenue**

A40

Masons Arms

Portland Place

Harley Street

Weymouth Street

New Cavendish Street

Howland Street

Tottenham Court Road

**③ FITZROVIA**

**VP3: Brewers Staircase – Heals**

**VP4: Pollocks Toy Museum**

**VP5: Colville Place**

Marquis of Granby

**VP6: Charlotte Street Hotel**

**VP7: Newman Passage**

Margaret Street

Wells Street

Rathbone Place

High Holborn

Holborn

Ship Tavern

B402

Kingsway

A5204

A4201

B506

A40  B406

**Bond Street**

**REGENT & OXFORD STREET**  ④

New Oxford Street

A40

**② BLOOMSBURY**

**VP1: Oxford Street**

Argyll Arms

Oxford Circus

The Clachan

**VP3: Carnaby Street**

Carnaby Street

Kingly Street

Regent Street

**VP2: Regent Street**

Conduit Street

New Bond Street

Grosvenor Street

Brook Street

Mayfair

Berkeley Square

Albemarle Street

Berkeley Street

Great Marlborough Street

Wardour Street

Dean Street

Brewer Street

Queen's Head

**⑤ SOHO**

Greek Street

**SEVEN DIALS & NEALS YARD**  ⑧

**VP1: Seven Dials**

**VP2: Neals Yard**

B401

Endell Street

Drury Lane

Drury Lane

**THE ROYAL OPERA HOUSE**  ⑦

Covent Garden

Long Acre

**⑥ COVENT GARDEN**

A4

**LEICESTER SQUARE**

Monmouth Street

Lamb & Flag

A4200

**⑩ Leicester Square**

**⑪ CHINATOWN**

Shaftesbury Avenue

St Martin's Lane

**VP2: St Martin's Lane**

**VP3: Godwin's Court**

**VP1: Cecil Court**

**ST MARTIN'S LANE**  ⑨

Strand

**CLEOPATRA'S NEEDLE**

Waterloo Bridge

**PICCADILLY CIRCUS**  ⑫

A4201

A4

Piccadilly

Jermyn Street

St James's Street

Haymarket

A400

**London Charing Cross**

Victoria Embankment

**⑭**

Embankment

Embankment Pier

St James's

Pall Mall

**TRAFALGAR SQUARE**  ⑬

Northumberland Av

Whitehall

Old Shades

**⑮**

**VICTORIA EMBANKMENT**

Green Park

Piccadilly

**The Green Park**

The Mall

**St James's Park**

A3212  A3211

Hungerford Bridge

# [1] KING'S CROSS & ST PANCRAS STATION

King's Cross station was built in 1852 as the terminus of the east coast line (operated by the Great Northern Railway) that ran between London and Edinburgh. This area was once known as Battle Bridge as legend has it that Boudicca's last battle with the Romans occurred here and that she is buried under platform 9 or 10. Her ghost allegedly still wanders the station! The area surrounding the station had earned a seedy reputation by the late 20th century but a huge renovation programme – of both the station and the surrounding area – has turned its fortunes around. The station is now most famous for being the one from which Harry Potter catches the express to Hogwarts from platform 9¾.

St Pancras, just a stone's throw from King's Cross, was built in 1868 by rival train company Midland Railway to service the Midlands and North West of England. The services were moved next door to King's Cross in the 1960s and St Pancras was due to be demolished, however a fierce campaign to save the station, led by Sir John Betjemen, saw the station saved and renovated. Today it is the UK terminus for the Eurostar, which joins London to Brussels and Paris.

With impressive architecture, statues, crowds of people and a light tunnel, both stations are worth visiting to photograph.

## What to shoot and viewpoints

### Viewpoint 1 – King's Cross ♿
The primary focus of your visit to King's Cross should be the main concourse; its huge lattice arcs over the entire area. Use a midrange or zoom lens to isolate sections of the roof and create abstract compositions. If you have a wide-angle lens, head to the point along the wall by the ticket office where the lattice meets a point at the floor, and shoot directly upwards to capture the entirety of the ceiling.

### King's Cross Light Tunnel ♿
Proceed downstairs to the Underground station, located along the tunnel that joins King's Cross to St Pancras and you will find the huge light installation known as the King's Cross Light Tunnel – a 90m-long gently curving tunnel with a backlit wall of pastel-coloured LED lights that shift and change. Position yourself at one end of the tunnel so you can't see the exit at the other end then, using a standard focal length, seek to capture the curve. This works especially well with just one person walking the tunnel ahead of you,

*VP1. King's Cross Light Tunnel, colour. Sony A6000, 16–50mm at 16mm, ISO 250, 1/60s at f/4. Oct.*

## How to get here

Take the Circle, Hammersmith & City, Metropolitan, Northern, Piccadilly and Victoria lines to the station.

| | |
|---|---|
| **Location Lat/Long**: | 51.530039, -0.1238 |
| **Location Postcode**: | NW1 2SB |
| **Underground & Lines**: | King's Cross St Pancras: *Circle, Hammersmith & City, Metropolitan, Northern, Piccadilly, Victoria* |
| **Main Station**: | King's Cross, St Pancras International |
| **Bus**: | 30, 46, 63, 73, 91, 205, 390, N63, N73, N91, N205 |
| **Cycle Hire**: | Belgrove Street, Birkenhead Street |

## Accessibility &#9855;

This location should present no accessibility issues.

## Best time of year/day

Any time of year works here. Ideally, visit on a sunny day as the light inside the buildings will provide good contrast.

*Left top: VP1. Giant Remembrance Poppy in King's Cross ticket hall. Canon 5D II, 17–40mm at 17mm, ISO 100, 1/40s at f/9. Oct. Left: VP1. King's Cross ticket hall ceiling. Canon 5D IV, 17–40mm at 17mm, ISO 400, 1/60s at f/6.7. Aug.*

*Opposite: VP1. King's Cross Light Tunnel, mono. Sony A6000, 16–50mm at 16mm, ISO 160, 1/60s at f/4. Oct.*

*VP2. The clocktower at St Pancras Station. Canon 5D II, 70–200mm at 70mm, ISO 200, 1/750s at f/5.6. May.*

*VP2. The stairs to St Pancras Station. Sony A6000, Fisheye 8mm at 8mm, ISO 200, 1/800s at f/8. May.*

roughly two thirds into shot so they act as the primary focal point for the composition. The most prominent colour is often a pastel pink and I find converting to monochrome most effective as this brought out the contrast in the image. Tone the monochrome to suit your own taste.

## Viewpoint 2 – St Pancras ♿

By way of contrast St Pancras is more about the original 19th-century aesthetic that was retained despite the renovation. Starting at the station's exterior, proceed to the entrance of St Pancras Renaissance hotel. If you have a wide-angle or fisheye lens, use it to exaggerate the imposing structure of the hotel and station facade as it curves away towards King's Cross station. Enter the station building through the entrance about 100m to the right of the hotel entrance. Shoot the entrance to the station with the deep red brickwork, the lines of the arches and the station beyond making a strong composition. On the concourse you will find *The Meeting Place*, a nine-metre bronze statue of a man and woman embracing. Use a zoom lens to isolate the upper portion of the statue or use a wide-angle lens to capture it all.

Again, the red brickwork provides a great backdrop. If you have a fisheye lens, you can capture the statue and the lines of the roof beams to create an unusual composition. Just around the corner from *The Meeting Place* is a statue of the saviour of St Pancras – celebrated poet, Sir John Betjemen. The figure is standing looking upwards and shielding his eyes. Shoot wide with the station wall behind or use a zoom lens to bring the statue's face into sharp focus, with the station clock behind to create a narrative.

*Opposite top left: VP2. Entrance to St Pancras Station. Sony A6000, Fisheye 8mm at 8mm, ISO 200, 1/60s at f/8. May. Top right: VP2. Exterior car park outside St Pancras Station. Sony A6000, Fisheye 8mm at 8mm, ISO 200, 1/640s at f/8. May.*

*Opposite left: VP2. Sir John Betjemen statue, St Pancras Station. Canon 5D II, 24–70mm at 28mm, ISO 200, 1/30s at f/8. May. Right: VP2. The Meeting Place sculpture, St Pancras Station. Canon 5D II, 24–70mm at 24mm, ISO 400, 1/20s at f/5.6. May.*

As well as a desirable and expensive place to live, Bloomsbury is home to many cultural establishments including the British Museum. The area gave its name to Bloomsbury Publishing, publishers of the Harry Potter series, and the Bloomsbury Set, a group of artists who met in the area in the early 1900s and included Virginia Woolf and John Maynard Keynes. This area was lived in and farmed well before the 1066 Norman invasion and was noted as a vineyard in the Domesday Book.

Although the area passed through many royal hands it was Henry VIII who seized the land from the clergy in the 16th century and gave it to the Earl of Southampton. During the 18th and 19th centuries descendants of the Earl developed the area into a place for affluent residents to live, and now, a wander round Bloomsbury's old streets, cafes, shops, formal squares, museums and historic buildings with a camera is time well spent.

## What to shoot and viewpoints

### Viewpoint 1 – Woburn Walk ♿

At the northern boundary of Bloomsbury close to Euston station is Woburn Walk. During the summer months this pedestrian street with its quaint little shops and cafes just begs to be photographed. If you have a wide-angle lens, this can help increase the perception of depth, but a standard mid-range lens will secure good images. Look to arrive late morning when the cafes are open and people will add life to your images. Shoot from either end of this street; there is busy traffic at one end but using a short focal length of 24mm or less will push that to the background.

### Viewpoint 2 – The British Museum ♿

Of much interest to the photographer is the incredible Great Court – the Museum's inner courtyard. This two-acre space is enclosed by a spectacular glass roof and has the world-famous Reading Room at its centre. On entering the museum you will find yourself in the Great Court; the key to shooting it is to capture the symmetry of the central Reading Room and the staircases either side. The museum opens the Great Court for visitors 20 minutes earlier than the rest of the museum, which eases the crowds in slowly

## How to get here

### VP 1 – Woburn Walk

Take the Circle line to Euston Square or the Victoria line to Euston and exit either station to Euston Road. Head east away from the stations until you reach the junction with the A4200 – you'll see St Pancras New Church on the corner. Turn right on to the A4200, cross over to the church side of the street and head south away from it. Woburn Walk is about 200m on the left.

| | |
|---|---|
| Location Lat/Long: | 51.52659, -0.12944 |
| Location Postcode: | WC1H 0JL |
| Underground & Lines: | Euston Square, Euston, Russell Square: *Circle, Hammersmith & City, Metropolitan, Piccadilly* |
| Main Station: | Euston |
| Bus: | 30, 59, 68, 73, 91, 168, 205, 390, N73, N91, N205 |
| Cycle Hire: | Endsleigh Gardens |

### Accessibility ♿

This is a street-level location that should present no accessibility issues.

## Best time of year/day

During spring, summer and autumn, when the cafes are open and the sun lights the walk, are the best times to visit.

### VP 2 – The British Museum

Take the Central or Piccadilly line to Holborn station. Exit the station on the corner, head north and past the old tramway that rises to split the road in two, and take the left side of the road. You'll pass Sicilian Avenue to your left. Head along the avenue and as you emerge on to the A40 you'll see Bloomsbury Square Garden opposite. Cross over or go around to the left side of the garden. Turn left and the museum entrance is approximately 100m to your left.

| | |
|---|---|
| Location Lat/Long: | 51.51966, -0.12692 |
| Location Postcode: | WC1B 3DG |
| Underground & Lines: | Holborn, Tottenham Court Road: *Central, Northern, Piccadilly* |
| Bus: | 1, 8, 14, 19, 24, 25, 29, 38, 55, 73, 98, 134, 242, 390 |
| Cycle Hire: | British Museum |

*Top*: VP1. Bookshop on Woburn Walk. Canon 5D II, 70–200mm at 70mm, ISO 200, 1/250s at f/8. July. ***Above***: VP2. Woburn Walk cafes. Canon 5D II, 17–40mm at 17mm, ISO 100, 1/125s at f/7.1. Aug.

## Accessibility 👤

Holborn station has no step-free access. Take the Central line to Tottenham Court Road station then exit the station and head north along Tottenham Court Road, past the Dominion Theatre. Take the next right turn into Great Russell Street and continue for 500m until you reach the museum. Most areas of the museum are fully accessible.

## Best time of year/day

The museum is open 10am–5pm but they may open the doors from 9.30am on busy days to avoid delays. Bright sunny mornings will ensure strong shadows in the Great Court.

## Opening hours

Mon to Sun: 10am–5.30pm. Fri: open until 8.30pm. The museum is closed 24th–26th Dec and 1st Jan. Go to: *www.britishmuseum.org* for more information.

## Admission prices (2019)

**Free**.

## VP 3 – Sicilian Avenue

Follow directions to the British Museum. Sicilian Avenue is on the way.

| | |
|---|---|
| **Location Lat/Long**: | 51.5185, -0.12134 |
| **Location Postcode**: | WC1A 2QS |
| **Underground & Lines**: | Holborn: *Central, Piccadilly* |
| **Bus**: | 19, 38, 55, 98, N19, N38 |
| **Cycle Hire**: | Southampton Place |

## Accessibility 👤

Follow accessibility directions from Tottenham Court Road, then head past the museum for a further 200 yards to Bloomsbury Square Gardens. Head south through the garden. Sicilian Avenue lies opposite. This is a street-level location that should present no issues.

## Best time of year/day

It can be shot at any time of year and any time of day, though sunny mornings (after 9am, when the cafes are open) will ensure people are present in your shots.

*Top left*: VP1. Woburn Walk cafe patron. Canon 5D II, 70–200mm at 70mm, ISO 200, 1/350s at f/9.5. July.

*VP2. British Museum interior. Canon 5D II, 17–40mm at 17mm, ISO 100, 1/200s at f/5.6. Sept.*

*VP2. Performer outside the British Museum. Canon 5D II, 70–200mm at 70mm, ISO 200, 1/250s at f/8. July.*

and allows you to get the images you want. If you find people in front of you, shoot just above their heads – this will allow you to capture the central area and the tessellated roof. Once you're done, head back into the entrance hall and take the stairs to the small viewing gallery. This offers a bird's eye view of the court below and brings you closer to the ceiling, thus changing the dynamic of your composition. Head back down to the ground floor and take the stairs at the centre of the court, (these lead round the back of the Reading Room) where you can shoot back towards the entrance. With few people taking the stairs, you'll have a clear view to capture the lead lines of the balcony, the strong light and marvellous shadows cast by the steel struts that hold the glass panels overhead.

Upon leaving, be sure to take time to wander around the streets directly south of the museum. You'll find all manner of interesting and eclectic shops and buildings. Be sure to shoot the Pied Bull Yard clock on Bury Place, and Fancy That of London – a gift shop on Museum Street.

### Viewpoint 3 – Sicilian Avenue ♿

This pedestrian avenue, tucked just out of sight close to Holborn station was built in 1906 using Italian marble throughout. If you have a fisheye lens, this is a great place to use it before the shops and cafes open. The focal points for your images can be the wonderful arcing lamp stands – shoot these as key points but also zoom in to capture the stunning colours and designs that adorn them. The repeating patterns of these designs makes for classic compositions, particularly when you use a zoom to isolate the details and compress the perspective.

*Opposite top: VP2. The Great Court inside the British Museum. Canon 5D II, 17–40mm at 17mm, ISO 200, 1/180s at f/8. June.*
*Left: VP3. Lamppost in Sicilian Avenue, Holborn. Sony A6000, Fisheye 8mm at 8mm, ISO 200, 1/640s at f/8. May.*
*Right: VP3. Lamppost in Sicilian Avenue, Holborn. Canon 5D II, 70–200mm at 135mm, ISO 200, 1/1000s at f/5.6. May.*

The name Fitzrovia was coined in the 1930s, when the area started to become more bohemian, with writers such as Virginia Woolf and George Bernard Shaw living there. It came from the Fitzroy family, who developed the area in the 18th century and from whom many of the area's prominent features (the Fitzroy Tavern and Fitzroy Square) took their name. It doesn't have the same cachet as Soho or Knightsbridge and, sandwiched as it is between Oxford Street and Soho to the south and Regent's Park and Marylebone to the north, it's often overlooked – a mistake in my opinion; Fitzrovia has some fascinating subjects and features worthy of a photographer's attention

## What to shoot and viewpoints

### Viewpoint 1 – Warren Mews ♿

Warren Mews is probably one of the most photographed mews in London. The entrance can only be described as picture-postcard. During spring and summer the entrance is festooned with foliage, beautifully contrasting with the dark paint on the brickwork. This is a simple shot to take: stand on the opposite side of the road and take it; it's best with no sky, and a standard wide-angle will suffice.

*VP2. Looking upwards to the BT Tower. Sony A6000, Fisheye 8mm at 8mm, ISO 100, 1/320s at f/8. July.*

### Viewpoint 2 – The BT Tower and Cleveland Mews ♿

For many years known as the Post Office Tower, this 177m (581ft) London landmark was built and opened to the public in 1966. The revolving restaurant at the top of the tower drew almost 5 million visitors until 1971, when a bomb was detonated in a toilet on the top floor; it has been permanently closed to the public ever since. The tower is so important to national communications that it's technically known simply as Location 23 and no one is supposed to confirm or even discuss it's whereabouts! There are many locations from which to shoot it but two key spots are from the western side of Fitzroy Square and right beneath it – standing on Cleveland Mews. Shoot directly up towards the tower. Using a wide-angle lens will allow you to capture the tower and its reflections in the glass building on the mews itself. Shoot on a clear-sky day or when there's textured cloud to ensure the structure stands out against this backdrop.

*Opposite: Monochrome wide-angle shot of the Brewer Staircase. Canon 5D II, 17–40mm at 23mm, ISO 400, 1/15s at f/7.1. May.*

## How to get here

### VP 1 – Warren Mews

Take the Circle line to Great Portland Street, exit the station and head east past the The Green Man pub. A hundred metres past the pub take a right into Cleveland Street, then the first left into Warren Street. Warren Mews is to the right.

| | |
|---|---|
| **Location Lat/Long:** | 51.52358, -0.14198 |
| **Location Postcode:** | W1T 5LX |
| **Underground & Lines:** | Great Portland Street, Warren Street: *Circle, Hammersmith & City, Metropolitan, Northern, Victoria* |
| **Bus:** | 18, 21, 73, 205, 390, N5, N20, N73, N253 |
| **Cycle Hire:** | Bolster Street |

### VP 2 – The BT Tower and Cleveland Mews

At Warren Street Tube station, exit into Tottenham Court Road and turn right heading against the traffic. Walk for 500m until you see the Fitzrovia Bell pub, then take Howland Street directly opposite and head west for about 500m, until you find Cleveland Mews to your right.

| | |
|---|---|
| **Location Lat/Long:** | 51.52162, -0.13873 |
| **Location Postcode:** | W1T 4JZ |
| **Underground & Lines:** | Goodge Street, Great Portland Street, Warren Street: *Circle, Hammersmith & City, Metropolitan, Northern, Victoria* |
| **Bus:** | 24, 29, 73, 390, N29, N73 |
| **Cycle Hire:** | Howland Street |

VP2. Looking up at the BT Tower from Cleveland Mews. Sony A6000, Fisheye 8mm at 8mm, ISO 100, 1/320s at f/8. July.

## VP 3 – Brewer Staircase, Heal's, Tottenham Court Road

Take the Northern line to Goodge Street – Heal's is on the opposite side of Tottenham Court Road – or take the Victoria line to Warren Street station. Exit the station into Tottenham Court Road, turn left and head south against the traffic. Walk for around 500m and you'll see Heal's store on the opposite side of the road.

| | |
|---|---|
| **Location Lat/Long**: | 51.52114, -0.13467 |
| **Location Postcode**: | W1T 7LQ |
| **Underground & Lines**: | Goodge Street: *Northern* |
| **Bus**: | 24, 29, 73, 390, N29, N73 |
| **Cycle Hire**: | Alfred Place |

## VP 4 – Pollock's Toy Museum

Take the Northern line to Goodge Street, exit the station, turn left and take the first left. Take the first left again and walk for about 50 yards, Pollock's is on your right. Alternatively, take the Victoria line to Warren Street station. Exit the station into Tottenham Court Rd, turn left and head south against the traffic. Walk for about 500m and take a left into Tottenham Street. Take the first left into Whitfield Street and Pollock's is about 50m on the right.

| | |
|---|---|
| **Location Lat/Long**: | 51.52035, -0.13516 |
| **Location Postcode**: | W1T 2HL |
| **Underground & Lines**: | Goodge Street: *Northern* |
| **Bus**: | 24, 29, 73, 390, N29, N73 |
| **Cycle Hire**: | Charlotte Street, Scala Street |

*VP3. Brewer Staircase, Heal's, Tottenham Court Road. Canon 5D II, 17–40mm at 23mm, ISO 400, 1/25s at f/7.1. May.*

## Viewpoint 3 – Brewer Staircase, Heal's, Tottenham Court Road ♿

Heal's furniture store on Tottenham Court Road opened in 1833 and it is famous for its Brewer Staircase, designed and installed by Cecil Brewer in 1916. If you have a fisheye lens, this is a perfect location to use it, especially at the top of the staircase looking down, as it exaggerates the sweep of the stairs. A wide-angle enables you to capture the spiral form and allows enough depth of field to ensure the chandelier is in focus. Use a midrange lens and look directly up into the lower lights of the chandelier, with a short depth of field to bring just one or two lamps into focus. This creates a very intimate image.

Heal's actively welcomes people taking pictures of the staircase but please appreciate that it is a working department store and use discretion. If you wish to take home your own small piece of the chandelier, individual lights exactly like those on the one in the shop, can be purchased in store.

## Viewpoint 4 – Pollock's Toy Museum ♿

Pollock's Toy Museum originally existed in an attic room over Benjamin Pollock's Toy Shop in Covent Garden. When the museum grew too large it was moved to its current site, 1 Scala Street in Fitzrovia. This is a very easy subject to shoot and a standard midrange lens will suffice to capture images of the museum and shop. You can include Pollock's printers next door to extend the image and add even more character to images of this little spot.

## VP 5 – Colville Place

Follow directions to Pollock's Toy Museum. Head past the museum and continue to the end of Whitfield Street. Cross Goodge Street and you'll see a police station to your left and a park to your right; to the right of the park is Colville Place.

| | |
|---|---|
| **Location Lat/Long:** | 51.519349, -0.13503231 |
| **Location Postcode:** | W1T 2BJ |
| **Underground & Lines:** | Goodge Street: *Northern* |
| **Bus:** | 24, 29, 73, 390, N29, N73 |
| **Cycle Hire:** | Charlotte Street, Scala Street |

## VP 6 – Charlotte Street Hotel

Follow directions to Colville Place, then walk to the end of Colville Place and turn left into Charlotte Street. The hotel is about 50m on the right.

| | |
|---|---|
| **Location Lat/Long:** | 51.518423, -0.13497074 |
| **Location Postcode:** | W1T 1RJ |
| **Underground & Lines:** | Goodge Street: *Northern* |
| **Bus:** | 24, 29, 73, 390, N29, N73 |
| **Cycle Hire:** | Charlotte Street, Rathbone Street |

## VP 7 – Newman Passage

Follow directions to Charlotte Street Hotel. To the left of the hotel take Percy Passage; directly ahead is the Newman Arms pub, and Newman Passage is to the left, opposite Percy Passage.

| | |
|---|---|
| **Location Lat/Long:** | 51.5178, -0.13509 |
| **Location Postcode:** | W1T 1EH |
| **Underground & Lines:** | Goodge Street: *Northern* |
| **Bus:** | 24, 29, 73, 390, N29, N73 |
| **Cycle Hire:** | Charlotte Street, Rathbone Street |

## Accessibility ♿

Most of these locations have level street-level access and should present no issues. Some streets have cobbles, which are slippery when wet and hard-going for wheelchair users. There is a lift in Heal's store.

## Best time of year/day

Spring and summer are best for flowering foliage but most of these are street locations and can therefore be shot any time of year and any time of day. An early morning visit generally means there will be fewer vehicles around.

*Opposite: VP3. The Brewer Staircase, Heal's, Tottenham Court Road. Sony A6000, Fisheye 8mm at 8mm, ISO 400, 1/80s at f/8. May.*

*Top*: VP4. Printers shop by Pollock's Toy Museum. Sony A6000, 16–50mm at 16mm, ISO 800, 1/160s at f/4. July.

*Middle*: VP4. Pollock's Toy Museum, Fitzrovia. Sony A6000, 16–50mm at 22mm, ISO 200, 1/160s at f/4.5. June.

*Bottom*: VP5. Colville Place, Fitzrovia. Sony A6000, 16–50mm at 16mm, ISO 125, 1/60s at f/4. Aug.

### Viewpoint 5 – Colville Place ♿

One the oldest residential walkways still in use today, Colville Place is tucked out of sight between Charlotte Street and Whitfield Street opposite the British Transport Police academy building. The street is lined with a variety of plants in pots. Look to use the widest angle lens you have and shoot from the Whitfield Street end of the street – this will increase the sense of depth in the scene and make the nearest plants appear much larger. This shot is best taken during spring and summer when the foliage is at its most vibrant.

### Viewpoint 6 – Charlotte Street Hotel ♿

Emerging from Colville Place into Charlotte Street, head to your left for about 100m where you will find the Charlotte Street Hotel. This five star hotel, which opened in 2000, was designed by Kit Kemp. It's easily shot with a normal midrange lens, although you may wish to use a wide-angle lens and crop the image later. Arrive early in the morning just after dawn when there are fewer vehicles parked out the front and the hotel is illuminated. The two prominent gas street lamps are lit each night and, when combined with the subdued street lighting, lend after-dark images a very intimate feel.

### Viewpoint 7 – Newman Passage ♿

Behind the Charlotte Street Hotel is the Newman Arms pub, now sadly closed, but directly adjacent is Newman Passage. Look up to the top windows (above the Newman Arms) and you'll see a painting of woman in period costume leaning out of the window. The pub dates back to 1730 and used to be a brothel … the lady is waiting for her next client! Proceed down Newman Passage just to the left of the pub; this will bring you out into a small yard where an interesting diorama is played out. Take the passage up the slope (away from where you first entered) and this will bring you out to Newman Street. The passages can be shot with normal midrange lenses or wide angle ones to make them appear larger than they are. During the morning, light comes into the yard between the passages; shoot into the passage from Newman Street and slightly underexpose to increase the shadows that hug the interior of the passage as it slopes into the yard.

Oxford Street and Regent Street are the most popular shopping streets in the UK. Oxford Street was originally a Roman road, which ran between the counties of Essex and Hampshire. Called Tyburn Road during the Middles Ages, the road was used for hanging criminals from nearby Newgate Prison. It was briefly a residential street during the 18th century, until it became synonymous with retail during the late 19th century.

Many well known chains have their flagship stores on Oxford Street and it attracts around half a million visitors a day. Regent Street is only half the length of one-and-half-mile-long Oxford Street but hosts more upmarket stores. Developed during the 18th and 19th centuries, Regent Street was designed from the start to host only shops of a certain distinction – that meant no 'common' trades such as butchers or grocers would be allowed. The two streets intersect at the famous Oxford Circus, under which lies the Tube station by the same name. It's one of the few stations to have an entrance at each corner of a square.

## What to shoot and viewpoints

Oxford Street lends itself to people photography, while Regent Street is more about capturing the architecture. Head to the southern end of Regent Street (in the morning) to capture sunlight on the buildings that curve into Piccadilly Circus. During the daytime – rain or shine – Oxford Street is a great place to find interesting characters and, with a diverse range of people, light and buildings, pictures will be more about capturing the rush of city life. Stand on a bench and use a zoom to capture the huge volume of people that crowd into Oxford Street mid-afternoon. Be sure to shoot other details, such as the ornate statue adorning Selfridges at the western end of Oxford Street. During the evening and into the night, there are several locations to shoot: one classic shot is to shoot from the traffic island at the top of Regent Street, looking north through Oxford Circus towards the church and BBC building in the distance. Wait until late evening, then shoot 10–15 second exposures. It can take a few shots to perfect your timing with traffics lights directly ahead but patience will pay off.

Take a short detour via Carnaby Street: from Oxford Circus head south down Regent Street, turn left into Great Marlborough Street (just past Liberty's) and turn right into Carnaby Street. This location is all about people but keep an eye out for the street decorations. It can be worth coming here in the hours before dawn to photograph the lights, especially at Christmastime.

## How to get here

Take the Central or Bakerloo line to Oxford Circus, or the Piccadilly line to Piccadilly Circus. Alternatively, there are many buses that stop at Oxford Circus and Regent Street. Carnaby Street can be found by exiting Oxford Circus station, heading south along Regent Street (for around 100m) until you see Great Marlborough Street to your left. Carnaby Street is to your right just after Liberty's.

### Regent Street/Oxford Street Junction
| | |
|---|---|
| **Location Lat/Long:** | 51.51529, -0.14201 |
| **Location Postcode:** | W1B 3AG |

### Oxford Street
| | |
|---|---|
| **Location Lat/Long:** | 51.51515, -0.14323 |
| **Location Postcode:** | W1B 3AG |

### Regent Street
| | |
|---|---|
| **Location Lat/Long:** | 51.51309, -0.14063 |
| **Location Postcode:** | W1B 4TB |

### Carnaby Street
| | |
|---|---|
| **Location Lat/Long:** | 51.51326, -0.13894 |
| **Location Postcode:** | W1F 9PS |

| | |
|---|---|
| **Underground & Lines:** | Oxford Circus, Piccadilly Circus: *Bakerloo, Central, Piccadilly, Victoria* |
| **Bus:** | 22, 38, 94, 98, 113, 139, 159, 390, N15, N18, N98, N207 |
| **Cycle Hire:** | Little Argyll Street |

## Accessibility &

All viewpoints have street-level access and should present no issues.

### Best time of year/day

These locations can be shot at any time of year and any time of day. During the daytime crowds make for interesting subjects, whilst in the late evening traffic streaks can be captured. At Christmastime shoot the lights with or without crowds – during the evening and before dawn respectively.

*Lower Regent Street light trails at Christmas. Canon 5D II, 24–70mm at 32mm, ISO 100, 15s at f/19, tripod. Dec.*

Exit at the south end of Carnaby Street and take a right turn along Beak Street back to Regent Street. As you emerge on Regent Street, you'll be at the start of the curve as it leads into Piccadilly Circus. This is a great place to capture traffic streaks late evening and early morning; the dynamic of the curvature and the lights in Piccadilly Circus illuminate the far end of Regent Street. Don't be afraid to head out in the rain and shoot Regent Street – the wet ground will reflect the light and make your images glow.

Safety: In 2014 it was revealed that Oxford Street was one of the most polluted streets in London due to the volume of traffic. It also emerged that it had one of the highest crime rates in the city, due to the number of potential targets for criminals. The exclusion of all traffic except buses and taxis, and the introduction of CCTV have improved these statistics but be aware if you have respiratory problems, and be vigilant of your belongings while on the street.

*Piccadilly Circus, end of Regent Street. Sony A6000, 16–50mm at 16mm, ISO 100, 1/500s at f/5. June.*

***Opposite****: Bus light trails in the rain. Canon 5D II, 17–40mm at 17mm, ISO 100, 20s at f/11, tripod, LEE ND 0.6. Oct.*

*Above*: Carnaby Street Christmas lights. Canon 5D IV, 70–200mm at 70mm, ISO 1600, 1/45s at f/4. Dec.

*Above*: Early morning rain in Piccadilly Circus. Sony A6000, 16–50mm at 16mm, ISO 640, 1/160s at f/4. Oct.

Soho was developed as a royal park by Henry VIII in 1536, with aristocratic residences being built in the early 18th century. It continued to be an affluent area into the middle of the 19th century, but the aristocracy had mostly left by the time a horrendous outbreak of cholera struck in 1854. Throughout the 20th century the area was mostly known as a centre for the sex industry with its striptease, peep shows, blue cinemas, sex shops, massage parlours and clubs. Theatres, music and film companies based themselves in Soho and, along with cheap accommodation, it became known as a bohemian neighbourhood, albeit one with a sinister underbelly of crime.

Since the turn of the 21st century the area has undergone a huge change: the sex shops have almost all gone and trendy cafes and bars have taken their place. London's gay community is centred around Old Compton Street and the gentrification of the parish has done much to improve this vibrant part of London. The word 'Soho' has been used to name bohemian areas of other major cities around the world, including New York and Hong Kong.

## What to shoot and viewpoints

Soho is a vibrant area – there is much to distract the eye so take your time as you walk around. If you want to shoot the crowds and the nightlife, look to arrive late afternoon or early evening. On summer days people will spill out of the pubs and cafes and move between venues. Use a small, fast lens of around 50mm with a short f/4 f-stop and keep the ISO high to ensure you keep that shutter speed fast. Use the vibrant displays in shop windows as backdrops; pride flags, erotic shop displays, bars and cafes all make good backgrounds to metropolitan London. And don't be put off if it rains – with so much gaudy lighting on display, the rain acts as a reflector, pushing light back on to people. Use a tripod to blur motion for something creative or shoot handheld to freeze the action around you.

Return at dawn to shoot the same spots and you'll find a very different place: some cafes might be open but the mood in the morning in Soho is subdued; this time you'll be looking to capture people quietly easing into their day over coffee. During the day, take time to visit Soho Square. This little park with a quaint hut at its centre has appeared in many films and, compared to the raucous streets that surround it, is a far gentler location.

## How to get here

Take the Central line to Tottenham Court Road station. Exit the station and take a left into Oxford Street. Walk for 150m then take Soho Street to your left – this leads directly to Soho Square. Exit the square via the southwest exit on Frith Street – this leads past Ronnie Scott's club and then to Old Compton Street, the main street at the heart of Soho. To the eastern end of Old Compton Street is Moor Street, which leads to the Palace Theatre. To the west of Old Compton Street are the clubs and shops. At the far end of Old Compton Street is Tisbury Court; this leads to Rupert Street, where there is a food market on Tuesdays and Thursdays.

### Regent Street / Oxford Street Junction

| | |
|---|---|
| **Location Lat/Long**: | 51.51411, -0.13446 |
| **Location Postcode**: | W1F 0DA |
| **Underground & Lines**: | Leicester Square, Oxford Circus, Piccadilly Circus, Tottenham Court Road: *Bakerloo, Central, Northern, Victoria* |
| **Bus**: | 14, 19, 24, 29, 38, 55, 73, 98, 390, N8, N25, N55, N73, N98, N207 |
| **Cycle Hire**: | Broadwick Street, Frith Street, Great Marlborough Street, Moor Street, Soho Square |

### Accessibility

This location is all at street level and should present no issues.

### Best time of year/day

Soho can be shot at any time of year. Late evenings are best to capture nightlife. In the early morning Soho is generally very quiet, and at weekends people visit the cafes along Old Compton Street.

*Opposite, clockwise from top right: Rupert Street food market. Sony A6000, 16–50mm at 23mm, ISO 100, 1/80s at f/5. Sept. •The famous hut in Soho Square. Sony A6000, 16–50mm at 16mm, ISO 100, 1/100s at f/5. June. •Shaftesbury Avenue at night. Canon 5D IV, 24–70mm at 27mm, ISO 100, 6s at f/11, tripod. Nov. •Dog walking in Soho. Sony A6000, 16–50mm at 16mm, ISO 100, 1/160s at f/4. Sept. •Rain outside the Palace Theatre on Shaftesbury Avenue. Canon 5D IV, 17–40mm at 17mm, ISO 3200, 1/30s at f/4. Mar. •Sunny morning at a cafe, Soho. Sony A6000, 16–50mm at 16mm, ISO 100, 1/500s at f/4.5. July.*

In the 18th Century the fourth Earl of Bedford asked architect Inigo Jones to redesign Covent Garden to attract wealthy residents. The Italianate-style design chosen by Jones greatly influenced how the buildings in London were designed and built from that point onwards. Once a fruit and vegetable market, today the area is a well known shopping arcade, famous for its open-air street performances. If you arrive by Tube at Covent Garden station, watch out for William Terriss. Terriss, an actor, was murdered in 1897, and over the years there have been numerous reports of his (very tall) ghost appearing in the station …

## What to shoot and viewpoints

A major tourist attraction, Covent Garden gets very busy from lunchtime onwards, so arrive early in the morning for fewer people in shot. The interior of the halls were designed to capture as much light as possible, but you may need to raise ISO on overcast days. Using a range of lenses and focal lengths offers different styles of image here; use your fisheye and wide-angle lenses to exaggerate the sense of space. Your midrange lens will allow you capture the building along with visitors and those who work there. Use your zoom lens to pick up details in the building and take time to capture and isolate people; using a short depth of field will bring out the character in people's expressions.

### The Covent Garden Halls ♿

The main building consists of two main halls with a covered shopping arcade in between. The central arcade is a great place to shoot on a quiet morning, just after the shops open. With few people around, isolating a single person in compositions is far easier at this time of day. Use a wide-angle lens both to exaggerate the archways at either end and to expand perspective, making the arcade seem far longer. At weekends and evenings street performers inhabit the open square to the north end of the halls. Use a zoom lens to isolate your subject and their expressions then move around to capture the crowd's reactions to the performance, using your midrange lens to include the crowd as a whole.

Be warned though, performers are not above ridiculing photographers who they suspect are not paying attention and they will happily act up for the camera. There are also acrobatic performances at the eastern end of North Hall and classical and operatic performances on the lower floors at the eastern end of South Hall. Shoot the facades on the north and south sides, which run the entire length of the main building. Crouch low and catch the shadows cast by the columns. The north facade is quieter than the south, where the restaurants are located. Finally, shoot images of North and South halls at dusk, when the big gaslights come on. Your wide-angle lens can be put to good use, exaggerating the height and size of the two main halls.

### St Paul's Church ♿

The front of the St Paul's Church (the actors' church) with its large columns makes the perfect backdrop; there may be as many as 300 people watching performances. You can access the rear of the church with its red brick and often capture people relaxing on the benches.

**Note**: Covent Garden is privately owned and run so whilst personal photography is permitted, tripods or commercial shoots without prior permission are not. Please ensure you give some change to the performers if you do take photos. They're working artists and deserve to be paid.

*Opposite top left: Busy afternoon in Covent Garden. Canon 5D IV, 70–200mm at 70mm, ISO 400, 1/350s at f/11. June.*
*Right: Performer in Covent Garden. Sony A6000, E 55–210mm at 55mm, ISO 320, 1/100s at f/4.5. May.*

*Opposite middle left: Performance in Covent Garden Square. Sony A6000, 16–50mm at 27mm, ISO 100, 1/320s at f/5.6. July.*
*Right: Performer in Covent Garden. Canon 5D II, 70–200mm at 200mm, ISO 200, 1/320s at f/7.1. Apr.*

*Opposite bottom left: Covent Garden South Hall. Sony A6000, 16–50mm at 16mm, ISO 100, 1/80s at f/4.5. July.*
*Right: A Charlie Chaplin lookalike performs in Covent Garden. Sony A6000, 16–50mm at 50mm, ISO 2000, 1/160s at f/5.6. Apr.*

## How to get here

Take the Piccadilly line to Covent Garden, turn right out of the station and head down the slight incline to the main building. Be aware that Covent Garden station has no step-free access. Take the Central line to Tottenham Court Road station, exit and take Charing Cross Road south for 500m to Leicester Square station. Take Great Newport Street (next to the station) and cross directly into Long Acre; this will lead you to Covent Garden station.

**Location Lat/Long:** 51.512061, -0.12296473
**Location Postcode:** WC2E 8RF
**Underground & Lines:** Covent Garden: *Bakerloo, Northern, Piccadilly*
**Main Station:** Charing Cross
**Bus:** 9, 13, 15, 23, 24, 139, 153
**Cycle Hire:** Bow Street, Russell Street, Southampton Street, Wellington Street

## Accessibility &

This location is on street level with ramps throughout so should present no issues.

## Best time of year/day

Any time of year is good for a visit. During the daytime crowds and performers will be present. In the evening the crowds thin out a little and people gather at the bars and cafes. With cobbles and paving stones, rainy evenings make for very photogenic images.

Theatre manager and director John Rich commissioned The Beggar's Opera (written by the poet and dramatist John Gay), which earned him enough money to build the Royal Opera House in 1732. After the theatre burned down and was rebuilt in 1810, it was the first theatre to use limelight, a heated block of quicklime, used to create a bright spotlight on the indoor stage. This is where the expression 'in the limelight' comes from. Since then, the theatre has been in an almost constant state of redevelopment, with the latest expansion completed in 2014, when a glass atrium was added to the entrance. The theatre hosts opera, ballet and plays.

## What to shoot and viewpoints

The best spot for shooting the Royal Opera House is at the northern end of Bow Street. Position yourself on the corner of Broad Court opposite Floral Street. From here you will be shooting towards the corner of the main building. Try using a midrange lens and adjust your position to include the building in frame, using a wide-angle lens if you have one. One great composition is to include Enzo Plazzoto's statue *Young Dancer* at the end of Broad Court; try placing the statue in the left of the frame and the Royal Opera House in the background. Shooting just before dawn or late in the evening with the statue illuminated makes this shot.

While on Broad Court make time to capture the five famous red telephone boxes, which are tucked just out of sight. There are two angles that work particularly well: either aim directly at all five telephone boxes and wait for a few moments for someone to walk through; catch them mid-stride to add life to your image – extra special if it's raining. Or position yourself at either end of the row of phone boxes and shoot with a short depth of field to isolate the second or third box in the row. Be careful not to use too shallow a depth – it can result in the out-of-focus box being too blurred.

## How to get here

Take the Piccadilly line to Covent Garden and exit the station. Turn right and head towards Covent Garden. Take Floral Street next to the Nag's Head pub – this will lead you along the side of the Royal Opera House. As you emerge on to Bow Street next to the opera house entrance, the statue of *Young Dancer* is on the opposite side of the road.

| | |
|---|---|
| **Location Lat/Long**: | 51.51295, -0.1222 |
| **Location Postcode**: | WC2E 9DD |
| **Underground & Lines**: | Covent Garden, Leicester Square: *Northern, Piccadilly* |
| **Bus**: | 9, 11, 13, 15, 23, 139, RV1 |
| **Cycle Hire**: | Tavistock Street |

## Accessibility &#9855;

Follow step-free directions to Covent Garden station from Tottenham Court Road station. There is street-level access, which should present no issues.

## Best time of year/day

Any time of year is good to visit. The best time of day is late evening when the opera house is fully illuminated. The statue and phone boxes can be shot any time – night or day – but rainy days will offer reflections from the paving stones in front of the phone boxes. Visit: *www.roh.org.uk* for more information.

*The Royal Opera House, Covent Garden. Canon 5D IV, 24–70mm at 24mm, ISO 200, 6s at f/11, tripod. Oct.*

*Early morning by the Royal Opera House. Canon 5D II, 17–40mm at 20mm, ISO 100, 15s at f/8, tripod. Jan.*

**Top**: *Broad Court telephone boxes in the rain. Sony A6000, 16–50mm at 16mm, ISO 320, 1/160s at f/4. Apr.*

# [8] SEVEN DIALS

Seven Dials is the junction where seven streets meet at the heart of the West End. The Seven Dials monument – a sundial pillar – actually has six sundials mounted upon it but has seven roads joining it, due to a planning error: an extra road was added after the column was designed and the unplanned seventh dial was turned into a gnomon.

Thomas Neale designed the Seven Dials area in the 17th century for wealthy residents but in fact, the area became one of the most notorious slums in London – there was a pub on every corner. Both Dickens and Keats wrote about how horrible the area was: Keats described it as a place "where misery clings to misery for a little warmth. Want and disease lie down side by side to groan together." Regeneration programmes in the mid- to late-20th century improved the area and it's now one of the more chic areas of London and is populated by cafes and shops.

Neal's Yard, named after Thomas Neale, is a courtyard connecting two streets at the heart of Covent Garden. It was renovated in the 1970s by entrepreneur Nicholas Saunders, who developed the area into an ethical and colourful shopping quarter with a bakery, coffee house and dairy all carrying the Neal's Yard name.

## What to shoot and viewpoints

### Viewpoint 1 – Seven Dials ♿

Seven Dials can be shot night and day. Look to shoot with a wide or midrange lens across the square. During the daytime there will be lots of people and traffic. Shoot from the corner of Monmouth Street facing north and try to place the Crown pub to the right of the gnomon in your compositions. Evenings are very busy so if you're using a tripod, you won't be able to put it in the centre of the square – shoot from one of the side roads instead. You can shoot long exposure images in the evenings by using the street furniture (such as the rubbish bins) to rest on.

*Above*: *VP1. The Seven Dials gnomon. Sony A6000, Fisheye 8mm at 8mm, ISO 200, 1/400s at f/8. May.*

## How to get here

### VP 1 – Seven Dials

Take the Piccadilly Line to Covent Garden. Leave the station on Long Acre and turn left. Walk for about 100m and take the right turn into Mercer Street – this leads directly to Seven Dials.

| | |
|---|---|
| **Location Lat/Long**: | 51.51377, -0.12699 |
| **Location Postcode**: | WC2H 9HD |
| **Underground & Lines**: | Covent Garden, Leicester Square: *Northern, Piccadilly* |
| **Bus**: | 14, 19, 24, 29, 38, 98, 176, 390, N19, N29, N38 |
| **Cycle Hire**: | Moor Street |

### Accessibility ♿

Follow step-free directions to Covent Garden station from Tottenham Court Road station. The location offers street-level access that should present no issues.

### Best time of year/day

Any time of year is good for a visit, although Christmastime means there are more lights in the main Seven Dials junction. Shoot midday and late evening for crowds or around dawn for fewer people and cars.

*VP2. Neal's Yard, Seven Dials. Canon 5D IV, 24–70mm at 24mm, ISO 200, 1/180s at f/8. June.*

## VP 2 – Neal's Yard

Follow directions to Seven Dials. Once at the main junction of Seven Dials proceed along either Monmouth Street or Short's Gardens, both roads have entrances to Neal's Yard, which is signposted about 50m from Seven Dials.

| | |
|---|---|
| **Location Lat/Long**: | 51.51445, -0.12633 |
| **Location Postcode**: | WC2H 9DA |
| **Bus**: | 14, 19, 24, 29, 38, 98, 176, 390, N19, N29, N38 |
| **Cycle Hire**: | Moor Street |

### Accessibility

Follow step-free directions to Covent Garden station from Tottenham Court Road station. The location has street-level access and should present no issues.

### Best time of year/day

Any time of year is fine. Residents prefer people do not enter the yard before 8am. It's best shot on bright sunny days or wet rainy evenings. Bright days will ensure blue skies and colourful paintwork are vibrant. On rainy days and evenings paving stones will reflect the light from the buildings, offering more light than on dry days.

*Above*: *VP2. Neal's Yard, Seven Dials. Canon 5D IV, 24–70mm at 24mm, ISO 400, 1/180s at f/8. June.*

## Viewpoint 2 – Neal's Yard ♿

Neal's Yard has wonderfully decorated buildings and a bohemian feel to the courtyard. On bright sunny days the colours, combined with the presence of a crowd enjoying the shops and restaurants, makes for a vibrant image of London life. The courtyard is quite small so a wide-angle lens is a must. You can shoot with a standard midrange 24–70mm lens but try to isolate people or small sections of buildings. Single out interesting people among the foliage and use the buildings as a colourful backdrop. A short focal length will help further isolate interesting characters.

Note that the residents of Neal's Yard request that people don't enter the courtyard before 8am, this is to discourage crowds gathering and making lots of noise in the morning.

*Top left*: *VP1. Seven Dials at Christmas. Canon 5D IV, 24–70mm at 24mm, ISO 100, 8s at f/11, tripod. Dec.*

St Martin's Lane runs south from Seven Dials to St Martin-in-the-Fields church on the edge of Trafalgar Square. It's an eclectic blend of second-hand bookshops, antique dealers, and high-class gentlemen's outfitters. The English National Opera, the Duke of York's Theatre and the Noel Coward Theatre are also based here, along with galleries and cafes. London's narrowest pedestrian alley is Brydges Place at the southern end of St Martin's Lane. It is 200m long and just 15 inches wide at its narrowest point.

## What to shoot and viewpoints

### Viewpoint 1 & 2 – Cecil Court and St Martin's Court ♿

Cecil Court with its Victorian shop fronts is a wide pedestrian shopping street that connects St Martin's Lane with Charing Cross Road. Here you'll find an assortment of old shops selling antique books, maps, medals and other memorabilia. It's a great place to shoot at any time; during the day people gaze hypnotically into shop windows; at night, lights illuminate the darkened street. I like to shoot here at dawn, especially just after a rainstorm, when the light is reflected from the ground. If you're here at a quiet time be patient: sooner or later someone will walk through and add a spark of life to your image.

### Viewpoint 3 – Goodwin's Court ♿

Goodwin's Court is one of London's best-kept secrets. As you head down Goodwin's Court from Bedfordbury, you'll notice that the left side of the street appears to have been caught in a time-warp; the windows and gaslights look like they're straight from the pages of a Dickens novel. Visit late evening to see the street lit by gas lamps. You'll need a relatively wide-angle lens to capture a good line of sight, but there's an office block at the far end, which you'll want to keep out of shot. A tripod is a must when it's dark as there's very little light here.

*Top: VP1. Wet morning in Cecil Court. NEX-C3, E 18–55mm at 18mm, ISO 1600, 1/10s at f/3.5. Jan.* **Bottom:** *VP3. Goodwin's Court, St Martin's Lane. Canon 5D IV, 24–70mm at 24mm, ISO 1600, 1/30s at f/2.8. Nov.*

*Opposite: Rainy evening outside Fogg's. Sony A6000, 16–50mm at 16mm, ISO 3200, 1/50s at f/3.5. Nov.*

## How to get here

Take the Piccadilly or Northern line to Leicester Square station. Exit the station on to Charing Cross Road, turn left and 50m south of the station is St Martin's Court. Go to the end and you'll emerge into St Martin's Lane. Opposite and to the right of St Martin's Court is the entrance to Goodwin's Court. Turn right into St Martin's Lane from St Martin's Court, walk 20m to Cecil Court. Continue to the southern end of St Martin's Lane, Brydges Court is situated just after the English National Opera building.

### VP 1 – Cecil Court

| | |
|---|---|
| **Location Lat/Long**: | 51.51073, -0.12696 |
| **Location Postcode**: | WC2N 4AT |

### VP 2 – St Martin's Court

| | |
|---|---|
| **Location Lat/Long**: | 51.51097, -0.12777 |
| **Location Postcode**: | WC2N 4AL |

### VP 3 – Goodwin's Court

| | |
|---|---|
| **Location Lat/Long**: | 51.51091, -0.12699 |
| **Location Postcode**: | WC2N 4EA |
| **Underground & Lines:** | Charing Cross, Embankment, Leicester Square: *Bakerloo, Circle and District, Northern, Piccadilly* |

| | |
|---|---|
| **Main Station**: | Charing Cross |
| **Riverboat**: | Embankment Pier |
| **Bus**: | 24, 29, 139, 176, 453, N5, N20, N29, N41, N27 |
| **Cycle Hire**: | William IV Street |

## Accessibility ♿

Tottenham Court Road station has step-free access. Take the Central line to TCR, exit the station and head south along Charing Cross Road – Leicester Square station is about 500m. There is street-level access for all locations except Brydges Court and as this alley is very narrow (at only 18 inches wide), it will not allow wheelchair access. For access to Goodwin's Court without taking the small steps, proceed up New Row (opposite St Martin's Court) and take a right into Bedfordbury. About 20m along here on the right there is street-level access into Goodwin's Court.

## Best time of year/day

Street photography here is good at any time of year and day.

*Top: VP1. Checking the news on Long Acre, St Martin's Lane. Sony A6000, 16–50mm at 27mm, ISO 100, 1/250s at f/5. Dec.*
*Above: VP1. Shadow figure on Cecil Court, St Martin's Lane. Sony A6000, 16–50mm at 16mm, ISO 100, 1/250s at f/4.5. Apr.*

*Opposite top left: A wee crafty swatch, St Martin's Lane. Sony A6000, 16–50mm at 25mm, ISO 160, 1/160s at f/4.5. May.*
*Top right: VP1. Window shopper in Cecil Court, West End. Sony A6000, 16–50mm at 50mm, ISO 3200, 1/100s at f/5.6. Apr.*

*Opposite left: VP3. Cobblers, St Martin's Lane. Sony A6000, 16–50mm at 25mm, ISO 640, 1/160s at f/4.5. Mar. Right: VP1. Checking out the art in Cecil Court, St Martin's Lane. Sony A6000, 16–50mm at 16mm, ISO 2000, 1/160s at f/3.5. May.*

Originally just another residential square, Leicester Square was home to artist William Hogarth. It was during the 18th century that theatres were built, which became world-famous cinemas. Today, this is where the latest Hollywood blockbusters are premiered. At Swiss Court to the northeast you'll find the Canton Tree, which marks 700 years of the Swiss Confederation and the enduring friendship between Britain and Switzerland. Due to its proximity to major West End attractions, Leicester Square is a popular place for people to meet and performers and artists populate the square on busy afternoons.

## What to shoot and viewpoints

There is always something happening in Leicester Square so my advice is to walk through the area slowly, keeping an eye on what's happening around you. When there's no movie premiere scheduled, street performers will be there. On very busy days there can be hundreds of people in the square so try not to be swept along by the crowds. Use a small, fast lens to isolate interesting people, visitors and performers. Move through the square's centre by the fountain and on hot days you'll find pigeons (and people) playing in the water. When it rains, the crowds thin out, umbrellas appear and wet pavements offer the perfect way to show the rain and its effects. Where Leicester Square joins Piccadilly Circus you'll find the Canton Tree. Try to arrive before midday to see the figures striking the bells.

*Opposite top left: Charlie Chaplin statue and shadow, Leicester Square. Sony A6000, 16–50mm at 16mm, ISO 100, 1/160s at f/4.5. June. **Right**: Shakespeare in Leicester Square. Sony A6000, 16–50mm at 26mm, ISO 640, 1/160s at f/4.5. May. **Bottom**: Puppet show in Leicester Square. Sony A6000, 16–50mm at 31mm, ISO 160, 1/160s at f/5. Apr.*

*Busy evening on Coventry Street. Canon 5D IV, 24–70mm at 24mm, ISO 800, 1/30s at f/4. Mar.*

## How to get here

Take the Piccadilly or Northern line to Leicester Square station, exit the station on to Charing Cross Road, cross over and walk into Leicester Square.

| | |
|---|---|
| **Location Lat/Long**: | 51.51039, -0.13011 |
| **Location Postcode**: | WC2H 7LU |
| **Underground & Lines**: | Charing Cross, Leicester Square, Piccadilly Circus: *Bakerloo, Northern, Piccadilly* |
| **Main Station**: | Charing Cross |
| **Bus**: | 24, 29, 176, 453, N5, N20, N29, N41, N279 |
| **Cycle Hire**: | Panton Street, St Martin's Street |

## Accessibility ♿

Take the Central line to Tottenham Court Road station for step-free access. Exit the station and head south along Charing Cross Road for 500m until you reach Leicester Square station. Leicester Square is opposite the station.

## Best time of year/day

The busiest times are afternoons and evenings and performers will be present during these times. The main square is usually locked between midnight and 6am but the rest of the square can be accessed at any time. Note the square may sometimes be closed for special events and film premieres

Chinese migration to Britain began at the start of the late 19th century, when many Chinese settled around the docks at Limehouse in the East End, selling food and catering for the passing trade from Chinese sailors. Sadly, the area became synonymous with opium dens and slum housing, rather than restaurants and shops. Chinatown's current location, centred around Gerrard Street, began in the early 1970s as more people arrived from Hong Kong. The area now has more than eighty of the finest Asian restaurants in London, as well as many wonderful shops and supermarkets selling authentic Asian food and other items. While you're here, I urge you to head to one of the bakeries and sample the wonderful confectionary, particularly the fried bread sugar sticks!

## What to shoot and viewpoints

Busy most times of day, one of the best times to visit Chinatown is early evening to catch the blue hour as the crowds begin to swell. This becomes even more interesting when it rains as wet pavements reflect the garish lights from the restaurants. If you visit during the day, the street signs and public notices in both English and Chinese make interesting subjects, as well as the shop window displays.

One of the best times of the year to visit is during the Chinese New Year celebrations at the end of January, beginning of February. Lanterns are strung across Gerrard Street, Lisle Street and Macclesfield Street, filling the normally empty sky.

The New Year parade is a vibrant event with dragon dancers, floats and all manner of interesting costumes on display as the parade circles Chinatown. The best view is had from the edge of the pavement along Shaftesbury Avenue, between the entrances to Gerrard Street and Wardour Street. The ornate gate to Chinatown (on Wardour Street) was made by Chinese artisans in the style of the Qing dynasty.

*Opposite top*: Meeting in Chinatown. Canon 5D II, 17–40mm at 33mm, ISO 800, 1/8s at f/4. Sept.

*Opposite bottom left*: Looking east along Gerrard Street, Chinatown. Canon 5D IV, 24–70mm at 24mm, ISO 100, 8s at f/11, tripod. Nov. **Right**: New China restaurant at night looking west along Gerrard Street. Canon 5D IV, 24–70mm at 24mm, ISO 100, 10s at f/11, tripod. Nov.

*Evening in Chinatown. Canon 5D IV, 24–70mm at 24mm, ISO 2000, 1/30s at f/6.7. Dec.*

## How to get here

Follow directions to Leicester Square. Enter Leicester Square and just past the Hippodrome Casino take the right along Leicester Court, which leads to Newport Place. Continue to the New China restaurant opposite the Q-Park car park, then turn left. This will lead into Gerrard Street, the main street through Chinatown.

| | |
|---|---|
| **Location Lat/Long**: | 51.5114, -0.13211 |
| **Location Postcode**: | W1D 6LU |
| **Underground & Lines**: | Piccadilly Circus: *Bakerloo, Piccadilly* |
| **Bus**: | 14, 19, 38, 98, 390, 453, N8, N19, N25, N38, N55, N98, N207 |
| **Cycle Hire**: | Wardour Street |

## Accessibility ♿

There is street-level access, which should present no issues. Follow accessibility directions from Tottenham Court Road station to Leicester Square.

### Best time of year/day

Shooting late in the evening, when crowds are present and the shops and restaurants are all lit up. It's even better if it's raining, as this will reflect light and offer the chance of reflections.

*Top*: Dragon dancer in Chinese New Year parade, Chinatown. Canon 5D II, 24–70mm at 34mm, ISO 400, 1/125s at f/5. Feb.

*Above*: Young dragon dancer in Chinese New Year parade. Sony A6000, E 55–210mm at 165mm, ISO 500, 1/320s at f/6.3. Feb.

*Top*: Chinese gifts, Chinese New Year celebrations. Canon 5D II, 24–70mm at 55mm, ISO 200, 1/80s at f/4.5. Feb.

*Above*: Dragon in Chinese New Year parade, Chinatown. Sony A6000, E 55–210mm at 210mm, ISO 1000, 1/400s at f/6.3. Feb.

*Top*: The Chinatown Gate on Wardour Street. Sony A6000, Fisheye 8mm at 8mm, ISO 125, 1/400s at f/8. May.

*Above*: Chinese lanterns, Chinatown. Sony A6000, 16–50mm at 21mm, ISO 100, 1/640s at f/5. Oct.

*Above*: Bilingual street sign in Chinatown. Canon 5D IV, 70–200mm at 180mm, ISO 800, 1/500s at f/5.6. Mar.

Piccadilly is named for Robert Baker, who was well known in 17th-century London for making *piccadills*, a type of lace collar, which was very popular at the time. Piccadilly Circus itself was designed and built by John Nash in 1819 to join Regent Street and Piccadilly; the name circus comes from the Latin for circle. The 'circle' was broken around 1886 when Shaftesbury Avenue was added and the area had to be redeveloped for the road to be 'attached'.

During Word Wur II, when the clubs around the area were visited primarily by off-duty US serviceman, there were so many prostitutes working here they earned the nickname the Piccadilly Commandos. The first electric advertisements appeared in Piccadilly Circus in 1910, and the world-famous neon and lit signs have been developed and improved ever since, until in 2017 when the multiple LED screens were replaced with one giant high-definition screen. The most famous resident isn't whom we might think; many people mistakenly believe the statue atop the Shaftesbury Memorial Fountain is Eros but it's actually a statue of his brother Anteros – the Greek god of requited love. It was the first statue in London to be cast from aluminium and not bronze.

## What to shoot and viewpoints

### The Reflecting Mirror ♿

At Piccadilly Circus it's almost impossible to create an original composition; no matter what you shoot, it will be something others have shot before. The key to making your own interpretation of this popular location is to visit at unusual times and during different weather. My favourite times to visit are early in the morning or during a rainstorm – ideally combining both at the same time. As with so many London locations, the tough Portland stone that paves the Circus transforms into a giant mirror when it gets wet. Position yourself on the south side of the Circus and use a wide-angle lens to capture Piccadilly, Regent Street and the giant screen directly ahead of you. If using a midrange lens, take several shots and using stitching software to put together a panoramic image.

### The Underground Entrance ♿

Just east of the fountain is an underground entrance. The railings curve slightly on the north side and this curve works as a perfect lead line towards the fountain and the curve is echoed by the buildings leading away up Regent Street. On clear mornings the sun will come along Coventry Street from Leicester Square. Catch this moment by standing with your back to Piccadilly with the fountain silhouetted in front of you.

### The Morning Clean ♿

There's a secret to shooting early morning blue-sky reflections in Piccadilly Circus. The circus gets very dirty during the day, so each morning around 7am the street cleansing department spray the area by the fountain with detergent and wash the dirt down the drains. This leaves the paving stones wet for about 20 minutes. In the summer, once they've completed the daily cleanup, get in quick, squat down low and place your camera about two inches off the ground – you'll get stunning reflections of all the buildings around Piccadilly Circus. The bonus is it's so bright you can shoot without a tripod, even at ISO 100.

*Opposite top*: Piccadilly Circus morning reflection. Canon 5D II, 17–40mm at 17mm, ISO 200, 1/180s at f/11. July.

*Opposite bottom*: Light trails through Piccadilly Circus. Canon 5D II, 24–70mm at 24mm, ISO 50, 15s at f/16, tripod, LEE ND 0.6 grad. Sept.

Close up of Anteros in Piccadilly Circus. Sony A6000, 16–50mm at 50mm, ISO 100, 1/640s at f/5.6. July.

*The Horses of Helios* early morning. Canon 5D II, 17–40mm at 24mm, ISO 100, 1s at f/11, tripod. Mar.

## Horses of Helios and the Three Graces ♿

Be sure to shoot the Horses of Helios statues located at the corner of Coventry Street and Haymarket. Visit on a late summer evening and place your tripod on the street corner. Shooting with a long exposure of 5–10 seconds will capture traffic streaks leading back to Piccadilly Circus.

Cross to the opposite side of the street from the Horses of Helios. At the top of the building, above the horses, are three golden statues of naked women leaping from the roof. You'll need a zoom lens of around 150mm to place them against a blue sky.

*Top*: Meeting in Piccadilly Circus snow. Canon 5D IV, 24–70mm at 70mm, ISO 1600, 1/60s at f/4. Dec.

## How to get here

Take the Piccadilly line to Piccadilly Circus, or bus number 88 from Oxford Circus.

| | |
|---|---|
| **Location Lat/Long**: | 51.510286, -0.13458100 |
| **Location Postcode**: | W1D 7ET |
| **Underground & Lines**: | Piccadilly Circus: *Bakerloo, Piccadilly* |
| **Bus**: | 3, 12, 88, 94, 159, 453, N3, N109, N136 |

## Accessibility ♿

There is no step-free access at Piccadilly Circus. Take the Victoria or Piccadilly lines to Green Park, exit the station and head east past the The Ritz hotel to Piccadilly Circus, which is along Piccadilly. The circus itself should present no accessibility issues.

## Best time of year/day

This location can be shot any time of year. For crowd-free shots, visit in the morning at weekends. After midday the crowds will swell and street performers will appear in the afternoons. Rainy days brighten the pavements and offer reflections.

*Above*: Heavy rain, early morning in Piccadilly Circus. Canon 5D IV, 24–70mm at 28mm, ISO 1000, 1/30s at f/4. Dec.

Piccadilly Circus light trail, early morning. Canon 5D II, 17–40mm at 17mm, ISO 100, 6s at f/22. Oct.

Trafalgar Square and Nelson's Column are located north of Westminster at the head of Whitehall. These famous London landmarks commemorate Lord Nelson's naval victory at the Battle of Trafalgar, during the Napoleonic Wars. John Nash was responsible for the design and the 169-ft (52m) Nelson's Column at the square's centre completed in 1845. Guarding it are the four 'Landseer Lions', designed by artist Edwin Landseer.

A number of statues and sculptures occupy the square, but the Fourth Plinth, left empty since 1840, has played host to contemporary art since 1999. The square used be fully tarmacked but that was removed in 1920 and the stone flooring we see today was put in place. The fountains were built to serve two purposes: to reduce both glare from the tarmac and 'the risk of riotous assembly'!

## What to shoot and viewpoints

### Early morning

The square is tied closely to photography as Henry Fox Talbot, the father of photography, took several exposures of the square and column while they were under construction during the early 1840s, when photography was in its infancy. If you arrive between 6am and 9am you can watch the bird handlers at work and take images of the birds of prey scaring the pigeons away. Many people assume the square must be constantly busy but if you're an early riser, you'll find the square empty just after sunrise during the summer months. The fountains, whether operational or not, provide superb foreground interest with the National Gallery at the rear, and they're perfect for capturing reflections when still.

*Sunny morning in Trafalgar Square. Canon 5D II, 70–200mm at 200mm, ISO 400, 1/80s at f/25. May.*

## How to get here

Take the Piccadilly Line to Piccadilly Circus, exit the station and head along Lower Regent Street. Turn left at the Crimea memorial on to Pall Mall – Trafalgar Square is 500m ahead. You can also take the District or Circle lines to Embankment station: exit the station northbound and immediately cross under the railway bridge to Northumberland Avenue, turn right and head to Trafalgar Square.

| | |
|---|---|
| **Location Lat/Long**: | 51.50846, -0.12823 |
| **Location Postcode**: | WC2N 5DN |
| **Underground & Lines**: | Embankment, Charing Cross, Leicester Square, Piccadilly Circus: *Bakerloo, Circle and District, Northern, Piccadilly* |
| **Main Station**: | Charing Cross |
| **Riverboat**: | Embankment Pier |
| **Bus**: | 9, 11, 12, 15, 88, 91, 159, 453, N9, N11, N15, N91 |
| **Cycle Hire**: | Craven Street, Pall Mall East, St Martin's Street |

## Accessibility ♿

For a step-free approach take the Piccadilly or Victoria Line to Green Park, head to the bottom of the park (near Buckingham Palace) then head along The Mall and through Admiralty Arch into Trafalgar Square. Trafalgar Square should present no accessibility issues.

## Best time of year/day

It can be shot at any time of year and any time of day. Artists and performers will be by the National Gallery mid-afternoon as the crowds swell. Rainy days offer reflections from the paving stones. Special events include the Passion Play on Easter Weekend, St George's Day celebrations in April, and Christmas lights in December, as well as many other smaller events that take place throughout the year.

*Above: Trafalgar Square at night during Christmas. Canon 5D IV, 70–200mm at 70mm, ISO 200, 8s at f/9.5, tripod. Dec.*

## Reflections

When it rains, the Aberdeen granite that paves the square provides fantastic opportunities to shoot reflections of the architecture and people. One of my favourite haunts is by the entrance to the National Gallery. From here, observe people passing through the square. The area directly in front of the gallery building is quite wide so even with a midrange lens you can capture enough background detail to add interest to any people shots you may take.

**Note** that tripods are not allowed in the square itself without permission. You can however use them on the roads around the square. I find the traffic island directly to the south of the square a great place to shoot from when it's dark. You can capture images of the entire square and this is worth visiting at Christmastime when the famous Norwegian tree is erected and decorated.

*Reflections and rain in Trafalgar Square. Sony A6000, 16–50mm at 16mm, ISO 100, 1/80s at f/4.5. Mar.*

**Opposite top left**: *Early morning rain in Trafalgar Square. Canon 5D II, 24–70mm at 24mm, ISO 1600, 1/60s at f/2.8. Jan.* **Top right**: *The city's smallest police station, Trafalgar Square. Canon 5D II, 17–40mm at 20mm, ISO 100, 4s at f/8, tripod. Apr.*

**Opposite left**: *Close up of fountain spray, Trafalgar Square. Canon 5D II, 70–200mm at 155mm, ISO 200, 1/500s at f/8. Oct.* **Right**: *Crossing Trafalgar Square in the rain. Sony A6000, 16–50mm at 16mm, ISO 100, 1/200s at f/5. July.*

*Each Good Friday at Trafalgar Square, The Passion of Jesus is performed. Sony A6000, 16–50mm at 16mm, ISO 100, 1/200s at f/8. Apr.*

*National Gallery reflected in Trafalgar Square fountains at dawn. Sony A6000, 16–50mm at 16mm, ISO 100, 1/250s at f/5. Apr.*

# ⓮ CLEOPATRA'S NEEDLE

Cleopatra's Needle has a wonderful yet sad history. Originally made for Pharaoh Thomas III in 1460 BC, the needle – a trophy of the Battle of the Nile – was brought from Alexandria in Egypt. A barge was made especially to bring it to London but foul weather in the Bay of Biscay in 1877 led to the deaths of six crewmen.

The barge was cut adrift and left floating around the Bay of Biscay for several days. A week later it was spotted, towed to London and finally erected on the Embankment, by the Thames. A plaque on the base of the needle commemorates the six crewmen. The sphinxes that sit at the needle's base are not Egyptian ones but Victorian copies. Keep an eye out as you walk along the Embankment; you will notice the benches have camels and winged sphinxes on them too.

## What to shoot and viewpoints

The dark bronze colour of the sphinxes make them tricky to shoot in darkness (bracketed shots can work) so the best time to visit is in the morning, especially in mid-autumn when the sun will rise directly over the opposite side of the Thames. The sun will cut through the buildings and by using a tight aperture you can cause it to starburst in front of one of the sphinx. Shoot from the other side of the road to capture the entire needle and its adornments; a zebra crossing in the foreground shot in mono acts as a great lead in. Shoot the base at an angle, incorporating

*Sphinx by Cleopatra's Needle. Sony A6000, Fisheye 8mm at 8mm, ISO 100, 1/160s at f/8. Oct.*

the line of the Embankment path leading away. If you have a fisheye, place one of the sphinx paws very close to the bottom of the frame. It will make it appear as if the sphinx is reaching out to you.

## How to get here

Take the Circle or District line to Embankment station, leave via the riverside exit, turn left and head back towards the Shard. The needle is approximately 250m north of the station.

| | |
|---|---|
| **Location Lat/Long**: | 51.5085, -0.1203 |
| **Location Postcode**: | WC2N 6PB |
| **Underground & Lines**: | Charing Cross, Embankment: *Bakerloo, Circle & District, Northern* |
| **Main Station**: | Charing Cross |
| **Riverboat**: | Embankment Pier |
| **Bus**: | 1, 26, 59, 68, 76, 139, 168, 172, 176, 188, 243, 341, 453, N11 |
| **Cycle Hire**: | Embankment, Northumberland Avenue |

## Accessibility ♿

There is street-level access, which should present no issues.

### Best time of year/day

The best time of day for a visit is around dawn in the middle of the year, when the sun rises behind the riverbank opposite the needle.

*Opposite: Cleopatra's Needle, Victoria Embankment. Canon 5D IV, 24–70mm at 24mm, ISO 200, 1/30s at f/19. June.*

WILLIAM ASKIN | MICHAEL BURNS
JAMES GARDINER | WILLIAM DONALD
JOSEPH BENBOW | WILLIAM PATAN
PERISHED IN A BOLD ATTEMPT
TO SUCCOUR THE CREW OF THE
OBELISK SHIP "CLEOPATRA" DURING
THE STORM OCTOBER 14TH 1877

During the mid-19th century the River Thames was nothing more than a giant sewer. This resulted in two cholera epidemics that killed over 25,000 Londoners. Jospeh Bazalgette, championed by Isambard Kingdom Brunel, was given the job of engineering a better sewage system to clean up London and reduce disease. One of three embankment projects, Victoria Embankment was the most ambitious and the most expensive. Completed in 1870, having overrun in both budget and time, the construction narrowed the Thames but ensured that London had adequate sewage facilities. The sewer that runs directly under Victoria Embankment is still in use today.

The embankment carries the District and Circle lines directly under the road running parallel to this beautiful riverside walk. In 1889, Embankment became the first street to be permanently lit by electric light, however in 1884 the lights were replaced by gas lamps, which were brighter and cheaper.

## What to shoot and viewpoints

### The walkway and its city views ♿

The primary feature of Victoria Embankment is the 90-degree curve it takes from Blackfriars to Westminster. Starting at Blackfriars Bridge you'll see 'the Boomerang building' (officially known as One Blackfriars) and Gabriel's Wharf directly opposite. The walkway is open with a clear view upriver towards Westminster. As it heads under the trees, it begins to curve. Pause every so often during your walk to admire the view: St Paul's Cathedral and the Shard lie behind you, and ahead, the London Eye and Big Ben. This is the secret to shooting this walkway: as you proceed, the vista constantly changes. Some of the best views are found around Waterloo Bridge; just before it, the City swells behind you and as you pass under the bridge, Westminster itself dominates.

### Street photography and Victoria Embankment Gardens ♿

Victoria Embankment is another superb place for street photography. Look for people caught in the early morning sunlight, simply walking under the trees or sitting on the benches. You won't need to be up close and personal for this; the long pavement will allow you to use a longer focal length to capture people in context with the Thames and the view behind them. Often a short depth-of-field works well on people – the shape of St Paul's or the Shard, even when blurred in the background, are distinct enough to stand out. On rainy days this is the place to get that quintessential shot of rain-soaked London. Try to capture someone with an umbrella strolling along the side of the Thames, with St Paul's or any of the landmarks in the background and the light thrown up by wet paving slabs. During sunny days in spring and summer, make time to visit the Victoria Embankment Gardens next to Embankment station. They're home to incredible floral displays and a huge variety of tulips appear in the spring.

*Couple looking east along the Thames from Victoria Embankment. Canon 5D II, 70–200mm at 81mm, ISO 400, 1/90s at f/5.6. Nov.*

## How to get here

Take the Circle or District line to Blackfriars, Temple or Embankment station, depending where you want to begin your walk.

**Location Lat/Long**: 51.50721, -0.12191
**Location Postcode**: WC2N 6NS
**Underground & Lines**: Charing Cross, Embankment: *Bakerloo, Circle and District, Northern*
**Main Station**: Charing Cross
**Riverboat**: Embankment Pier
**Bus**: 1, 26, 59, 68, 76, 139, 168, 172, 176, 188, 243, 341, 453, N1
**Cycle Hire**: Embankment

## Accessibility ♿

There is street-level access, which should present no problems.

## Best time of year/day

Any time of year works here. Visit at dawn to catch sunlight on the tree-lined river path, or evening for the lights that line the river. Spring and summer are best for visiting the gardens.

*Opposite: Cyclist heading towards Parliament, Victoria Embankment. Sony A6000, 16–50mm at 16mm, ISO 100, 1/500s at f/4.5. Sept.*

*Dawn along the Thames. Sony A6000, 16–50mm at 22mm, ISO 100, 1/200s at f/4.5. Jan.*

*Morning snooze, Victoria Embankment. Sony A6000, 16–50mm at 25mm, ISO 100, 1/800s at f/5. Sept.*

*Above*: *Victoria Embankment Gardens. Canon 5D IV, 70–200mm at 135mm, ISO 200, 1/500s at f/4. May.* **Above right**: *Canon 5D IV, 70–200mm at 200mm, ISO 200, 1/500s at f/4. May.* **Below**: *Canon 5D IV, 70–200mm at 169mm, ISO 200, 1/1000s at f/4. May.*

*Light trails along Victoria Embankment. Canon 5D II, 24–70mm at 70mm, ISO 100, 37s at f/16, tripod, LEE ND 0.9 grad. May.*

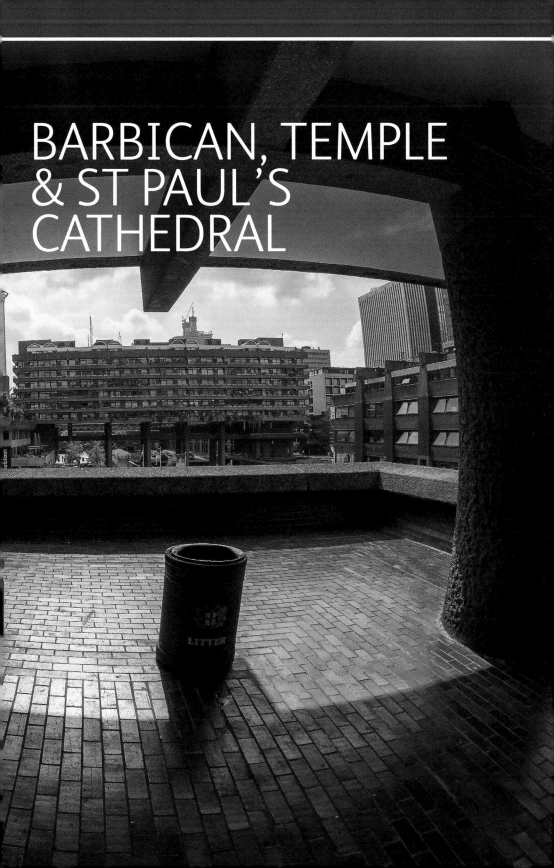

# BARBICAN, TEMPLE
# & ST PAUL'S
# CATHEDRAL

**This final section covers the Barbican, Temple and St Paul's Cathedral area, and whilst it's not quite as hectic as the previous locations – Covent Garden, Fitzrovia and King's Cross – it's certainly no less important.**

We begin at the Millennium Bridge, which, along with Tower Bridge, is now one of London's iconic bridges, especially among photographers. Countless images are taken on and around what is commonly known as the 'Wobbly Bridge'. Its useful lead-lines to St Paul's Cathedral to the north are a blessing; there is an almost symbiotic relationship between St Paul's and the Millennium Bridge in fact – a winning combination. Then it's on to Sir Christopher Wren's masterpiece of design, St Paul's Cathedral, which along with Tower Bridge, ranks as one of the key iconic shapes on the London skyline.

Moving eastwards, we'll begin to wind down and visit some quieter places that lie in the eastern half of the central city area: the Barbican Estate – a wonderful place for architectural photography; Smithfield Market – now much quieter than it was many years ago but still offering some wonderful images and Holborn Viaduct, which deserves attention for its ornate and vibrant decoration.

We visit Blackfriars pub and then move on to Temple and Lincoln's Inn, the home of London's legal profession and a place steeped in history. We conclude our journey with a visit to Somerset House and the stunning Nelson Stair, another of London's hidden gems.

*Previous spread*: Barbican Estate, City of London. Sony A6000, Fisheye 8mm at 8mm, ISO 100, 1/400s at f/8. July.

*Next spread*: Night bus waiting by St Paul's Cathedral. Canon 5D IV, 24–70mm at 24mm, ISO 100, 20s at f/11, tripod, LEE ND 0.9 grad. Oct.

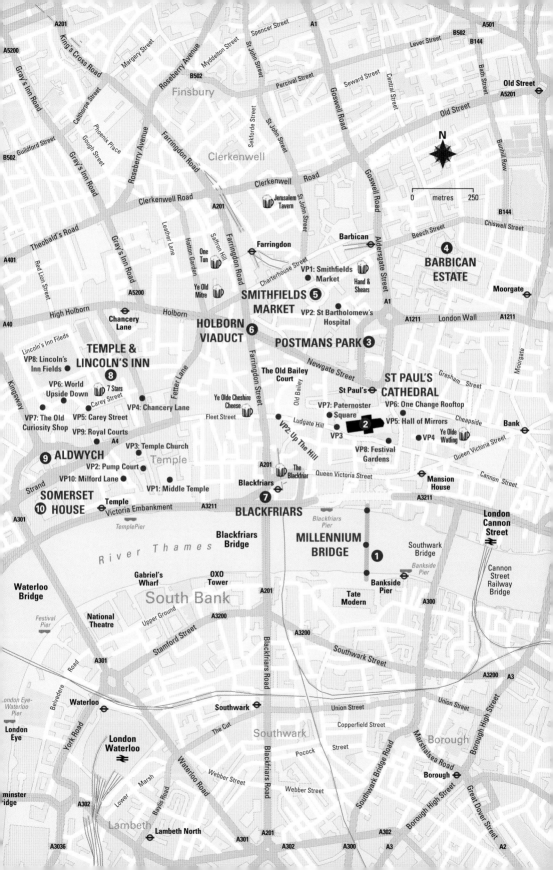

Officially known as the London Millennium Footbridge, it is often referred to by its nickname, the Wobbly Bridge because it vibrated when people walked across it. This steel suspension bridge was initially opened for just one day as it was considered too dangerous to use – it was closed for two years while modifications were made to stabilise it. The bridge links the southern Bankside with the City of London and is now one of London's iconic bridges and probably one of the most photographed.

## What to shoot and viewpoints

### Viewpoint 1 – South under bridge, looking north to St Paul's ♿

This is probably one of the two most photographed angles of the bridge, especially at dawn and dusk. The key is to use the lights on the bridge as lead lines towards St Paul's as they add strong compositional lines. Boats moving up and downriver will cause streaks in long exposures, so you may need to take several shots. The riverside railing here is very useful as a platform – using just a jumper and the railing to rest my camera on, I was able to shoot a 20-second exposure of the view towards St Paul's one evening. It's one of the best images I've taken.

### Viewpoint 2 – North under Bridge, looking South ♿

This time, shoot from the north looking south to the Tate Modern. On rare foggy days the north-to-south viewpoint is perfect as the bridge disappears into the fog, allowing you to produce a high-contrast mono image. Under the north side of the bridge, at low tide steps lead down to the riverside, which allows a more extreme angle of the bridge above and on a slack-tide you can catch its reflection. One good composition is made by tightly cropping the bridge and Tate Modern, excluding other details. Please be careful when walking by the riverside; it is very muddy and strewn with substantial pieces of rubbish.

### Viewpoint 3 – The Centre of the Bridge ♿

From this position you can shoot either towards St Paul's to the north or the Tate to the south. Use a zoom lens – especially for St Paul's – as this helps compress perspective.

St Paul's is quite a way from the bridge; it also removes distractions from the frame. Be aware that pedestrians on the bridge will create small vibrations, so time your long-exposure shots for when fewer people are close by. Head here early in the morning on weekends, when there are only a few people around. The human element adds a sense of scale to the strong geometric shapes of the modern bridge and the stone of the cathedral.

## How to get here

Take the District and Circle lines to Blackfriars underground station. Exit the station and turn to your right into Queen Victoria Street. The Blackfriars Pub should be on your left. Walk for 500m until you pass the College of Arms to your left. You will see St Paul's Cathedral to your left and the Millennium Bridge to your right. You can take the Central line to St Paul's and walk round the cathedral to get to the bridge, however St Paul's station does not have step-free access to street level.

| | |
|---|---|
| **Location Lat/Long:** | 51.50952, -0.09852 |
| **Location Postcode:** | EC4V 3TT |
| **Underground & Lines:** | Blackfriars, Mansion House, St Paul's: *Central, Circle and District* |
| **Main Station:** | Blackfriars, Cannon Street |
| **Riverboat:** | Blackfriars Pier |
| **Bus:** | 4, 11, 15, 17, 26, 521, N11, N15, N21 |
| **Cycle Hire:** | New Globe Walk, Tate Modern, Queen Victoria Street |

### VP 1 – Southeast, under Bridge
**Location Lat/Long:**  51.50841, -0.09773

### VP 2 – Centre of the Bridge
**Location Lat/Long:**  51.50968, -0.09853

### VP 3 – South Ramp, Looking towards St Paul's
**Location Lat/Long:**  51.50827, -0.0986

### Accessibility ♿
There is street-level access that should present no issues.

### Best time of year/day
Dawn and dusk all year round are the best times for good skies. Shoot at night from the bridge when it's quiet to get views downstream towards Tower Bridge and the City. Shooting when it's raining during the day will offer atmospheric shots. I have not experienced any restrictions on tripod use and you're free to shoot as many images as you wish, using whatever camera kit you prefer. Do note that the bridge is popular, space is limited and you may find the good spots already in use, so if possible, visit early in the morning when there are very few people around.

*Top*: VP1. View to St Paul's by Millennium Bridge. Canon 5D IV, 24–70mm at 34mm, ISO 200, 20s at f/16. July. ***Above***: VP1. Looking north towards St Paul's from south side of the Thames. Canon 5D IV, 24–70mm at 45mm, ISO 400, 1/90s at f/11. Apr.

*Middle*: VP2. Person resting by Millennium Bridge. Sony A6000, 16–50mm at 16mm, ISO 100, 1/125s at f/11. Feb. ***Above***: VP2. Millennium Bridge in the mist. Sony A6000, 16–50mm at 16mm, ISO 100, 10s at f/11. Nov.

*VP3. Southwark Bridge from Millennium Bridge. Canon 5D II, 24–70mm at 46mm, ISO 100, 20s at f/8, tripod, LEE ND 0.9 grad. Oct.*

*VP3. Harpist taking part in a morning photoshoot on Millennium Bridge. Canon 5D IV, 70–200mm at 111mm, ISO 400, 1/750s at f/6.7. June.*

## Viewpoint 4 – South ramp, looking towards St Paul's ♿

This is one of the most iconic spots to shoot in London: the on-ramp view to St Paul's with the bridge's glass panels acting like an arrowhead shooting towards the cathedral. Shoot this particular location with a long exposure of a few seconds to blur the motion of the people as they cross the bridge. Busy times are early evening and during rush hour on weekdays. On rainy days wait for people to cross with umbrellas. Use a wide-angle lens and crouch down – this will exaggerate perspective and make the people appear more dynamic as they head over the bridge.

## Viewpoint 5 – Art on bridge ♿

Not a viewpoint as such but a treat if you know what to look for. As you walk on to the bridge from the St Paul's side and continuing for about 50m, look at the floor: dozens of tiny little pieces of 'gum art' have been carefully drawn on the bridge. They are painted pieces of chewing gum stuck in between the metal grips. Many were created by local artist, Ben Wilson, who was followed in turn by others. Some reveal intricate designs of people and animals, some the dates people visited London, their names and home countries. Most people never even see this art, even those who cross the bridge every day.

# [2] ST PAUL'S CATHEDRAL

St Paul's Cathedral, along with Tower Bridge and the Houses of Parliament, is one of the definitive, iconic sights in London, with its 365-ft-high dome framed by spires dominating the skyline. There has been a church dedicated to St Paul on this spot in London since AD 604, however it wasn't until Sir Christopher Wren's career-defining masterpiece was built in 1670, after the Great Fire of London destroyed the previous structure, that London gained the majestic building we see today.

## What to shoot and viewpoints

### Viewpoint 1 – Millennium View &

Standing on the Millennium Bridge and shooting north towards the cathedral offers one of the now iconic and classic views of the bridge and cathedral. The bridge forms the perfect lead line to St Paul's. Shoot on a bright and slightly cloudy day, perhaps with an ND grad to hold back the light, and the texture in the sky makes a superb backdrop to the cathedral. Return in the evening when cloud catches the dying sun, then stay to capture the lights of the city and the illuminated dome of the cathedral. Note the lights of the dome are switched off after midnight.

### Viewpoint 2 – Up the Hill &

Cross Ludgate Circus (where Fleet Street and Ludgate Hill adjoin) and position yourself on the south side where Ludgate Hill curves. Wait for the number 15 red London bus to pass into view on a sunny, blue-sky afternoon for a classic image of this great landmark.

*Top*: VP1. Pink dawn sky over St Paul's from Millennium Bridge. Canon 5D IV, 70–200mm at 70mm, ISO 800, 1/45s at f/4. Oct.

VP1. St Paul's Cathedral at Christmas from Millennium Bridge. Canon 5D II, 70–200mm at 70mm, ISO 800, 0s at f/5.6, tripod, LEE ND 0.6 grad. Dec.

*Opposite left*: VP2. Looking east up Ludgate Hill towards St Paul's. Sony A6000, 16–50mm at 24mm, ISO 100, 1/400s at f/5. June.
*Right*: VP8. Bus stopping by St Paul's Cathedral. Canon 5D II, 17–40mm at 17mm, ISO 400, 1/60s at f/16. Oct.

*VP6. St Paul's at night from One New Change. Canon 5D IV, 17–40mm at 21mm, ISO 100, 30s at f/13, tripod, LEE ND 0.9 grad. Aug.*

### Viewpoint 3 – Up Close ♿

Head to the churchyard around the cathedral; the perspective on the northeast side offers tranquil images with the rich greenery. The trees in spring and summer allow you to construct natural frames around St Paul's dome and the small paths that lead through the churchyard. Working up close to the cathedral will require a wide-angle lens if you wish to capture the entire building. Using a mid-range lens isolates the dome among the trees.

### Viewpoint 4 – On to St Paul's ♿

Head east from the cathedral to Watling Street. This is one of my favourite views of St Paul's: stand roughly halfway along the street and shoot back towards the cathedral; on a busy morning you can catch commuters rushing in the direction of St Paul's and they add some lively foreground interest, combining well with the slight curve of the street. See the section on Watling Street (see page 102).

### Viewpoint 5 – Hall of Mirrors ♿

To the east of St Paul's Cathedral is One New Change (with its shops, restaurants and offices) and the western entrance allows for a hall-of-mirrors-effect shot. It's best shot on a bright sunny day with lots of blue sky, as the blue will reflect from the many glass panels. Visit again on a rainy day and the ground provides an additional pavement mirror.

### Viewpoint 6 – One New Change Rooftop ♿

Be sure to take the lift up to the rooftop of One New Change, where the sixth-floor public viewing gallery puts you on a level with the dome of St Paul's. There are lots of glass panels all around the viewing gallery balcony that catch the colours during a sunrise or sunset (entry is free and it opens at 6.30am). You'll get a view of the London skyline that allows you to shoot not only St Paul's up close and at height but also the Shard and others.

VP5. Reflections of St Paul's in One New Change. Sony A6000, 16–50mm at 16mm, ISO 100, 1/500s at f/4.5. May.

**Top left**: VP8. St Paul's Cathedral puddle reflection, Festival Gardens. Sony A6000, 16–50mm at 16mm, ISO 100, 1/640s at f/5. Apr.
**Right**: VP4. Rain on Watling Street. Sony A6000, 16–50mm at 25mm, ISO 1600, 1/160s at f/4.5. May.

VP3. Infrared image of St Paul's from the churchyard. Canon 5D II, 17–40mm at 17mm, ISO 200, 1/90s at f/8. June.

## Viewpoint 7 – Paternoster Square &

To the northwest of St Paul's, just past the main front entrance, is Temple Bar gate – a large stone arch that leads into an open square. Head to the far north of the square behind the pillars and on clear days shoot so St Paul's dome lies between the pillars. Using a standard midrange lens of 24–70mm, shoot in portrait and process the final image as a high-contrast monochrome.

## Viewpoint 8 – Festival Gardens and Lord Mayor's Parade &

To the south east more brash images are on offer, with the stark lines of the sunken water garden and the meticulously arranged flowerbeds providing strong and precise foregrounds. Use a classic red phone box to give that true London feel to your shot. Cross over to the other side of the road to allow you to assemble a composition encompassing the entire building and some foreground interest. This location offers a perfect opportunity to capture the number 15 bus passing by the cathedral; nothing says London more than a red bus in front of a famous landmark. Return at dusk to capture the number 15 completing its last run. A darkening sky and traffic streaks add a dynamic element to the image. The Lord Mayor's parade happens twice a year (check when at *lordmayorsshow.london*) and always passes St Paul's. Grab a spot along New Change just next to Festival Gardens – it's the perfect place to capture people on the parade route and if you're lucky, you might get a shot of the Mayor and his carriage. The Lord Mayor of London is head of the Corporation of London and apolitical; the office is concerned with promoting business interests in the city. The role is not to be confused with the Mayor of London, who is elected for four-year terms and governs the strategic interests of London: police, fire, civil defence and so on.

## Inside The Cathedral &

Photography is allowed inside, but there are restrictions: no photography whilst masses or services are being conducted and no photographing people without their consent. For a full list visit: *stpauls.co.uk*. The Cathedral Trust organises official open evenings for photographers during summer months, tickets are first come first served and while no tripods are allowed, you can use any handheld camera equipment. Images must be for personal use only, not for commercial purposes. Check the official St Paul's website for dates.

## How to get here

Take the Central line to St Paul's station, exit the station and St Paul's Cathedral is right next door. St Paul's station has no step-free access, so if you're mobility is limited, it's best to take the Circle or District line to Cannon Street station, exit the station on to Cannon Street and head west to St Paul's, which will be clearly visible about 500m ahead.

| | |
|---|---|
| Location Lat/Long: | 51.51377, -0.09826 |
| Location Postcode: | EC4M 8AD |
| Underground & Lines: | Cannon Street, Mansion House, St Paul's: *Central, Circle and District* |
| Main Station: | Blackfriars, Cannon Street |
| Riverboat: | Bankside Pier, Blackfriars Pier |
| Bus: | 4, 8, 11,15, 17, 23, 25, 26, 56, 76, 100, 172, 242, 521 |
| Cycle Hire: | Cheapside, Newgate Street |

### VP 1 – Millennium View
| | |
|---|---|
| Location Lat/Long: | 51.51045, -0.09846 |
| Location Postcode: | EC4M 8AD |

### VP 2 – Up the Hill
| | |
|---|---|
| Location Lat/Long: | 51.51396, -0.10232 |
| Location Postcode: | EC4M 8AD |

### VP 3 – Up Close
| | |
|---|---|
| Location Lat/Long: | 51.51423, -0.09755 |
| Location Postcode: | EC4M 8AD |

### VP 4 – On to St Paul's
| | |
|---|---|
| Location Lat/Long: | 51.51304, -0.09378 |
| Location Postcode: | EC4M 8AD |

### VP 5 – Hall of Mirrors
| | |
|---|---|
| Location Lat/Long: | 51.51384, -0.0957 |
| Location Postcode: | EC4M 8AD |

### VP 6 – One New Change Rooftop
| | |
|---|---|
| Location Lat/Long: | 51.51409, -0.09618 |
| Location Postcode: | EC4M 8AD |

### VP 7 – Paternoster Square
| | |
|---|---|
| Location Lat/Long: | 51.51472, -0.09902 |
| Location Postcode: | EC4M 8AD |

### VP 8 – Festival Gardens and Lord Mayor's Parade
| | |
|---|---|
| Location Lat/Long: | 51.51296, -0.09647 |
| Location Postcode: | EC4M 8AD |

## Accessibility &

Use Cannon Street station directions. There is street-level access and lifts into the building.

## Best time of year/day

Dawn and dusk are best for distance shots (from the bridge and St Peter's Hill). Spring and summer (during opening hours) are best for the churchyard gardens.

The Lord Mayor of London's carriage during the parade. Canon 5D II, 70–200mm at 85mm, ISO 400, 1/125s at f/5.6. Nov.

**Top left**: VP7. St Paul's Cathedral from Paternoster Square. Sony A6000, 16–50mm at 16mm, ISO 100, 1/125s at f/4.5. Apr.
**Right**: VP8. Festival Gardens, St Paul's Cathedral. Sony A6000, 16–50mm at 16mm, ISO 100, 1/200s at f/5. Sept.

Lord Mayor of London, Dr Andrew Palmly, Lord Mayor's Parade. Canon 5D II, 70–200mm at 116mm, ISO 400, 1/125s at f/4. Nov.

# 🄸 POSTMAN'S PARK

Just north of St Paul's Cathedral is Postman's Park, a former churchyard and burial ground. In the late 19th century it opened as a public park and contains George Frederic Watts's *Memorial to Heroic Self-Sacrifice*, a memorial to ordinary people who died saving the lives of others.

The centrepiece memorial is in the form of a loggia – an external gallery attached to a building – which houses many ceramic tablets with the name, date and details of the heroic deed for which the person gave their life. Not only is it a fascinating subject to shoot, it's very humbling to read the tablets and learn about those who lost their lives simply doing a good deed.

## What to shoot and viewpoints

The garden is quite small and in addition to the loggia has several interesting features. Enter the park from the eastern side by St Botolph's church and you can shoot the park's entire length, using the small fountain as foreground interest. During spring and summer, flowerbeds will add colour to your compositions. Just beyond the fountain is the loggia containing the ceramic tiles. I find selecting just one or two to photograph has more impact than trying to shoot the whole collection. On the western side of the park there's more scope to shoot compositions using the trees and shrubs with the benches as focal points. Look to get down low if you can, as this will help fill the frame with more greenery.

*Below: Postman's Park garden. Canon 5D IV, 24–70mm at 24mm, ISO 200, 1/90s at f/8. Apr.*

## How to get here

Take the Central line to St Paul's Tube station, exit the station and cross the interchange (via the crossings). Head north away from the station along St Martin's Le Grand. The park entrance lies just before the turning into a street named Little Britain. You can get a number 76 bus from Waterloo Station that stops outside St Paul's station.

| | |
|---|---|
| **Location Lat/Long**: | 51.51676, -0.09771 |
| **Location Postcode**: | EC1A 7BT |
| **Underground & Lines**: | Liverpool Street, St Paul's: *Central, Circle and District, Hammersmith & City, Metropolitan* |
| **Main Station**: | Moorgate |
| **Bus**: | 4, 56, 76, 100 |
| **Cycle Hire**: | King Edward Street, Newgate Street |

## Accessibility ♿

St Paul's station has no step-free access. If required, take the Central or Circle line to Liverpool Street, exit the station onto Liverpool Street and take Old Broad Street by The Railway Tavern pub. Turn right at the end on to London Wall and head towards the Museum of London. Take the first left off the Rotunda roundabout into Aldersgate Street; the park is to your right with street-level access.

## Best time of year/day

The park is only open during the daytime. Spring and summer are best as the flowerbeds are more vibrant and the sun lights the park during the longer summer days.

Postman's Park memorial wall plaques (top image):

P.C. HAROLD FRANK RICKETTS
METROPOLITAN POLICE
DROWNED AT TEIGNMOUTH
WHILST TRYING TO RESCUE
TWO BATHING AND SEEN
...11 SEPT 1916...

P.C. EDWARD GEORGE
BROWN GREENOFF
METROPOLITAN POLICE
WHO LIVES WERE SAVED BY HIS
DEVOTION TO DUTY AT THE
TERRIBLE EXPLOSION AT
SILVERTOWN · 19 JAN 1917

P.C. PERCY EDWIN COOK
METROPOLITAN POLICE
VOLUNTARILY DESCENDED HIGH
TENSION CHAMBER AT KENSINGTON
TO RESCUE TWO WORKMEN
OVERCOME BY POISONOUS GAS
7 OCT 1927

FREDERICK MILLS A RUTTER
ROBERT DURRANT & F DUNES
WHO LOST THEIR LIVES IN
BRAVELY STRIVING TO SAVE
A COMRADE AT THE SEWAGE
...WORKS EAST HAM
JULY 1ST 1895

ELIZABETH BOXALL
AGED 17 OF BETHNAL GREEN
WHO DIED OF INJURIES RECEIVED
IN TRYING TO SAVE
A CHILD
FROM A RUNAWAY HORSE
JUNE 20 1888

HERBERT PETER CAZALY
STATIONER'S CLERK
WHO WAS DROWNED AT KEW
IN ENDEAVOURING TO SAVE
A MAN FROM DROWNING
APRIL 21 1889

HERBERT MACONOGHU
SCHOOL BOY FROM WIMBLEDON AGED 13
HIS PARENTS ABSENT IN INDIA LOST
HIS LIFE IN VAINLY TRYING TO RESCUE
HIS TWO SCHOOL FELLOWS WHO WERE
DROWNED AT GLOVERS POOL CROYDE
NORTH DEVON · AUGUST 28 1882

SAMUEL RABBETH
MEDICAL OFFICER
OF THE ROYAL FREE HOSPITAL
WHO TRIED TO SAVE A CHILD
SUFFERING FROM DIPHTHERIA
AT THE COST OF HIS OWN LIFE
OCTOBER 26 1884

DAVID SELVES
...OF WOOLWICH
...CLASPED IN HIS ARMS...
SEPTEMBER · 12 · 1886

FREDERICK ALFRED CROFT
INSPECTOR AGED 31
SAVED A LUNATIC WOMAN
FROM SUICIDE AT WOOLWICH
ARSENAL STATION BUT WAS
HIMSELF RUN OVER BY THE TRAIN
11 JAN 1878

HARRY SISLEY OF...
ELEVEN, AGED...

JAMES HEWERS
AGED...

GEORGE BLENCOWE
AGED 16...

ERNEST BENNING
...

ALICE AYRES
DAUGHTER OF A BRICKLAYER'S LABOURER
WHO BY INTREPID CONDUCT
SAVED 3 CHILDREN
FROM A BURNING HOUSE
IN UNION STREET BOROUGH
AT THE COST OF HER OWN YOUNG LIFE
APRIL 24 1885

*Above left*: Postman's Park memorial. Canon 5D IV, 24–70mm at 38mm, ISO 400, 1/125s at f/6.7. Apr. **Above**: Postman's Park gravestones. Canon 5D IV, 24–70mm at 30mm, ISO 200, 1/15s at f/8. Apr.

*Top*: Postman's Park memorial wall. Canon 5D IV, 24–70mm at 28mm, ISO 200, 1/20s at f/6.7. Apr.

*Postman's Park memorial plaque. Canon 5D IV, 24–70mm at 32mm, ISO 400, 1/350s at f/6.7. Apr.*

G.F. WATTS'S MEMORIAL
TO HEROIC SELF SACRIFICE

UNVEILED IN 1900, THIS MEMORIAL TO HEROIC SELF-SACRIFICE WAS
CONCEIVED AND UNDERTAKEN BY THE VICTORIAN ARTIST
GEORGE FREDERIC WATTS OM RA (1817-1904).

IT CONTAINS PLAQUES TO THOSE WHO HAVE HEROICALLY LOST
THEIR LIVES TRYING TO SAVE ANOTHER.
WATTS BELIEVED THAT THESE 'EVERYDAY' HEROES PROVIDED
MODELS OF EXEMPLARY BEHAVIOUR AND CHARACTER.

'THE MATERIAL PROSPERITY OF A NATION IS NOT AN ABIDING
POSSESSION; THE DEEDS OF ITS PEOPLE ARE.' G.F. WATTS
'GREATER LOVE HATH NO MAN THAN THIS, THAT HE LAY DOWN HIS
LIFE FOR HIS FRIENDS.' JOHN 15:13

WATTS GALLERY, COMPTON, SURREY

LEARN MORE ABOUT THE WATTS MEMORIAL
WWW.POSTMANSPARK.ORG.UK

The name Barbican comes from the Latin for fortified gateway: *Barbecana*, and the site was originally a Roman fort. The area was almost completely obliterated by bombing during World War II with considerable loss of life, however during the 1960s construction of a 'model of modern living' began at this 40-acre site. The Barbican Estate consists of three tower blocks, thirteen terrace blocks and various courtyards, as well as the Barbican Centre (an arts, drama and business venue), the Barbican public library, the City of London School for Girls, the Museum of London, and the Guildhall School of Music and Drama. It's considered a perfect example of British Brutalist architecture due to its stark lines and heavy use of concrete as a primary building material. The estate is now Grade II Listed.

*Opposite bottom: Barbican Estate, City of London. Sony A6000, Fisheye 8mm at 8mm, ISO 100, 1/400s at f/8. July.*

*Below: Stairwell in the Barbican Estate on a bright morning. Sony A6000, Fisheye 8mm at 8mm, ISO 100, 1/250s at f/8. Mar.*

## What to shoot and viewpoints

At first, the complex may not seem worth shooting but once there you become immersed in this concrete jungle and one can't help but think of dystopian novels such as *Brave New World*. The harsh lines and architecture offer bold compositions. It's not a prime tourist location but the dark and harshly lit areas are superb for those wishing to practise or just dabble in the art of architectural photography. There are dozens of long walkways, stairwells and courtyards – it's essentially a sprawling estate and although it's private land, it's unlikely you'll be stopped from using a tripod. The underground areas can be tricky to shoot as they are dimly lit so high ISO and fast lenses are advisable. Look for interesting plays of light, in both the textures it covers and the shapes the concrete forces light and shadow to take. It can take time to find the flow but it's a superb place to practise your understanding of contrast and shape. If you're not convinced, I was able to secure a shot on my very first visit, shooting with a handheld pocket camera, and it earned me a place in the prestigious Landscape Photographer of the Year competition!

## How to get here

Take the Circle or Metropolitan lines to Farringdon, exit the station and turn right on to Farringdon Road. Turn left and head south away from the station towards the red bridge of Holborn Viaduct. Continue for 100m and turn left into Charterhouse Street. Walk to the end, passing Charterhouse Square (a park) on your left. Turn right on to the A1 and the Barbican Estate is about 100m ahead of you – you'll see the high-rise tower blocks.

| | |
|---|---|
| **Location Lat/Long**: | 51.52044, -0.0938 |
| **Location Postcode**: | EC2Y 8DS |
| **Underground & Lines**: | Barbican, Farringdon, Moorgate: *Circle, Hammersmith & City, Metropolitan* |
| **Main Station**: | Farringdon, Liverpool Street, Moorgate |
| **Bus**: | 4, 56, 153 |
| **Cycle Hire**: | Barbican Centre, Fore Street |

## Accessibility &#9855;

There is street-level access to and around the Barbican complex.

## Best time of year/day

Any time of year works well here. During the day is best as strong light is required for bold compositions. Be aware that the Barbican is a residential complex so please respect residents' privacy.

*Above*: Barbican Estate, City of London. Sony A6000, Fisheye 8mm at 8mm, ISO 100, 1/320s at f/8. July.

*Above*: Infrared image of the towering Barbican apartment block. Canon 5D II, 17–40mm at 22mm, ISO 200, 1/180s at f/6.7. Mar.

Smithfield was known as Smooth Field in the Middle Ages when the area was used to graze livestock. From that, a livestock market grew with many of the local streets named after animals such as Cock Lane, Duck Lane and Goose Alley. Meat has been traded at Smithfield Market for more than 800 years, making it one of the oldest markets in London.

In 1381 Wat Tyler, leader of the Peasants' Revolt, met the king (Richard II) at Smithfield to make his demands but a skirmish broke out and he was stabbed by William Walworth, the Mayor of London. Seriously wounded, Tyler was taken to St Bartholomew's hospital but Walworth dragged him from his deathbed, beheaded him and put his decapitated head on London Bridge as a warning. Smithfield was also the site where Scotland's most famous revolutionary William Wallace was put to death. Having been captured in Scotland and brought before King Edward I for trial, Wallace was hung, drawn and quartered near St Bartholomew's Hospital. St Bart's Children's Hospital as it is more commonly known, is the oldest hospital in Europe still located on its original site, having been founded as a hospital for the poor in 1123.

## What to shoot and viewpoints

### Viewpoint 1 – St John's Gatehouse ♿

The 16th-century gatehouse on St John's Lane houses the museum of the Order of St John, which in 1887 is where the St John's Ambulance organisation was founded to train and offer first aid. The Order of St John sent knights to the Holy Land in the 12th century to treat those wounded fighting the Crusades. Essentially, the gate is similar on both sides although the south-facing side is more enclosed and offers a wider shot that includes more lampposts. Shoot mid-morning to mid-afternoon to ensure the gate is lit by the sun; the pale stone walls reflect light into the enclosed area in front of the gate, allowing you to shoot lower ISO and faster shutter speeds. During the spring and summer, use the trees in front of the gate as natural frames to hold back the bright sky above.

### Viewpoint 2 – Smithfield Market ♿

The market is much smaller than it was in its heyday in the early 20th century – the public area primarily consists of the Great Avenue, a small road that bisects the Smithfield Market building. Use a zoom lens to shoot the painted dragons that keep watch over the entrances each end of the Great Avenue. Head through the building to the northern end and you'll find five red telephone boxes of different sizes. Shoot the phone boxes head on and capture someone in full stride walking past to give your compositions a touch of life. The vivid red of the boxes against the green and purple of the railings behind works well. Shooting all the phone boxes can look messy, so isolate two for a more balanced image. Finally, look up: in the ceiling is the Smithfield clock. Position yourself at either end of the Great Avenue and shoot the clock with your zoom lens. Set it off-centre and use the ceiling's cast-iron supports as a repeating pattern around the clock.

*Opposite*: VP1. St John's Gate, Clerkenwell. Canon 5D IV, 24–70mm at 24mm, ISO 200, 1/20s at f/6.7. Aug.

VP2. Dragon decorations at Smithfield Market. Canon 5D IV, 70–200mm at 160mm, ISO 200, 1/500s at f/8. Apr.

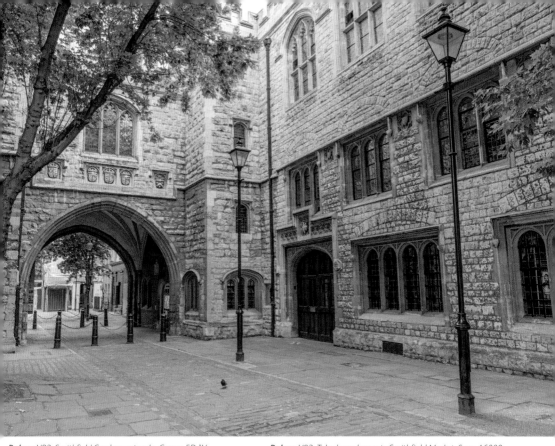

*Below*: VP2. Smithfield Gardens rotunda. Canon 5D IV, 70–200mm at 200mm, ISO 200, 1/60s at f/8. Apr.

*Below*: VP2. Telephone boxes in Smithfield Market. Sony A6000, 16–50mm at 25mm, ISO 2000, 1/160s at f/4.5. Oct.

## Viewpoint 3 – Cloth Fair ♿

Just to the north of St Bartholomew the Great church is Cloth Fair. Once home to a community of weavers, this quaint little street was also home to poet laureate Sir John Betjeman – the saviour of St Pancras station. The pub, the Hand and Shears, has been on the site since 1532. Shooting along the street from either end will offer interesting images. Use a zoom to compress perspective and remove some of the modern street signs. During mid-morning in spring, sunlight enters the street and the south-facing houses catch the light perfectly.

## Viewpoint 4 – The Wallace Memorial ♿

Situated to the south of the central rotunda and park and on the exterior of St Bartholomew's Hospital building is the memorial to William Wallace. This is an easy shot to make but an interesting one as the memorial is often bedecked with Caledonian flags and notes left by those paying their respects to one of Scotland's legendary heroes.

*Above left: VP3. Cloth Fair on a sunny morning. Canon 5D IV, 24–70mm at 24mm, ISO 200, 1/125s at f/8. Apr. **Above middle**: VP3. Cloth Fair, home of Sir John Betjemen. Canon 5D IV, 24–70mm at 24mm, ISO 200, 1/15s at f/8. Apr. **Above right**: VP4. William Wallace memorial, Smithfield. Canon 5D IV, 24–70mm at 28mm, ISO 200, 1/45s at f/6.7. Aug.*

## Viewpoint 5 – St Bartholomew-the-Less church and square ♿

Two key points of interest are located here: the church of St Bartholomew-the-Less and the hospital courtyard. The former is a beautiful chapel located in the hospital grounds, it's open most days and anyone can go in. On bright days the church is brightly lit – the whitewashed

## How to get here

Take the Circle or Metropolitan line to Farringdon, exit the station and turn right on to Farringdon Road. Turn left and head south away from the station towards the red bridge of Holborn Viaduct. Continue for 150m then turn left into West Smithfield; the Smithfield rotunda is about 250m ahead of you. The Great Avenue is through the market to your left; St Bartholomew's Hospital and the Wallace Memorial to your right. The hospital entrance is to the right of the Wallace Memorial. You can see the church of St Bartholomew-the-Less through railings set into the wall. The Cloth Fair is on the far eastern side of the rotunda.

| | |
|---|---|
| **Underground & Lines:** | Barbican, Farringdon: *Circle, Hammersmith & City, Metropolitan* |
| **Main Station:** | Farringdon |
| **Bus:** | 8, 17, 25, 40, 46, 63, 341, 521, N8, N63 |
| **Cycle Hire:** | Snow Hill, West Smithfield |

### VP 1 – St John's Gatehouse

| | |
|---|---|
| **Location Lat/Long:** | 51.52198, -0.10274 |
| **Location Postcode:** | EC1M 4BU |

*VP5. Entrance to St Bart's courtyard. Canon 5D IV, 24–70mm at 24mm, ISO 200, 1/45s at f/11. Apr.*

interior means you won't need to up the ISO too much to get some shots. It's a small chapel so a wide-angle lens works well to capture the pews, altar and the striking chandeliers. To the east through the arch lies the courtyard of the hospital. Visit on a bright sunny day in spring or early summer to see blossom on the trees by the fountains. Shoot with a zoom lens to isolate the blossom and details of the fountains, or use a wider lens to take in the whole scene with its combination of light and shade provided by sunlight through the trees. Note this is a working hospital – patients and staff use the courtyard to rest so please be respectful when taking photographs.

*VP5. Blossom by St Bart's fountain. Canon 5D IV, 70–200mm at 165mm, ISO 200, 1/125s at f/11. Apr.*

## VP 2 – Smithfield Market
**Location Lat/Long:**   51.51952, -0.10141
**Location Postcode:**    EC1A 9PS

## VP 3 – Cloth Fair
**Location Lat/Long:**   51.51901, -0.09979
**Location Postcode:**    EC1A 7JQ

## VP 4 – The Wallace Memorial
## VP 5 – St Bart-the-Less Church and Square
**Location Lat/Long:**   51.51824, -0.10036
**Location Postcode:**    EC1A 7HD

## Accessibility ♿
There is street-level access that should present no issues.

## Best time of year/day
Any time of year is good for a visit but the hospital and church are only open during the daytime.

The Holborn Viaduct was built in 1864 as part of improvements to ease traffic in central London and reduce traffic congestion at Holborn and Ludgate circuses and it was one of London's first modern flyovers. A railway station was added in 1874 at the eastern end of the bridge, though this was replaced in 1990 by the City Thameslink station. Gracing the bridge is a statue of Mayor William Walworth, best known for killing Wat Tyler, leader of the Peasants' Revolt, in 1381 at Smithfield. Today, the bridge still serves its original purpose of reducing congestion.

## What to shoot and viewpoints

During the day this beautiful scarlet iron bridge offers multiple decorations to shoot; cast iron lions at either end of the bridge, statues, crests and painted dragons – the emblems of the City – all make wonderful points of interest. However the best time to shoot the viaduct is at night, especially during the week when plenty of traffic flows underneath. Using a tripod, position yourself on the side of the road, try to frame the shot to remove any distractions from the top of the bridge and concentrate on the lines: the buildings' upright lines, the curves of the bridge's underside and (with long exposures) the lines of light that will appear under the bridge. You may think the underside of the bridge is too dark to shoot but the traffic doesn't move very quickly and with even with a 5–10 second exposure the light from the traffic will illuminate the underside of the bridge, bringing out all the glory of its engineering. Move in tighter with a wide-angle lens and stand directly under the bridge to really emphasise the lines of light. Buses and small vans are worth waiting for as their light-lines always fill the frame, although smaller cars and bikes will keep the light-lines lower in the shot and allow you to capture more of the bridge's detail.

*Griffin decoration on Holborn Viaduct. Canon 5D IV, 70–200mm at 70mm, ISO 400, 1/20s at f/5.6. Mar.*

*Opposite top: Light trails under Holborn Viaduct. Canon 5D II, 17–40mm at 17mm, ISO 100, 5s at f/5.6, tripod. Jan.*

## How to get here

Take the Circle or District line to Farringdon underground station, exit the station and turn right on to Farringdon Street. Turn left and head south towards the river. You'll pass under Holborn Viaduct but use the stairs to reach the road above.

| | |
|---|---|
| **Location Lat/Long**: | 51.51712, -0.10491 |
| **Location Postcode**: | EC4A 4AN |
| **Underground & Lines**: | Farringdon: *Circle and District* |
| **Main Station**: | Farringdon |
| **Bus**: | 8, 25, 46, 521, N8, N25, N242 |
| **Cycle Hire**: | Snow Hill |

## Accessibility ♿

Follow directions from Farringdon station. If you wish to go to the top of the viaduct, turn right at the junction with Charterhouse Street just before the viaduct. Charterhouse Street leads to Holborn Circus; turn left at the circus and head east to the top of the viaduct.

## Best time of year/day

Any time of year is fine. Shoot midday when the sun it out, to capture the statues and decorations on the bridge. Shoot the bridge's underside late in the evening or early morning to photograph light streaks from the traffic.

*Below*: Holborn Viaduct adornments. Canon 5D IV, 70–200mm at 89mm, ISO 200, 1/750s at f/8. Aug.

*Below*: Holborn Viaduct adornments. Canon 5D IV, 70–200mm at 183mm, ISO 200, 1/350s at f/8. Aug.

Blackfriars lies north of the river, just to the south west of the City of London. The area was established in the 14th century when the Dominican Friars, known for their distinctive black robes (Black Frères from the French *frère* meaning 'brother'), moved their priory from Holborn to just south of Ludgate Hill. Blackfriars has been witness to key moments in history, including the divorce between Catherine of Aragon and Henry VIII in 1529. It was also the birthplace of Henry VIII's sixth and final wife, Katherine Parr. Henry VIII closed the priory during the Dissolution of the Monasteries.

In the intervening 500 years the area has been host to Blackfriars Theatre, built on the grounds of the former Dominican monastery. The theatre was in direct competition with Shakespeare's Globe, which stood directly across the river. The Worshipful Society of Apothecaries (an early type of pharmacist) established itself in the area but their building was destroyed by the Great Fire and then rebuilt as the beautiful Apothecaries Hall, which still stands today. Blackfriars is now best known for the train stations, the bridge and the incredible pub: The Blackfriar, which stands by the Blackfriars underground station (on the north side of the Thames by Blackfriars Bridge). It's well worth a visit if you're hungry and thirsty. See page 208 for Blackfriars Bridge – South Bank.

## **What to shoot and viewpoints**

### **Viewpoint 1 – Apothecaries Hall** &
The beautiful Apothecaries Hall stands on Black Friars Lane, just off Playhouse Yard, around the corner from Blackfriars underground station. Visit during the week, when the main courtyard is open to the public. This will enable you to capture the view from the courtyard looking through the main doors back to the street; the archway makes a perfect frame.

### Viewpoint 2 – The Blackfriar pub
I highly recommend a visit to the Blackfriar pub, just opposite the station. The exterior, with its ornate decoration and wonderful statue of a jolly Black Friar, makes for some great photographs, though the real secrets lie inside … the pub's interior is a work of art: frescos adorn the walls wherever you look. The light is dim inside so you will be working at very high ISOs. Stay for a drink or the superb cooked breakfast. When it's quiet, you can rest your camera on one of the tables and shoot much lower ISO and slow shutter speeds.

### The Boomerang – One Blackfriars
Leaving the pub behind, make your way down the northeast side of the bridge to the Thames path below. From here you can get a superb shot of the Boomerang skyscraper, (Londoners love to give their buildings nicknames!) using Blackfriars Bridge as a lead-line. This shot works well at sunrise, when the building's glass plates reflect the warm orange light of the rising sun. It's also spectacular at night, when both the Boomerang and bridge are illuminated and the latter can act as a lead-line.

### Queen Victoria statue
If you head over Blackfriars Bridge (see page 208 for the south side of Blackfriars Bridge), take the western path but before you begin crossing, there's a shot to be had: align the statue of Queen Victoria with the Shard in the distance. This juxtaposition makes one of those classic old-and-new images that can often be found in historical cities like London.

*Opposite top left: Commuter framed in doorway. Sony A6000, 16–50mm at 18mm, ISO 3200, 1/160s at f/3.5. Mar.*
*Top right: VP1. The Apothecaries Hall, Blackfriars. Sony A6000, 16–50mm at 16mm, ISO 125, 1/160s at f/4. May.*

*Opposite left: VP2. Blackfriar Pub in Blackfriars. Sony A6000, 16–50mm at 23mm, ISO 100, 1/125s at f/5. Apr.*
*Right: VP2. Breakfast in the Blackfriar Pub. Sony A6000, Fisheye 8mm at 8mm, ISO 3200, 1/40s at f/8. May.*

## How to get here

Take the Circle or District line to Blackfriars station, exit the station and take a right – you'll see the Blackfriar pub across the junction. Head under the railway bridge to the right of the pub, then turn immediately left into Blackfriars Lane. Keep walking north, the yellow building directly ahead of you is Apothecaries Hall. The 45 and 63 buses both depart from King's Cross station and stop at Blackfriars – stop L on the north side of the bridge and stop D on the south side.

| | |
|---|---|
| Underground & Lines: | Blackfriars: *Circle & District* |
| Main Station: | Blackfriars |
| Riverboat: | Blackfriars Pier |
| Bus: | 45, 63, 388, 388, N63, N89 |
| Cycle Hire: | Milroy Walk, Poured Lines |

## Accessibility &

The viewpoints are on fully accessible streets with street-level access for wheelchairs and those with limited mobility. Note some parts such as the steps from the bridge to the Thames Path may not be directly accessible and you may have to make a short round-trip at street level to connect back to the Thames Path. Apothecaries Hall is up a small set of steps, which may present issues for some.

## Best time of year/day

Blackfriars can be visited at any time of year and at any time of the day. As advised, there are various times of the night and day when some shots will work better than others.

## Opening hours

The Apothecaries Hall courtyard is only open Mon to Fri from 9am–5pm and may be closed when special events are taking place.

## VP 1 – Apothecaries Hall

| | |
|---|---|
| Location Lat/Long: | 51.51292, -0.10325 |
| Location Postcode: | EC4V 6ER |

## VP 2 – Blackfriar pub

| | |
|---|---|
| Location Lat/Long: | 51.512162, -0.10367131 |
| Location Postcode: | EC4V 4EG |

*Above*: VP2. Blackfriar pub interior, Blackfriars. Canon 5D IV, 24–70mm at 24mm, ISO 800, 1/20s at f/6.7. May.

*Opposite top*: Between Blackfriars bridges. Canon 5D IV, 24–70mm at 24mm, ISO 200, 101s at f/19, tripod, LEE ND 0.6 grad. Oct.
*Left*: The Boomerang building catching the dawn light. Canon 5D IV, 70–200mm at 121mm, ISO 200, 1/90s at f/4. Oct.
*Right*: Statue of Queen Victoria by Blackfriars Bridge. Canon 5D IV, 70–200mm at 200mm, ISO 400, 1/350s at f/4. Oct.

Temple is an area bound by King's College, Fleet Street, Blackfriars and the Thames Embankment. The area is named after the church that still stands there and was once the home of the Knights Templar – a Catholic military order, famed for fighting in the Crusades and for developing an early form of banking.

After the Knights Templar was disbanded in the 12th century, the area passed through several hands becoming ever more important as the centre of English law. It consists of two main sub-districts: Inner Temple and Middle Temple. When the Thames Embankment was built, it extended the Temple area; the stairs at the bottom of Essex Street next to Milford Lane mark the spot where the bank of the Thames was before the Embankment was built. One common motif on a lot of the buildings around Middle Temple Lane is the lamb and flag. The lamb with a halo and staff – a religious symbol – is known as *Agnus Dei* or Lamb of God. It is the adopted emblem of the Middle Temple. Note that most areas of Temple are closed at weekends. The Middle Temple Lane embankment entrance is only open Monday to Friday, when the local courts are in session.

*VP1. Temple insignia, Temple. Canon 5D IV, 24–70mm at 54mm, ISO 200, 1/250s at f/4. Aug.*

## What to shoot and viewpoints

### Viewpoint 1 – Middle Temple ♿

The entrance to Middle Temple that faces the Thames can be shot with a standard midrange lens. During spring and summer the trees dapple the light over the grand entrance and its cobbled road. In autumn the leaves turn so shoot in the warm light of early morning to enhance the colours.

### Viewpoint 2 – Pump Court ♿

Proceed north along Middle Temple Lane into Temple. About halfway along the lane look for the arched entrance tunnel into Pump Court. Shoot this tunnel with someone passing through. A wide-angle lens will exaggerate the size of the tunnel and the light at each end will help place the person in silhouette.

## How to get here

Take the Circle or District line to Blackfriars, exit the station and head west along Victoria Embankment to the entrance to Middle Temple Lane opposite the submarine war memorial by the river. If you don't require step-free access then you may alight at Temple, exit the station and head east back towards Blackfriars along Victoria Embankment, Middle Temple Lane entrance is only around 100m from Temple station.

| | |
|---|---|
| **Underground & Lines:** | Blackfriars, Holborn, Temple: *Circle and District, Central, Piccadilly* |
| **Main Station:** | Blackfriars |
| **Bus:** | 1, 11, 15, 26, 59, 68, 76, 91, 168, 188, 341, N11, N15, N21 |
| **Cycle Hire:** | Arundel Street, Houghton Street, Kingsway, Lincoln's Inn Fields, Sardinia Street, Strand |

### VP 1 – Middle Temple
| | |
|---|---|
| **Location Lat/Long:** | 51.51237, -0.11105 |
| **Location Postcode:** | EC4Y 7AN |

### VP 2 – Pump Court
| | |
|---|---|
| **Location Lat/Long:** | 51.51297, -0.11061 |
| **Location Postcode:** | EC4Y 7AA |

### VP 3 – Temple Church
| | |
|---|---|
| **Location Lat/Long:** | 51.5132, -0.11036 |
| **Location Postcode:** | EC4Y 7BB |

### VP 4 – Chancery Lane
| | |
|---|---|
| **Location Lat/Long:** | 51.51482, -0.11135 |
| **Location Postcode:** | WC2A 1PL |

### VP 5 – Carey Street
| | |
|---|---|
| **Location Lat/Long:** | 51.51502, -0.11295 |
| **Location Postcode:** | WC2A 2JB |

VP1. The lane north out of Temple. Sony A6000, 16–50mm at 16mm, ISO 800, 1/160s at f/4. Aug.

**Top**: VP1. Thames end of Middle Temple Lane at the entrance to Temple. Sony A6000, 16–50mm at 21mm, ISO 400, 1/160s at f/4. Apr.

VP2. Pump Court tunnel leading to Temple Church. Canon 5D II, 17–40mm at 17mm, ISO 200, 1/60s at f/4. Aug.

## Viewpoint 3 – Temple Church &

Head through Pump Court to Temple Church – it's a wonderful circular shape. Shoot the whitewashed undercroft with its repeating pattern of columns. The church courtyard is quite small so if you wish to capture the whole church in one shot, a wide-angle lens will pay dividends here.

## Viewpoint 4 – Chancery Lane &

Exit the church courtyard by taking the left hand path past the church rotunda. This will lead along a path directly on to Fleet Street. Directly opposite is Chancery Lane, which will take you into the Lincoln's Inn area. Around 100m along Chancery Lane and on the left is the Law Society building with several gilt lions sitting on the railings. Use a large aperture (a small f/stop) to create a short depth of field to bring just one lion into focus with a background bokeh (out of focus).

## Viewpoint 5 – Carey Street &

Continue north along Chancery Lane until you reach the left turn into Carey Street. Proceed along Carey Street for about 100m. To your right you'll find the blue entrance to New Square and four red telephone boxes at the rear of the Royal Courts of Justice. Shoot square-on for an almost symmetrical, wide composition, or move in closer to isolate two of the boxes. I would suggest the two to the right as you can use a short depth of field with the arches and entrance of the court behind – the bold shapes will cut through the bokeh.

## Viewpoint 6 – World Upside Down &

Proceed to the western end of Carey Street as it bends to the right; you're now in Portugal Street. Turn left, walk for about 50m and follow Portugal Street to the left. As you reach Sheffield Street, you'll find a huge upside-down globe – this is the artwork *The World Turned Upside-Down* by Mark Wallinger. It's a big object so you'll need quite a wide lens if you're standing close to it. One option is to shoot from the roadside with Australia facing towards you, and try to keep the buildings behind separate from the globe. Move around and shoot from the eastern with Portugal Street leading away to the left of the frame.

*Opposite top left: VP3. Temple Church in the morning sun. Canon 5D II, 17–40mm at 17mm, ISO 200, 1/60s at f/8. Aug. Top right: VP3. The Temple Undercroft. Canon 5D II, 17–40mm at 17mm, ISO 800, 1/60s at f/4. Aug.*

*Opposite left: VP4. Lions atop the railings outside the Law Society building, Lincoln's Inn Fields. Canon 5D IV, 70–200mm at 200mm, ISO 400, 1/90s at f/8. Mar. Right: VP5. Phone boxes to the rear of the Royal Courts of Justice. Canon 5D IV, 24–70mm at 45mm, ISO 200, 1/60s at f/8. Aug.*

**VP 6 – World Upside Down**
**Location Lat/Long:** 51.51443, -0.11731
**Location Postcode:** WC2B 6LE

**VP 7 – The Old Curiosity Shop**
**Location Lat/Long:** 51.5149, -0.11729
**Location Postcode:** WC2A 2ES

**VP 8 – Lincoln's Inn Fields**
**Location Lat/Long:** 51.51627, -0.11666
**Location Postcode:** WC2A 3BP

**VP 9 – Royal Courts**
**Location Lat/Long:** 51.51354, -0.11317
**Location Postcode:** WC2A 2LL

**VP 10 – Milford Lane**
**Location Lat/Long:** 51.51237, -0.11105
**Location Postcode:** WC2R 3BD

## Accessibility &

There is street-level access to all areas that should present no issues.

## Best time of year/day

The best time of day is between dawn and dusk, except for the Royal Courts of Justice, where a late-evening shot is on offer. Rain works well in such locations where you find cobbles and wet pavements that reflect the surrounding architecture. Temple itself is only open to the public Monday to Friday but all other locations can be accessed at any time.

*Opposite bottom left: VP5. Entrance to Lincoln's Inn Fields chambers. Sony A6000, 16–50mm at 16mm, ISO 320, 1/160s at f/4. Apr. Bottom right: VP6. The World Turned Upside Down artwork, Lincoln's Inn Fields. Canon 5D IV, 24–70mm at 24mm, ISO 200, 1/500s at f/8. Aug.*

*VP7. Old Curiosity Shop in Lincoln's Inn Fields. Canon 5D II, 17–40mm at 25mm, ISO 400, 1/60s at f/4. Aug.*

### Viewpoint 7 – The Old Curiosity Shop ♿

At the globe, turn and head north between the buildings and after 50m you will arrive in front of The Old Curiosity Shop. There is some doubt as to whether this inspired Dickens to write his novel of the same name or if it was the other way around but either way, it's a wonderful find. Shoot directly in front of the shop or, if blocked by parked vehicles, use a wide angle up close from the street corner. In the rain, the shop is reflected in the pavement on the opposite side of the street.

### Viewpoint 8 – Lincoln's Inn Fields ♿

Lincoln's Inn Fields park and garden is directly ahead of you. It's a large town square with a wooden gazebo at the centre, which makes an interesting subject to shoot on sunny days.

### Viewpoint 9 – Royal Courts ♿

Head back to the globe by the LSE building then continue west to the main road Kingsway. Turn left and head south towards Bush House and Aldwych. Turn left and continue along the eastbound curve towards Australia House. Continue past Australia House and return to the Royal Courts of Justice. Here you'll find a statue to the great literary figure Dr Samuel Johnson, the first person to compile and publish a dictionary of the English language.

There's also a superb view looking east along the Strand past the Royal Courts of Justice. This location makes for a great evening shot as the light begins to fade and the city lights are switched on. Traffic passes both sides of you offering long-exposure light streaks. Shoot 20-second (or greater) exposures. Shoot early in the morning just after dawn during the blue hour, capturing the large lamppost directly in front of the Twinings tea shop, with its distinctive wattle 'n' daub construction.

### Viewpoint 10 – Milford Lane ♿

Finally, leaving Samuel Johnson's statue behind, take the south Strand road back past the church of St Clement Danes then take a right into Milford Lane. Follow this all the way back to Victoria Embankment. Where Milford Lane emerges, you'll see a red telephone box. This spot is perfect for catching people heading north into Temple or Lincoln's Inn via the Essex Street steps. Use a wide angle to exaggerate the sense of space. The spot is especially good when it's raining as people rush past with their umbrellas and the bright red phone box acts as a counterpoint to the rain-soaked people and pavement.

*Opposite top: VP9. Light trails by the Royal Courts of Justice. Canon 5D IV, 17–40mm at 25mm, ISO 200, 30s at f/9.5. Oct.*

*Above left*: VP9. Statue of Dr Samuel Johnson, Aldwych. Canon 5D II, 70–200mm at 200mm, ISO 200, 1/90s at f/8. May.
*Above right*: VP10. Gent passing through Milford Lane. Canon 5D II, 17–40mm at 17mm, ISO 100, 1/60s at f/4. Aug.

Aldwych is both a road and small district within Westminster. The main focus is a 600m, semi-circular stretch of road that's joined to the Strand at both ends. The traffic runs eastbound only, moving traffic from the West End and Bloomsbury towards the City.

Aldwych is home to Australia House, the Indian High Commission, the Waldorf Hotel, theatres and shops. During the day it doesn't appear to offer much, apart from the chance for some street photography, but late evening and at night is when this great little street shares its secrets. During the night the Indian High Commission building is illuminated with the colours of the Indian flag; both the Aldwych Theatre and the Waldorf Hotel are brightly lit up and there are two great spots for shooting traffic streaks.

## What to shoot and viewpoints

### Viewpoint 1 – Aldwych &

There are several great viewpoints here: the Indian High Commission can be shot from the opposite side of the road. Avoid overexposing or the colours will bleed – around 2–3 seconds is enough. A wide-angle lens works best as the building is quite tall and by including the pavement in the foreground, you'll add scale to your image. At the traffic island in the middle of the road outside the Waldorf Hotel, there's a taxi rank where black cabs wait in a line. Look towards the line of cabs, wait for buses to make their approach along Aldwych and look to shoot 10 seconds or greater exposure; this will freeze the cabs and hotel but provide an explosion of wonderful lights from the rear of the cabs. At the corner opposite the Aldwych Theatre, include part of the road and shoot 20 second or greater exposure to capture traffics streaks whilst freezing the lights on the theatre's exterior. Finally, make your way to the far eastern end of Aldwych, opposite Australia House, and shoot looking back along the road. This gives you quite a long view back up towards where Kingsway joins and again offers the chance to capture long light streaks.

*Opposite: VP1. Light trails from buses, Aldwych. Canon 5D II, 17–40mm at 31mm, ISO 100, 13s at f/9 , tripod. Jan.*

### Viewpoint 2 – St Mary le Strand &

On the southern side of Aldwych runs the road known as the Strand. In front of King's College, the Strand splits in two with the church of St Mary le Strand standing forlornly on an island. The church isn't open very often, but in spring the blossom on the trees lining the front path explode into colour. If the gates are closed the bars are wide enough to poke your lens through and get a shot of blossom in front of the church. A wide-angle lens will allow you to capture the whole scene. Using a midrange lens of about 35mm so you can capture the trees, their blossom and the church in the background.

*Opposite top left: VP1. Indian High Commission. Canon 5D IV, 24–70mm at 25mm, ISO 200, 4s at f/8, tripod. Oct. Top right: VP2. St Mary le Strand church. Canon 5D II, 17–40mm at 19mm, ISO 200, 1/60s at f/13. Mar. Middle left: VP1. Waldorf Hotel doorman. Sony A6000, 16–50mm at 34mm, ISO 500, 1/160s at f/5. May. Right: VP1. Bus passing Aldwych. Sony A6000, 16–50mm at 16mm, ISO 100, 1/320s at f/4.5. May.*

## How to get here

Take the Circle or District line to Temple station, exit the station and head left away from the river. Head uphill along Arundel Street to Australia House where Aldwych begins.

| | |
|---|---|
| **Underground & Lines:** | Charing Cross, Covent Garden, Holborn, Temple: *Bakerloo, Central, Circle and District, Northern, Piccadilly* |
| **Main Station:** | Charing Cross |
| **Bus:** | 1, 4, 6, 9, 11, 13, 15, 23, 26, 59, 68, 76, 87, 91, 168, 171, 172, 188, 243, 341 |
| **Cycle Hire:** | Kingsway Southbound, Wellington Street |

### VP 1 – Aldwych
| | |
|---|---|
| **Location Lat/Long:** | 51.51268, -0.11711 |
| **Location Postcode:** | WC2B 4DF |

### VP 2 – St Mary le Strand
| | |
|---|---|
| **Location Lat/Long:** | 51.51222, -0.1168 |
| **Location Postcode:** | WC2R 1ES |

### Accessibility &

There is no step-free access to Temple station. If you require it, take the Circle, District or Northern line to Embankment, exit the station and head away from the river. Take Villiers Street or Northumberland Avenue, then you can take the Strand east; Aldwych curves away to the left.

### Best time of year/day

Any time of year works here though spring will reward you with blossom on the trees. Evening or before sunrise are good times to visit.

Somerset House has a long and varied history. Originally established in the 16th century, and situated in the area between the Strand and the River Thames, it was the residence of many royals.

For 130 years, until 1970, it was the UK's main centre for registration of births, marriages and deaths. It is now a centre for art with galleries and studios, and hosts live performances, films and exhibitions throughout the year, including some excellent photography exhibitions. Each year the main courtyard is transformed into an ice rink, bar and cafe area for the duration of the Christmas season. Somerset House has also featured in a number of movies including the Bond films *Tomorrow Never Dies* and *Goldeneye*.

## What to shoot and viewpoints

### The Building &

The building's facade and courtyard are very worthy of attention. One perspective is to shoot through the entrance's high vaulted archway, placing the southern buildings in the arch. There's often an installation in the main square, which can add an interesting focal point at the centre of the arch. If the sky is bright and causing highlight blowout, wait from someone to walk past and frame them in the bright light. This will capture both the building and the scale of the entrance in relation to the solitary figure.

### The Courtyard and Ice Rink &

The central courtyard often hosts art installations, except at Christmas when the ice rink is installed. At all other times the fountains will be in operation. Once again a wide-angle lens, while not required, will pay dividends. Shoot from one side or another to capture the breadth of this grand courtyard. If you're there early in the evening, increase your ISO and capture the lamps at the courtyard's edge. At Christmas you can walk in off the street and take pictures of the decorations, the skaters and the tree.

### Nelson Stair

One special place hidden away in the west wing is the famous Nelson Stair, also known as the Navy Staircase. It's reminiscent of Escher as it twists and turns towards the glass ceiling at the top. If you have an ultra-wide-angle or better still a fisheye lens, this is the perfect time to use it. There are several places you can shoot the staircase from but I like the simplicity of shooting from the bottom and allowing the lens to exaggerate the steps closest to you – it makes the staircase look vast. As you ascend, use your widest lens to shoot the twists and turns of the flights of stairs.

*Opposite top*: Somerset House main courtyard. Canon 5D II, 17–40mm at 17mm, ISO 200, 1/60s at f/22. Mar.

*Below right*: Lamps outside Somerset House. Canon 5D IV, 70–200mm at 200mm, ISO 400, 1/250s at f/11. June.

*Below left*: Christmas skating at Somerset House. Canon 5D IV, 24–70mm at 24mm, ISO 2000, 1/30s at f/2.8. Nov.
*Middle*: Entrance to Somerset House. Sony A6000, 16–50mm at 27mm, ISO 100, 1/320s at f/5. June.

*Below: Nelson Stair, Somerset House. Sony A6000, Fisheye 8mm at 8mm, ISO 400, 1/25s at f/8. May.*

## How to get here

Take the Circle or District line to Temple station, exit the station and head left away from the river. Head uphill along Arundel Street to Australia House and turn left in the Strand. Walk for 250m – Somerset House is signposted to your left, just past the King's College entrance.

| | |
|---|---|
| **Location Lat/Long**: | 51.51098, -0.1171 |
| **Location Postcode**: | WC2R 1LA |
| **Underground & Lines**: | Charing Cross, Covent Garden, Embankment, Temple: *Bakerloo, Circle and District, Northern, Piccadilly* |
| **Main Station**: | Blackfriars, Charing Cross, Waterloo |
| **Riverboat**: | Embankment Pier |
| **Bus**: | 1, 4, 6, 9, 11, 13, 15, 23, 26, 59, 68, 76, 87, 91, 139, 168, 171,172, 176, 188, 243, 341, 521, RV1, X68 |
| **Cycle Hire**: | Arundel Street, Somerset House, Strand |

## Accessibility &

There is no step-free access to Temple station. If you require it, take the Circle, District or Northern line to Embankment, exit the station and head away from the river. Take Villiers Street or Northumberland Avenue, then you can take the Strand east. Stay on the Strand until you see Somerset House signposted to your right. Note that the upper floors of the Nelson Stair are not accessible but you will be able to shoot the classic angle at the foot of the staircase with no issues.

## Best time of year/day

Somerset House is generally only open during the day and entrance is free, though some events charge an admission fee. It sometimes opens until late evening when certain events are on, such as the Christmas ice rink. Tripods are not permitted within Somerset House itself – you must shoot handheld.

## Biography

**George Johnson is a professional photographer who was born in London. Photography is in his blood: his great-great-grandfather was a professional landscape and portrait photographer in the late 19th century and both his parents were hobbyist photographers who introduced George to photography at the age of four.**

George has been taking photography seriously for over 10 years, and his landscape and urban photographs have appeared in *Amateur Photographer*, *Digital Camera*, *Black and White Photography*, *Digital SLR Photography* and *Photography Week* magazines, as well as *National Geographic Traveller*.

He has also enjoyed considerable success in national photography competitions; his images have been commended several times in the prestigious Landscape Photographer of the Year competition.

George is an official contributor at Getty Images and his clients have included Microsoft, Boeing and Japan Airlines, as well as Visit Britain and Visit London.

When not out taking photographs, his time is spent either with his family or attending extremely loud heavy metal gigs at London's rock clubs.

George uses Canon and Sony cameras and lenses, and LEE Filters.

To find out more about George, his workshops or to buy prints visit: ***www.syxaxis.com***

## PHOTOGRAPHING **LONDON** (VOL. 2) – OUTER LONDON & SECRETS OF STREET PHOTOGRAPHY
BY GEORGE JOHNSON

The second volume of George Johnson's *magnum opus* explores beyond Central London to the London boroughs a short Tube or bus ride away. Although Vol. 2 takes you largely off the beaten track, Greenwich, Richmond Park (with its famous deer rutting), Kew and Hampton Court Palace will be familiar to many. The locations are a mix of urban and semi-rural, including woodland parks, cemeteries, leafy residential streets, old houses and the skyscrapers and docks of East London but prepare for some surprises as you journey through this guidebook.

Finally, George reveals his secrets of street photography, sharing his tips and techniques, as well as a stunning gallery of his best street photography work.

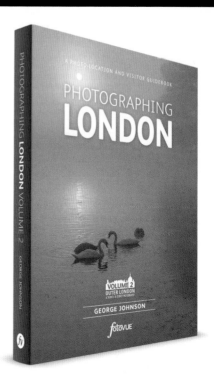

# Order at: **www.fotovue.com**
# use code: **GEORGE** at checkout
# to get:   **15% OFF** all books <small>FREE UK SHIPPING IS STANDARD</small>

## PHOTOGRAPHING **LONDON** (VOL. 2) – CONTENTS

### OUTER LONDON – NORTH

# ABOUT FotoVUE

If you are a keen photographer or want to take the best photos when out and about or on holiday, fotoVUE guidebooks show you where and how to take photographs in the world's most beautiful places.

## Forthcoming titles

- *Photographing Northumberland* – Anita Nicholson
- *Photographing The Cotswolds* – Sarah Howard
- *Photographing Wiltshire* by Robert Harvey
- *Photographing West Ireland* – Carsten Krieger
- *Photographing The Yorkshire Dales* – Lizzie Shepherd
- *Photographing Iceland* – James Rushforth, Geraldine Westrupp and Martin Sammtleben

- *Photographing Kent* – Alex Hare
- *Photographing Dublin and Wicklow* – Adrian Hendroff
- *Photographing The Hebrides* – Chris Swan
- *Photographing The Night Sky* – Alyn Wallace
- *Photographing Surrey and Sussex* – Beata Moore
- *Photographing Family* – Sarah Mason and Suzi Garlick
- *Photographing Liverpool* – Geoff Drake
- *Photographing Lancaster* – Lee Metcalfe
- *Photographing Weather* – Stephen Burt

## Local knowledge books

fotoVUE photographer-authors use their local knowledge to show you the best locations to photograph and the best times to visit.

Order at: **www.fotovue.com**
use code: **GEORGE** at checkout
to get: **15% OFF** all books

FREE UK SHIPPING IS STANDARD

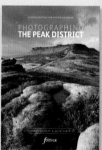
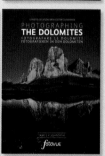
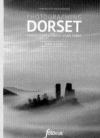

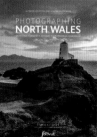
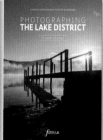

Contact: *mick@fotovue.com*

*Tre Cime di Lavaredo and the Milky Way in the Dolomites, Italy. Photograph by Alyn Wallace, author of the forthcoming PHOTOGRAPHING THE NIGHT SKY (published by fotoVUE). This location also features in PHOTOGRAPHING THE DOLOMITES by James Rushforth (published by fotoVUE).*

# LOVE HILL WALKING & PHOTOGRAPHY?

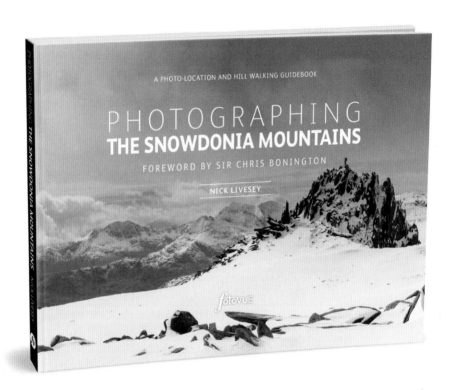